To say that but for my wife, Helen, I could never have written this book, would be a serious understatement, for without her struggle, first to try to save the lives of Ethel and Julius Rosenberg, and then to gain my freedom, the events related in this book could never have happened.

ON DOING TIME

MORTON SOBELL

CHARLES SCRIBNER'S SONS □ NEW YORK

Library of Congress Cataloging in Publication Data

Sobell, Morton.
  On doing time.

  Autobiographical.
  1. Sobell, Morton. 2. Political prisoners—United
States—Personal narratives. 3. Espionage—United
States. I. Title.
HV9468.S7   365'.6'0924 [B]   74–11203
ISBN 0–684–13938–3

Even as I was writing this book, and after it was finished, there were many instances where I wanted to "explain myself" to the reader, but I have always felt that any book must ultimately explain *itself*—otherwise the writer has failed. However, lest any reader gain the impression that I have a photographic memory, let me explain that Helen, my wife, saved every letter I sent her from prison. These served to help me recall many of the events related in the book.

After I finished writing a first draft, covering the entire span of years of imprisonment, it became apparent that I could not include it all in one volume. Accordingly I have synopsized the period following my Alcatraz experience—in this volume. However a second volume covering that rather interesting period in prison reform is being worked on. At various phases in the writing of the book I sought the advice of friends, but in the end, as one friend put it, "writing is a lonely task." However I did have the invaluable editorial assistance of two good friends, Ms Pat Anderson and Dr. Annette Rubinstein. And if it hadn't been for the thousands of pages of typing of Ms Edna Reiter, my task would have been immeasurably more difficult.

June 7, 1974

PROLOGUE

On April 5, 1951, Julius and Ethel Rosenberg were both sentenced to death, and Morton Sobell to thirty years imprisonment. They had all been tried and convicted of a single count, conspiracy to commit espionage.

On June 19, 1953, despite worldwide protests, the Rosenbergs were executed, and Sobell imprisoned on Alcatraz. After more than eighteen years behind bars, he was released from the federal penitentiary at Lewisburg, Pennsylvania, on January 14, 1969.

This is an account of the trial and his imprisonment.

CONTENTS

Part One

UPHEAVAL

1 Kidnapped

TWO days after we left for Mexico the Korean war broke out. Events moved swiftly during the next two months and our anxieties kept apace with the mounting repression back home.

Several weeks after we arrived here, while Helen and I were trying to figure out what to do, Julius Rosenberg whom I had known since my City College days was arrested for allegedly stealing the secret of the atom bomb and transmitting it to the Soviet Union. I was absolutely certain that Julius had had no connection with the atom bomb, and I couldn't conceive that he could possibly have been involved in any espionage. I panicked; I foresaw the FBI swooping down on everyone with a left-wing political past, and filling up the concentration camps which had previously contained the Japanese during World War II.

Helen and I were both apprehensive now of returning to the States, because possible perjury indictments faced us for having falsely signed non-Communist affidavits when we had gone to work for the Reeves Instrument Company three years earlier. But there was no way out. I had explored all the possibilities, with negative results; we had neither passports nor influence. Then, just as we were preparing to re-

[3]

turn, Ethel, Julius's wife, was arrested on the identical charge—stealing the atom bomb. We hesitated, momentarily, to regain our equilibrium, then decided to spend a last few days in Mexico as if we were truly on a vacation before plunging into the maelstrom which we were sure awaited us on our return to the States.

The weather was exquisite. I had never before experienced the perfect climate that Mexico City had to offer; we had been taking walks to the parks regularly ever since we had settled in our apartment on Cordoba. On the morning of August 16, 1950 we all went to one of the nearby parks where we strolled and sunned ourselves leisurely, as if we had not a care in the world. Mark had just learned to walk and we let him exercise his new-found skill. It felt good to watch him maintain his precarious balance as he plunged ahead without fear. Sydney, ten, always seemed to find new interests in the scene.

Shortly before noon we started back, stopping off briefly at the *Super-Mercado* to shop for the evening meal. It was easy to eat well in Mexico, what with the tremendous variety of fresh fruits and vegetables that were commonly available. After lunch Helen, Mark, and I took off for another one of the District's innumerable parks. Sydney remained behind to do some reading. The variety of the parks was amazing. This one had a large, imaginatively designed children's playground which had fallen into an obvious state of disrepair. It looked like a relic from some other age or civilization, with every single piece of equipment broken, standing like artifacts on a surrealistic landscape, monuments to some political administration, but neglected by its successors. But the greenery of the park hadn't suffered this same fate of neglect; the flowers were all blooming in tropical splendor and the trees were full.

We sat down on the plush velvet carpet of grass while Mark scampered about, running and falling, having a joyous time. Helen and I played games, I the voyeur and she the temptress, occasionally broken off while I went to fetch Mark who had gone too far afield. We enjoyed ourselves even though we were afraid that once we returned to the States such lighthearted *kinderspiel* would become a thing of the past. In fact, knowing this made it imperative that we not allow ourselves to be deprived of whatever happiness we could gain. Suddenly the sky became overcast; the prelude to the now familiar midday tropical downpour. This always left behind an unmatched freshness in the already clean air. I quickly put Mark in his stroller and we began to run. It was fun, trying to beat the rain, but halfway home the skies opened up. We sought shelter under a nearby canopy, but it was quite useless. With the wind whipping the rain around, in a few minutes we were soaked to the skin. It felt so good to be so carefree, even while burdened with thoughts of the future.

As soon as the rain began to let up we started home again, arriving there just as the rain stopped. Once in our apartment we shed our wet clothing, and I opened one of the two large, hinged windows in our living room to let in some of the rain-refreshed air. Unhappily a sudden gust of wind slammed the window closed with such a force that it shattered the window pane. I looked down and saw no one; fortunately the streets were still deserted. After covering the opening with newspapers I went down and arranged for a glazier on the same block to replace the shattered pane. By that time we were all famished. Helen put Mark to sleep in the upstairs room of our duplex and I put a large red snapper in the oven. We had decided to make this a gala occasion and dine by candlelight. Although Sydney was young in years she joined our dinner conversation, which covered a broad range of topics. We talked about almost everything—except the subject which concerned us most at the moment; our impending return to the States. Eight o'clock found us still at the dinner table, Helen and I sipping our coffee and all of us indulging in the exquisite Mexican pastries.

There was a sudden knock on the door, and Sydney got up to open it. We couldn't see the hallway from our seats in the dining alcove, but when we heard a commotion we both got to our feet and began to move toward the door. Three men with drawn guns confronted us. I'd never have guessed what my reaction to such a situation would be. None of us was frightened by the men and their stubby, ugly guns; it was as though we had routinely encountered such situations. And yet I had never conceived that it might come this way—our arrest.

Rather aimlessly, the men began to look around the apartment. When I demanded an explanation, the leader of the trio announced that I was one Johnny Jones, wanted for a fifteen thousand dollar bank robbery in Acapulco. Naively taking him at his word I denied the whole thing offering to show him my identification. He then showed me a badge, and identified himself and his cohorts as Mexican Security Police. All the while the men were unsystematically looking around the downstairs rooms, opening closet doors, lifting cushions. They still had their drawn guns in hand, but were not pointing them anywhere in particular. It seemed rather Hollywoodish.

After some minutes the chief started up the stairs to continue his search. Helen and I protested that he would wake our baby and I asked to be allowed to call the United States Embassy. Their reaction to this request was quite violent; they began pushing me out of the apartment. It took a moment before I realized what was happening; then I began to resist. The three of them literally carried me down the stairs to the street level, by which time I had aroused the whole building with my shouts. When we passed the door of the street floor apartment, I yelled to the tenants that I was being kidnapped and for them to call the police or the Embassy. By this time I was apprehensive about the men who had identified themselves as Security Police. Naturally I had no idea that they wanted to keep the Embassy out of the operation so that later on at the trial the prosecution could say that I had simply been deported by the Mexican Government. Involving the Embassy would have made the thing even stickier.

When they finally got me out on the street I began to yell for the police in an even louder voice, and a cluster of people gathered around us. Strangely enough the Security Police didn't have an auto waiting to take us away. They flagged a cab, but when they tried to shove me in, feet first, I simply spread my legs apart. I evidently resisted them well enough to frighten off the cab driver. Police or no police, he didn't want any trouble.

Suddenly I saw Helen in the street with another cop who, I later learned, went into the apartment shortly after I had been snatched to pick her up. She had apparently been inspired by my struggle to bite the thumb of the man who escorted her down and yell as I was doing. Mark and Sydney were still up in the apartment, alone. Many years later I learned from Helen that they had underestimated our daughter. She had heard me ask permission to call the Embassy, so after they left her in the apartment this was precisely what she did. Unfortunately she was able to get no one but an unhelpful nightwatchman on the phone. One can only speculate as to what might have happened if she had been able to reach a responsible officer.

After the cab had moved off I was left standing for a short while, although well surrounded by police. Finally they flagged down another cab but before I could repeat the scene with an even larger onlooking crowd one of the cops hit me over the head with a revolver butt.

When I woke up I was lying on the floor of the cab at the feet of the three. All the way to our destination they kept muttering vague threats. When we finally got downtown and the cab stopped in front of their office, the leader of the expedition warned me that if I raised any rumpus when I got out of the cab, "I'll plug you." I was too tired and beaten to react to this. He didn't know he no longer had to threaten me; I had had all the fight knocked out of me by the blow on my head.

I got up as instructed and walked quietly into the building, which I recognized from my many wanderings downtown. It was some kind of government building, with a post office on the street floor. We went up to the fourth floor by elevator; there I was escorted into an office and ordered seated. It was quiet here. In a couple of minutes a tall, slim, nattily attired man with an air of authority came over. From the way the others acted it was apparent he was the boss, and when I asked for an explanation of what had transpired, he slapped me sharply across the face and said, "I'll ask the questions around here." He was doubtless a little angry with me for the way I had behaved earlier. Then he left.

Soon Helen was escorted into the room, and as she passed close to me I told her not to be frightened. The tall, slim man, who came back in with her, rewarded me with another one of his professionally administered slaps; Helen winced and gave him a piece of her mind. It hadn't really hurt me; for the moment I was beyond being hurt. Helen was then taken past me to another room.

After a while I tried to relax and take stock. First I discovered that there was a gash in my scalp, and when I explored the gash with my finger it was so deep I didn't believe it. I thought that the skull itself must be dented. The blood had coagulated and my hair was matted. Then I became aware that I no longer had my eyeglasses. I didn't know when I had lost them, probably during the scuffle in front of our house. I suppose it was lucky I didn't have a mirror in which to see myself. I asked my guards for a doctor to sew up my scalp, and they promised they would get one as soon as possible. Of course they never did.

I had no idea what was going on behind the scenes during this next period. Men came into the room, some stayed for a while and then left, others stayed longer. I tried to engage some of them in conversation, hoping that they might drop an unguarded word, but had no luck. They were evidently well trained.

Some years later I learned from an attorney that this was the period of bargaining, during which the tall man negotiated with the FBI for his "reward." It was supposed to be around seventy-five hundred dollars. It would have been a coup if we could have brought this out at the trial, but such delicate negotiations are not usually susceptible of proof.

I don't know how long I had been kept in the room when I heard the pained cry of a child. I soon realized that it was my own son, but his cry did not come from the room into which I had seen them take Helen. Helen told me later that she had heard me denounce my captors for keeping Mark and her apart (I had no recollection). Actually he was with Sydney. They had been left alone for quite a while in the apartment before the police sent someone to fetch them. Poor Sydney, alone with the baby in the midst of nowhere! I don't know if my protests had anything to do with it, but after a while they brought Helen to the children and even offered them a cot.

As the evening wore on I completely lost track of time. At one point they photographed me, and when I saw that the photographer was using a Leica camera, for a fleeting moment I felt that this was my camera, which they had appropriated. Then I remembered that all Leicas look alike—and that it was highly improbable that they would insult me by taking a mug shot of me with my own camera. At another point I asked to go to the toilet. I was escorted to a public men's room, on the floor above, after being duly warned not to try to make a break. At some time during the evening they asked me for the combination to the safe in the wall of our apartment—threatening to smash it open—but I couldn't even begin to remember it. My mind was an utter blank. When I told them that Helen could probably recall the combination, they agreed to let me shout to Helen, over the partitions of the office, asking her to give it to them, which she did. We didn't really have much in the safe, outside of some money and such documents as the tourist permits, marriage license, and birth certificates. They must have expected to find more "incriminating evidence" than these items, none of which was introduced at the trial.

Around midnight the coming and going slowed down, but there were still about a dozen police who hung around, as if they had no place to go and were marking time. They sent down for sandwiches and coffee, offering to get me some. I thanked them but declined the offer. I couldn't have eaten. I had a watch in the watch pocket of my trousers, but had forgotten about it until I pulled it out about one in the morning. This was a big mistake. It was a seventeen-jewel Bulova which my mother had given me some ten years earlier. One of the policemen came over and asked to see it, and I innocently handed it to him. That was the last I ever saw of it. Of course this sort of petty larceny was common police practice both in Mexico and in the States. It seems sanctioned by all the agencies involved in the "orderly administration" of justice; the cops are never censured by their superiors or by the courts.

The next two or three hours passed uneventfully. Everything was quiet around me and I simply sat and thought. When would it end? Where and how would it end? My thoughts were on the future; the past was past.

Finally I was taken downstairs and put in a heavy Packard, between two policemen whose open jackets displayed shoulder holsters. The streets were totally deserted and the sky was beginning to show the first signs of daybreak. From inside the auto I could see Helen and the children getting into an identical Packard a short distance ahead. Helen carried Mark in her arms and I knew she must be exhausted. I wanted to ask the police to let me take Mark from her, but felt I had to remain unencumbered—in case an opportunity arose where I could make a break, or whatever else. Anyway, they would probably have thought it a trick if I had asked to care for our child. Before we started the tall, slim, slap-happy chief came over to the side of the car and told my guards in English, "If he makes any trouble shoot him." I didn't take it seriously. I felt that they did not want a shot-up Morton Sobell on their hands. Whatever was going on, I knew it was highly irregular, and hoped for an opportunity to make trouble.

The policeman on my left was apparently the leader of this two-car safari, for when he gave the signal we took off, our car in the lead. The autos kept in sight of each other throughout the whole trip. As soon as we started moving through the streets of the Federal District they told me I was being taken south to the chief of police, for further action. A short time later I saw the sun rising on my right and knew we were going north, not south. I didn't point this out to Julio, as the leader was called. Why antagonize him needlessly; better to let him think he had misled me. Anyway it was going to be a long trip to the border.

There were four of us. The driver up front, my two guards, and myself. The two guards were very sociable throughout the journey, and soon I learned that the guard on my right had not fathered any children by his wife and held her responsible for the failure. He was now engaged in negotiations which would eventually lead to his having a child by another woman. Julio also had matrimonial problems. I was rather surprised that they discussed these intimacies before a stranger. Every few hours, when we came to a small village, the autos stopped while the men refreshed themselves, and

Julio called his chief to report on the progress of the expedition. He made no secret of this. Since these were strictly Mexican eating establishments, I declined all offers of food and water. Helen had a hard time with Mark. She had only a single baby bottle, and all she could give Mark during the entire trip was some condensed milk which the police bought, since they would never stop long enough for her to get some water boiled. They were evidently under a time pressure—not simply trying to be unkind. It became stiflingly hot that August day, and we were thoroughly dehydrated. But between the lack of sleep and the traumatic events of the previous evening I was past being discomforted by thirst and hunger.

Even after the sun fell it was still terribly hot in the car; Julio dozed, and when I leaned over to his side to open his window wider he jumped up in alarm. I had committed a faux pas of the first magnitude. I hadn't realized that his gun holster was near the window crank. The other guard told me he had been watching my every move, and would have shot me if I had reached for Julio's gun. Getting involved in gunplay had been furthest from my mind. I had never shot a hand gun, and didn't know how.

As it grew late the stops became less frequent. I had no idea of where we were, or at what time we were supposed to reach the border. They told me about an hour before we were to arrive in Monterrey. It was near eleven o'clock when we arrived in Monterrey, and all the shops were closed except for one apothecary. For the first time since we had been kidnapped they allowed me to speak to Helen and the children. There wasn't much to say except a few words of encouragement. Mark finally got his bottle of pure water. Helen,

I, and even Sydney at least had some understanding of the situation, but poor Mark had to suffer without reason. It hurt me to watch him gulp his bottle in record time before it was refilled for the rest of the journey.

By this time I realized that it was sheer fantasy to think in terms of getting away. I couldn't have gotten very far in this strange country. It wasn't as though it were New York City, with which I was familiar. After about fifteen minutes we all got back into the autos, much refreshed, even though we still hadn't eaten a thing all day.

For the last leg of the trip our driver stepped up his speed to about seventy-five miles an hour. It was all flat country, a straight road with almost no traffic. When we arrived at Nuevo Laredo about 1:30 A.M., Julio made his last phone call to his chief, returning to tell me I was to be released across the border. Then he returned the envelope containing seven hundred dollars which he had taken from the safe in our apartment. He had taken two hundred dollars, which he explained quite seriously was to cover the expenses his men had incurred during this expedition. I didn't argue. If he had taken it all it wouldn't have mattered. It was already Friday, and I had been up since Wednesday. I was past caring.

We started for the border where we stopped at Mexican customs. Julio got out and talked with the customs officer, apparently marking time until an appointed time of rendezvous. When he returned to the car we started up immediately and began to cross the Rio Grande. At midpoint on the bridge our car stopped and an American, badge in hand, got into the front seat with the driver; we proceeded until we reached the United States customs. I got out of the car and the customs inspector motioned me to follow him into his office.

Why didn't I cry out that we had been kidnapped by these men who were with us in the autos? I suppose our situation was not too different from that of the German Jews, who, even as they were about to enter the gas chambers, were hoping for some kind of miracle. Unrealistic as it seems in retrospect, I thought that perhaps nothing further would happen, that the worst was over. Anyway, since it was apparent that the Americans were a part of the kidnapping conspiracy, there was no point in protesting. Of course, I could have cried out "for the record," but at this stage I was not aware of such subtleties. I did not usually act on impulse, and Helen, watching me for cues, also kept quiet.

The customs inspector filled out a card on the typewriter listing my name, address, and other minor information, and then asked me to sign it, explaining that this was required of *all* returning citizens. I complied with his request since there was nothing on the card which was in any way detrimental. How was I to know that he would later write on the card "Deported from Mexico," and claim at the trial that he had explained to me "that our regulations required that any person who was being deported from Mexico, there be a record made and that I would like for him to furnish me with the necessary information"?—all of which was pure fabrication. Having signed the card I began to leave, but found the doorway blocked by a man who flashed a card, identified himself as an FBI agent, and pronounced the fateful words, "you are under arrest," snapping handcuffs on my wrists. At that moment the world did not collapse around me. I don't think my heart rate even accelerated. I had been hoping, and when my hopes did not materialize I accepted what came. Until then I had never experienced handcuffs; in Mexico the police had not used them. I later learned that Mexicans considered handcuffs uncivilized.

I looked over, momentarily, at the customs inspection area, and saw that Helen was standing there with the children, apparently free, and breathed a sigh of relief, although not too deeply. Then I was taken into another room where I was stripped and searched. My wallet, with the money, my keys, and other odds and ends were taken away; they said that the money would be returned to me the following morning after it had been examined. Examined for what? It was all legitimate. Helen didn't have a penny on her.

That search over, I was taken to witness the meticulous examination the customs inspector gave our luggage, under the doubly watchful eyes of some FBI agents. I suppose they wanted me to be present during the customs examination for legal reasons. Our things had been so thrown together by the Mexicans that it was a wonder they all fitted into the bags. My return had obviously been timed to minimize the possibility of witnesses, although I did not then know why.

It was a hot, dry night in Laredo, Texas, and the baggage search took the better part of an hour. Seeing a drinking fountain I asked the FBI agent who was standing next to me if I could quench my thirst. He assented, but another agent, apparently a local man, dressed like the Texans I had seen in movies, warned me in all seriousness, "I'll shoot you dead if you make a false move." Since I was legally under arrest, I thought he might welcome the opportunity to do so, if I gave him the least excuse. Throughout the years, no matter how grim the situation, the officials would almost always provide some such unintended but appreciated comic relief. At the moment, thoughts of escape were furthest from my mind; Texas or Mexico were equally foreign to me.

The only items from our luggage which the FBI retained were some letters I had written Helen from Vera Cruz, the rent receipts, various identification papers, and Syd's return flight ticket. There was no sign of our Leica, Bolex movie camera, or the leather briefcase which Helen had given me on my last birthday. But it was the small piece of electrical equipment, which I had taken with me as a sort of conversation piece in case I met any electrical engineers, that was really the most important missing item. I had kinder thoughts about the petty-thieving Mexican police when I realized the FBI had not found that synchro in our luggage! I'm sure it would have been a star exhibit at the trial.

After the customs examination I was taken to the local jail. Helen, at least for the moment, was still free and she left, with the luggage, for the local hotel.

At the jail, by the time I was processed (which included being sprayed with DDT, as though I were a plant) it was already four in the morning of Friday the eighteenth. It all seemed to have begun ages ago— eight o'clock in the evening of the sixteenth. The intervening period was unlike anything I had ever before experienced—or even imagined. What charges would be leveled against me? What did the future hold in store for me?

Early that morning I was awakened and told to dress. Without benefit of breakfast or washup I was led to a large room in the jail where I was greeted by two FBI agents. One of them, Rex I. Shroder, whom I recognized as the man who had boarded our auto halfway across the bridge, presented me with the complaint, an affidavit he had sworn out against me, which was the legal basis for my arrest.

In it he swore that I had had five conversations with Julius Rosenberg, on various dates from January 1946 until May 1948, during which he alleged we had conspired to violate Section 31 of Title 50, United States Code, that we had conspired to transmit information to the Soviet Union relating to the national defense. The complaint alleged that I had joined the conspiracy on or about July 1944 while the United States was at war.

It was on the basis of the wartime aspect of the charge that the FBI agents told me I faced the death penalty—unless. This was the first in a long series of inducements: it was suggested that things "would go easier" for me if I cooperated. Besides, they assured me, I was much better off here than in the "salt mines" in Russia, where I would have been sent had I ever succeeded in getting to Eastern Europe. The agents never made explicit their meaning for cooperate, or for the benefits I would gain.

I don't know how long they talked to me (I don't think I said anything the entire time), pulling out their complete bag of shop-worn tricks. When they tried the good guy–bad guy routine, I smiled inwardly. It was so obvious. I knew that they were both my enemies, and nothing they said or did could change that certain knowledge.

The whole meeting with these FBI men had an unreal quality. Of course I had not conspired with Julius to transmit information etc., but beyond this I wondered how Shroder had picked the five dates on which I was supposed to have had conversations with Julius? The first three were when I still lived in Schenectady. I used to come into New York City on occasion, and would sometimes visit Julius and Ethel, but upon what information could he possibly arrive at the dates of those visits much less the conclusion that Julius and I had conspired? Only if Julius had told Shroder that he had met me on these dates and that we had conspired together could Shroder honestly swear that he had information to this effect. The thought that Julius had lied and told him this never occurred to me, and yet Rex Shroder swore that I had met Julius, which left me bewildered: I couldn't then believe that an agent of the United States Government would deliberately commit perjury. I still thought of the government as above outright perjury.

The visit with the two agents was terminated by the arrival of the United States Commissioner. I was told I would be given a preliminary hearing. I didn't know what the preliminary hearing was supposed to be and understood nothing about the function of the Commissioner. (I hadn't studied it in civics or government.) Reporters and photographers were allowed into the room for the occasion.

How can I possibly explain, even to myself, how I could have remained silent during the so-called hearing that morning? First there was the matter of the kidnapping, then the complaint, with its fabricated allegations. Why didn't I denounce these? My head was still split open from the gash the Mexican police had inflicted. This was obviously the occasion to tell what had transpired since Wednesday evening—but I remained mute. And to top it all, I "waived" removal proceedings to New York when the Commissioner gave me his word that the proceedings were purely formal, and that I could do nothing to interfere with my removal to New York. Later I discovered that he was quite right, but that in so advising me he had acted as my counsel, which was entirely illegal. And in fact, some years later, an opinion by Supreme Court Justice Douglas stated that no one should ever be put in a position where he could waive his constitutional rights.

After signing the waiver I was returned to my cell with the Commissioner's assurance that my removal to New York would be expedited. And what I most wanted now was to get to New York where I had friends and could find an attorney to expose the fraudulent complaint. I did not think any Texas lawyer would help me.

Miraculously, the door to my cell opened shortly after I was returned to it and Helen walked in, explaining that we were allowed a visit. Apparently we were not even being watched and we talked freely, as though the cell were not bugged. We had no secrets.

Helen told me she had been awakened early by a phone call from the FBI agents, who invited her to join them at breakfast, offering to have a woman take care of the children so she could speak with them undisturbed. They were courteous, but she declined. However when she sat down in the coffee shop the agents came to her table uninvited and began to talk. Why didn't she tell them to leave? That wasn't her style, and it is difficult to break one's style. After breakfast the agents followed her to her room, telling her how glad she should be to be back in the States since if we had succeeded in getting to Eastern Europe, which they had apparently assumed we were trying to do, we would now be in the salt mines—the same as they had told me. They also told her that she would be surprised at how much she could remember, if she only worked at it. This was their euphemism for "cooperation," a process whereby the cooperator is fed the bare outlines of a story, picks it up and elaborates on the details, trying to keep as close as possible to both the real facts and the outlined story. It was a game at which they were experts, and when the cooperator was finished he had usually lost track of where the facts ended and the fantasies began.

Before the agents left she asked them about visiting me, and was told that visiting was not scheduled until Saturday but that they would make an exception and allow her a visit that afternoon.

There wasn't even a chair in my cell, so we sat down on opposite beds, knee to knee and talked— mostly about what to do. At no point did the thought of "cooperating" with the FBI ever arise, and so it never came up in our conversation.

We agreed that she would fly to Washington on the next available plane, leave the children with her mother, and go immediately to New York to find a lawyer. I asked her to contact the American Civil Liberties Union, as well as Edward Kuntz, a lawyer who had come to my attention some years earlier when he defended Morris Schappes, a former City College English instructor. Helen also said that she would arrange to have my suit pressed so that I would look more presentable when I got to New York and was confronted by press photographers. She had already undergone that experience that morning. One other task I gave her—to have my eyeglasses duplicated and sent to me wherever I was. I could read without them but everything else was out of focus. She had been told she would be able to pick up the money that had been taken from me the previous night, and we agreed that she would leave me fifty dollars for contingencies. All that business transacted, we talked just for a little while about ourselves, as though to prove to ourselves that we were still human beings—even under these circumstances. We kissed, and then she left. And I was alone in Texas.

I was alone in a smallish, four-man cell with two double bunks and could start no conversation with any of the other prisoners as they passed by my cell. The way they avoided me indicated that they had been warned not to get too close. I was amazed that I didn't feel frightened by what had transpired. I felt no pain, nor did I experience any overt anxiety. I must have been anaesthetized. I sat or lay on my bed, completely removed from the outside world and the past ran through my mind as though I were about to be executed, except that it lasted for four days; time enough to encompass a brief lifetime like mine.

2   My Life

WHO was Morton Sobell? What was he doing here, locked up in a Texas jail facing the death penalty? Where had he come from?

Louis Sobel was born in 1889, in a small Russian village; six years later Rose Pasternack was born in the same village. Both families were uneducated, landless peasants who spoke Yiddish rather than Russian; as Jews they were forbidden to own land or to move to the cities. However Louis managed to find employment as an apprentice to an apothecary in a larger neighboring town, where he learned Russian.

Shortly after the turn of the century both families emigrated to the United States and took up residence among their compatriots in lower Manhattan. Unlike her older sisters, Rose Pasternack attended elementary school and high school; there she was an involuntary drop out, leaving to go to work as a sewing machine operator.

Louis Sobell (who had added an extra "l" to his name) worked as a cigar maker, attending school evenings. In 1910 he entered Cooper Union evening engineering school, still continuing to work as a cigar maker. In 1915 he graduated as a civil engineer and shortly afterwards married Rose. On April 11, 1917, shortly after the United States entered World War I, Morton Sobell was delivered in the Lying In Hospital in lower Manhattan.

Our one and a half room cold water flat on the east side of lower Manhattan is my earliest memory; during the winter of 1921–22, when I was not yet five. My maternal grandmother had the half room, with its shaftway for light and air. She was a small, frail woman, who sat most of the day in her tiny living space, occasionally eating milk-softened bread. My parents and I lived in the other room.

We used a common toilet in the cold hallway. A gas meter which had to be fed a quarter every time the gas pressure began to go down was our sole source of energy for illumination, cooking, and heat. That winter the gas meter consumed an enormous number of precious quarters. We had no bath and no ice box. The perishables were stored on the window sill, but as soon as the weather warmed up, my mother had to buy them from meal to meal.

With the postwar inflation, the Sobell family didn't prosper. Thus in 1921 my father decided to become a pharmacist. He entered the Columbia College of Pharmacy, which he attended for the next two years, working at the same time as a non-graduate pharmacist.

That summer of 1922 my mother took me to the country to a farm owned by a relative. Here were several cows which had to be milked daily: since my relatives were orthodox, they would not violate the Sabbath by milking. This task became my mother's—the only one who did not light candles and pray on Friday evenings.

I went to school shortly before I was six. The large, fat teacher would walk up and down the aisles with a ruler in her hand, brandishing it as a weapon. If anyone dared move she ordered him to put his hands on his desk, palms down, and then brought the ruler down on them. I was terrified. When I told my mother what went on in class she immediately took me out of school.

In 1923, as soon as my father graduated from Columbia with his Ph.&G. we moved uptown to the Bronx and I re-entered school there. Shortly afterwards my sister was born. I have almost no memory of my first three years at school. I must have been a very mediocre student.

My father became an entrepreneur in 1927. He purchased a drug store, financed by loans from a relative, since we didn't have a penny of our own. It was a run-down, one-man store in a shabby neighborhood, a block from the railroad tracks. He never hired anyone, working from eight in the morning until after eleven at night, seven days a week, fifty-two weeks a year, my mother and I helping him when we could. I would deliver prescriptions or travel to the wholesale drug house.

Initially we rented an apartment in a new building about two blocks from the store. But economic conditions worsened and we moved three times—each time into a lower-rent apartment.

I didn't find school very interesting. My fifth-grade teacher complained to my mother that I seemed absorbed in daydreaming. Actually, I constantly brought in projects which I had made at home, usually with my father's help; maps with gelatin capsules designating the products of the area; models of villages; a model of a famous Civil War boat. Anything to try to make school a little less boring. However, in junior high school I began to do better work and even enjoyed algebra. During these years I saw more of my father than most children do, but always in the store; we never sat down all together to a meal.

Ever since I can remember my father read the *New York Times*. On Sunday he would buy both the *Times* and the *Herald-Tribune* (they were only six cents each). We also read the *Daily Worker* and the *New Masses*, regularly.

My mother's brothers, Louis and Morris, were the real radicals. Louis had started out, like my father, as a cigar maker, but became a labor organizer, traveling a great deal. Our family album held a picture of the adventurer seated on the bank of some river out West, wearing high leather boots. Morris had originally been a chemist but was now deeply immersed in radical politics. Both of these uncles were close to us and their influence was an important factor in our political orientation.

My parents both belonged to the International Workers' Order (IWO), a left-wing fraternal and insurance group. However, tied down as he was in the store, my father could never attend meetings. Consequently his revolutionary ardor was directed toward the salesmen who came into the store to sell him pharmaceuticals, and toward his customers, some of whom he must have offended. I used to listen as he talked about how socialism would cure all the evils of our system. His main source of information for what was happening in the USSR was *Soviet Russia Today*. He also took correspondence courses in Marxism and political economy from the Communist Party's Workers' School, typing out his lessons on an old beat-up Underwood typewriter.

Sometime during these years my mother joined the

Communist Party and about once every five or six weeks the meeting was held in our house. There was always a lot of Party literature at home, as well as copies of the *Daily Worker*, to be distributed by my mother.

There was little political activity at Stuyvesant High School which I attended. Several attempts were made to organize radical students and I attended some meetings, but no functioning group ever developed out of them. I tried taking a course at the Workers' School in Engels's *Anti-Dühring*, but found it meaningless and never really learned who Dühring was until many years later. I did become an amateur radio operator at school and when a workers' radio club was organized, I became a member. But it never really got off the ground. I recall putting everyone to sleep at one of the Friday evening meetings talking about electric meters.

At Stuyvesant I first met Max Elitcher and William Danziger, who were to figure in the trial. We were in the same graduating class. I knew Elitcher lived in a very poor neighborhood in mid-Manhattan, although we never visited each other at home. We all had several classes in common. I envied Bill's easy manner, his poise; he was also bright. But my closest friend in high school was Meyer Ebert, a fellow radio ham. Our friendship was not based only on this common interest, as we saw eye-to-eye politically, went to concerts— usually free ones—and sometimes attended the opera at the old Hippodrome, where for twenty-five cents we could sit in the balcony and listen to Verdi. Afterwards, going home on the subway, we'd sing the arias at the top of our voices. Meyer's family was apolitical and didn't understand him. I felt lucky to have the parents I did.

Graduation night was particularly happy, since I won two gold medals—one in physics and one in mathematics. Afterwards we all went home on the subway.

I entered CCNY in February 1934, the bottom of the depression. My father's business continued its steady decline. He worked the same hours as always, but we had less and less money and ended up living in an old run-down linear apartment on St. Ann's Avenue, across the street from the store. One advantage of this place was that for the first time my sister and I each had our own rooms, even though they were small. Since my bedroom was cluttered with radio apparatus I did my school work in the otherwise unused dining room. The large mahogany dining table was my desk and the china closet my bookcase.

College was a terrible disappointment; my teachers seemed disinterested or incompetent. For a miserable two years I struggled through the required liberal arts program—the engineering courses I wanted so badly dangled temptingly before me. One irrational, perhaps compulsive, aspect of my behavior was that I never cut class during those first few years of college. It just never occurred to me not to attend a class, no matter how boring it was.

While I was ideologically opposed to the ROTC, I nonetheless enrolled in my freshman year. There was a lot of talk during this period about manning the barricades to fight for socialism and I felt that I had better learn to shoot a rifle if I was going to become politically involved. But they didn't teach you how to shoot, you only drilled. I already had too many dull courses, so I dropped it at the end of the semester and never did learn to shoot a gun. I recall all the anti-ROTC ferment going on, and the outcry over one of the ROTC pamphlets, containing the statement, "democracy leads to mobocracy."

The years at City were politically active for me. I first became a member of the National Student League, the Communist-leaning student organization. When the League merged with the Socialist student group to form the American Student Union I joined that. We had no center or rightist organizations on the campus, but we did have President Robinson, who didn't think it proper for students to demonstrate against the ROTC and expelled twenty-one for doing so. Then, against the desire of the student body, he invited some Italian students who were touring the country propagandizing for Mussolini to be his guests at a gathering in the Great Hall. When one of the student leaders, Eddie Alexander, took the microphone away from Robinson and began to greet the Italian students as "entricked students of Fascist Italy," our president turned livid and called him a gutter-snipe. Within a day almost every student on the campus wore a button, "I am a gutter-snipe." The whole student council was then expelled. Much of our political activity during this period was directed against Robinson and what he stood for. After I graduated the students finally succeeded in forcing his resignation.

During my first two years at City I was involved in all the political action, attending meetings on the campus and off. I took the Oxford Oath—pledging myself never to fight for my country under any circumstances—and joined student strikes whenever they were called. There were May Day parades with student contingents; and in 1936, when I started my engineering courses, I joined the Young Communist League (YCL). My mother was also politically active, helping in the organization of unemployed workers councils in the lower Bronx. My own involvement was taken for granted by my parents.

When I joined the YCL at City College it was set up on a schoolwide basis, but wasn't a very formal organization. We had our meetings Friday nights. Discussion centered on fascism in Germany and Italy and the fight going on in Spain. There wasn't much talk about school issues. The American Student Union was the organization for that. There was no attendance taken at YCL meetings. One could always invite friends (outsiders were generally present) and meetings were lively, often with intense political arguments.

City College was not easy, a grind from early morning until late at night, weekends and Christmas included. I never knew if my eyes would make it through the semester. At the end of the school year I was completely worn out. Summers I worked as a maintenance man (electricity, water supply, sewerage, and mechanical equipment) at Camp Unity, a Communist interracial summer camp located in Wingdale, New York, about sixty miles from the city.

My Uncle Louis was the manager, but my employment was a case of nepotism in reverse. I worked well over eight hours a day, seven days a week—something was always breaking down. For this I got room and board and seven dollars a week. I usually lost fifteen pounds during the summer, although I ate well, but I didn't mind working hard. The respite from study was welcome. And camp wasn't all work. I would manage to take a half hour a day to go swimming, the only sport I really liked, and I acquired further political education. By the end of the summer I generally managed to save about sixty dollars, but more important, my health was restored so I could take another year of the school grind.

Going to school in the Thirties was strictly an act of faith or a manifestation of love of learning for its own sake. We were all aware that City College engineering graduates were not hired by the large corporations. For one thing, we were considered too radical; for another, most students were Jewish (to many people this was redundant).

The courses offered by the Engineering School did not meet our needs. I had to take a year of "machinery, A.C." and a year of "machinery, D.C.," although I wasn't really interested in machinery at all. I wanted electronics, as did so many other students. Nonetheless, we all worked at these courses with an unbelievable intensity, cranking out two or three thick laboratory reports a week.

Thursday afternoon from twelve to two was set aside for the Engineering Society meetings. These were generally devoted to technical subjects, and no political discussion was permitted. Here juniors and seniors mixed, and I got to know members of the engineering classes of 1937, 1938, and 1939.

During my last year at school we organized the Steinmetz Society at the engineering school, which was very loosely connected with the YCL, and not formally affiliated with it. (Steinmetz was an electrical engineer who worked for General Electric in the Twenties. Although he was known to be a Socialist, Steinmetz's political leanings were ignored because his work put General Electric so far ahead in the development of high-voltage electric transmission lines.) About half the electrical engineers—twenty-five or thirty of us—came to the meetings held in a small hall a few blocks off the campus. I remember that Julius Rosenberg functioned as a leader in this group; I was only a rank and filer. (The other engineers I knew well—Elitcher, Danzinger, Joel Barr, William Mutterperl—attended meetings too, and all of them figured in the trial in one way or another.) We discussed the situation in school, as well as the broader political questions of the day—German fascism and the Civil War in Spain.

The Federation of Architects, Engineers, and Technicians (FAECT), the radical engineers trade union, held some organizational meetings on the campus at this time, but nothing came of it. Julius became quite involved with the FAECT after graduation, but the organization didn't exist in Washington, where I went to work after graduation.

There wasn't much socializing among the electrical engineers. Sometimes, during the finals, we would meet at the home of a colleague to study together, but otherwise we were in contact only at school. During my last year I came to know Julius Rosenberg better. He was in the class of 1939, a year behind mine, and had just begun his engineering courses. We were never in the same class, but we sometimes would get together over lunch. To save time we used to eat on the instrument tables in the electrical engineering labs. We both brought sandwiches from home and purchased containers of milk in a nearby grocery. Julius, like all the other students then matriculated in the City College Engineering School, was very bright but his prior technical background was slight. I don't think he had ever fixed a radio or an electrical appliance. I suppose he chose engineering because, despite the remote employment possibilities, it seemed the most "practical" course of studies available at City. He might more suitably have become a Greek scholar, but this offered no means of earning a living. Since his family was even poorer than my own, and lived in the slums of the Lower East Side, the need to earn a living undoubtedly loomed even larger in his calculations than it did in mine. We talked of the gloomy international situation and of engineering and of what we would do if we couldn't find jobs. Emigrating to the Soviet Union, where at this time engineers were desperately needed, was one of the alternatives we discussed.

In the middle of my last semester we learned of a forthcoming civil service examination for the position of junior engineer at two thousand dollars a year—a fantastic salary for any of us. My father wasn't making that much in his own store. As soon as school exams were over, we got together at the meeting rooms of the American Labor Party in upper Manhattan and conducted our own classes for a whole week, reviewing questions from past civil service tests. We shared information, taught each other, and studied as if our lives depended on it—which wasn't far from the truth.

That summer was the last one I spent at Camp Unity. I worked hard as usual but now I had a college degree—and no job after camp closed. I had placed thirteenth on the civil service examination in my district, with a grade of ninety-six and a half. I had only to wait for an assignment. While I waited I looked around, read the want ads in the *Times*, and made the rounds of the employment agencies where I was told, without any apology, that no Jews were wanted. Shortly before Christmas, I did get a couple of weeks' work, installing radios for the Davega Radio Company, and I earned about six dollars a day.

I was getting impatient. It had been six months

since my graduation. Elitcher, Danziger, and many others who had placed below me on the civil service list had already received job assignments in Washington and elsewhere. I went to see Si Gerson, a well-known Communist who had been athletic director at camp. He was a wheel now. He worked in the office of the Borough President of Manhattan. I told him the story and he wrote to S. H. Ordway, one of the civil service commissioners. I then took a bus to Washington to present my letter to the Commissioner. The following week I received an appointment to the Bureau of Ordnance in the Navy Department in Washington, where Elitcher, Danziger, and a number of other former classmates were already working.

I arrived in Washington at the end of January 1939 and was assigned to a large drafting room in the Navy Department building on Constitution Avenue. From where I sat I had a magnificent view of the Washington Monument. Over a hundred other men worked in this room. The only good thing about my job was the pay, and I found I was able to send about half of my salary home to supplement the dwindling income from my father's store. Although I was paid as a junior engineer, I was doing drafting. Since this was my first actual "engineering" job, I said nothing and waited, assuming the state of affairs to be temporary. I found an apartment that had formerly been the upstairs of a one-family house. It consisted of two large rooms, a tiny kitchen, and an enclosed porch—more than I could use alone. Danziger was already married and since I knew Elitcher next best, I asked him to share it with me.

A former classmate invited me to join the Young Communist League group in Washington which he himself had found only a couple of months earlier. I did. The group consisted of about twenty members—all government workers. I had no idea whether similar groups existed in Washington. At times we operated in *sub-rosa* fashion, and at other times quite openly. Political discussion (conducted like a seminar with each of us taking a turn as leader) was our principal "activity." I started reading the *Daily Worker* again, buying it at a newsstand next to the *Washington Post* building on Pennsylvania Avenue. It was not without a certain trepidation that I purchased the Party paper, always wondering if any police observers were posted near by.

When I took the *Worker* home, Elitcher also read it. I never tried to proselytize him, but we frequently discussed the events reported. After a few months Elitcher followed me into the YCL group.

At the beginning of the summer of 1940 I bought a 1936 Dodge for three hundred dollars. For me it was an active summer socially, and on weekends I traveled to the Sky Line Drive and other resort areas near Washington. A girl I had known casually in New York came to work at the Census Bureau, together with many others from Hunter College to whom she introduced me. We had our wild parties, such as midnight picnics at Rock Creek Park, where much milk was consumed; canoe jaunts along the stinking Potomac, concerts at the Watergate, and lawn parties. I would sometimes use the high fidelity set that I had built for an out-door recorded concert.

Sometimes relatives or friends would come to Washington and stay for a few days. During the summer of 1940 Max's younger brother visited us and while we were all at Hain's Point Swimming Pool we ran into Julius and his wife, Ethel. They had come to Washington when Ethel secured a job with the Census Bureau.

However, shortly after our meeting at the pool, the Rosenbergs returned to New York.

Part of my expanding social life revolved around people connected with the YCL and another part was completely separate from politics, though here too my acquaintances were generally progressives. I wanted the freedom of an apartment without a landlady on the premises, so in September 1940 we rented one, unfurnished, in a building on N Street across Rock Creek Park from Georgetown. It was only twenty minutes' walk from work, in a largely black neighborhood, although our building was strictly white. Elitcher and I each had a large room and shared a small kitchen in between. In my room I had a bed, a chest of drawers, a work table, and my high fidelity radio set, with a cheap linoleum rug on the floor.

By this time I realized that my job with the Navy Department was not going to improve and I started looking around for another. I visited the Bureau of Standards and almost got a job there. They were most interested in my amateur radio background, but it wasn't recent enough. I then went to Langley Field in Virginia and stayed overnight with William Mutterperl, my former classmate. Here, too, they found my radio background not recent enough. I started going to school again, taking courses in radio engineering and ultrasonics.

Elitcher had followed me into the YCL and subsequently we had transferred to the Communist Party which underwent several organizational changes. During one period, we met in cells of about four or five for discussions; at other times the group expanded to about fifteen. Even when we met in small cells, special classes of some twenty people were set up to study the newly published *The History of the Communist Party of the Soviet Union.* This negated the security which might have been provided by the small cell arrangement. I believe there was even a mixing of governmental and non-governmental people in these classes, but no one questioned it, though I did have qualms about losing my government job, should my Communist Party membership be revealed.

This was the period of the Soviet-Nazi pact and the Party's efforts were aimed at keeping the United States out of the European war. Washington was unique in that very few open organizations of the Left existed there, because of the intimidation of the government workers who constituted a major part of the population. Elsewhere Communist Party members frequently functioned in other organizations, but in Washington the Party's mission was almost exclusively educational. It did provide support for kindred organizations whose members visited Washington. Our apartment became a hotel for people who came to Washington to picket or lobby. We would frequently put up three or four people for a week-end, and would sometimes have a guest for several weeks. I joined the American Peace Mobilization near the end of 1940; it was the only open organization of its kind in Washington.

In the 1940s the question of Communist Party membership was considered a personal matter, at least in the circles in which I traveled. I can't recall ever asking anyone if he was a member of the Party, or anyone ever asking me. My own ambivalence toward some of the positions taken by the Party made me especially reluctant to recruit anyone; I did not feel I could defend every shift in the Party line.

My own reason for joining the Party was simple: I

felt it was the only organization which got down to fundamentals and called for an overthrow of the system and the evils which were inherent in the capitalist structure. The liberal reformist organizations, in my view, concentrated only on individual obnoxious facets of the system rather than the essence.

I was well aware that the Communist Party U.S.A. was following the lead of the Russian Communist Party, often subordinating the needs of the American workers to the interests of the Soviet Union. I also believed that the security of the Soviet Union was a paramount concern at this time since, if the USSR were overthrown, the Parties of all the other countries would be immeasurably weakened. From any long-range point of view the interests of the USSR seemed to coincide with those of the workers of all other countries, but this didn't resolve the short-range problems that arose to plague me from time to time. If forced to argue I could almost support any position, but in my heart I felt that the Party was the way. It was, I suppose, a matter of faith.

I met Helen early in 1941. I liked her from the very beginning. A friend, Shirley, who was a Communist Party member, moved into a room in Helen and Casey's (Helen's husband) house in a pleasant section in the outskirts of the city, and through her I got to know the family (including their one-and-a half-year-old daughter Sydney) well. I was impressed with little precocious Sydney and Casey seemed like a nice easy-going guy. Subsequently I learned from Helen that she was unhappy in her marriage. My feelings were very confused since I soon found myself in love with Helen and she with me. Helen had graduated in 1939 from Wilson

Teacher's College but had failed the license exam by one-half point. She felt that her exam papers had been down-graded in view of her radical political acitivity at school and she was now studying, intending to take the exam over again. From time to time when I dropped by I would help Helen with her math review; she had majored in science which made it easy for us to talk.

When Germany invaded the Soviet Union in June, 1941, the whole orientation of the Communist Party changed. The American Peace Mobilization had pick-eted the White House until a week before the invasion, to protest Roosevelt's aid to Great Britain. Now there was a call for getting as much help as possible to the Allies. I didn't find this reversal difficult to accept. My thinking was conditioned by the international events of those years: the West's betrayal of Spain to the Fascist powers and the acquiescence of England and France to Germany's take-over of Czechoslovakia. I had read Herbert L. Matthews's heartbreaking dispatches from Spain in the *New York Times* and also those of Geyde from Czechoslovakia, at the time of Hitler's invasion, and I remembered them well. So when the Soviet Union sought to gain time for survival by making a pact with the devil, I wasn't surprised or disturbed. And now that Hitler attacked the only Socialist country in the world, imperfect as it was (and I was well aware even then of its shortcomings), I felt it had to be saved: it would be a long time before another Socialist nation arose. The capitalist nations had learned their lesson and would, I believed, play their cards more shrewdly the next time.

In any event, for American Communists the political world became "simpler" with the German attack on the Soviet Union. The period of the non-aggression pact, the source of painful conflict for so many Party members, was over. Once again the Nazis were clearly and unambiguously the enemy.

June 22, the night of the attack, I was at a party in Helen's house. Everyone remained until the small hours of the morning, ears glued to the radio. There weren't enough chairs and at one point in the evening I lay down on the carpet. Helen came over and put her head on my belly, using it as a pillow. It was casual and yet so thrilling. I knew she felt as I did.

A few weeks later, I decided to get away from Washington for a while. I headed south in my Dodge, stopping off at Langley Field to see Bill Mutterperl, and then continued on to Augusta, Atlanta, and Wrens, Georgia. In Wrens, I explored the locale of Erskine Caldwell's play, *Tobacco Road,* in the company of Caldwell's father, a minister. I had never seen such poverty and disease: families of ten living in a one-room shack with a single bed, and everyone diseased from undernourishment.

I stayed several days in Birmingham, Alabama visiting the nearby coal mines, and similar attractions. Then I headed for New Orleans, where I had a letter of introduction to a couple who ran a beauty parlor in the French Quarter. I stayed with them for a while, exploring the city and taking them for a ride along the Gulf.

I started back by way of Pensacola, Florida. It was summertime and there were only a handful of people on the beach. One of them was Ephraim Cross, my erstwhile French teacher from City College. He was headed for a vacation in Mexico. We exchanged a few words, but nothing important. That night, before I fell asleep, I suddenly found the solution to my dissatisfaction with my job and the troubling relationship with Helen: I would simply go back to school.

Since I had been sending all my surplus earnings home to assist my parents and to help with my sister's education, I didn't have any accumulated capital. I sold my high fidelity set and my auto. This, plus my accumulated leave money, netted me seven hundred dollars. It was enough to pay for Michigan, but not M.I.T.

I had been granted an occupational deferment by the draft board in Washington, and they indicated they wouldn't change my status if I returned to school for a year.

During my last month in Washington Elitcher and I had an argument and we didn't even talk to each other until the day I left. On the surface it was one of those absurd quarrels. I had told him that his socks stank up the house and that he should wash them more frequently. But obviously more lay beneath the surface of his hurt feelings. I never figured out what it was.

I was relieved to be leaving Washington. In one fell swoop I had "solved" all my problems. I was leaving a job in which I was unhappy and I was leaving Helen, with whom I was by now deeply in love. She had no teaching license and was working as a sales girl in a dry goods store. I hadn't told her of my quarrel with Elitcher and she invited us both to dinner the day before I left Washington. I resented Elitcher's being there. I tried to feel gay, but too many unspoken thoughts flashed through my mind as Helen and I looked at each other during the meal.

I found school at Michigan almost idyllic; different from any of my previous school experiences and I resolved not to be diverted from my studies by any need to earn money. With careful economy I knew I could stretch my $700 to last for the year. Together with another student, I rented a two room suite, a small bedroom and a large living room in a boarding house next to the campus. My share of the rent was $4.00 a week. For an additional $5.40 a week I ate all my meals except Sunday supper at the cooperative dining hall. Tuition was only $150 for the whole year.

At Michigan, as a graduate student, I no longer had to take required courses. Every class I enrolled in was one I myself selected. Since I was primarily an experimentalist, I began working on my thesis project from the first semester—the measurement of radio frequency power at high frequencies. I also did another small project in the physics department on the volume-expander used in high fidelity audio equipment.

Besides the courses and my experimental work, there was the campus atmosphere which was entirely novel and delightful to me. At the cooperative dining room I ate with graduate students from other disciplines: psychology, mathematics, biology, and physics. There were also concerts, lectures, and an occasional graduate dance. The classes were small but the students weren't as bright as those at City.

Sunday, December 7, 1941, I was at home studying and listening to the philharmonic, when the news bulletin came through that the Japanese had bombed Pearl Harbor. After that things were not the same at school. The pace became frantic. M.I.T. set up a crash program of instruction for the electrical engineering professors. Christmas they came back to Michigan with blueprints of equipment which had to be built for radar courses scheduled to start in February.

I returned East for the Christmas vacation, stopping first at the home of my parents who were now living in Philadelphia. My father had finally given up his drug store and obtained a civil service appointment as an engineer at the Philadelphia Navy Yard where he was much happier. After a few days I left for Washington to visit with old friends. Elitcher and I had forgotten our quarrel and we went over to Helen's house together. She asked me to go to a party with her that evening. I wanted very much to be with her but knew it would only make us both miserable. I took the train back to Ann Arbor that very evening, returning to school a whole week before classes began.

Living on a deserted campus was strange. I needed to get equipment built for my ultra-high-frequency generator and had to do all the work myself, since the machine shop personnel were busy making equipment for the new radar courses. But I enjoyed it and working twelve hours a day gave me little time to think about Helen.

The second semester at Michigan was even more exciting, intellectually, than the first. To my great delight I was able to take a course with a mathematician of the first rank, Anton Zygmund. I also learned glass blowing, to construct the lamps I needed for my thesis experiments. My teacher was an old German glass blower.

As soon as the war began industrial and government recruiters visited the campus in droves. I was pleasantly surprised to receive an offer from General Electric. However both Bell Labs and the M.I.T. Radiation Lab turned me down. In the meantime I was offered a seven hundred dollar fellowship. I would have liked to remain at school working for my doctorate, but finally told Professor Dow, who had submitted my name, that difficult as it was for me to refuse the opportunity, I could not in good conscience continue to study when I felt that I could contribute to the war effort. A week after my last exam I finished my thesis, and left the campus several days before graduation.

I stopped in Washington for a day and found that Helen had obtained a position as a scientific aide at the Bureau of Standards. Then, after a quick visit in Philadelphia, I headed for General Electric in Schenectady.

In Schenectady I rented a room within walking distance of G.E. As a test engineer I was given four "test" assignments, each of three months' duration, in various parts of the "works," before being permanently placed. My starting salary was $34.50 a week: a come-down from the $2,600 per annum I had been earning in Washington. My first three assignments didn't turn out very well and for nine months I struggled to find a niche for myself in the sprawling G.E. enterprise.

The other test engineers were hard working, competent, convivial men. I got to know a few of them well and we frequently ate together in the evenings and went to a movie or sometimes to a tavern. That was all Schenectady had to offer. Our discussions ranged from engineering problems to politics and religion. However I never felt entirely comfortable in the company of these men. Theirs seemed a different world. I saw the war primarily as a fight against fascism, while they saw it in terms of fighting for their country. The overthrow of capitalism was a basic premise of my existence. They never questioned our system. I felt best when we discussed engineering problems.

From almost the beginning I spent weekends in New York City every couple of weeks. Since we worked a six-day week, this meant catching the late afternoon train out of Schenectady Saturday, arriving in New York in time to catch a show with one of several girls I knew there. Sometimes I would drop in to see Julius and Ethel Rosenberg who had just moved into a new apartment on the Lower East Side. Generally we talked about the progress of the war and what the future held for us. I always felt at ease with them; Ethel radiated a warmth one didn't find in many people. Sometimes I would also visit the Danzigers who had returned to New York. But in 1943 they moved to the West Coast and I didn't see them again until 1950.

I always took a late Sunday evening train back to Schenectady, arriving just in time to get home, shave, and go to work. Despite the long tiring journey, I found my jaunts to New York revivifying.

In April of 1943 I received my fourth job assignment, this one in the aeronautics and marine engineering department. Here I at last found myself. Though I had never worked on servo-mechanisms (automatic control devices) before, my general background in engineering and mathematics stood me in good stead. I was given several problems for which I found elegant solutions, and at the end of this three-month assignment, it was agreed that I would stay on. I now had a desk and a lab bench, and, most important, I was doing *real* engineering.

Helen had written during this period, to keep me apprised of events, and, sometimes, of her feelings. But when I answered I was deliberately restrained. In late August of 1943 I went to Washington for a one-week vacation. Bill Mutterperl, with whom I had been corresponding, agreed to come up from Langley Field so we could spend a couple of days together. I also visited Max Elitcher and his recent wife, as well as other

friends. Two days before I was due to return to Schenectady I went out to Helen's place. Casey left early in
the evening and Sydney was asleep upstairs. We talked
about everything except our feelings for each other. I
gathered that her marriage had further deteriorated. We
went down to the basement and played a game of Ping
Pong. Afterwards we were talking about the game when
I suddenly took her in my arms and kissed her and
asked her if she would marry me. It seemed as though I
had planned it. There wasn't a moment's hesitation before she assented.

In September we met in New York for a three-day
vacation, staying in a borrowed apartment. They were
three days such as I had never before experienced. We
went to plays and concerts, ate in good restaurants, and
made love. Helen had told Casey she was leaving him.
While waiting for her divorce she and Sydney moved
into her parents' home in Arlington, Virginia. I had broken up an unhappy marriage.

Since we were both basically conventional people
we agreed that Helen would continue to stay with her
parents for the eighteen months necessary to secure a
final divorce decree. I phoned her every week and
every six weeks traveled to Washington to spend a
blissful eighteen hours with her.

Sydney accepted me as a friend and Helen's
parents embraced me as one of the family. I tried to get
a job at the Johns Hopkins Applied Physics Laboratory
near Washington, but failed. Around Labor Day the
Elitchers, Helen, and I took our vacations together at a
state park in West Virginia. We had several intensive
political discussions about Earl Browder's then recent
opus, *Victory and After,* in which he predicted that, as

a result of their wartime cooperation, the United States and the Soviet Union would work together in peace and friendship. I wasn't so sanguine.

In the fall and winter, as our marriage drew nearer, I visited Helen more frequently. She was having trouble at her job at the Bureau of Standards, where she had been confronted with evidence of past membership in the Communist Party. However the issue was never resolved because she left the Bureau when she received her final divorce decree.

Several days later, on March 10, 1945, we were married in Arlington, Virginia, with the Elitchers as witnesses. After a party for Helen's relatives, we headed for Schenectady where I had rented a furnished apartment on the ground floor of a two-family house. It contained three large rooms, living room, dining room, and kitchen and three tiny bedrooms. That first afternoon we bought our first groceries, got some ice for the ice box, and Helen, Sydney, and I started our life together.

The cold weather was over and spring was particularly lovely where we lived in Schenectady, on the outskirts of town close to a park. In April Helen got a job at G.E., working on the development of vibration instruments.

In a short while we had established our daily routine. We would take Sydney to the child care center a short distance from our house, and then drive to G.E., where we both put in a six-day week. When the weather was good I would meet Helen at our car, lunch time, and would drive to one of the nearby locks of the Erie Canal—the canal my father was surveying when I was born. We would sit on the grass eating our lunch and watch the barges being lifted or dropped in the lock. I would never have believed that life could be so beautiful.

After several attempts at socializing in Schenectady, Helen and I gave up. Anything beyond superficial communication was virtually impossible with the people whom we met. The one exception was a solid friendship we established with Dr. P. and his wife, refugees from Hitlerism. It was infinitely easier to talk with them than with our fellow Americans.

I had not re-joined the Communist Party at Michigan because my stay was to be so brief, and when I came to Schenectady the war was already on. In the circumstances the Party seemed superfluous, at least for the moment. I couldn't conceive of a meaningful Communist Party except in opposition to the capitalist system, but during the war, because of the need for unity between the Soviet Union and the United States, the Party ceased to function as a revolutionary organization. I didn't get the *Daily Worker* in Schenectady either, since it would have been delivered by mail and I didn't feel a need to flaunt my inclinations in a small town. When I was in New York, I generally picked up a copy at a newsstand.

For our one-week vacation in August 1945 we took a trip to Montreal and then followed the St. Lawrence river to Ottawa. It was here that we awoke one morning to learn that the United States had dropped an atomic bomb over Japan. I had heard mention from time to time at G.E. about the uranium diffusion plant at Oak Ridge, but this casual gossip hadn't made much of an impression. Of course, it never occurred to me when I heard the news in Ottawa that five years later the A-bomb would figure so prominently in our lives.

I tried to work on non-military projects after the war and for several months I worked on the development of a new transcription turntable for broadcast studios and came up with a design based on principles opposite those on which the turntables then in use were operated.

In December 1945 the Electrical Workers' Union went out on strike, and set up massive picket lines around the works. General Electric didn't ask the engineers to come to work although they paid us and required us to remain in Schenectady. Since Helen and I were both being paid our full salaries, we felt it only fair to make contributions to the strike fund. For two months we had an extended vacation at home. We arose each morning at our regular time and filled the day largely with study and reading. We also went to a wood-working shop in a local school one or two evenings a week. Helen learned how to operate the wood lathe.

I suppose the studying Helen did during the strike influenced her decision to go back to school instead of returning to work when the strike was settled. She enrolled in Rensselaer Polytechnic Institute (RPI) in Troy, a town about fifteen miles from Schenectady.

After the strike the G.E. management evidently became worried when they learned that efforts were being made to organize the engineers. They called a meeting of all the engineers, at which top level officers warned the men about the harmful effects of unionization for engineers; namely it wasn't professional, and would be degrading to their status. One union organizing meeting was held, at which two of G.E.'s top research scientists spoke. Over a hundred engineers showed up but the meeting was disrupted by company stooges. Naively, I hadn't realized that G.E. would play that dirty. Another meeting was held at which Jim Mc-Manus of the Newspaper Guild spoke. Several hundred attended this meeting but nothing ever came of it. None of the men who worked with me seemed to be interested in joining a union, despite the miserable wages we were being paid. I was making thirty-five hundred dollars a year during most of 1945. I considered trying to help organize, but felt that since I was a junior engineer my influence would be negligible. Besides I was never one of the boys.

After the war, Harry Belock, a government engineer whom I had run into on and off during the war, quit his job and set up his own concern, the Reeves Instrument Company, in New York. He offered me and one of my co-workers a job at a considerable increase in salary. My co-worker accepted, but I stayed on at G.E. I had just started development of a new radiosonde tracking system which was more interesting than the one I had recently completed. I set this one up on the roof of the lab building and conducted many flight tests during its development. This was how I really enjoyed working, testing my designs before they went into production.

Both Helen and I wanted to get away from Schenectady. While it was a very easy town to live in, it seemed a dead end for us. Yet I didn't particularly want to go back to New York. I knew that things were much too hectic there and living was a constant hassle. Nonetheless we decided to return to New York, but only for a limited period of time.

In June of 1947, after Helen had taken her finals at Rensselaer, we moved to New York City and I went to work for Reeves at a salary of seven thousand dollars a year.

The housing shortage in postwar New York was acute. My parents, who were living once again in the city (my father was now working at a chain drug store), turned their own apartment over to us while they moved into one vacated by a cousin. It was hot—especially in the small, top-floor Bronx apartment, but our situation was momentarily eased by the fact that Sydney was away at camp.

Hunting for an apartment proved very discouraging. We finally made a deposit on a cooperative garden apartment under construction, but when the building was completed and we were ready to move in, we were informed that it could not be set up as a cooperative under existing federal housing regulations. Our money was returned and, at year's end, we found ourselves back where we had started. We ended up doing what I had said I never would do—buying a house; in February of 1948 we moved into our new home in Flushing, Long Island.

When I started to work at Reeves, I was asked to sign an affidavit that I wasn't a member of the Communist Party and never had been one. I complied without giving it a second thought. By then my past membership seemed far away. In the meantime Helen, too, had gone to work at Reeves, and she also signed the non-Communist affidavit. However, while Helen found her job at Reeves fairly interesting, she decided that she would rather be a physicist. She quit her job and registered at Columbia University.

At Reeves I was project engineer in charge of the development of a plotting board which was used to track airplanes by radar and to plot the actual flight path on paper. Technically it was a fascinating project, but since 1947 marked the acceleration of the cold war, this was not the kind of work I wanted to do. However, I convinced myself that everything was only temporary and coasted along.

Once we were back in New York I began to renew ties with some of my old friends, including Julius and Ethel. Since my marriage I had only seen them infrequently, on the fly, generally when I was in New York on G.E. business. We visited them in their apartment in Knickerbocker Village. It was pleasant but inadequate for them and their two children; one smallish bedroom, a living room, and a tiny kitchen. Julius wasn't doing well. He had been fired from his government job, accused of being a Communist Party member. He had then gone into business with some relatives, and eventually set up a small machine shop. I didn't ask Julius why he didn't try to obtain a non-security engineering job, since I knew that such jobs were not easily available and Julius had no real engineering experience. He had been employed as a government inspector, but that wasn't truly engineering work. As a matter of fact, we never discussed engineering, though he would sometimes speak of technical problems encountered in his machine shop venture. We generally talked politics, art, or, in a broad sense, the sciences. Ethel was interested in child psychology, as was Helen, and this became an important topic of conversation when we all got together.

While Julius's movements and speech were rather staccato, giving an appearance of definiteness in whatever he did, Ethel appeared much more soft spoken. She expressed herself with a certain tentativeness, which belied the fact that by this time her ideas were actually well formulated. Despite what the trial judge and Eisenhower later said about her, nothing in their relationship suggested that she dominated Julius. I never asked Julius whether he was a member of the Communist Party, and he never asked me.

I wasn't reading the *Worker* regularly nor had I given any consideration to rejoining the Communist Party since our move to New York. Perhaps it was because my energies were fully absorbed by my job and family. I had also begun to feel a slight uneasiness about the affidavits Helen and I had so unconcernedly signed at Reeves. When Julius had been accused of membership in the Party, in 1945, the only consequence (serious enough for him) was the loss of his government job. But by 1947 the federal loyalty program had been instituted. The result of a federal employee's being accused of falsely signing a loyalty oath was not simply a lost job: it was a perjury charge, carrying a possible five-year prison sentence. The same was true for an employee of a company like Reeves, with military government contracts.

Early in the summer of 1948 I received a letter from Max Elitcher. When I had seen him a year earlier he told me that things were not going well between him and Helene, and that they would probably have to be divorced. From our conversation I gathered that Helene was bearing down too hard on him; she had a tremendous drive. In his letter, however, Max made no reference to his marital difficulties but wrote that he and his family would be coming to New York in a week to look for a house. He had decided to leave his Navy Department job and work for Reeves.

The Elitchers arrived at our home at suppertime.

We had plenty of room since both Edie, Helen's sister who had been staying with us, and Sydney were away for the summer. After they had put their child to bed, Max told me that he had been followed by what he presumed to be the FBI from Baltimore all the way to New York. Initially I found this story implausible but when he said he had stopped to buy some dinnerware at Baltimore and had afterwards noticed a car following him through all the turns of the Baltimore streets, I began to believe him. I slowly became angry at him for having continued on to my home, possibly drawing the FBI to me. With my Communist background I did not wish to be an object of the FBI's attention. In any event I thought it had been unfair of him to come under the circumstances, and then to wait until they had settled and their child was asleep before telling me about it.

Max and I discussed the incident for some time without confiding in Helen or Helene. Both of us, of course, were keenly aware that thousands of people with left-wing backgrounds were currently being investigated by the FBI.

Halfway through the evening I decided to see if my house was under surveillance. I told Max I was going to take a ride and see if I were followed. He offered to come along as an observer and we drove around Queens for about twenty minutes before returning home. Since the traffic was light it was fairly easy to determine that we were not being followed. (At the trial Max Elitcher gave this whole incident a different ending, hurting me more than anything else during the trial.)

The Elitchers stayed at our place a week while househunting. In the end they decided to buy a house exactly like ours, which was being built on the next street, with a back yard adjacent to ours. I wasn't happy about this since it would bring our families into intimate contact and I remembered the animosity that had developed after our close association in Washington.

When the Elitchers moved in we socialized with them minimally. Max and I drove to work together, yet Helen and I never fell into the habit of visiting them to watch TV, which was the thing to do in 1948, nor did we ever have dinner together. It was a distant relationship, which deteriorated with time.

In commuting to work with Max every day (we would alternate, using his car and mine), I felt a change in him; he had become more like Helene—aggressive and not as easy to talk with as before. Our discussions became quite trivial, and in fact, we both remained silent a great deal of the time. We had definitely grown apart.

I was deeply troubled by the worsening state of Soviet-American relations and the possible use to which the work I was doing might be put. But I never discussed this with Max; I didn't want him to be privy to my inner thoughts. His job was entirely different from mine. He was more or less a paper-shuffler, as he had been in Washington, taking care of all the details of a contract. He worked by himself at a desk and never in the lab. I don't know how much of the technical details he was required to know for his part of the job.

One of the reasons that I had enjoyed working on the radiosonde weather balloon project at G.E. was that it had no intrinsic war capabilities. When I heard that there was another meteorological project in the offing, I tried to interest Reeves. However, this was simply a developmental project without funds for follow-up production, so the Reeves front office was uninterested. After that fell through, I had an idea for an automatic electron trajectory-plotter and did some preliminary paper design work on it, but again I couldn't interest Reeves.

By the end of the summer of 1948 the most interesting part of my work on the plotting board was completed. I had gotten the bugs out of the prototype and from then on most of my work had to be done in the office where I would have to "make like an executive," coordinating many of the engineering details of production. I didn't enjoy this. Halfheartedly I looked around at some of the other companies in the area, but couldn't find anything I really liked or which would have taken me out of the war industries.

That September Helen became pregnant but finished her semester at Columbia, leaving at the end of January 1949.

As soon as the first production model of the plotting board was completed, I began to work out of the old Roosevelt Field from which Lindbergh had taken off on his flight to Paris when I was ten years old. Here we tested the plotting board, tracking an old B-17 of World War II vintage. This would have been fun if I hadn't been aware of the part this equipment might play in future situations.

Mark was born in June 1949 and Helen, with greater understanding of child psychology than I, did not send Sydney off to camp that summer. My Leica camera took on a new lease on life. Sometimes on Saturday or Sunday I would shoot a whole roll of thirty-six pictures of Mark and spend the rest of the day in the cellar developing and enlarging them.

Helen and I continued to visit Julius and Ethel and

I met Julius for lunch on several occasions. In 1949 his machine shop wasn't doing well and he was looking for business. He thought I might prevail on Harry Belock, my boss, to sub-contract some work to him as it was quite usual at Reeves to farm out such work. But when I visited Julius's shop I realized that none of his equipment was adequate for the kind of precision work that Reeves required. I tried to explain to him, without hurting his feelings, that it would be useless for me to approach Belock under the circumstances. He spoke of his shop with such obvious pride.

I found myself thinking increasingly of going back to school and wrote several universities to find out the possibilities, both for student and teacher, but I realized that Helen would have to obtain her master's before I could consider going for a doctorate. In the meantime, I began taking a mathematics course at N.Y.U. under a good mathematician, Professor Johns.

In February 1950 Helen returned to her studies at Columbia and I had an opportunity to teach a graduate course on feedback amplifiers at the Brooklyn Polytechnic Institute. I had never taken such a course myself, and there wasn't even a good book on the subject. But I put together a course, lecture by lecture. It was hard work, but it was also fun, and I felt well-rewarded by the experience.

In the early spring of 1950 Julius called me at work and asked if I could lend him some money. He had to meet bills at the machine shop and was short of cash. He had never before come to me for financial help; I knew he must have felt very embarrassed. We met for lunch that afternoon. Our discussion about his predicament was uncomfortable for both of us; I had no idea that he was in desperate financial straits. After lunch I went to my bank and withdrew three hundred dollars, which I gave him without setting any time for repayment. I knew he would repay me as soon as he could.

About this time Bill Danziger and his wife moved back to New York City after a long absence, and visited us at home. When Bill mentioned that he was working for a firm which farmed out rough machine shop jobs, I told him that Julius was now in that business and looking for work. (I gave him Julius's address. This figured in the trial.)

In April, I took a trip to the Carswell Air Force base in Texas, where the military was going to use the plotting board I had designed. This was the first time I had been to Texas. It was an awesome feeling to stand under the tail of a mammoth B-36. However, I felt ill at ease surrounded by all the brass; it brought home to me, better than anything else could, the military significance of my work over the past three years.

My admission to Carswell had been made possible because Belock had applied for an increase in my security clearance—from "confidential" to "secret." As I have said, for some time I had been worrying about the non-Communist affidavits which Helen and I signed, and with Belock's action my concern was greatly increased.

One peculiarity of my character is that I have always felt a compulsion to finish a job, whatever the consequences. When I was a child and brought my father his meal, at the store, in a valise, the Gentile children of the neighborhood would taunt me with epithets like "kike" or "Christ killer" and sometimes threaten me. On more than one occasion they pelted me with stones and I ran for my life, carefully holding the valise horizontally so as not to spill any of the soup in the pot.

The thought of abandoning the valise or swinging it so that I might run faster never occurred to me. Even when I was hit and my ear gashed, I still hung on to the valise as if it were dearer than life itself.

For the last two years at Reeves this side of my personality had dominated as I single-mindedly devoted myself to completing the plotting board project. All around me an anti-Communist mania was raging, instigated and manipulated by the Establishment. First had come the Truman Doctrine, proclaiming the support of the United States for all right-wing counter-revolutionary forces. Then the House Un-American Activities Committee stepped up its hunt for spies in the government. The Attorney General came out with his list of "subversive" organizations and the leaders of the American Communist Party were arrested. Richard Nixon, then a member of the House, began his ugly career pursuing his prey relentlessly. I had been aware of everything that was happening, deeply dismayed by it, and yet, somehow, the full import of these events had not properly impressed themselves upon me.

In June of 1950, however, there came a moment when I felt that all my tasks had been completed. The course I was teaching had ended, and, more important, the last of the plotting boards had been shipped. Helen's semester at Columbia was over, as was Sydney's school year. With all my obligations discharged, I relaxed—and then the wild emotions of the domestic witch hunt closed in. I was again the little boy who arrived at his destination with valise intact, and noticing that his ear was gashed, suddenly realized that he was afraid.

In truth, given the times, there was much for us to fear. Helen and I had both committed perjury when we signed the "loyalty oaths" at Reeves, and many of our relatives and friends had also been members of the Party. I had recently been granted "secret" clearance with no apparent difficulty, but I was certain at some point to be the subject of an FBI investigation. Helen, of course, had long ago been officially accused of Communist Party membership when employed in Washington by the Bureau of Standards.

In addition to this realistic fear there were other apprehensions which pervaded the American Left in 1950, and which I shared. The belief was widespread that World War III was in the offing. It seemed to us that America was veering toward fascism, a fascism that would be much the same as that of Nazi Germany. We saw mass roundups, concentration camps, and death ovens, à la Hitler.

Today, with the advantage of hindsight, we can see that the Establishment faced no mass opposition. The Left was already weakened, isolated, and impotent. Repression by congressional committees, blacklists, loyalty oaths, and a few thousand firings, deportations, arrests, and trials, were all that was necessary to provide an atmosphere of silent conformity for the massive military buildup our country was undertaking. But I, as well as other more astute political observers, did not perceive this at the time.

The evening newspapers on Friday, June 16, carried headlines about a former army sergeant who had been arrested for the theft of the atom bomb. I saw it as more fuel for the rising temperature of the cold war.

The next evening Helen and I took Sydney and her cousin, Sandy, to Coney Island for an excursion we had promised Sydney weeks before. This was the first time since my childhood that I had been there and it was the first time that I had ever gone on so many different rides. When I was a child I never had enough money for more than one or two of the attractions. But while I was going through the motions of amusing myself, my mind was elsewhere; how should we respond to the menace I felt in the political situation? I knew I had to leave Reeves; but where to go; what alternative way of life?

I had been considering the possibility of our living abroad but it seemed an enormous step. Mexico seemed most practicable. We had talked of going there on vacation. It was close and living there was inexpensive. If we went, perhaps it would be merely a long summer vacation. We could go with an open mind, look around, and then decide our course of action. It was crazy, I knew, but I felt we had to get away to some place where the air would be cleaner, where we could relax—psychologically as well as physically.

By the time we left Coney Island I felt that this was the way. When Helen and I discussed it she agreed with me. She seemed pleased and relieved.

I went to work at Reeves that Monday and Tuesday, cleaning up some last minute odds and ends. On Wednesday I withdrew most of the money from our bank accounts, cashed our defense bonds, and obtained our tourist permits from the Mexican Consulate. I bought the airline tickets, sixty-day excursion, return trip tickets for us and Sydney. Hers was good for six months. We started packing Wednesday evening. It was only then that we told Edie, who was living with us, our plans, that I was taking a leave of absence and that we were going to Mexico for a while. We decided not to tell our parents about our trip while our ultimate plans were still so uncertain. Thursday, Bill Danziger came over to borrow my electric drill and I told him where we were going. One of the last things I did was to write Harry Belock, my superior at Reeves, asking for an indefinite leave of absence. We left from La Guardia Thursday, on an evening flight.

3   Mexico

THERE was something unreal in the all-night flight to Mexico City. The first stop, Washington National Airport in Virginia, was only a stone's throw from Helen's mother. I wanted very much to say, "let's get off and see the folks for a while," but instead we stayed in our seats and chatted about old times—my periodic visits to wartime Washington, from Schenectady and spending barely eighteen hours with Helen before starting back, to be at work the following morning. I almost yearned for those "good old days" when everything seemed so simple, and we were all united in the struggle against fascism; when there were no witch hunts for Reds, when . . . But as soon as the plane took off again these thoughts were put aside, and I began to wonder what lay ahead.

As the hour got late the seat lights were extinguished, one by one, until most of the travelers were sleeping. Mark had long since gone to sleep, lying on top of me. Helen was at my side, Sydney across the aisle. From time to time I would close my eyes, doze off for a moment and re-awaken with a start, as though I should instead be thinking of what was to come. Helen and I ought to be planning our next move. Why were we leaving the States? Would we come back? Unuttered questions. Questions that were not even internally formulated with this precision.

It must have been after midnight when the plane landed in Dallas, Texas and we all disembarked to go through customs. It seemed uncivilized to awaken a planeload of people for these formalities. I registered our Leica and Bolex movie cameras, as well as some additional lenses, so that I would not have to pay duty on them when we returned. When we returned? Were we returning? At this time I didn't know. We might manage simply to have a fine vacation in Mexico, at the end of which we would find that we had exaggerated things in our minds and return to the States, ready to pick up where we had left off.

The only concrete worry concerned the statements Helen and I had signed when we went to work for the Reeves Instrument Company. Up until now the government had gone after the wheels, and not bothered much with little fish. Now we might be indicted for perjury. With the accelerated pace of witch-hunting, we felt that it was only a matter of time, and perhaps events, before all Communists, ex-Communists, and progressives would be persecuted.

Not quite knowing what we feared made rational decisions difficult. This was probably what lay behind my equivocation. Why didn't we go to Europe instead of Mexico? This seemed like a more drastic step, and besides, it would have cost much more to get to Europe and to live there. Who could imagine that later, at the trial, David Greenglass would testify that Julius had told him to flee the United States by way of Mexico, through some elaborate scheme involving the Soviet Embassy in Mexico?

With daybreak people began to move about the

cabin, and the unreal phantasmagoric atmosphere gradually evaporated; Mark was chipper as he crawled up and down the carpeted aisle. We had never thought of making ourselves inconspicuous on this trip and had only told Sydney we were taking an extended vacation, probably for the summer. The fact that her school was over made it seem natural, but she probably had her own doubts.

As soon as we cleared customs at Mexico City I began to inquire about rooming houses in the city, and after a few phone calls located one which sounded promising. When we got to the house, on Minatitlan, we found it everything the landlady had claimed on the phone and we settled temporarily into two rooms—a large one and a small one—with kitchen privileges. This would do until we had a chance to look around.

We tried some of the nearby restaurants and all picked up the usual tourista diarrhea. After that we confined almost all of our eating to the rooming house. Shopping for food was not difficult and we were easily able to adapt to what was available in the local stores. We had been warned about the fresh milk, but made good whole milk from a dry Nestles product. I wondered that it was not available in the States. We took several trips to tourist attractions and familiarized ourselves with the neighborhood—just as though we were ordinary tourists.

I concentrated on finding a suitable apartment. Every morning Helen and I would scan the newspaper ads, and then I would look at the most likely. It took a couple of days to learn the overall situation and I became an expert apartment hunter. I was surprised at how expensive some of the places were—three and four hundred dollars a month for nothing extraordinary.

After about a week I found a pleasant, furnished apartment on Calle de Cordoba, a working class neighborhood not very far from Insurgentes and Obregon, two of the major avenues. It was a duplex, three flights up. On the lower level was a living room, in which Sydney would sleep, a small kitchen, a dining alcove, and a maid's room, hardly bigger than a large closet; the upper level, a bedroom and a bathroom. It was adequately furnished and was quite reasonable—under a hundred dollars a month, although we found that a maid came with the apartment, and her wage was an additional forty dollars a month. Later I learned that she lived downstairs in a basement located at street level, with about a dozen other members of her family. It was pitiful to see the family all living in what would have been a boiler room—if the house had had a boiler. They seemed to have no furniture, sleeping on mattresses on the floor.

Helen and I were both concerned that our families would worry and decided to write them. We didn't want to burden them with the knowledge of our location, for fear that they might be questioned about us, and would be torn between the desire not to betray our whereabouts, and fear of the law. Since I had seen my friend Bill Danziger just before we left the States I wrote him enclosing messages for our parents, and asking him to re-mail them. For some reason, in the return address, I used the name Morty Sowell, a real pseudonym, although giving our correct address! Yet in renting the apartment, I had used my real name, even though I had learned in the course of my apartment hunting, that under Mexican law all rentals had to be registered with a government agency. When I wrote Danziger a second letter, with some more enclosures, I used still another pseudonym, Morty Levitov (Helen's maiden name). Coming down to Mexico, we had left a trail as wide as Fifth Avenue, and now we were registered in government files at this address. What possessed me to use these so obvious pseudonyms? I suppose I couldn't quite make up my mind whether or not I was trying to hide.

We met Manuel de los Rios, a neighbor, across the hall. The name de los Rios struck a familiar chord almost from the moment he introduced himself, and when I asked, he informed me that he was indeed the nephew of the last foreign minister of Republican Spain. I remembered de los Rios as a heroic figure in the Republican government, one who did not waver when the government came under attack by the western democracies as communistic.

Our families quickly took to each other and within a few days he invited us to a party of confreres, former Spanish Loyalists who were now living in Mexico, awaiting the day when Franco would be overthrown and they could go home again; people who under the guise of neutrality had been betrayed by the democratic governments of the West. This was the first opportunity Helen and I had had to discuss the civil war in Spain with those who had participated in the struggle and I warmed up to these Spaniards as though I had known them all my life.

Manuel told us how he had fled from Spain after the defeat of the Loyalists and had lived in New York City for a while, teaching Spanish in DeWitt Clinton High School. Here in Mexico he had his own business, designing furniture and doing interior decorations.

During the next couple of weeks Helen and I relaxed. We bought a stroller for Mark and explored the city. Since taxis were relatively cheap it was easy to get around with the kids and we visited the usual historical sites, the museums, and various market places, sampling some Mexican foods. There was one small park a block away from our apartment, and it was there that we first let Mark practice walking without support. We also visited some of the larger parks which were within walking distance. The Super-Mercado was only six blocks from the house, making grocery shopping convenient for the *Norteamericanos*. Initially we had had some problems, like Mark's diaper rash, but locating the omnipresent diaper service solved that. Gradually we found ourselves really enjoying the scene.

I visited some places by myself including the National Institute of Cardiology, about which I had heard while in the States. I should have liked to work there, but things were too much up in the air even to think of it.

We were able to buy the International Edition of the *New York Times,* which was flown in from Europe, and with my knowledge of French, read the local Spanish press well enough to make out the major news.

We read about the Korean War every day, but it was like reading of events on a distant planet. The war didn't appear to affect the Mexican people at all, and the language barrier made our distance from it even greater. Nevertheless I was aware of what was going on in the States—even if at the moment I didn't feel myself to be involved.

At the trial the prosecution claimed that our "flight" was triggered by the announced arrest of the former army sergeant, David Greenglass, who was Ethel Rosenberg's brother, but I could make out an even better case by claiming that I saw the Korean war coming and was afraid of the resultant repression. Just before we left the States I had a definite feeling that the movement toward repression was accelerating, and now, with the war, I was certain that they would begin rounding up all known Communists and progressives, to be interned in concentration camps, just as the Japanese had been during World War II. I was well aware that Constitutional safeguards were always suspended during times of conflict. Had I remained in the States I would have quit my job at Reeves. I was very skeptical that North Korea had launched an attack against the South. Manoeuvering events to justify attacks on other countries was fairly standard procedure: witness the *Maine,* the *Lusitania,* and as we were to see in the mid 1960s, the Tonkin Gulf resolution.

There was no question but that the cold war was becoming more heated. Congressional committees were busy trying progressives in the press. It was apparent that anyone who doubted the official Washington version of what had allegedly transpired in Korea would be branded a traitor. We were relaxing—but with bated breath, waiting for the next shoe to fall. It was a totally unreal situation and we didn't have to wait long for that other shoe.

I was so shocked when I picked up the newspaper and read that Julius Rosenberg had been arrested, on charges of having stolen the atom bomb for the Soviet Union, that I walked back to our apartment numbed, handing the paper to Helen without a word. Putting aside the whole espionage business, I knew that Julius had never had anything to do with the atom bomb project. This was also the first time I learned that ex-GI, David Greenglass, who had been arrested the week before we left the States, was Julius's brother-in-law, and had been involved with him in the Houston Street machine shop venture.

Our worst fears of the turn of events back in the States seemed realized. Julius's arrest was announced jointly by the Attorney General and J. Edgar Hoover, from Washington, as if it were an event of great national importance—a political event. Since the start of the cold war, many accusations of treason and espionage had been loosely flung around. Elizabeth Bentley had made the headlines over the years with a lot of wild stories of espionage committed by government officials in fairly high positions; Whittaker Chambers had testified to being a member of a Communist underground in the 1930s; and some notable scientists had been accused by the House Un-American Activities Committee of having been members of a spy ring. But nothing had ever come of these accusations, except that they made life miserable for a lot of people who were powerless to defend themselves. But since the arrest of Klaus Fuchs in England early in 1950, and subsequently, of Harry Gold in the United States, events had taken a different turn. These were no longer the rhetorical accusations of the preceding period; here they were talking of the "atom bomb secret" having been stolen. It was almost inevitable that accusations like this would be leveled— the Soviet Union had exploded its first atom bomb, in 1949, well before United States officials had predicted it would have one ready.

Helen and I didn't even discuss the arrest. What could we say to each other? Unbelievable, unbelievable. What else was there to say? What was there to speculate on?

We had left the States somewhat in fear of being indicted for signing the non-Communist affidavits. In

Mexico the start of the Korean War made us even more fearful, but we had managed to relax. Our days of relaxation were now over. In our minds there was little question that we could ever go back to the States and pick up where we had left off. I was sure that my former association with Julius would arise, and God only knew what they would make of it. I would obviously have to take the Fifth Amendment before a Grand Jury since I could never testify on my Communist associations. What should we do? Sit and wait here? For what? Settle here? It was too close to the States for real comfort. I felt we had to leave.

That same evening I spoke to Manuel. I asked him bluntly if he knew any way in which Helen and I could get to Europe, with the kids, without a passport. I intimated that with the sharpening political climate in the States we could not afford to return. No, he didn't know how I could get to Europe, but suggested that if I wanted to hide for a while a friend of his in Guatemala had a plantation which might be ideal. Once a week his friend flew up to Mexico City in his private plane, and he probably would have room for us on the return flight. Luckily the following day the friend was scheduled to arrive, Manuel tried to call him, but the telephone circuits weren't working properly and after several poor connections he gave up. It was tantalizing and I don't know why he didn't suggest riding over to his friend's place in Mexico City. It was all very strange— almost like one of those dreams, where the object pursued keeps eluding one.

Then Manuel came up with another idea. He suggested I go to Campeche, an isolated minor seaport on the east coast, where a sea captain, who was his friend, stopped regularly. He explained that he had once done an interior decorating job on a movie theater in Campeche and had had to stay there for some time while the work was in progress; that was how he had become acquainted with the sea captain. But it sounded very tenuous. Manuel didn't know exactly when the boat came into port, or where it came from, or where it went. He didn't even know the size of the boat. It reminded me of Wagner's Flying Dutchman.

I hadn't depended solely on getting help from Manuel. The afternoon I read of Julius's arrest, I made the rounds of travel agencies, to learn what I could about ship transportation from Mexico. The picture wasn't encouraging. Aside from the required passport; only one lone passenger ship was due to call at Tampico and Vera Cruz in August and a Polish freighter was supposed to call at Vera Cruz once a month. When I visited the Polish trade mission, however, I learned that the ship from Poland called only several times a year, not on any regular schedule, and was not due within the next month or so.

While making the rounds of the travel agencies I picked up literature and maps. Occasionally, mainly during the winter months, cruise ships would call at Vera Cruz or Tampico for a day. All of this literature was eventually seized by the FBI. Of course it was evidence of "flight to avoid prosecution." Prosecution for what?

After a couple of days I had covered all the travel agencies in Mexico City and knew that there was nothing more to be learned there. I felt trapped, and in desperation decided to go to Vera Cruz in the hope of finding some way of getting to Europe. I discussed the move with Helen, since it meant I would have to leave her and the children behind. We decided that if I found a way for all of us going to Europe together that would be fine, but that I should not miss any opportunity of going alone, and once in Europe, I would help Helen and the children get there. This decision was not arrived at without a great deal of soul searching, for it meant that Helen might wind up in prison, while I would escape, but the alternatives seemed worse.

Manuel was very helpful when I told him I intended to go to Vera Cruz. He suggested I make the trip at night, to avoid the heat of the tropics. He came down to the bus station with me, having advised me to get there well ahead of time to get a good seat. After I was settled in my window seat I saw why. As soon as the regular bus seats were filled, the bus driver started to place removable seats, suspended from the arm-rests of the fixed seats, in the center aisle of the bus. Before the bus left, every square inch of space in the vehicle was occupied, and no one could budge. We pulled out of the terminal about 7:00 P.M., on July 21, three days after I had first read of Julius' arrest. During those three days I had run around Mexico City, looking, searching, hoping to find somehow, somewhere, an answer. None was forthcoming,

Before I left Helen I told her it would probably be best if she cashed in the return portion of our round-trip airline tickets, so she would have more cash available, should the need arise. I didn't think we would be returning to the States anytime during the next four weeks, when the tickets expired. However since Sydney's ticket was good for six months we held on to it. When I was arrested, the FBI also seized this ticket and for several years refused to return it, thus depriving Helen of any refund.

The bus trip proved to be more of an adventure

than I had anticipated. We made a couple of brief stops at small towns close to the Federal District, after which we took off for the climb over the mountains which separated us from the sea coast. All night long the driver kept steering the bus around blind hairpin curves cut out of the mountainside, at what seemed like breakneck speeds. Any slight miscalculation or obstacle would have sent us toppling down to total destruction. There were absolutely no posts or other restraints anywhere along the road; nor did the bus seem particularly sturdy.

At night high up in the mountains even the tightly packed mass of humanity was not sufficient to warm the unheated bus. I put on my rubberized raincoat to keep warm, and immediately began to perspire, but found this preferable to the sharp chill of the night mountain air. Finally, after a miserable night during which I don't think I slept for even a moment, we started the descent to the coast. With the coming of daybreak I could see the small Mexican villages we passed through as we approached the coast. They were all picturesque, in the tourist sense, but I was aware of what lay behind the picture card façade, and couldn't appreciate their architectural qualities.

As we pulled into the village square at Vera Cruz at quarter to eight in the morning I looked up to the baggage rack for my Spanish grammar. It was gone. When I stepped from the bus I could already feel the oppressive tropical heat of the day, despite the early morning hour. The Diligencias, where Manuel had advised me to stay (there were only one or two other hotels in all of Vera Cruz) was located right on the square, only a few steps from the bus stop.

I had not even thought about signing the hotel reg-ister until I was poised above it, pen in hand, and on the spur of the moment I decided to use a pseudonym, and to make it easy to remember wrote Morris Sand. Thus I wouldn't be faced with the potentially embarrassing situation of having forgotten my registered name. The idea that this impulsive act would some day be used at my trial to prove that I was guilty of espionage would never have seemed possible, even if someone had then tried to point it out to me. Flight is always taken as evidence of guilt by the courts, I was to learn. Again—guilt for what?

Vera Cruz was a hot, blazing, burning town in July, and it took only one look around the docks, which were only a couple of blocks from the hotel, to realize the futility of my having gone there. A single lonesome freighter tied up at the docks was being unloaded, at leisure, and only a couple of souls were visible in all the area. I wondered what manner of commerce could be carried on in this fashion? I spent the next week wandering around those docks, looking, hoping to discover some small miracle that would allow us to all go to Europe together.

On the more practical side I quickly discovered that I could not buy anywhere in Vera Cruz the Halazone tablets we had been using to purify our drinking water, even though I found several surprisingly large apothecaries. I immediately wrote Helen, asking her to send some, telling her what I had done thus far.

The days dragged. In the morning I would awaken quite early, drink some milk which I made from the powdered milk, and eat a bun which I had bought the previous evening. Then I headed for the docks, wandered around, looked for people to talk to, hoping to run across someone who could give me some kind of lead. It was totally without plan. I made the rounds of the shipping offices. One of the companies had posted a ship schedule, covering all the docks, and projecting well into the fall. I found nothing encouraging. Every two or three days a coastal frieghter was listed to call there, and less frequently a transatlantic freighter would be listed. But all of these were also scheduled to stop at American Gulf ports, like Galveston, before crossing the Atlantic.

After my morning expedition I would lunch lightly at a restaurant. I would set out again for more of my wandering. I found the midday tropical sun so hot that I had to get a broad-brimmed straw hat for protection. I also ordered a pair of prescription sunglasses since I felt a pair of slip-on glasses would put the tourist stamp on me. To be consistent I used the pseudonym Morris Sand. This too was documented at the trial, as though having used it twice would make it twice as damning.

The afternoon was more of the same aimless wandering around the docks. Almost all of the workers took a two hour siesta after lunch. And many could be seen dozing in the midday heat around the dock area. In speaking to a stevedore I learned that he made between $1.50 and $2.00 a day—when he worked. I had little difficulty in communication because most of the Mexicans, even the less educated, spoke English. Within a few days I developed a deep tan.

I discovered that Vera Cruz was a tourist town for Mexicans. Each morning small fishing boats would put out with their parties of sportsmen, and each afternoon they would return with their loads of red snappers and other Gulf fish. There were also commercial fishermen who had their fish iced at a local station and then shipped by rail to the capital.

Among the many people I met was a Mexican capitalist engaged in the manufacture of lamp fixtures, who complained quite volubly about the amount of graft he had to pay merely to conduct a legitimate business. I must have met and spoken to hundreds of people, sounding out each one, looking for a way to Europe without a passport. I never got a single encouraging response.

About six o'clock I usually ate a good meal, either at the hotel or at one of the other better restaurants. My living expenses were really quite modest. The hotel room ran twelve pesos, meals around eleven pesos, beer and soda three or four pesos, and magazines and newspapers two pesos—altogether less than four dollars a day. After the evening meal I usually relaxed. There wasn't much more I could do. Most of the time I simply stood around, watching the nightly ritual promenade around the village square. Two counter-rotating rings of people encircled the square, the outer ring rotating clockwise. Each ring was formed by groups walking six abreast, the space between the groups dependent on how crowded it was. Most groups were of one sex, and were composed mainly of the younger people. The older inhabitants sat on the benches surrounding the square. I'm sure that I missed much of the play that must have gone on in this ritual, which seemed to be so thoroughly formalized.

The marimba played all night long in front of the hotels, usually accompanied by percussion instruments. After the first few nights its novelty wore off and it got on my nerves. The same tunes, night after night after night, and even the different tunes had a certain sameness about them and I wondered if the music were really as poverty stricken as it seemed.

One evening I went to a concert given by a band at the local marine academy. It was the usual small band concert, but a blessed relief from the marimba. Another couple of evenings I spent at the movies, and several evenings I went "slumming." The stench was almost unbearable because of the heat. The slums of Vera Cruz were not very different from the slums of Harlem; street lighting was almost non-existent, and where I could peer behind the curtains I saw a bareness that meant the same all over. The light which emanated from these houses was like that of another period, yellow and flickering. A huge coffee shop, painted antiseptically white, was located on the corner opposite the Diligencias. Here the nightly habitués sat all evening over their cups of *café con leche* or cups of chocolate whipped up by the expert twirling of a long wooden paddle between the palms of the hands. There must have been hundreds of tables here, some within and many spread out over the sidewalks. Night after night the same scene repeated itself, including the same beggars, the same cripples, and the same blinded—until, by the end of the week, it had become part of my whole life.

After a week of this unproductive routine, as a last resort before going back to Helen I decided to take a look at Tampico. Inquiry revealed that the bus trip was sheer torture; there was no direct route. I decided to take the plane, which was scheduled to fly once a week, on Sunday mornings.

I wrote Helen a letter, telling her of my plans, but didn't address it to her. At the bus station in Mexico City Manuel had suggested that I send mail to him since our name was not on our mailbox. I was glad to take him up on this. (At the trial the FBI came up with

this letter, as well as the earlier one, and Manuel testified that when he got the letter and opened it, he was
surprised to find it addressed "Dear Helen.")

The night before I took off for Tampico I called
Helen on the phone. I felt I had to talk with her and
after I hung up I experienced an overwhelming loneliness, for these few minutes brought back with painful
sharpness the reality of our situation.

I awoke early Sunday morning, glad to be leaving,
and took a cab to the airport. It wasn't much of an airport; a dirt runway and a small hangar. There wasn't
even a waiting room for passengers. While I waited for
my plane to arrive I saw a large group take off for Cuba
on an old DC-4. I had considered the possibility of
Cuba as an intermediate point, but decided it wouldn't
simplify the problem. Watching these people take off, I
wondered if I could have somehow slipped into their
midst, unnoticed. Finally my DC-3 arrived, three-and-
a-half hours late. We took off for Tampico at once, hug-
ging the coastline all the way down at under five thousand feet altitude, and landed at Tampico in less than
two hours.

When I bought the airline ticket I used the pseudonym M. Sand. At the Hotel Tampico I made it Marvin
Salt, probably thinking this would help break my trail.
The decision to change my pseudonym was made at the
last moment, and I again chose a name I'd have little
difficulty recalling. Had I planned ahead even a little
bit, I would have chosen a less obvious name, written it
down well ahead of time and memorized it by the time I
registered at the hotel. Haphazardness characterized all
my efforts to get to Europe. Of course, the FBI had no
difficulty in tracking down M. Sand who took the flight
to Tampico, and connecting him with Marvin Salt who

registered in the hotel. (At the trial they brought up all the Mexican witnesses who were able to identify me through all those sinister transactions.)

As soon as I registered I took off for the docks. Tampico was more spread out than Vera Cruz, and I was advised to take a bus to the beach, from which I then walked to the docks. I immediately saw what I already knew: Tampico was mainly a port from which Mexico exported its oil. In the harbor I noticed a couple of familiar freighters at anchor; ships I had seen earlier in the week in Vera Cruz. (It was only a one-day run between the ports.) But there were no cruise ships there. Somehow I had the notion that I might manage to get aboard a cruise ship.

Even though Tampico was north of Vera Cruz the heat there was much worse. After a night of tossing about I took a bus out to the beaches where I simply walked around, absorbing some of the cool Gulf breeze. I should have loved to swim and really cool off but felt that this would be impermissible self-indulgence. A little resuscitated I walked back to the hotel, passing through what must have been the worst sections of town. Huge oil storage tanks and oil refinery equipment were spread out over the fields adjacent to the river where the tankers docked. In the midst of this were dilapidated wooden houses in which people lived. The stench was an unbearable combination of petroleum products and sewage, aggravated by the heat.

The name of the government agency that controlled the Mexican oil industry, PEMEX, was painted in huge letters on the storage tanks. I was well acquainted with the history of the Mexican petroleum industry, and it went through my mind as I walked along the road under the hot tropical sun. At one time the oil industry had been controlled by big American oil monopolies, who, in their avarice, had pumped the wells so hard as to all but ruin them. In 1938 the government of President Cárdenas expropriated the wells, whereupon the United States Government made all sorts of threats to attempt to regain the oil for the American companies. But Cárdenas didn't scare easily. This was part of the unorthodox history of our country which I learned when I was still quite young—but not in school. I picked it up from the *Daily Worker* and other radical papers which we always had at home, while my teachers at school were dishing out the standard version of American history.

Since Tampico was so much larger than Vera Cruz, investigating any potentialities which may have existed appeared futile. After a couple of days I was so discouraged, probably by the heat as much as anything else, that on August 2 I took a DC-3 flight back to the Federal District, too worn out to return by bus. (At the trial the prosecution brought out that I had used still another pseudonym when registering for this flight—Morton Solt. Dolt might have been more appropriate.)

I didn't return to our apartment when I landed in Mexico City. Instead I rented a small attic room in a downtown hotel, and spent a week in further search for passage to Europe. Of course, I used another pseudonym in registering at the hotel, and for once the FBI wasn't able to track it down. At least they didn't bring it up at the trial. They probably never looked, assuming that I returned to our apartment when I got back to the city. However, after the first couple of days loneliness made me visit Helen and the kids in the apartment each evening at about nine. I left in the morning before seven.

My reasons for taking the hotel room in the first place were a little fuzzy. I was afraid the apartment was being watched, and I also thought that I could operate more efficiently if I were by myself, and not involved in the day-to-day details of family life. Sydney was of considerable help, and Helen was able to manage without too much difficulty. When I decided to come home evenings, I reasoned that by avoiding the neighbors (I didn't even let Manuel know I was back), I would avoid being found. (Actually, I had nothing upon which to base my fears in this direction, other than the general feeling that things would be getting hotter back in the States.) I spent the days, from early morning to late at night, in intense activity—searching for the magic carpet to Europe. Again I visited travel agencies, collecting literature, asking all sorts of questions, hoping, hoping that something would turn up. I also made concrete moves. For instance, I visited the editor of a newspaper whose editorial position had impressed me, but his distrust was so obvious that I left after a short while. Much later I learned Mexico was filled with police agents, and the editor had probably felt I was one.

I also went to see Toledano, the head of CTAL, the Confederation of Latin American Workers, the big left-wing trade union of Latin America. Some years earlier Toledano had been a considerable power, but by the time I saw him his strength was waning. I spoke to his secretary, explaining that I had to see Toledano himself, since the matter was delicate, and was most pleasantly surprised when after being frisked by a man who sat outside the entrance to the office, I was ushered into Toledano's office within a short while. Inside I recognized Toledano seated at a large desk with a bodyguard standing at either side of him. I didn't waste any time. I told him I had to get to Europe—for political reasons—but that I didn't have a passport. Could he help me? He listened very courteously, but in the end told me that there was nothing he could do. I couldn't tell from his expression whether this was in fact the case, or whether he too thought I was some kind of provocateur. Perhaps he didn't want to get involved in anything illegal. I hoped that somebody might approach me subsequently without involving Toledano, to feel me out. But that didn't happen.

Earlier, when I was still in Vera Cruz, I had written my Uncle Louis, asking him if he knew anyone in Mexico who might help us. After waiting a week without getting a reply, I tried calling him from a downtown telephone depot, but when I finally got through the connection was so poor that I couldn't really understand a word he was saying. However he did write me immediately afterwards, and I got his letter a couple of days later, addressed to N. Walter, at our apartment, telling me that he was working on the problem—whatever that meant. Nothing ever came of this, except that he was later called to testify before the grand jury, and threatened with all sorts of penalties for not cooperating with the prosecution. However I didn't learn about that until many years later. For the first ten years after I was convicted I knew almost nothing of what had gone on in this regard prior to the trial.

Every day I read thoroughly the International Edition of the *New York Times*, hoping to discover what was happening back in the States. But this was no more productive than any of my other efforts. After scurrying around for a useless week, trying to find someone with the connections to help me, Helen and I decided that in these circumstances it would be best if we returned to the States. *Que sera sera.* We really had no alternative. Without ever having verbalized the thought, in back of our minds lay the idea that if we were going to be arrested it would be best if we were arrested in the States and not in Mexico, where we were unfamiliar with the laws. Besides in the States we had family and friends. We knew that Mexico and the United States had an extradition agreement but the idea that a charge of perjury might be considered a political crime never occurred to us. Besides we didn't know that political crimes were excepted by the extradition agreement. Neither did we think that my efforts to flee would be used against me at a subsequent trial. That, I suppose, was very naive, but sophistication in such matters comes only with experience.

Once the decision was made I moved back to Cordoba, and outwardly we picked up the casual style of living which had been interrupted by Julius's arrest. We all got our smallpox vaccinations, and I was about to buy our return flight tickets when the second bombshell burst. Picking up the newspaper on the morning of August 12, I found Ethel Rosenberg's picture on the front page, with the announcement that she too had been arrested and charged with being a part of the atom bomb conspiracy. I rushed back to the apartment to tell Helen. It left us speechless and frightened. What was there to talk about? Poor Ethel, poor children, where could they get help? What madness was there back home that could lead to such a situation? There was a feeling of total helplessness, as though I'd been punched in the solar plexus, and now was experiencing the numbness and the dull ache that followed.

When we finally decided that there were no alternatives open to us but to return to the States and face the mad situation, we delayed a moment too long. After the brutal kidnapping and arrest, I found myself in the Webb County Jail in Laredo, Texas anxiously waiting to be taken back to New York, where I thought I would not feel as helpless, where I hoped I would find a lawyer who would expose the falseness of the complaint that was the basis for my arrest.

I wasn't allowed newspapers in the jail so I didn't know then that the *New York Daily News* and other newspapers were calling me an atom spy. Almost as soon as Helen left I tried to get a pencil and paper to write her, but it wasn't until Sunday that I succeeded. And it wasn't until Monday that I was finally permitted to see a doctor about the gash the Mexican police had made in my head. He advised me that it was best not to sew it up, since it had already begun to heal. Early Tuesday morning I was taken out of my cell for the first time, to shave under the watchful eye of a guard. I was then given a special meal of beans topped with two eggs, a going-away present. Two marshals took me by auto to the Houston jail. It was an uneventful ride and since I still had no eyeglasses I couldn't see much of the countryside.

In Houston I was placed in the federal tank of the county jail. This was essentially a dormitory, enclosed by walls and iron bars, which housed only federal prisoners being held prior to trial. I was intrigued by the very simple security mechanism used at the entrance to the tank. It was an interlocking double door, arranged to limit the number of men who could enter or exit from the tank at one time. The prison guards never entered the tank, it was run entirely by the inmates.

The food was shoved into the tank in large slop buckets, and the inmate wheels dished it out into pitted aluminum bowls. They also handled the inmate commissary orders. It was a hot night in Houston, and all the men in the tank walked around in their undershorts. Thirty or forty men were trying to cool off under the one filthy shower. Everyone was friendly, and one inmate, a lawyer, tried to give me advice. Everyone knew who I was since I was still news.

The following day I was picked up by the head marshal for transfer to New York. When I checked out of the jail I found I had five dollars less than the $50 with which I had arrived. The officer in charge claimed that I had purchased commissary to that amount. This was my first encounter with the petty corruption that I later found to exist in the whole prison system. It was a good measure of my state that I didn't even utter a word of protest against this high-handed thievery. I simply accepted it as inevitable.

The head marshal himself took me to New York because he probably knew there would be a great deal of publicity attached to my arrival and, as I learned on the trip, he was very much involved in politics. He was accompanied by a deputy whom, he told me, he had sworn in specifically for this mission because of his sharpshooting prowess. Escape was so remote from my thoughts that it didn't than occur to me he was warning I had better not try it.

We landed at Newark Airport without incident; the sharpshooter hadn't had to prove his abilities. The photographers were on hand en masse. As I stood on the airfield in my newly pressed suit with my hands manacled in front of me, the big Texan snuggled up to my side and put on his most solemn expression for the press and photographers. Look this way, look that way, look look look. Finally the marshal ordered me into a waiting automobile while he talked to the press. The photographers came over to the car and took some more pictures, trying to call my attention by addressing me as "Morty." It worked the first couple of times. Then I realized that these vultures were not friends.

Presently the marshal and his deputy joined me and we were driven to the Federal House of Detention, at 427 West Street, Manhattan. Here security regulations required that I pass through a fluoroscopic X-ray machine for the detection of any weapons I might have. Today use of this type of X-ray machine is forbidden since it spews out large quantities of dangerous radiation over the entire body—including the gonads—while one of the officers peers at a fluoroscopic screen. Since the examining officer had not taken adequate time for his eyes to become dark-adapted, the radiation I was subjected to was even greater than it would ordinarily have been. To impress the Texan with their latest scientific marvel the jail officials ordered me into the path of the X-rays a second time for a demonstration/examination. Then I was issued the standard federal prison blues and locked into a cell for the night.

Early the following morning, Thursday August 24, I was "dressed out" in my own clothes and taken to the United States Attorney's office in the federal courthouse, on Foley Square. Here I was interrogated chiefly by Myles Lane, an assistant to United States Attorney Irving Saypol. Several other United States attorneys, including Roy Cohn, were present in the large office as well as a number of FBI agents. They all worked on me for well over an hour, threatening, cajoling, trying every tactic. I knew they were experts and didn't attempt to outwit them. They showed me snapshots of Julius and Ethel, and their friends, at the same time talking familiarly about them—as if to impress me with the extent of their knowledge. They mentioned various City College classmates who had been active in radical affairs, including Joel Barr, who I knew had gone to Europe to study: they told me they had Barr cornered in France and would soon arrest him. All this affected me as deeply as it was supposed to, but I remained mute.

As a climax they re-enacted the death penalty scene, holding out the probability of a lesser penalty if I cooperated. At no point did they make any concrete promises, everything was done by suggestion. Before it was over everyone had acted his part, including the FBI agents who had been standing around apparently uninterested, looking out of the window, or casually fingering some objects. This was undoubtedly a theater piece which they had acted many times before, and I had to acknowledge to myself that it was a skillful performance, but I had had almost a week to steel myself for this ordeal.

Throughout the interrogation I repeatedly asked to be allowed to see my attorney, but got no response. Although I hadn't been in contact with Helen since I had last seen her in the Laredo jail, I was certain she must already have obtained a lawyer. When they saw they would get no place with their interrogation they took me to their boss, Irving H. Saypol.

Saypol was brutal, coarse, and completely without finesse. In a threatening voice he immediately came on strong with the electric chair line and then led me down to the United States Commissioner's office, where I was once more arraigned without benefit of counsel. During the proceedings I disputed Saypol when he reported to the Commissioner that I had told him something which in fact I hadn't, whereupon the Commissioner advised me not to say anything, since I had no counsel present. Of course, there were newspaper reporters present ready to take down whatever Saypol said.

Later I learned that Helen had indeed already hired Eddie Kuntz as my attorney and that he had been trying to see me all that morning, but the officials had outwitted him in this rather unequal legal game. He hadn't been allowed to see his client before, during, or after the arraignment! Of course the law enforcement officers knew that a client was supposed to see his lawyer at the first opportunity. Yet they continued to disregard the law with absolute impunity. (Later the Supreme Court censured this practice in the *Miranda* case, but with little practical effect.)

That afternoon the marshals took me back to the Federal Detention House, where I managed to get to a medical assistant to ask him for five drops of belladonna for my tightly knotted stomach—a remedy I had learned from my father. Surprisingly he gave it to me without question. Only after my stomach relaxed did I fully realize how deeply I had been affected by the afternoon's proceedings.

4   The Tombs

JULIUS ROSENBERG was kept at the Federal House of Detention after his arrest but I wasn't able to see him, and an hour after I got back from my arraignment I was once more ordered to put on my civilian clothes, this time for transfer to the Manhattan County Jail, more commonly known as the Tombs. It had evidently been decided that Julius and I should not be kept in the same jail. Unlike the House of Detention the Tombs was no makeshift jail. From the outside it looked like a mighty fortress, standing more than a dozen stories high, with walls of bricks and glass blocks. After going through more than a half dozen locked gates I was admitted to a private cell on the fourth floor, where I lay down for a welcome respite. I wasn't used to the pace of events. During this period, while I was accessible to photographers, and while the United States Attorney had me very much on the front page of the newspapers, I was completely cut off from my family, friends, and the attorney I knew Helen must have secured. My most urgent thoughts were directed toward re-establishing communications with Helen. Even though I was emotionally exhausted I was surprised when I fell asleep as soon as the lights were extinguished, and slept well all night.

The next morning I didn't have to wait long for the visit to which I had been looking forward with such terribly high expectations. It turned out to be an exercise in sheer frustration, and a totally dehumanizing experience. When I got down to the visiting room the guard locked me into a steel cubicle the size of a telephone booth but without a top, and without any sound-absorbing material. Through a small glass window about five by eight inches in area I could see Helen standing on the other side of the booth. Her eyes barely reached the window, beneath which was a plate with several dozen small holes, evidently meant for talking through. Somehow the baffling which was designed to prevent the transmission of material objects also impeded the sound, so as to make it impossible to carry on a conversation. The only way we could communicate was for one of us to shout into the perforations, while the listener placed his ear over the holes on the other side of the wall.

Sixty-odd men were trying to communicate with their loved ones, all shouting in attempts to make themselves understood, creating a din that made communication even more difficult. The system had obviously not been designed by an acoustical engineer—at least not a competent one.

At the moment I was overwhelmed with tender feelings I wanted to convey to Helen, and I was powerless to communicate them. After a short while we both acknowledged defeat and gave up trying to talk. We stood there and simply looked at each other, smiling and managing to make ourselves understood without the spoken word. We learned the meaning of phatic communion as never before. From the very first visit Helen would open her blouse or dress, for me to see her breasts, or more—even under the most impossible conditions. Looking at her this way never ceased to intoxicate me. I became a voyeur through necessity.

Late that afternoon, when we were locked in the cells for the night, I lay down on my cot and relived the whole brief visit with Helen. Again and again I reconstructed the scene and the images; thus the fifteen or twenty minutes we were together served as the source of material for many intimate fantasies during those long hours I spent in the cell alone. I was not the first to observe that after one is deprived of all freedom he still retains the freedom to think and dream. I knew it was indulgence to allow myself such sensuous fantasies, but in the circumstances this was the only way I knew to stay alive. And that was what I meant to do.

It was a full week after my arrest in Texas before I was permitted to meet Eddie Kuntz, my lawyer. During that week I had been held in four different jails; been intimidated; been interrogated by government agents on three occasions; appeared at two different arraignments; and photographed endless times by hundreds of photographers. But my attorney couldn't see me.

The attorneys' visiting room didn't have booths for separating the attorney from his client, but there was a wide table with a barrier in the middle, presumably to make the passing of papers more difficult. And trying to talk across a wide table wasn't easy; the room was noisy and fully packed. Our initial conference didn't go well. I couldn't establish any rapport with Kuntz and I felt that he was uncomfortable and wanted to terminate the visit as soon as possible. He seemed totally unresponsive in regard to possible steps to be taken about the Mexican kidnapping and pushed my questions aside. He wasn't at all like the lawyer I had expected.

He didn't advance a single thought. Unfortunately my initial impression never changed, even at the last visit on Alcatraz, some years later.

At our first meeting, I learned that he had obtained another lawyer to join with him in the case. So I now had two lawyers with whom I expected to be in daily contact in order to discuss questions of strategy and tactics. But after that first visit I didn't see Kuntz for a week, and I saw nothing of Harold Phillips, my second attorney, for even longer.

The next visit was like the first: general discussion, nothing specific, no plan of action. Eddie wasn't keen about going into court to attack the kidnapping, hinting that I had made a serious mistake in waiving extradition from Texas. (I discovered much later it was only removal proceedings, since the federal government, unlike state governments, does not need extradition proceedings.)

My bail was still one hundred thousand dollars, and Kuntz assured me getting it reduced was out of the question. If I should succeed in raising the sum, he said, the government would promptly ask the court to increase the amount. This didn't prevent Helen and my mother from trying. However, with all my family and all Helen's family helping, not even a half of it could be raised. A professional bail-bondsman was out of the question; none would put up security for a political prisoner.

Knowing that I was going to be here for months, I immediately inquired about obtaining reading material. A helpful prison guard told me about the library, situated on another floor, and how to gain access to it. The Tombs did indeed have a library, but it was strictly for show. Many jails have inaccessible showplace libraries.

Another guard told me to put in a request to the warden asking for permission to receive books from the outside, and I was agreeably surprised when I received permission. This was probably better than having access to an impoverished prison library, Helen brought me the first book at hand, Hogben's *The Loom Of Languages,* and I felt great relief once I knew I could get reading material.

Fortunately there was no limit on the number of letters I could write, and I wrote Helen every day. From the start I numbered my letters, fearful that she might not get one and we would not be aware of it. Helen also wrote me almost every day. I would get her letter around noon, shortly after I had seen her, would glance at it, and put it away. It was too precious to consume all at once. Our letters were of course censored, but it wasn't too difficult to circumvent the censor: we had our own private language.

My day was now measured from visit to visit, each one renewing me like some magical elixir. It felt so real, standing together, although separated by steel and glass, watching Helen smile, uttering familiar words, or stroking her breast for my eyes—her hand becoming my hand. It seemed so utterly real, for the moment I forgot where I was.

The visits, the books, and the letters—these were the elements of which my life would henceforth be woven. They became my sustaining life force. Never before had my existence been reduced to such an elemental level.

In the morning the time before the visit passed quickly, in anticipation. At night, before I fell asleep I would feel close to Helen. The hours between were bridged by letters and books. Only much later did I become aware of how fortunate I had been during this traumatic period, in that I was never confronted with the dilemma of whether or not to confess: I had nothing to confess. Nothing at all! Moreover I was even spared consideration of whether to cooperate with the prosecution, assenting to whatever story they concocted for me. The idea of cooperating was beyond my limited imagination, a totally foreign concept. Never, not even in passing, did Helen and I ever touch on the subject.

After the first week at the Tombs I became aware that my sense of the passage of time had gone awry. The week hadn't felt like a week at all—nor like a day or a month, or any other period. It was as though time were suspended, as I was here suspended in space. Many times during the next years I would have occasion to make similar observations concerning this strange phenomenon, where time lost all meaning. And until the day I was freed it never ceased to amaze me.

The fourth floor of the Tombs was known as "bum's row" because it housed the Bowery derelicts and others picked up for "crimes" like vagrancy. I made several futile attempts at conversation, but couldn't find any common ground. I found the inmates quite noisy and without any redeeming qualities, a rather harsh judgment. Later, after I had grown accustomed to their style, I began to pick up tid-bits of information from these men. I learned all the ramifications of "copping a plea"; how the DA threatened to throw the book at them if they demanded a trial, and so got them to plead guilty to a lesser charge. And the "Pen-indef" sentence. Penitentiary-indefinite meant that a so-called parole board would mete out sentence after observing the inmate for six or more months. This frequently meant a thirty-six month sentence for pleading guilty to a misdemeanor. I learned about the "connection lawyer," who was said to have an in with the DA, for which he charged an appropriate fee. I learned a lot about criminals and justice.

Life at the Tombs wasn't easy for a white middle-class Jew. It was strictly regulated, while at the same time anarchistic. The place was filthy, men (inmates and guards alike) spitting on the floor as though they had always done it at home. But it was the noise that bothered me more than any other single aspect. All of the surfaces in the cell house were hard: the vitreous tile on the wall, the concrete floor, the glass bricks through which the subdued light entered, and the steel walls and bars of the cells. All calculated to reflect every bit of sound through the length and breadth of the cell house. It was as though the hardness of the atmosphere was symbolized by these building materials.

The cell—five by eight, with a seven foot ceiling— was constructed of steel plate, with the usual bars on the front. I had a cot without a mattress, a toilet without seat, a diminutive wash basin with a single cold water spigot, a steel seat and a table, hinged to the wall. I was locked in the cell nineteen hours a day. It was hot in the Tombs in August—and it smelled. No air moved near the ventilator opening in the wall. After breakfast I was permitted out of the cell for two hours, when I could walk up and down the aisle in front of the cell. After lunch I could promenade for three more hours. That was the extent of my recreation. I didn't have my eyeglasses during my first week at the Tombs and everything was blurred. Perhaps it was just as well—except that I couldn't see Helen too well.

The complete emptiness of my new life was accentuated by the realization that I no longer had any responsibilities. Helen was now shouldered with the daily chores of bringing up the family, and all the additional tasks that arose from my imprisonment. Others have noted that when a father is locked up, his family is frequently punished far more than he, but this aspect of imprisonment has been disregarded, since it would interfere with the orderly administration of justice.

The day I arrived at the Tombs I began to bombard Helen with frantic letters, alternately cajoling and threatening, in an effort to convince her of my need for a conference with my lawyers. Shortly before Labor Day, when I learned that Phillips would not be able to make it until he returned from the long weekend, I felt as though my world would explode. I was beyond anger or bitterness. Two weeks after I had arrived at the Tombs a meeting was finally arranged. All day I waited for the lawyers, my ears keenly attuned to the telephone bell in the officer's booth around the corner from my cell. Every time it rang I expected to be called out for the visit. When four o'clock came and visiting time for lawyers was over, I was emotionally exhausted and a feeling of frustration and powerlessness overcame me. I lay down on my cot and fell asleep—wishing I didn't exist.

Kuntz and Phillips showed up the following afternoon. I wasn't even interested in the reason for the delay, and since they apparently had nothing to tell me, I opened the questioning, determining that they were apparently agreeable to my active participation in the case; yet upon discussion of the kidnapping, it was obvious that they had already reached a decision— without my knowledge, much less participation. On the basis of a Supreme Court decision of the last century, and without investigation of the circumstances, they had decided not to raise the kidnapping in court. It was a disastrous conference.

The next couple of days I wrote to Helen complaining about my lawyers, their lack of frankness, and how they virtually ignored me, their client. A short time later Kuntz came, alone, for a conference. As a result of this I wrote Helen that all was well once more: our respective positions had been clarified. Even as I wrote, I was aware that I wanted so much to believe this that I had deluded myself. It was at this conference that Eddie told me that some of his former clients were now avoiding him, but I felt I couldn't allow this to affect my judgment of the situation.

Helen sold our house in Flushing to pay the lawyers the initial fee of five thousand dollars. An additional five thousand was raised from our relatives. Helen and Mark then moved into an apartment in the Bronx. Sydney temporarily went to Washington to live with her father, which made things a little easier for Helen.

Around the middle of September Helen was handed a subpoena to appear before the grand jury. My lawyers lost no time in bringing Saypol before a judge to quash the subpoena, on the grounds that it was tantamount to asking Helen to testify against her husband. The judge did not quash the subpoena outright, but severely limited Saypol's area of questioning. Thus when Saypol did get Helen before the grand jury, he was stymied in questioning her about anything concerning me. It wasn't that we had anything to hide, but we knew that a prosecutor gained an advantage over the defendant if he could compel the defendant, or his wife, to give him any information whatsoever. (Ethel Rosenberg's lawyers were not as astute and immediately prior to her arrest she was compelled to take the Fifth Amendment before the grand jury, without benefit of the directive my lawyers had gotten from the judge. This cost her dearly at the trial.)

I didn't know it at the time, but Helen was threatened with indictment if she resisted testifying before the grand jury, although as Kuntz had pointed out to Saypol, if he could indict Helen, he would. I was also unaware that my parents and various other relatives had been brought before the grand jury. Neither Helen nor my parents told me about this, for they wanted to spare me any additional pain.

From time to time my parents would visit, as well as write. I was grateful that my mother did not cry when I saw her. My father was in a state of shock and appeared completely lifeless. I could only wonder what he thought.

On September 18 two United States marshals took me to the courthouse at Foley Square. Since it was only about four blocks away we walked. I had on a set of handcuffs, with a marshal at each side. Even though I thought I was going to be presented with an indictment, it felt wonderful to get out of the Tombs and to walk in the streets of New York. A whole month had passed since my arrest and I had had absolutely no information about the charges against me, other than the five alleged conversations with Julius and what Saypol had been telling reporters.

But instead of an indictment, the government asked for, and got, a two-week postponement. In a sense I was disappointed, since I was anxious to know the accusations against me. As a result of Saypol's press conferences the newspapers had labeled me an atom spy. Yet I hadn't had the remotest connection with the atom bomb, and I felt they would have to prove more than those five alleged conversations with Julius. Now I would have to wait two more weeks for the answer.

In an effort to get mileage from the request for the postponement, the government made some lengthy arguments. Phillips spoke for me, and I was so disturbed by his inept presentation that I wrote Helen he would have to be dismissed. What I didn't know and couldn't appreciate, was that when Kuntz took on the case he knew he would become a pariah in the legal community, and so Phillips was to become his connection, as it were. Kuntz was shunned and Phillips, with less of a history of left-wing association, was his claim to respectability. But I had only a slight inkling of what was going on outside, and couldn't understand, as Helen did, the need for respectability. She didn't dismiss Phillips; neither did I. I argued with Kuntz that we should get rid of Phillips, but that was as far as I went.

Two weeks later I was again taken to court, and again the indictment was postponed. It was all a mystery to me.

Meanwhile I was enduring my days at the Tombs as well as I could. Theoretically this was a jail, a facility for holding men for a short time prior to trial. Thus it had no yard, and no indoor recreational facilities. There were some old battered decks of cards around, and occasionally someone would produce a checker set out of nowhere. That was it. Somehow the men were supposed to pass the time doing absolutely nothing. Later, when I met men from upstate prisons, they told me it was much more difficult to do time in a jail than in the regular prisons.

Our routine was fixed. Awakened at six, breakfast

at six-thirty in the cell, as were all the meals. Lumpy, watery, cooked cereal mixed with stewed figs or prunes, and coffee. Or dry cereal with skim milk, again with the stewed fruit, and coffee. Sometimes we had some synthetic jelly. The quality of the stewed fruit left something to be desired, and the crew of the fourth floor mixed the fruit with the cereal in order to cut down on the number of bowls used. No other floor had this. I wrote Helen complainingly, and since the warden or his aide was censoring my mail, the situation was rectified within a couple of days. The power of my letters . . .

For lunch we usually had a soup made from leftovers, like hot dogs and cereal or beans. The stews, watery and tasteless, had precious little meat. The main meat dishes were hot dogs and baloney, both of which seemed to be made from the same material and bore little resemblance to meat. I felt that graft was involved. The meat balls were hard and indigestible. The best meal was Friday's lunch, when we usually had a big piece of boiled carp. Few of the men ate it and I had no difficulty getting extra pieces. Sunday's lunch would have a *pièce de résistance* like roast beef or bully beef or ham—about one or two ounces. The only fresh vegetable was cabbage.

Supper usually consisted of dishes like beans, spanish rice, spaghetti, or mysterious concoctions that defined analysis. Pickled beets and souplike Jello rounded out the meal. In addition we had five slices of foul-smelling white bread at each meal, most of which was flushed down the toilet.

The skim milk in the morning was made from powder, usually freshly mixed and still warm. The coffee at dinner was foul tasting, and the tea at supper insipid.

However, once a month the lunch was decently cooked. It was the regular menu, only it had been prepared with some TLC. Rumor had it that that was the day the place was inspected by a group charged with overseeing the operation.

When I first arrived I ate everything indiscriminately. In fact, after Laredo it tasted good. But after about a month my stomach rebelled; luckily I was able to buy a couple of containers of milk from the commissary cart, drinking one with my lunch and the other at supper. Somehow I managed. Everything was so flat, I wondered that salt was not available. An investigation revealed that the salt did indeed come up from the kitchen with each meal, but the "runners," the men who were in charge of dishing out the food, put the salt aside and peddled it for cigarettes. I paid my pack of cigarettes and got a container of salt, enough to last at least a month. However, on the following weekly shakedown, the hack who inspected my cell picked up the container and emptied it down the toilet. After this happened a second time I realized this was part of a petty conspiracy between the runners and the guards. The guards depended on the runners for the orderly maintenance of the institution, and this was their payoff.

The runners, unlike all of us on the fourth floor, were sentenced prisoners. They slept in dormitories and did not mingle with the unsentenced prisoners, whom they considered subjects for prey. On weekends the runners would sell cigarettes, for three times the regular price. Or if a new arrival came in after suppertime, they might bring him a sandwich for an appropriate price. The runners rationalized such peddling on the grounds that, since they were not paid, this was the only way they could get smokes.

Men who came to the Tombs with money had it deposited in an account from which they could withdraw up to two dollars each day, in change. Paper money was considered contraband. With the money one could purchase food, candy, drinks, ice cream, cigarettes, and newspapers from the commissary cart which came around twice each day. Most of the men on the fourth floor didn't even have a nickel for a cup of coffee; the same miserable coffee that was served with meals. I found the sandwiches inedible. The *New York Times* was usually sold out by the time the cart got to our floor, so I would end up reading the *New York Daily News*. I restricted my buying to ice cream and milk.

The operation of the commissary was a mystery, as I was to find with most prison commissaries. Almost all of the food items came out of the inmate kitchen supplies, yet the whole operation was strictly entrepreneurial. The chief was an old man, Rifkind, whose brother was the federal judge, Simon Rifkind. Everyone knew that the pork chop sandwiches that were sold for forty-five cents were supposed to be served to the inmates at mealtime, but never appeared. Who was going to complain? And to whom? One quickly learned the feeling of powerlessness, and went along with the system and its corruption.

Lights went out at ten, and if I fell asleep immediately I would awaken around four or five in the grayness of the morning, which was depressing and stirred up many dormant anxieties. Consequently I would try to remain awake after the lights went out, when I could reconstruct Helen's visit of that morning, or review her last letter, or just daydream.

My sleep was filled with all sorts of dreams. One was a frequently recurring dream in which I went out looking for a job, an obvious wish-fulfillment. In another I discussed a sole-warmer with another engineer. This device was a heating element mounted on a piece of mica, like a bread-toaster. I pointed out that if the heater were placed too close to the feet the mica would block the evaporation of the perspiration, on the other hand if it were placed too far away, this would result in a loss of heating efficiency. Was this an unconscious wish to warm my soul, coupled with fears of the electric chair?

While I was struggling with the daily problems of my new life, the prosecution finally managed to get an indictment, which I first learned about from the pages of the *New York Daily News* of October 11. Later I discovered that my lawyers were apprised of it the same way.

Even though the indictment was available to the press on the eleventh, I didn't obtain a copy until October 15. It was identical to the indictment that had been handed down earlier against Ethel and Julius, except that my name had been added to the list of defendants. Now I knew absolutely nothing more. What was I accused of doing? Conspiring to transmit information to the Soviet Union. The indictment had a list of overt acts, but none involved me in any way. They were all about Julius, Gold, and Greenglass.

The following day the marshals came to take me to Foley Square. How many times had I rehearsed in my mind the words "not guilty"? Over and over again I said them: softly, loudly, imperiously, threateningly —every way imaginable. So when I came into court, without having spoken to either Kuntz or Phillips, and the judge asked how I pleaded, and Phillips informed the court that I would not plead at this time, I was ready to hit the roof. When would my lawyers learn that I was a human being? Without having an opportunity to talk to them in the courtroom, I was whisked to the holding cell in the basement. Nor did they drop by to see me there. Presently the marshals took me back to the Tombs.

The following day, after I had complained to Helen about the behavior of the lawyers, Kuntz visited me, and he agreed that things had been handled badly. He explained that they had agreed to defer the plea in order to prepare some pre-trial motions. This didn't seem very convincing to me.

Having lost confidence in my lawyers, I asked Kuntz for some law books. This would be impossible, he said. I then asked him for some titles that Helen might get, but he remained adamant. When I asked Helen to look into the matter of law books I might study, she also wasn't helpful and I felt that Kuntz had persuaded her against it.

Immediately after the bomb had been dropped, Helen and I had read the Smythe Report on the development of the atomic bomb, and now, in order better to prepare myself on what I assumed to be the subject of the accusations against me, I asked her to bring me a copy. Kuntz forbade this on the theory that the government might somehow use it against me at the trial. Based upon Saypol's statements to the press Kuntz thought that I would in fact be accused of atomic espionage. He apparently did not believe my assertions that I had never, in any way, legal or illegal, been connected with the atom bomb. It wasn't until November that Kuntz began to have some faith in what I was telling him, admitting his initial stand-offish attitude had been dictated by prudence—thinking that I would collapse under the pressure and become a government witness against the Rosenbergs, à la Greenglass.

I've often wondered if the outcome of the trial

would have been different if I remained at West Street and had access to the inmate prison lawyers there. I could then have obtained information about legal texts, and cases pertaining to conspiracy law. Julius Rosenberg had this opportunity, but didn't take advantage of it. He had faith in his lawyers, a misplaced faith as subsequent events proved. But even if it wouldn't have changed the course of the case, having access to legal material would greatly have lessened my frustration and made life somewhat more bearable, for Helen as well as myself. As it was, all my frustrations were vented on Helen.

After awhile we developed certain patterns and rhythms and thus we could anticipate the character of a visit, making it more delightful. In fact visiting took on the character of a game we played, a game which had one main function—to enable us to survive until such games were unnecessary.

There wasn't a day I wasn't aware of myself, what I was doing, how I was acting, and I knew that the intensity of a visit with Helen and my preoccupation with sex was not the way a political prisoner should be acting, but I also knew that with absolutely no one to talk to, I had to do something to keep myself going, and Helen agreed that anything which worked was permissible, so long as I did not violate my fundamental ethos. I could not have formulated my ethical norms, but I had acquired a well developed sense of values which clearly defined what was permitted, what forbidden. For instance, literally, even to save my own skin, I could never have testified against Julius and Ethel.

With no responsibilities, except to keep myself together, I tried to create them. I imagined the details of Helen's present life, discussing those things in which I saw possible problems. For example, I was concerned about the heat in the apartment. Reading in the *Times* that the price of wool would skyrocket, I advised Helen to anticipate her wool clothing needs over the next few years and make the necessary purchases; I concerned myself with all the details of Mark's and Helen's diet. But, of course, my picture of life outside was terribly distorted. I was aware of this but it didn't prevent me from trying to lead that vicarious existence.

But there were things that did make life a little easier. For instance, I learned that for a bribe of fifty cents, I could use one of six visiting booths that was equipped with a telephone. It was such a joy for Helen and myself to talk like human beings. Even the thought that the phones might be bugged was irrelevant; let them hear what we said! We were again able to talk in soft tones, lovingly and tenderly, as we looked at each other. Helen even solved the problem of the window height by bringing in a small box on which she stood during the visit, and which she parked under a guard's desk the rest of the time. For this guard she brought cigars. Since the other booths at this end of the visiting room were never used, we were alone, allowing Helen greater latitude in indulging my voyeurism.

I usually managed to see Helen for about twenty-five minutes each visit and when she would come five times in one week I would feel like a glutton. But then if for any reason I missed a visit with her, I would feel a constant torture which would be relieved only when I saw her again. My precarious equilibrium was such that I would move from the heights of ecstasy to the depths of despair, and back again, at the slightest provocation. A single wrong word from a guard was enough to spoil a whole visit. More than anything else I dreaded the visitless weekends. So Monday was a very special day. The relief I felt on seeing Helen after a weekend of nothingness was indescribable. The visits on other days were preceded by a genuine joy of anticipation; on Mondays by anxiety. Friday again was special, for I tried to make it concentrated enough to last until Monday.

I began working on the first of a series of paper engineering projects, an automatic analytical balance. Today these are commonplace. Since it was basically a servo problem, it was well within my province of expertise. Another servo problem I tackled was a pen recorder. These paper studies gave me the mental stimulation I had sorely missed.

Hitherto life had been too busy to think about the past. Now I recalled long forgotten incidents, including the model flying airplanes I built when I was about twelve. I asked Helen to get me a model airplane magazine to compare the then with the now, and discovered that like most things, the field had outgrown its simple beginnings, to the point where I couldn't recognize my hobby any more. What a pity, that the youth of today were so encumbered with complexity, in every facet of their existence, including their hobbies. I thought of the first crystal radio set my father had built when I was five.

One had to search for the sensitive spot on the galena crystal with the cat whisker, then tune three knobs and adjust a sliding coil. We used a bedspring for an antenna. It was thrilling, but I found the programs themselves meaningless.

Later, shortly before I entered Stuyvesant High School, I myself became intensely interested in short wave radio. At Stuyvesant, when I finished my regular school day I would head for the radio shack where I studied the Morse code and radio theory. It was a proud day, in December 1931, when I passed my examination for a radio amateur license and received my "ticket" with call letters W2DPH.

Within a month I was on the air. I had managed to scrounge around for almost all the parts for my receiver and transmitter. The transmitting tube and power transformer I had had to buy; each cost four dollars, a huge sum during the depression.

For the next two and one half years, until I graduated, I operated my station, rebuilding my transmitter and receiver many times. I didn't get any scholastic credits for this activity because it wasn't an official part of the curriculum, but it was the most useful part of my learning during that period. In my last term at school I was elected president of the radio club. All these pleasant memories came back to me.

I don't think I could have managed even with the games Helen and I played, if it hadn't been for the books she brought. The whole time I was in the Tombs I didn't stop reading. When tensions were unbearable, when the noise of the cell house almost drove me crazy, when I was in the depths of despair—I kept reading. It was the only escape I had from the realities I couldn't face, though I didn't indulge myself in escapist literature.

I read Freud and, for the first time, Thomas Wolfe who later became my favorite American novelist. He and Proust were alike in that each described a sector of society with which he was intimately familiar. Jacob Wasserman's *The Mauritius Case* affected me deeply, since it concerned a young man, Etzel, who had been unjustly convicted of murder. In the end Etzel is freed, but commits suicide shortly afterwards because he finds he has no real desire left to live. For the rest of the time I was imprisoned, I wondered if perhaps I might not myself be burned out by the time I was released. I found Thomas Mann's discussion of subjective time in *The Magic Mountain* exceptionally pertinent in my present circumstances: how time, under conditions of monotony, assumes a timelessness which in retrospect becomes only a moment. Before I was freed I reread the book twice, each time with even greater delight.

Reading about Madame Curie made me wonder why it was that experimental physicists during this period were awarded Nobel prizes quite promptly while the theoreticians, like Einstein, had to wait so many years for their prize. And then Einstein didn't receive it for either of the Relativity theories. Ibsen really excited me but it was *The Wild Duck* that became my favorite. His presentation of that universal question that every thinking person must have at one time pondered: does anyone have the right to destroy the illusions of others? was masterful. In my youth I'd have had no hesitancy in giving an affirmative answer, but now I could only say that each case had to be examined individually, because people are individuals.

But Ann Segher's *Transit* was depressing. The story of refugees from Hitler trying, against opposition from the western democracies, to leave France in 1940, and the conniving of the refugees to stay alive, to evade the law, and to get the necessary documentation to leave, was little different from what went on in prison.

What is Life? by the physicist, Irwin Shrödinger, became one of my scientific favorites. The line of demarcation between physics and biology became blurred as Shrödinger wrote about the age old riddle of life, until one lost all sense of the separation. What a contrast with the biology I was taught in school, where we had only to memorize the names of things and functions and understanding the whys never became a subject for study.

I also read Gide, Hemingway, Tolstoy, Saroyan, Strindberg, Hersey, Fromm and many others. But in George Bernard Shaw I found my true love. Reading Shaw was like the enjoyment of listening to Beethoven. His plays were well developed intellectual exercises, no less complex or masterfully plotted than a Beethoven symphony. Over the years *Saint Joan* became my favorite, and I waited for the day I would be free and could see it on the stage.

I always welcomed a good joke and here it was especially important. One day I was called out of my cell and U.S. marshals presented me with a notification that my "secret" clearance had been withdrawn, and wanted me to sign an acknowledgment. It was ludicrous. Did they think I might apply for a sensitive job? I didn't sign. So what could they do to me—put me in prison?

Each cell in the Tombs was like a tomb, a place of interment. The exception was the eleventh floor, commonly known as "canary row," where they sent men who were singing for the DA, for their protection as well as added inducements: regular size twin beds, with mattresses and springs; individual radios; wooden tables; and other amenities of life. Most important of all: two-hour "bench visits," which meant that the inmate and his visitors could sit down on a bench and talk like human beings. Cooperating witnesses were well-treated, at least while their cooperation was necessary.

David Greenglass and Harry Gold were housed there, even though, like myself, they were Federal prisoners. At least (by the time they testified at the trial) these two witnesses would make sure their stories had no discrepancies.

It was ironic that while I was a victim of the wave of repression that later became known as McCarthyism, I had little real idea of what was going on during the 50s. I read in the newspapers that the Senate wanted to set up "constitutional concentration camps," and thought it was a joke—akin to pregnant virgins. I couldn't see the havoc that was being raised with the lives of so many people simply because they had known me, despite the fact that I myself was imprisoned. I suppose I considered my case exceptional—*sui generis*, as the lawyers say.

Later, when I was at the Atlanta penitentiary, I ran across mimeographed documents on the Bureau of Prisons' procedures for dealing with large numbers of prisoners. It mentioned processing one hundred thousand per day. The Bureau had actually set up concentration camps, located mostly in the West, and had used federal prisoners, trustees, to set them up. This even though the Senate had never passed a bill. Undoubtedly there existed a list of people who were to fill these constitutional concentration camps.

After much deliberation, my lawyers, on November 14, filed a "Motion to Dismiss the Indictment", on the grounds that the indictment did not list any of the "essential facts" constituting the offense, as required by the Federal Rules of Criminal Procedure. Nor did it list any overt acts of which I was accused, despite the fact that the arrest warrant had listed five overt acts—the five mythical conversations with Julius, in furtherance of the conspiracy. It had taken my lawyers a whole month to draw up this simple motion, but I was ecstatic.

Kuntz refused to let me make any independent judgment of the motion; I had to take his word that we had a winner—that the government would not be able to uphold its faulty indictment under his blistering attack. The motion was duly argued on November 20, without my presence. Such motions were considered purely technical, not requiring the presence of the defendant, since he was presumed to have no voice in the argument.

In retrospect, I was amazed at how easily I accepted this perverted thinking of the courts. I was later able to ascertain that the memorandum of law which Kuntz and Phillips filed to support the motion was far from expertly drawn, but I don't think it would have made any difference if the foremost constitutional authority had drawn that motion. The prosecution was determined not to let the defense know, until trial time, what the case was about. Despite Kuntz's optimism, we lost.

If we were going to get any more pre-trial motions filed we had to do it quickly, since the trial was now scheduled to begin on January 4. Thus on December 11th my lawyers filed a "motion for a bill of particulars," once more to try to ascertain exactly what the accusation would be. The law is very explicit on the right of a defendant to be apprised of the nature of the crime, and to be given enough information to enable him to prepare to defend himself. In my case, however, the indictment simply quoted from the vague general language of the statute. The government countered that to give me a bill of particulars would be tantamount to giving away their case.

Sylvester J. Ryan, a political hack of a judge before whom our motion was argued on December 29, granted the motion in part. He required that the prosecution supply the date they claimed I joined the conspiracy, and a list of dates when I was supposed to have committed the overt acts in furtherance of the conspiracy; he gave the prosecution ten days in which to comply with the court order.

Now at long last I was to discover what it was all about. I didn't even try to think *why* the judge granted the motion. It was true that he and Kuntz had once practiced in neighboring offices, but surely that wasn't a sufficient basis for explaining such an unparalleled miracle as this. Miracle? I was only being given a small part of the information I truly deserved, under the law. I knew that political trials were outside the law, but I had difficulty in understanding that this was a political case. After all I wasn't a leading Communist, surely my political past wouldn't warrant such action against me, or against Julius and Ethel. At this point I still didn't understand this case in terms of frightening all progressives. I didn't understand that the government was going to use this case to mount a red scare, not unlike how Hitler used the Reichstag fire trial to frighten all the German liberals. It's always easier to see such things in terms of others rather than oneself.

The government now had until January 8 to comply with Ryan's order. In the meantime I went to court on January 4. Kuntz had assured me that the trial would not begin then so I wasn't surprised when the prosecution asked for a postponement. I saw Ethel and Julius in the courtroom, but didn't have a chance to talk with them. However I did have an opportunity to visit with Helen, through the wire mesh that separated the prisoners' section from the rest of the basement in Foley Square. I actually touched Helen, through the mesh, and for about twenty minutes we talked together, as we hadn't been able to do since Laredo.

But that night I felt cheated. Because I had not been prepared for the occasion, I didn't feel I had fully utilized the opportunity. And I wrote Helen that I felt as "one who had been on bread and water all these months, suddenly presented with an exquisite eclair, or like a blind person, suddenly given sight in the midst of an ocean of colored flowers." After a siege of poverty such richness is too much to be grasped all at once.

I led almost a double life. Most of the time I was in my cell, but from time to time I would be taken out from safekeeping and thrust into the limelight. I found it a trifle bewildering to be faced by reporters each time the marshals and I approached the courthouse on foot. What could I tell them? "I am innocent"? "It was a frameup"? I hadn't been accused of anything yet, I felt that to protest my innocence would sound phoney.

January 8 came and went and the government did not respond with the bill of particulars. It had not occurred to me that the government could act in this fashion. I had been so keyed up that I couldn't believe it when night came and I hadn't had any word. I don't think I ever again experienced the tension that I did on this occasion—not even when I was waiting for the jury verdict. I had spent five months in prison, and at last, I thought, I'd find out why.

But the expected miracle never took place. Instead, on January 11, the government filed a motion to re-argue the whole matter anew. They said that "the particulars which Judge Ryan has directed the Government to furnish the defendant Sobell is tantamount to giving Sobell a complete blueprint of the Government evidence against him." The responding affidavit that our attorneys filed did absolutely nothing to meet the issues raised by the government.

The motion was re-argued in front of Judge Ryan and he "amended" his initial order; tantamount to a complete reversal of his earlier position. Obviously the "boys" in the backroom had collared him and given him a good talking to—as is supposed to happen only in the corrupt city courts, not in the federal courts.

The new bill of particulars the government filed and to which Saypol swore, alleged that I had joined the conspiracy on or about June 15, 1944, and that the five overt acts (alleged conversations with Julius) listed in the original complaint were still valid. Now we had the prosecution as well as the FBI swearing that I had had five mysterious conversations with Julius. We were no further ahead now than we had been, except that my puzzlement over the five overt acts increased. Let me say here that at the trial the government never tried to prove these five conversations I was supposed to have had with Julius. They were thrown in strictly for camouflage. Nor was the prosecutor indicted for perjury, for swearing that he *would* prove these, *when in fact he didn't*. All is fair in this game called the trial, all that the prosecutor can get away with. As events would prove, there was no limit.

The trial which was originally scheduled for January 4 had been set back for January 14, and then on January 14 it was again set back for February 13. The government apparently had the power to manipulate the trial date, almost at will. But why were they delaying it? My lawyers were as much in the dark about it as I was, which wasn't saying very much. In the meantime life went on in the Tombs.

Initially I had found the noise of the inmates shouting from cell to cell unbearable, after we were locked up for the evening. There were usually many long distance conversations going on at the same time, all evening long, and some of them would get pretty heated. After a few months I learned to accommodate myself to this cacophony, as through the years I learned to accommodate to all sorts of annoyances. However, I knew I would not be staying there indefinitely and this, more than any other single factor, made it bearable. It is only the endless that becomes intolerable.

I also managed, for a packet of cigarettes, to get the lighting fixture in my cell cleaned. The lighting fixture was only accessible from a corridor outside the cells which was out of bounds to inmates like myself. The fixture had become so dirty that after the cleaning, the forty watt bulb made the inside of the cell look positively brilliant. I acquired, too, a piece of heavy canvas to smooth out the pressure of my bedspring. Until now I had used a blanket. The canvas was much better. The only bedding at the Tombs was dirty blankets and a straw pillow. Of course there were no linens. This wasn't the Waldorf, as the officers were so fond of pointing out.

Comparing prison to the Waldorf Hotel seemed to be a universal trait of prison guards. Years later, when I was in the hospital on the Rock, burning up with fever, and complained about the oversalty soup, I got the identical response.

While awaiting trial we wore our own street

clothes. Few of the men on my floor had the opportunity to change their clothing while they were there that I did. Helen would leave a package of clean clothes with the guard in the visiting room, and I would give him my soiled clothing to be picked up by Helen at the next visit. For some unknown reason I was not permitted two pairs of trousers or two shirts in the cell and each time I asked the guard for permission to make the exchange, he would look me up and down and ask why I wanted to change trousers I had worn only two months. When I learned that the usual reason was not acceptable, I told him I expected to go to court shortly. That he understood.

I didn't usually give a damn about being cleanly shaven, but under these oppressive conditions I felt I had to hold onto something that bound me to my prior existence. Besides, I wanted to appear handsome for Helen. But it would often be a week between shaves, making me miserable when I went to see Helen with the growth of stubble. Ordinarily we were sent in groups of about six to the balcony, with its warm-water sink and two-by-three-foot mirror hung vertically. While one group was shaving in front of the mirror, we were given brushes and soap to lather up. As soon as one of the men who was shaving was finished, he handed his razor to one of the lathered men, under the watchful eyes of the guard. To expedite the operation, so the two hundred–odd men on the floor could finish within an hour, we went back to the cell block to wash off the remaining soap at the mop basin, where warm water was available. The blades in the six razors were made to last for all the men on the floor. I never shaved without experiencing that pulling and tearing of the skin characteristic of a dull, dull blade.

On one occasion a guard took it upon himself to streamline the procedure, having us shave in the cell block, using a single bucket of water for rinsing the razors and shaving brushes. I knew what the response would have been if I had complained, so I used my "private line" to the warden. I wrote Helen a detailed letter telling her what had happened. The next time we shaved we were back at the sink with its fresh flowing water. One never knew how good things were until they got worse. (Many years later at the Lewisburg penitentiary, toward the end of my bit, I overheard one guard telling another "you make your own rules here, and then hope they're right.")

A practice which was calculated to degrade was carried out on the fourth floor. If a prisoner chose to leave his cell at noon, he could not re-enter until 3:25. If he needed to use the toilet he would have to suffer until then; no cell doors were opened until that hour. Later, again on the Rock, I ran into a similar practice. The guards would open or close all twenty cell gates on a tier in unison, by means of a long mechanical lever. The inertia of all the gates and the linkages that tied them together was tremendous, and once the system was set in motion it became a veritable monster, impossible to stop suddenly. As a result a number of men received painful injuries when they got their arms caught between the bars of the moving gates and the fixed bars, injuries which could have been minimized if the guards had chosen to move the gates more slowly. Of course a simple hydraulic damper could have remedied the situation, but it would have made the guards expend more energy.

The shakedown squad continued to visit once each week. I would have to step out of the cell and submit to a personal examination, then wait while my cell was searched for contraband. The efficiency of the procedure varied from officer to officer, some guards tearing the cell apart as if avenging themselves for the misdeeds of the miscreants, while others went through the routine perfunctorily, and a few professionally.

The real bastards amongst the guards could easily be discerned whenever a prisoner was brought in after midnight. They would slam open the cell gate and slam it shut, waking up everyone in the process. They might even shout a few words of obscenity for good measure. Of course the inmates would retort in kind—or perhaps the other way around.

In the Tombs the guards thought nothing of shoving an inmate around to emphasize a point. When it happened to me I felt it best not to complain; only my dignity had been hurt. This was in marked contrast with the federal prisons, where the guards had been taught never unnecessarily to lay their hands on an inmate. Of course this did not prevent their beating up inmates whenever they thought it was necessary. Once I saw an inmate beaten up in the Tombs in full view of the other inmates. An older and wiser guard finally intervened; he knew that such things were best done in the stripped cell, with no witnesses. I wrote Helen a lengthy description of the scene—and waited. Sure enough I was called to the warden's office, where he and his deputy were seated with my letter in front of them. In a direct confrontation a warden will almost always back up his guard, no matter how outrageous his behavior. Wardens feel it is necessary to allow their guards a certain latitude to maintain their morale. First the deputy tried to convince me that I was in error and had never witnessed the scene I described, but when that failed he tried another tack. Some time earlier I had requested permission to buy cheese in bulk from the commissary cart. At the time my request had been denied, but now the deputy indicated that permission would be granted if I would not write any more such letters. I assented without a moment's hesitation. I didn't feel there was a question of principle involved; I could always tell Helen about further brutality during our visits. And for the remainder of my stay I was able to buy cheese, which was a welcome supplement to my diet.

The men on the fourth floor of the Tombs weren't novices, but since they were generally charged with misdemeanors they usually did less than one year. This meant they were in and out of jail many times, so the turnover was much higher than on the other floors. Over a weekend the population would frequently double, since the courts were not open to dispose of the cases. This led to a doubling up in the cells. With two men in a cell and only one cot, one man had to sleep on the floor. Since I was a federal prisoner, being boarded out, no one was ever put in my cell.

The amount of food that came up on the food carts seemed to be fixed, not at all responsive to the changing number of men on the floor. As a result, whenever it got crowded the portions were proportionately smaller.

The first question asked of a newcomer to the fourth floor was, "where did you hang out?" This was the means used to establish identity. In a way, the Tombs was also a hangout, almost a rest home, for those who had been living on wine.

Saypol had not been entirely idle while he was holding Ethel, Julius, and me in jail. In November he tried Abraham Brothman and Miriam Moskowitz on charges of conspiracy to obstruct justice, using Gold and Elizabeth Bentley, the Red Spy Queen, as his main witnesses, and then in January he tried William Remington on perjury charges, again using Bentley as the star witness, all the while beating the anti-Communist drums louder and louder. Isolated as I was, and with mostly the *Daily News* for my news source, I couldn't relate my case to these. Somehow the hysteria that was building outside did not mean anything here. My immediate problem was one of survival. Even though I was aware that Gold would probably appear as a witness in our trial, I couldn't relate this to his role as a witness in the Brothman trial. I hadn't had a damn thing to do with all this—what were they trying to do to me?

From the February 1 newspaper I learned that a new indictment had been handed down against us. It was essentially the same as the previous indictment, except for one additional overt act, which allegedly involved Julius. Now the indictment had an even dozen overt acts, and I was still not mentioned in any. But it did give me an opportunity to go to Foley Square where I was able again to see Helen through the wire mesh. In court Phillips made his bumbling, fumbling presentation, again upsetting my equilibrum. I felt powerless to do anything but let him continue.

Even with the knowledge that the day of the trial was approaching, I still felt more like an interested onlooker than a defendant whose life was at stake. But those five alleged conversations with Julius bugged me.

On February 13, I again went to court, prepared for the trial to begin. This time it was moved forward to the twenty-eighth. On the twenty-eighth the new date set was March 6. Kuntz said he felt that this would be it.

I had told Helen how the marshals walked me to the courthouse on Foley Square and she took advantage of this by waiting in front of the Tombs until the marshals had escorted me out and then following about ten or fifteen feet behind. What could they do to us? They knew Helen wouldn't try to set me free, yet it made them nervous. Such a situation had probably never before occurred. It was exciting to walk with Helen following close behind me. After the long separation that had occurred, this was almost like walking hand in hand—almost.

I saw very little of Julius and Ethel during the courtroom appearances, nodding and smiling to each other as we stood facing the judge. The authorities never let us occupy the same holding cell, before or after going to the courtroom. On this point the orders from Washington must have been underlined.

While I felt no outward tension, with the approach of the trial date, I experienced a dramatic rise in sexual energy. At my urging, Helen and I conducted further "experiments" in sex together/apart. We each did our act alone, and related it to each other in our letters and during our visits. Of course the letters were couched in language we felt the authorities would not understand. This made us feel so close together at times that it was unbelievable. Real or unreal? In these circumstances who could say? When I left the Tombs I was never searched, so the night before the twenty-eighth, when I knew I would be going to Foley Square, I wrote Helen a lengthy intimate letter and gave it to her the following day. I don't know which gave me more pleasure, outwitting the authorities, or giving Helen the letter.

There was also an opportunity to visit with my mother, Mark, and Helen in a large holding cell. It felt good to see Mark as he moved about, to hear him talk, and to be close to him; a beautiful unhurried visit, completely unexpected. And I did not know whom to thank. After the family visit, my mother took Mark away while Helen remained with me. It would have been better if it had been a small warm room, but we extracted every last ounce out of that visit—as though we knew we would not see each other so closely again for a long long time. That night I thought that although everyone is aware of the significance of men without women, few think of the hardship for men to be in an environment without children.

With the Kefauver Committee bearing down on Frank Costello, whom I got to know later; the Foreign Minister's Conference; and the City College basketball fixing scandal (some of the players from my alma mater became fellow inmates at the Tombs), I thought that Saypol might be hard-pressed to make headlines with his red atom-spy stories. But his press conferences made headlines, before the trial and during the trial. The newspapers served as a forum for "evidence" he could not get into the courtroom. Thus we were tried twice, once in the press and once in the courtroom. (Many years later, when one of my attorneys taped a press interview in connection with a pending appeal, he was threatened with disbarment proceedings if he permitted it to go on the air. What was sauce for the government was not necessarily sauce for the defendant.)

What were my thoughts the last weekend before the trial? I hardly realized the significance. I read from morning to night—Hemingway, Ibsen, Sean O'Casey. When I stopped reading, or writing Helen, I found my mind seething with nothingness, a tumult and a whirring.

I wrote Helen:

I guess one of the difficulties in writing is that no matter what I say it becomes so trivial against the impending storm. According to the newspapers, a mother who sold her two children committed a horrible crime. Yet I know of another mother [Ethel Rosenberg] whose two children were taken away from her, needlessly, and with the same law's blessing. . . . What a strange period we are living through.

Good night, sweet love. Four kisses for you. Your Morty.

The morning of the day before the trial proved eventful: I was sentenced to be confined to my cell for five days, having been "convicted" of showing disrespect for an officer. As a result I didn't see Helen that last visit. Of course on the following day I was allowed to leave my cell to go to trial.

Part Two

THE TRIAL

1   The Jury

AFTER a good night's sleep, I awoke on the morning of March 6, 1951, feeling as though it were just another day. I wondered why my heart was not pounding with anxiety; I was to go on trial for my life. Had my sensibilities already become so dulled that I could no longer respond normally? Presently two marshals came for me and we walked together (I in handcuffs, of course) to the federal courthouse on Foley Square. They called it Foley Square—not, say, Cardoza Square. As usual we entered the courthouse through the rear (I didn't even know what the front looked like). I was locked in one of the holding tanks in the basement until the appointed time; then I was taken upstairs in a tiny elevator and admitted to the courtroom. The trial began promptly at 10:30.

> C.134–245
> The United States of America
>   v.
> Julius Rosenberg, Ethel Rosenberg,
> Anatoli A. Yakovlev, also known as "John,"
> David Greenglass and Morton Sobell.

This was the title of the case as it started. Actually neither Greenglass nor Yakovlev was tried with us.

Greenglass had pleaded guilty but his sentencing was held up until he had finished cooperating with the prosecution (testifying at our trial), and Yakovlev, a Soviet consular official, had left the country to return to the Soviet Union years before. His inclusion was for "technical reasons."

It was a large courtroom, and looked much like courtrooms I had seen in the movies. I sat on the extreme left of a long table, with Eddie Kuntz and Harold Phillips to my right. Julius and Ethel were at the opposite end of the table, and their lawyers, Emanuel Bloch and his father, Alexander Bloch, to their left. Thus the lawyers could confer, but we defendants were as separated as we had been all along. None of the lawyers had had much experience in felony cases; none had ever before tried a capital case, the lawyers' touchstone for separating the boys from the men. Eddie Kuntz had the most experience as a trial lawyer, but he hadn't practiced much in federal court. Phillips had once defended a client in federal court, but had almost exclusively practiced insurance law. Manny Bloch's criminal law experience was meager and his father was known as a business lawyer. This, then, was the defense team on whom three lives hung. Where were the more competent and experienced lawyers? Hiding some place, fearful of becoming involved in this case; fearful that it might wreck their professional careers.

In front of us was the prosecution table. Irving H. Saypol, the United States Attorney for the Southern District of New York, the busiest district in the nation, headed the prosecution team. Myles Lane, his chief assistant (an intimate of Three-Finger Brown, one of organized crime's colorful figures) was seated next to him. Then came a whole group of lesser lights, including Roy M. Cohn, a brash youngster who was soon to leap into prominence, first as an investigator for Senator Joe McCarthy, and then as his defense counsel at congressional hearings. Each of these younger attorneys could probably run rings around all of our attorneys put together when it came to federal law; they had all participated as a group in many of the recent political trials and were all well read in federal law. And it was *their* court; they were at home there. The judge, Irving Kaufman, was a youngster by federal court standards. He had only recently had himself and his law partner appointed to the federal bench, after vacating the position of dispenser of federal patronage. It was said that no other judge wanted this case and that Kaufman, the youth, had eagerly volunteered for it. As many have observed, notorious cases made bad law, and the more mature judges probably didn't want to have a role in the making of this bad law.

Throughout the trial Helen came early and got a seat in the first row, barely ten feet behind me. I could turn around and look at her any time I wanted to. It was good that she was there among the spectators, and not with me at the defendants' table, where Saypol had threatened to put her. But my parents were not permitted in the courtroom. They were named on the long list of over one hundred prosecution witnesses which the government was legally required, in all capital cases, to give the defense several days before the trial. Those named on the list would testify for the government and might tailor their testimony if they heard others testify. This was another of the many myths surrounding trial procedure which was religiously accepted by the courts. I couldn't imagine my parents testifying for the government—even if their son were truly guilty.

The game known as picking the jury began, and Kaufman set the note of ostensible fairness when he told the jury panel: "It is our purpose and object to secure a jury that has no feeling, no bias, no prejudice, as to either side of the controversy. To put it another way, the minds of the jurors should be the same as a white sheet of paper with nothing on it with respect to the case." How they could select such a jury, after all that Saypol, J. Edgar Hoover, and the attorney general had told the press about the case in recent months, was one of the many enigmas. The *Tabula Rasa* analogy had as much substance as Rousseau's *Savage Man*. Kaufman then informed the panel: "The following persons *will be* [emphasis added] called as witnesses for the government in this case . . ." and proceeded to read the list of about one hundred names, including a number prominently connected with the development of the atomic bomb. I didn't know it at the time, but in a front page story in the *New York Times,* Meyer Berger reported: "This nation's outstanding physicists, including Dr. Robert Oppenheimer and Dr. Harold C. Urey are expected to be called within a week or ten days." Major General Leslie Groves, the army man who had been in charge of administering the bomb project and Dr. George Kistiakowski, another top scientist, were also named on this list. This was the first big lie of the trial: but none of us knew it at the time. Not one of these eminent scientists was called to testify. Moreover, in later years we learned that they had never even been questioned by the government, or notified that they were on the government's list of witnesses. Clearly Saypol had never really intended to call them but listed them solely for the effect. Everyone—the jury, the public, and even the defendants and their lawyers—was properly awed by these names. I don't know if our lawyers had ever intended to call any scientific witnesses. It might have been sticky. There were questions of security clearance. And what defense witnesses could they have possibly secured to match the names on the prosecution's list?

Unlike procedure in the state courts, examination of the jury panel was conducted exclusively by Kaufman, not by the attorneys. He read off a long list of publications and organizations and asked if any of the panel members had read them or been associated in any way with them. They included the *New York Daily News* and the *Worker*, the *American Legion Monthly* and the *New Masses*. It was well balanced. Also included were the Abraham Lincoln Brigade, which had fought in the Spanish Civil War, and the International Workers' Order. And to balance these, the Ku Klux Klan was listed. Then Kaufman had yet another list read to the panel by the clerk of the court: this was the attorney general's subversive list. It included many of the same organizations and some additional ones. He then asked the panel: "Now, the question is whether any juror has been a member of, contributed to, or been associated with, or any member of his family or close friend, with any of these organizations?" The government was going to be absolutely certain that no one with any left leanings, or even associations, would get on the jury. He then asked the panel members if, as a result of anything they had read or heard on the radio, they had become so prejudiced that they could not render a verdict based on the evidence alone. I have yet to meet a racist who admitted to being one, or a person with any kind of prejudice who acknowledged it. The whole procedure was a comedy that a writer of fiction would have found difficult to match. From the day of our arrest until the day the trial ended the various agencies of the government including the FBI and the prosecution, constantly fed prejudicial stories concerning the case to the various media. And now the judge was asking the jury panel if they had been prejudiced by this material, which the prosecution had designed to prejudice them. A classic Kafkaesque scenario. When Kaufman asked, "Has anybody got any prejudice or bias against the government's loyalty program?" I felt like laughing. I didn't feel at all like a defendant at a trial, but rather like a spectator at a grand farce. But this was only the beginning. Kaufman then asked, "Have you ever formed or expressed an opinion concerning the work of the House Committee on Un-American Activities?" This was of course 1951, and the judge was permitted to ask such a question of a prospective juror. Political opinion was a legitimate area of inquiry.*

Saypol was as afraid of intellectuals as of working people. When a former writer for *Radio Free Europe,* a CIA-sponsored anti-Communist propaganda organization, turned up on the panel, I told Kuntz we would have to get rid of him. But Kuntz said wait and see. He proved right; Saypol used one of his peremptory challenges to get rid of the writer. Longshoremen he didn't like either, especially if they were black.

The system the government had for picking the jury panel worked well, for no one indicated that he had dared form an opinion, pro or con, on the work of the infamous House Committee. There were many

---

* Transcript of Record as filed in the Supreme Court of the United States, October Term, 1951, No. 111 and 112, pages 35–75. The trial record will henceforth be designated as R. followed by the page numbers.

questions the lawyers wanted to put to the jurors to ascertain their ideas, but were forbidden under *their* rules.

After a day and a half the jury was picked; the defense still having one challenge left. The government never let us forget this. Whenever any question about the jury came up in post-trial proceedings, the government always contended that we must have been satisfied with the jury since we hadn't even used up all our challenges. Actually the lawyers didn't use the last challenge because they were unwilling to risk a new juror's coming into the box with no challenge left.

The jury that was selected to hear the case was certainly not a cross section of the Southern District of New York. It consisted of two accountants, two auditors, a bookkeeper, a restaurant owner, a caterer for a tennis club, an estimator for a printing plant, a state employee, a lone black employed by Consolidated Edison, and a single retired woman, formerly a switchboard operator, who had recently served on a grand jury. The panel had included few blacks or manual workers, so it was relatively easy for Saypol to use his allowed challenges against those who survived the original screening. Consolidated Edison workers, as proved by past experience, were prosecution minded. He could afford to "integrate" the jury with this one.

After the selection of the jury the defense lawyers made their motions to dismiss the indictment, in order to "protect the record," for later appeals—just in case the jury should find us guilty. And then Saypol began the trial in earnest with his opening speech to the jury. No sooner did he finish talking about the fair trial we would get, when he told the jury, "The significance of a conspiracy to commit espionage takes on added meaning where the defendants are charged with having participated in this conspiracy against our country, at this, the most critical hours in our history, in time of war, around 1944."

One would have thought we were being tried for giving aid to Nazi Germany, not the Soviet Union, which had been our ally in 1944, at the most critical hours in our history. This was so blatantly dishonest that I was amazed our lawyers did not object; it was also objectionable from the legal point of view because the indictment did not charge us with having conspired to commit espionage *against* our country as Saypol claimed, but "to the advantage of the Soviet Union." The distinction was important, because the law allowed the prosecutor to have indicted us the other way. Finally, when Saypol said: "The evidence will show that the loyalty and the allegiance of the Rosenbergs and Sobell were not to our country, but that it was to Communism, Communism in this country and Communism throughout the world." (R. 180) Emanuel Bloch objected, because, as he put it, "Communism is not on trial here." But Kaufman allowed this to stand; "For purpose of establishing motive."

From Saypol's appeal to the jury's "patriotism," one might have concluded that we were being tried for treason. The disloyalty theme permeated the whole trial, from his opening statement to Kaufman's sentencing speech.* The jury of course equated disloyalty with treason as Saypol had intended. This was ironic, since

---

* Judge H. R. Tyler, in an opinion on a suit against Louis Nizer, wrote, "Plaintiffs are natural children of Julius and Ethel Rosenberg, who were executed in June, 1953 after their trial for treason in this court." Even a learned federal judge was mistaken on this point. (73 Civ. 2720 July 18, 1973, page 2.)

treason was the one crime defined in the Constitution, with the method of proof also prescribed; there have to be two witnesses to the same overt act. The founding fathers knew that George III and other monarchs had tried dissidents for "treason," which was in fact anything they chose it to be. Now, Saypol and Kaufman, while ostensibly trying us for conspiracy to commit espionage, were actually trying us for treason. And since the media had fully cooperated with the Establishment, spreading the news of the Red Peril from abroad, this accusation of disloyalty against us undoubtedly had a powerful effect on the jury. There was nothing we could do about it. Saypol went on, "The evidence will show that Sobell and Julius Rosenberg, classmates together at college, dedicated themselves to the cause of Communism."

Of course the evidence the government presented during the trial showed no such thing, but Saypol's false accusation had undoubtedly found its mark. Time and again he spoke of our betraying our country, of these traitorous Americans, these traitorous activities, treasonable acts ad nauseum. And our attorneys sat on their hands, mute. They would object, during the trial, to innumerable technical points which had little meaning in the final outcome, but while Saypol and the judge were having us pre-tried for treason, our lawyers didn't even raise the mildest objection.

Not given to understatement, Saypol told the jury that the Rosenbergs stole, through David Greenglass, "this one weapon that might well hold the key to the survival of this nation and means [sic] the peace of the world, the atom bomb." (R.183) And that, at the behest of the Rosenbergs, "Greenglass stole and turned over to them . . . sketches of the very atom bomb itself." In conclusion Saypol said, "The evidence of the treasonable acts of these three defendants, you will find overwhelming." But the Constitution clearly defines treason as giving aid and comfort to an enemy in time of war. Saypol had it both ways—he used all of the prejudice of the treason accusation, but we had none of the Constitutional safeguards.

And fifteen years later, when the hoax of the theft of the atom bomb had been exposed, the United States Attorney would completely reverse the government's position and tell the court: "So in the last analysis, the whole discussion of the value of the evidence [sketch of the atom bomb], and the government, I want to make it clear, has taken no position whatsoever with respect to that." (Morton Sobell v. United States, 66 Civ. 1328, U.S. District Court, Sept. 12, 1966, page 98.)

Bloch made a formal motion for a mistrial, but not because of the talk about treason, but on the ground that Saypol had brought up the Communist issue. Poor lawyers, they were so fixated on the Communist issue that they let all else pass unnoticed. From the start Bloch showed himself foolishly obsequious. "Let me assure Mr. Saypol that I didn't want to be discourteous [for interrupting him to object], but I wanted to reserve my right on the record." (R.185) The courtesy was never reciprocated throughout the trial; both Kaufman and Saypol took his turn in insulting our lawyers, but Manny Bloch never stopped being the "perfect gentleman." Perhaps that was why Nizer made him the hero of his book on the case.

A defense lawyer is generally at a disadvantage in an opening speech, because he usually hasn't much to talk about. He must wait until the evidence is in before he has something concrete to say—unless he is a political thinker and understands the issues. Manny Bloch could have told the jury what he had read about the case in the newspapers, pointing out that it had already been tried in the press; but he didn't. He could also have taken apart the prosecutor's treason opening. Instead he asked the jury to give his client, Julius Rosenberg, a "fair shake," and not be swayed by emotion. It was a far cry from Saypol's pointed, inflammatory accusations. Then Alex Bloch, representing Ethel, delivered his opening. He said even less than Manny. Phillips opened for Morton Sobell. He tried to attack Saypol for painting the picture "so much blacker than it is." (R.190) Outside of the implicit racism of the remark (of course few were conscious of it then), it was flawed because it acknowledged a certain degree of culpability. "I am not trying to minimize the fact that it is a criminal offense [the charge], but for heavens sake, why maximize it?" he went on. Phillips knew, Phillips sensed, that there was something false about Saypol's opening, but he didn't put his finger on it. Instead he went into a detailed analysis of the indictment, which made no impression on the jury. Saypol had delivered a blistering, fraudulent attack on the defendants, and our lawyers had countered only with vague generalities about prosecution and defense lawyers standing as equals before the court.

The selection of the jury, the formal motions, and the opening remarks had consumed two days. The following day, Thursday, March 8, the trial would begin in earnest.

2

Elitcher, My Friend

THE government's first witness was Max Elitcher. I had noticed his name on the list of witnesses, but thought nothing of it since there were so many other names there of people I knew, including my parents. Helen had last seen the Elitchers in Queens, when she put up our house for sale to raise money for legal fees. Max and Helene had immediately demanded payment for their share of our common washing machine, then located in our basement. They followed Helen through the house and selected as barter various items: our piano, the flagstones in our back yard, and miscellaneous small bits. The piano was especially dear to me because I had remodeled it myself giving it a modern and unorthodox appearance. After that episode Helen didn't see them again; there was no reason to—we hadn't been too close during the last half year or so while I was still free.

Saypol lost no time in getting to the heart of the government's case: communism! After a few short questions about Elitcher's background, Saypol asked him:

Q. Do you recall a conversation sometime in 1939 with Sobell regarding the Communist Party?

When Phillips and Manny Bloch objected (Alex Bloch said very little during the entire trial, and it would sometimes have been better if he hadn't said anything), the judge invited them up to the bench for a conference. Even though our attorneys had engaged in bench conferences before this, I had never been so acutely aware of the absurdity of this procedure until now. Julius, Ethel, and I were on trial for our lives, yet we were not permitted to hear what was taking place at these bench conferences where our attorneys were supposed to be protecting our interests. Moreover, though my attorneys were getting the previous day's trial transcripts daily, at the beginning of each day's proceedings, not once during the whole trial did they ever show me the trial transcript, in which I could at least have read about the bench conferences. Even if I had seen the transcript it would not have told me all, since much of what took place at the bench was "off the record." It was at this bench conference that Saypol promised the court he would prove my Communist Party membership right down to the time of the conspiracy. (R.199) This he never did. I had left the Party in 1941 when I went back to school and the conspiracy was alleged to have started in 1944, some three years later. But Kuntz never asked me about it, and so Saypol's lie remained unchallenged.

Kaufman admitted Elitcher's testimony concerning my Communist Party membership, "subject to connection," and if the promised connection was never made, who would remember it weeks later? Meanwhile the jurors were being prejudiced and there was little we could do.

Elitcher went on to testify that when we shared the same apartment in Washington, D.C., I asked him to join the Young Communist League. "At the time I said no, and for some period he continued to ask me about it and I finally did make such a move." He added that when he succumbed and did make the move, "it turned out that the group was being organized as a group or cell of the Communist Party and it was this which I joined." (R.205)

In admitting to Party membership—which he said continued until 1948—Elitcher made himself liable to two indictments for perjury: first, when he had taken the Navy Department loyalty oath, denying such membership and again when he had signed a similar form at Reeves. Thus he was testifying while facing a possible ten-year prison term—if Saypol chose to indict him. But it all had been pre-arranged and he wouldn't go to prison as long as he carried out his part of the bargain to cooperate. And cooperate he did.

At the meeting, he said he was asked if he would agree to such membership: "I don't recall the exact oath or whatever procedure was used, and from that time on, in attending meetings, I knew I was a member of the Communist Party." Saypol asked Elitcher if the Party cell had any connection with the Navy Department, in any way, knowing full well that the answer would be negative since he had questioned him at length beforehand. But the idea of a connection between the Party cell and the Navy Department had been implanted in the minds of the jury before Elitcher could even respond.

I had never asked Elitcher to join the Young Communist League (YCL) or the Party. I felt that Elitcher would be ready to join sometime, but that my asking wouldn't hasten that day. When he was ready, *he asked me*, and I took him to a meeting of the YCL. There wasn't any oath, or any other formality, and it wasn't a cell. It was quite open in fact and we met in a large group of about twenty or twenty-five. Some months later it was decided to split up the group and to transfer most of the members into the Communist Party.

Saypol then asked Elitcher to tell about my inquiring whether he knew any progressive engineering students who could be approached for espionage work. It was ludicrous on the face of it. Elitcher had not agreed to participate in espionage, according to his own testimony, yet I asked him for the names of others who would participate. What could I say to rebut this accusation if I took the stand? Simply denying it, I felt, would not be enough, and yet I could do nothing more. Saypol then took Elitcher back to our City College days, asking him if Julius or myself had had any conversations with him in 1937 or 1938, whereupon Elitcher dutifully recalled that we had *both* then asked him to join the YCL. He killed two birds with one ersatz stone. We had had a left-wing political group at engineering school, the Steinmetz Society, and it was never officially affiliated with the YCL. I knew that I had never asked anyone to join the YCL, neither Elitcher nor anyone else. Now I had to prove that I hadn't asked Elitcher to join at City College, as well as in Washington. With ten years staring him in the face it was easy for Elitcher to weave these lies into the real fabric of daily existence. In the end it was these small lies that made up the whole of the government case against me. A little lie here, a little lie there, and with some puffing from the prosecution, it added up to a huge conspiracy.

Once more Saypol took Elitcher over the events in Washington which were supposed to have led to my inducing him to join the Party. He said that I talked to him about the need to join the Party on many occasions, until he finally succumbed. Now I could see why Saypol went back and forth so much; it allowed him to have the testimony repeated. Nor did my lawyers object while the same testimony was given over and over again, each time with a little added embellishment. Saypol then asked Elitcher for some details of the weekly meetings which were held in the homes of the various members, and continued:

Q. Was there a time when Sobell acted as chairman of the group?

A. Yes, at the beginning, at these first meetings he was chairman.

Q. Do you recall incident to his presiding or acting as chairman whether any dues were paid to him by you, or did you see others pay him dues?

A. Well. The dues were paid to the chairman only. The chairman transferred the dues to other people. I don't recall the payment of dues to him specifically. (R.225)

The truth of the matter was that I was not chairman, certainly not at this time; I had only joined a short time earlier myself. Odd how Elitcher couldn't get himself to say that he recalled the payment of dues to me specifically. But he did recite the script that Saypol had written, which called for my having some official standing, otherwise the Appeals Court might question whether I was in fact a Communist or only an onlooker who happened to be present. To avoid this legal pitfall, I was made chairman. Then Elitcher told how we discussed readings from the *Daily Worker* and Marxist and Leninist theory. This wasn't enough, however, and Saypol asked him: "Did you receive any official instructions at these meetings?" With this cue Elitcher told that he did receive official instructions from me, as chairman. What were these instructions? "There was a suggestion, recommendation, to join certain organizations in Washington . . . one of them was the American Peace Mobilization. When the American Youth Congress had its congress in Washington [with Eleanor Roosevelt providing the Department of Commerce auditorium for some of its functions] there was a suggestion to assist them, to help in the activities." (R.226) Such were the activities which Communist Party members were directed to undertake (under orders from Moscow, no doubt).

For a while I wondered why Elitcher didn't tell about our going around, slipping leaflets under the doors of the houses in our neighborhood, or about our going to a nearby barber shop, which served as a party literature depot, collecting the literature for our group as well as that of several other groups; and about how we then rode around town distributing the various packets of literature. I saw he thus managed to disassociate himself from any Party activities; it was always *I* who was the chairman, or giving instructions, or collecting dues. And of course Elitcher's joining in the first place was made to appear nebulous. He was obviously averse to categorically admitting any of the things we had done together.

While Elitcher was testifying I began to worry how Kuntz would cross-examine him on this, since we had never discussed Elitcher, or much else for that matter. In the end my fears proved useless since neither Kuntz nor Bloch cross-examined Elitcher on anything remotely connected with the Communist Party. While the prosecution made the Communist Party a major issue, and the defense kept objecting to it, our lawyers none-theless pretended it hadn't even been mentioned during their cross-examinations. My lawyers never told me, and I don't know if Manny Bloch ever discussed the question with Julius and Ethel on a serious plane. In effect, my lawyers took the Fifth Amendment for me, without informing me, much less asking me.

Then, out of the clear blue, Saypol asked:

Q. At this time do you recall what the situation was in respect to the Hitler–Stalin pact? (R.226)

I could hardly believe it when Kaufman over-rode Bloch's objections to such a clearly provocative and loaded question. Then Saypol made the question more specific, asking if a chairman (meaning Sobell of course) issued any instructions in this regard. Dutifully Elitcher told the court that the instructions were to talk to people and gain support for the pact. Saypol followed up with:

Q. In the course of the pact, of course, Russia was an ally of Hitler, wasn't that so?

Finally the judge upheld Bloch's objection to this "question." It was odd that although Elitcher was talking about me, my lawyers were not the ones who were objecting. What a barrel of worms Saypol opened up when he got into the realm of international politics. But alas our lawyers never picked up the challenge. It would have been fair game to show that the United States and its European allies actively supported Hitler when he over-ran democratic Czechoslovakia and Austria and reacted only when he invaded feudal Poland. It would have made interesting cross-examination which under the ordinary trial rules should have been allowed.

The apparently small lie, that I was chairman of our group, was repeated over again and again, and each time Elitcher responded in predictable fashion.

When Saypol asked Elitcher on how many occasions he saw me after I left Washington, Elitcher responded that I had visited Washington twice. I couldn't believe my ears. Why should he lie about this? I must have visited Washington well over a dozen times during this period. During 1943 and 1944 I went down to Washington regularly, at least every six weeks, to see Helen. In addition I went down on several trips in connection with my work at G.E. Most of the times Helen and I would visit the Elitchers. Frequently they would let us have the key to their apartment, which was within walking distance of the Union Station, where we would spend the last few hours of our visit together. At the time of the trial I didn't understand the reason for this blatant lie, which seemed without purpose, but later it occurred to me that the prosecution was wary about showing our relationship as one in which we had casual social meetings. If every encounter between us was conspiratorial, the story would be tighter and more serious. Moreover, Saypol claimed that Elitcher had been approached by Rosenberg, rather than myself, to enlist as a spy. But if I was seeing Elitcher constantly this wouldn't make much sense. But unfortunately my lawyers never cross-examined Elitcher in this area; they could have torn him apart.

Elitcher's testimony against Julius was much the same. There was a lot of talk about espionage, but nothing came of it. However in telling the story of the June

1944 meeting with Julius, Elitcher forgot to include a very important "fact"—that Julius had told him I was supplying classified information for transmission to Russia. Saypol found it necessary to lead Elitcher over the story again and prod him with hints before he responded according to script (R.235–237). After this bit of tortuously drawn out testimony I was officially a member of the conspiracy.

The first substantial testimony was Elitcher's account of going to Schenectady in 1946 in connection with a Navy Department project and staying overnight at our house. He said we discussed our work and that I asked whether there was any written material on his project. He said he told me that the really important ordnance pamphlet on the subject would not be completed until the end of the year. Later that same year, he said, he stayed overnight again, and when I again inquired about the pamphlet, he again told me that it had not yet been completed. Thereupon, he said, I suggested that he see Rosenberg. Saypol asked him:

Q. Did he state to you the purpose for which you should see him [Rosenberg]?
A. Well, he said, I don't know in what words, or implied, that it had to do with this espionage business, but I don't recall the exact nature of the words. (R.247–249)

Phillips immediately objected that Elitcher had given the jury a conclusion—that I wanted the material in connection with this espionage business, whereas under the law a witness was only allowed to state facts, and it was for the jury to draw conclusions. But Kaufman was right there with a very recent decision (the *Petrone* case) from the Court of Appeals.

The Court. In effect they tell the district court not to adhere to the old form of law book teaching . . . that a conclusion should necessarily be excluded; the important thing, the important function of the district court is to attempt to elicit the truth from the witness. (R.249)

Saypol put it more simplisticly when he said: "After all, aren't we getting at the truth here, by trying to get impressions from the witness?"

The only problem with this is that impressions are hardly susceptible to cross-examination. What of the witness who testified that it was his impression that the accused was a witch? How does a lawyer cross-examine such a witness? Rules of testimony were laid down so as to give the defense a chance to subject the witness to questioning on the facts he related. Examination on impressions is usually impossible, hence can hardly lead to the truth.

It was of course true that Elitcher had stayed at our place in Schenectady as he related. He was our guest when he came up to visit G.E. on business. It was also true that in the course of conversation we talked not only about politics but also about the Mark-56 gun director on which he was the Navy Department project engineer. The development work on the project was done at the M.I.T. radiation lab, and the aeronautic and marine engineering division, for which I was working at G.E., was now engineering it for production. A prototype of the system was located on the ground floor of building 28, where I worked, and I had a badge that permitted me to visit that part of the plant at will. Generally speaking the situation was the reverse of Elitcher's description. It was he who was coming to G.E. for information to take back to Washington. In fact I worked on several aspects of the overall system; we had had seminars on it at which the whole Mark-56 system was discussed in great detail. Thus it was a natural subject for our conversation when Elitcher visited. It was also true that I had asked him about the ordnance pamphlet, but it was absolutely untrue that I had implied "that it had to do with this espionage business," or that I had suggested he see Julius. What was it that I said that gave him this impression? If I took the stand what could I do to defend myself against such a nebulous, incriminating impression? This was the pattern of a great deal of Elitcher's testimony—using a basically truthful incident upon which to attach a relatively small lie—a lie that changed the whole complexion of the event, a lie that proved sufficient to convict me.

Under Saypol's guidance Elitcher went on to claim that he had followed my suggestion to see Julius— about a half a year later. (Our meeting took place in early 1946 and the meeting with Julius either the end of 1946 or early 1947 according to his testimony.) (R.251) Saypol didn't think it necessary to have him explain the lengthy delay in carrying out "Sobell's suggestion." But on summation he put it this way:

. . . Sobell pumped him [Elitcher] for information concerning the new secret program of the government for fire control on our war weapons; how when he drew from Elitcher the admission that this secret program would be described in writing in the near future, Sobell instructed Elitcher to go *at once* [emphasis added] to Rosenberg and tell him that his material was in preparation and might be available; how Elitcher in fact did go to Rosenberg and tell him that. (R.1532)

Several times in the course of asking Elitcher about his meeting with Julius, Saypol emphasized the point that this visit was a direct outcome of our meeting—as if for fear the jury might forget.

Elitcher testified that at the end of July 1948 he drove to New York City with his family to look for a place to live. He told how he had gone to my house, after stopping off in Baltimore, and how he had been followed all the way to the city by two automobiles. He told the jury that I became angry when he told me about his being followed. Everything up to this point was essentially true, but then he said I told him that I had some material in the house which was too valuable to destroy, but too dangerous to keep around, and that I wanted to deliver it to Julius that very night. And despite his protestations I decided to make a trip into Manhattan. He continued:

> However, he insisted and said that he was tired. He asked me to go along. He said he was tired, and that he might not be able to make the trip back. I agreed to go after argument, and we left the house. Upon leaving I saw him take what I identified then as a 35 mm. film can. (R.361)

Elitcher continued, saying, I drove to Julius's neighborhood, where I left him in the car, taking the film can with me. On returning, he said I told him:

> He [Rosenberg] said "it's all right; don't be concerned about it; it's OK." [Sobell] then said Rosenberg had told him that he had once talked to Elizabeth Bentley on the phone but he was pretty sure that she didn't know who he was and therefore everything was all right. We proceeded back to the house.

Saypol then asked him about some photograph equipment in the basement of my house: a 35 mm. Leica camera, an enlarger, and some film processing equipment (Elitcher himself had similar equipment). Elitcher told of his having moved to New York City, becoming my neighbor, and going to work for the same company, the Reeves Instrument Company. I wondered what the jury made of this: with all of New York to move to, the Elitchers chose to become my backyard neighbors—under the somewhat unusual circumstances that existed between us, in terms of espionage.

Elitcher said that on one occasion, when we were driving to work together, I asked him if he knew any engineering students who were *not* involved in progressive activities, who might join our espionage ring. This contrasted with a previous request he said I had made for progressive engineering students. He who had not participated in any espionage was being asked to supply recruits: first progressives and then non-progressives.

Going back and forth, Elitcher then said that when he planned to leave the Navy Department, both Julius and I tried to dissuade him. (In view of the excellent espionage he had been carrying out?) The last question Saypol asked him was one Kuntz called poisonous.

Q. In the time you worked with Sobell at Reeves Instrument Company, or at any time, did you ever see Sobell take any papers or documents?
A. . . . I know that he did have a briefcase and he took material out, but what it was, or what the material was, I do not know.

Now all I had to prove was that I never took out material for espionage in that briefcase. Instead of the burden of proof being on the prosecution, I now had to prove that I was innocent.

After such a performance I suppose I should have been angry with Elitcher, yet I found myself without any strong feeling toward him. Not that I was turning the other cheek, or anything like that, but it was like watching someone doing something stupid. I knew he was weak, but he was far from stupid, and yet the prosecutor had had to refresh his memory so frequently that it angered the judge. I wondered if perhaps his unconscious was not fully cooperating; was he ashamed of what he was doing? But I was angry with my lawyers for the way they had been fumbling and bumbling, objecting to the picayune and allowing what I felt to be really important to pass without objection. Manny Bloch began the cross-examination of Elitcher. He first tried to establish the casual relationship between Julius and Max at college, making the point that Elitcher hadn't known Julius any better than hundreds of other students at school. Next he brought out his having signed the non-Communist affidavit in order to take the civil service examination in 1938. He then developed the sequence in which Elitcher had been questioned by the FBI and by the grand jury, and exactly how he had been questioned.

Elitcher related that he had been picked up by the FBI at work, before noon, one day toward the end of July, after Julius had been arrested: confirming what I thought while in Mexico, that everyone who attended engineering school with Julius would be picked up for questioning. He was taken down to the FBI offices where he was questioned briefly, and then driven home where they continued to question him while searching his house. Presumably Helene was also in on the questioning, though this was not mentioned. It was past midnight when the agents wrote out a statement which he signed; they then left him until the following day.

When Bloch asked him:

Q. Did you pass any information, secret, classified, confidential or otherwise, of the government of the United States, to the defendant Julius Rosenberg, at any time?

He drew a negative response. Bloch then elicited that after he had been questioned by the FBI, Elitcher had hired a lawyer from O. J. Rogge's law firm, the same one that Greenglass had hired. Rogge, former assistant attorney general, was a "connection lawyer"; that is, he had rapport with the United States Attorney's office. He could bargain with, and reach agreements with, the United States Attorney. He was a good man for one in Elitcher's position. I thought Bloch scored a point when he brought out how ludicrous Elitcher's story was—that he had been asked for confidential material for years, ever since 1944, and that although he had never turned anything over, he had retained Julius's confidence. Bloch then went on to elicit the admission that Elitcher had signed a loyalty oath while working for the government in 1948, and that he was in fact now fearful of being prosecuted for perjury.

But a lot of Manny's cross-examination went into trivial details concerning the exact procedure the FBI had used in questioning Elitcher. I couldn't see much point to this and became bored and impatient; I wanted to see the real questioning begin. Elitcher maintained that despite the perjury he had committed in signing the loyalty oath, no promises had been made to him and that he still didn't really know what action, if any, the government would take against him.

Elitcher said he had talked with the FBI agents on "many occasions," and had also gone over his testimony, preparatory to the trial, with Saypol, Roy Cohn, Myles Lane, and other members of the United States Attorney's staff. About three and one half weeks after the FBI's first visit to him at Reeves, Elitcher testified before the grand jury that subsequently indicted Julius and Ethel—but not me. My interpretation of these events (which is similar to that of many others who have studied the case) is that the prosecution initially viewed me, like Elitcher, as a vulnerable person who was a potential witness against the Rosenbergs. The government was not interested in additional defendants at this point; Julius and Ethel had been arrested with great fanfare; afterwards a mad scramble for witnesses to build the case was begun. The FBI naturally turned to Rosenbergs' left-wing associates.

When Bloch finished the examination that day, probing Elitcher's trip to New York in the latter part of 1946 (or early 1947), Kaufman reminded the jury that the trip had been taken at my suggestion. Strangely, Elitcher could remember nothing concerning the trip except that he had gone to see Julius about espionage at my suggestion. He didn't recall if his wife had accompanied him or how long he had stayed, explaining: "I was in New York quite often, so I don't recall the particular circumstances . . . I just recall the incident." But Bloch didn't ask why it had taken him so long to see Julius after he said I had suggested it, if he visited New York so often.

Court adjourned on that note, with Elitcher still on the witness stand. Since Kuntz would cross-examine the following day I expected to see him before court resumed. There was so much I could have told him about Elitcher and our relationship to help destroy his credibility, but Kuntz never came and I had to tell the story to myself.

The next morning Bloch tried to get some clarification from Elitcher about that New York trip, but without success; Elitcher still failed to recall a thing about it, though he must have discussed it with his wife after his first day on the stand.

When Bloch asked Elitcher whether he had told the FBI about the 35 mm. film can incident, or had mentioned Bentley's name during the first day's interview, Saypol objected that he didn't understand the question. When Kaufman asked Elitcher if *he* understood it, he answered in the affirmative, but this didn't deter Saypol, who persisted that *he* didn't understand it. Elitcher still maintained that he understood it, not taking Saypol's cue. After Elitcher repeated several times that he knew what Bloch meant by the question, with Saypol still objecting, Bloch told the court, "I think the question is proper, Your Honor, but I want to satisfy Mr. Saypol." (R.332) Bloch had obviously hit on a sensitive spot, and Saypol was trying to obfuscate the question. What emerged, with some ambiguity, was that Elitcher had not brought up the 35 mm. film can story until the second day of questioning, and had not brought up the report of Bentley's speaking with Julius until the third time he was questioned, more than three months later (R.332, 339), and then only after someone had directed his attention toward the name Bentley. (R.338) Under further questioning Elitcher acknowledged that he had been asked to resign from Reeves several days before he was scheduled to testify, and that he was now unemployed. Nonetheless he had purchased a new automobile a couple of weeks earlier. The Elitchers seemed strangely unconcerned about their financial future. What we didn't know, but should have suspected, was that the FBI would recompense him for his services by getting him a new job.

The crucial admission that Elitcher had not told his Bentley story until late in October, after he had been interrogated many times by the FBI and the U.S. Attorney's office, was damaging to the prosecution. This was why Saypol had objected so vigorously to the question. The jurors might have asked why it had taken him so long to recall a relatively recent incident, when he seemed easily to remember happenings of more than a decade ago. Bloch tried to clarify Elitcher's ambiguous testimony as to exactly when and how he had first told the Bentley story, asking him:

Q. Did you mention the name of Bentley at any time during your interrogation before the grand jury?

The court intervened, blatantly misstating the testimony in an effort to lessen the effect of Elitcher's admission on the jury:

The Court. Don't answer. It has already been answered. He said he wasn't asked, but he had already told the FBI about it before. (R.341)

Elitcher had *not* told the FBI the Bentley story when he first testified before the grand jury. (R.339) Nor had he said that he had not been asked the question before the grand jury. (R.341) That Kaufman could go to such extremes to distort the record indicates how serious he felt this to be. Bloch persisted in trying for clarification but the court told him:

The Court. It has been answered, let us have no further argument. Proceed Mr. Bloch. He said no he wasn't asked before the grand jury. (R.341)

How absurd to think that the grand jury would not have explored this crucial incident if Elitcher had already told the FBI about it. Yet Bloch was prevented from going into it. This is only one of many instances in which the judge teamed up with the prosecution.

When Bloch tried to explore Elitcher's financial unconcern, despite the possibility that he might be prosecuted, Saypol objected that it was irrelevant. Finally, after some badinage between Kaufman and Saypol about what Alfred E. Smith had said in similar circumstances, Elitcher was allowed to answer the question. Yes, he admitted, he was worried, but he didn't feel it made any real difference whether or not he bought a car. I felt he was lying. Elitcher would not have bought the car if he were really worried. He knew that everything had been arranged before he took the stand; that was why he had hired Rogge.

As soon as Bloch finished his cross-examination, Kuntz took over and my worst fears were realized. He asked Elitcher:

Q. So when you visited General Electric, you didn't only visit Sobell as a friend, but you visited him in connection with your work, did you not? (R.351)

Elitcher responded with a flat denial—which was of course the truth. The one rule that I had learned concerning cross-examination was that a question should not be asked unless the answer is known with a reasonable certainty. And Kuntz had absolutely no basis for asking this. It would have been so simple for him to have discussed the matter with me before he cross-examined Elitcher. Then he asked him:

Q. So that when Sobell asked you in Schenectady whether there was any material on certain phases of the work, you took it that he was asking you as a scientist, did you not?

And again Kuntz was rebuffed with a flat no! The heartbreaking aspect of this question was that if he had not proceeded so clumsily, he might have gotten Elitcher to agree, because this was in fact so. I couldn't understand why Kuntz referred to me as a scientist. I had never considered myself one; I was an engineer. Was my lawyer trying to play the prosecution's game of puffing up credentials? Undaunted Kuntz plowed ahead, asking:

Q. Sobell's job also for the government was to get you personnel was it not?

God almighty, what was my lawyer doing to me? After getting a *no* and getting into an argument with the judge, I was thankful that the questioning took a different tack.

At times the confusion which arose from Kuntz's questioning reached stunning proportions. He attacked Elitcher's testimony that I had asked him to suggest students for espionage by indicating that I was actually looking for engineering students to do legitimate work at Reeves. To my utter amazement, he got Elitcher to admit that this was so. The amusing, if bewildering, part was that *I had never asked Elitcher* about engineering students for Reeves, either for espionage or for any other purpose. I was on the lookout for promising young engineers for Reeves, and had in fact hired one on the recommendation of a former City College professor of mine, but since Elitcher had no special access to students, I had never mentioned this to him. Why he gave a positive answer to Kuntz's question was beyond me. Kaufman had to intervene at that point to remind Elitcher to add that I had also asked for students for espionage. (R.358–360) As a matter of fact our judge intervened in the cross-examination consistently, and always, it seemed, to score points for the prosecution.

Kuntz went on to show that Elitcher had hardly pursued his espionage "activities" with a sense of urgency; that when Rosenberg had initially spoken to him about my own alleged activities, asking him to join, he had waited several months, when we happened to be vacationing together, before bringing up the matter with me. Each of the encounters seemed to be more chance than calculation. He then brought out that each time Elitcher visited me in Schenectady, and we discussed the uncompleted ordnance pamphlet, he came on his own initiative.

By this time Kuntz had things under control and was able to get Elitcher to admit that I had never asked him for anything outside of the as yet unprepared ordnance pamphlet. Much of this talk about espionage reduced to this, and the 35 mm. film can incident. Kuntz showed the jury how silly it would have been for me to ask Elitcher to accompany me on a ten-mile trip to Manhattan, because *I* might get tired, when it was Elitcher who had driven in from Washington that day. He got Elitcher to admit that he hadn't told the FBI about the incident initially because he was consciously trying to conceal it, but when he finally decided to tell about the trip, now he said it was *he*, not *they*, who had brought up the name of Bentley. (R.370)

At this Kaufman became angry and told Elitcher that he, Kaufman, was now confused, since this apparently contradicted his previous testimony. When Elitcher tried to clear up the matter he only confused it more. This crucial matter, of Julius's alleged telephone conversation with Elizabeth Bentley, had been badly handled, and Elitcher was very confused. I didn't feel that any amount of questioning could have resolved it, since the confusion was in Elitcher's mind: a result of imperfect perjury.

I found it of more than academic interest that Kuntz assumed that it was fact that Elitcher and I had only seen each other twice during 1943 and 1944, as he had testified. It would have been very easy to get Elitcher to admit that this was untrue, and even though it wasn't very meaningful in itself, it might have served to damage his credibility. I recalled that during the trial I assumed that Kuntz must have had some lengthy conversations with Helen in areas where she was knowledgeable; much later I discovered, amazingly, that this was not so.

Kuntz hadn't taken much more than an hour for his cross-examination of Elitcher, after which Bloch made a motion for the production of all the written statements made and signed by Elitcher, all notes of the FBI and prosecution staff, and the grand jury testimony of Elitcher. The legal basis for this motion lay in Elitcher's contradictory testimony about Bentley. Kaufman indicated that he didn't think enough of a showing had been made by the defense lawyers, but that he would take the matter under consideration. Then there was the re-direct examination, and the re-cross examination, and it was late Friday afternoon when Elitcher was temporarily excused as a witness, subject to recall if Kaufman decided to let the defense lawyers have the requested material. Monday morning, minutes before court resumed, our attorneys were served with the statements Elitcher had signed for the FBI, dated July 20, July 21, and August 3, 1950. Kaufman was adamant in not allowing defense counsel any more than their lunch hour to read them. (R.430–434)

I never saw these statements, though I would probably have been more sensitive to any inconsistencies than the lawyers. Besides, they may have contained material about which Elitcher had not been examined, which may have been useful to us. On the basis of the hasty lunch hour perusal the lawyers decided not to use Elitcher's signed statements.

3

The Machinist
and the Atom Bomb

FRIDAY AFTERNOON, when Elitcher finished testifying, the government immediately brought in their
next witness, David Greenglass. As soon as he was
sworn in, Roy Cohn, who was going to examine him,
told the open court that a Dr. Dodson, chairman of the
chemistry department of the Brookhaven National La-
boratories, was going to be seated at the prosecution's
counsel table, "for technical purposes for some of the
technical testimony at the trial." The prosecution had
already received permission to have Dodson at their
counsel table, so Cohn's announcement was a grandstand play for the benefit of the jury, the defense, and
the public. Without his saying a word, Dodson's presence lent an air of credibility to the "technical" testimony which would be forthcoming from Greenglass.
This was a part of the orchestrated buildup of Greenglass's atom bomb testimony.

The obvious question is why didn't the defense
have experts at their counsel table? Did our lawyers
make a conscious decision not to get into the technical
aspects of the testimony because they felt that the government could not possibly make a mis-step here? Or
did they simply default through a lack of understanding
of the issues? Why didn't they consult with a physicist

before reaching any decision? They could have asked the court to get them one, and the court would have been compelled to comply.

Cohn began the examination by trying to puff up Greenglass's credentials. He said he had attended a machinist school, Pratt Institute, and the Brooklyn Polytechnic Institute. Cohn had the formidable task of supporting Saypol's promise of showing that an ordinary machinist had been able to steal the secret of the atom bomb.

Greenglass was sloppy in both speech and appearance. He struck me as a typical New York wise-guy as he testified with a broad grin on his face; a product of the Lower East Side. He told of having gone into the army in April of 1943, and after various stints as a machinist, having been assigned in August 1944, to work at Los Alamos, New Mexico, on a secret project. He said that he first learned of the nature of the project from his wife, Ruth, who visited him in November of the same year; Julius had told her. Greenglass told about working in "E" group, which was headed by Dr. Kistiakowski, and Cohn asked him:

Q. Did you have any other superiors in addition to Professor Kistiakowski?

I wondered if the jury believed that Kistiakowski was really Greenglass's superior. This was the way the prosecution built him up, by implied association with an eminent scientist. Yes, Greenglass said, he had other superiors such as the foreman of the machine shop in which he worked. After going over some of the details of the structure at Los Alamos, and the secrecy of the work, Greenglass told how he had learned the identity of such leading physicists who were working there, as Niels Bohr and J. Robert Oppenheimer. Cohn briefly touched on the atom bomb explosion at Alamogordo, and then asked Greenglass:

Q. Now did you have any discussion with Ethel and Julius concerning the relative merits of our form of government and that of the Soviet Union? (R.414)

Bloch objected, but Cohn cited a treason case in which the Supreme Court had ruled that such a question was permissible. Yet this wasn't supposed to be a treason trial! Greenglass told of hearing such discussions, several times a week, from 1935 to 1946, with Julius and Ethel expressing a preference for Russian socialism over American capitalism.

It is impossible for anyone who did not experience that bleak period in our history fully to realize how devastating such a charge was in 1951. This was not unlike the heresy of an earlier period of our country's history. Greenglass then said that when Ruth visited him in November 1944, she told him that Julius had told her he was engaged in espionage for the Soviet Union and to ask David to supply information about the atom bomb project, on which he was working.

I found it difficult to believe that a wise-guy like David wouldn't have known he was working on the atom bomb project until his wife told him about it, as he testified. But this had to be the testimony, otherwise the defendants might say that David had already started his espionage, even before Ruth was supposed to have asked him. He gave her the actual names of the scientists, who were known by pseudonyms, which was ludicrous, since the only reason for keeping their names secret would have been to hide the nature of their project. Yet, by David's own testimony, it was Julius who told Ruth what was actually going on at Los Alamos.

Greenglass described arriving in New York on furlough on January 1, 1945, and said Julius had asked him to write up a summary of the work he was doing. Again Cohn lost no opportunity of associating Greenglass with the real scientists. After Greenglass said that he had been working on high explosive lens molds (metal molds, used to cast liquid high explosive into a precise shape), Cohn asked him:

Q. That is lens molds in connection with Dr. Kistiakowski's work that you told us about? (R.428)

The jury would soon think that David Greenglass, the machinist, was Dr. Kistiakowski's right hand man.

The prosecution soon asked the judge to call it a day, despite its being early afternoon, because, Saypol said, "we are going into a new phase and I don't want to break the continuity." Actually Cohn had just started on the new subject, the lens molds, and had said enough to make the headlines that evening. Monday everybody would forget Saypol's statement about going into a new phase.

The United States marshals had given Helen permission to have my lunch sent in from a nearby restaurant (otherwise it would have meant baloney sandwiches during the whole trial). Of course they wouldn't let her bring in anything herself. When she had beef stew sent in, early during the trial, I found my stomach had shrunk so much that I could only eat a fraction of it. It contained more beef than I got at the Tombs in a whole month of beef stews. Helen and I were also permitted to lunch together twice a week, in a small closet-like room used for fingerprinting prisoners. We met this way for a leisurely forty-five-minute visit-lunch, five or six times during the course of the trial. I had never dreamed that a commonplace lunch could be so meaningful. It was the return to the near normal that gave these encounters their special flavor. We didn't discuss the trial at all; we had such a real need simply to relax into ourselves that we behaved as though visits were an everyday part of our existence. It felt good to pretend that nothing was amiss.

Every day, when I returned to my cell at the Tombs, I was beat, emotionally, and it was a relief to be able to stretch out and relax, even there. As a result I wrote Helen very little during the trial. But the weekends were long and dragging; the contrast couldn't have been greater—no visits, nothing. I couldn't even get interested in reading a book. That first weekend was also the sixth anniversary of our marriage. It passed by almost unnoticed; no reveries, nothing. Kuntz came a couple of times on Saturdays, and we had some general discussions. But he seemed to avoid getting down to brass tacks and I didn't have enough energy to push. I questioned him about my taking the stand, but he kept putting me off, telling me he would have to wait and see how things developed. In the meantime we made absolutely no preparation for this contingency.

Monday morning the trial continued, David Greenglass on the stand, again telling about the flat-type high explosive lens mold, about which he had testified on Friday, going into it in greater detail.* The

* Flat lens molds were used to cast high explosives (like a Jello mold casts Jello), which were used in implosion experiments in connection with the design of the atom bomb detonating device. I had read the Smythe report issued after the war, in which Smythe mentioned the gun method of detonating the atom bomb. Otherwise I knew nothing about it.

prosecution knew how to get the most press coverage for their witnesses. They then offered some of their "documentary" evidence, government exhibit 2, a sketch of the lens mold that Greenglass had specially prepared for the trial the day before, and which was supposed to be a replica of the one he gave to Julius. (R.439)

I never saw exhibit 2 during the trial. Kuntz probably was trying to shield me from any involvement in the atom bomb, since thus far the prosecution had only pointed the finger at Julius and Ethel. Whenever I tried to make some point to Kuntz while Greenglass was testifying, he made it clear that he thought it was unwise for me to give the jury the impression I was in any way involved in this area of the case.

All through the testimony the lawyers for the prosecution confused the lens mold with the actual high explosive implosion lens itself. The sketch of the mold was finally passed to the jury, as if it could somehow be meaningful to them. The replica aspect was probably soon forgotten and it became the real thing.

Greenglass was thoroughly confused on the subject, like someone who had picked up a smattering of ignorance. He didn't seem to know the difference between the lens mold and the lens. (R.459, 460, 462) An egregious error, like confusing the Jello mold and the Jello, which in the hands of an expert, would have sufficed to destroy his credibility. Here his examination by Roy Cohn was like a conversation between two illiterates.

The "technical" testimony was interrupted to introduce the dramatic Jello box. Greenglass said Ruth was given one half of one side of a Jello box by Julius. Here the prosecution introduced some more so-called evidence; two halves of a Jello box, which were cut in the courtroom precisely as Greenglass indicated. These two halves became government exhibits 4a and 4b.

Greenglass said a man came to visit him at his apartment in Albuquerque the first Sunday in June, and used the second half of the Jello box to identify himself. Exhibit 5, a photograph of Harry Gold, was shown to Greenglass, and he identified him as the man who had come to see him. He did not tell the jury that he had been staying on the eleventh floor of the Tombs with Harry Gold for the past several months.

Greenglass said that when he opened the door to his apartment Gold stepped through the door and said, "Julius sent me." (R.457) At this critical point, where Julius had to be unmistakeably identified, no pseudonym was used. Greenglass said that he then drew some sketches of an experiment in connection with the flat-type lens, which he gave to Gold. The prosecution introduced replicas of these sketches which Greenglass said he had drawn after his arrest, more "documentary" evidence.

Greenglass was an eager witness, very eager to please the government. When the judge asked him whether exhibits 6 and 7, connected with the experiment, were an "advance" over exhibit 2, the lens mold, he answered affirmatively. But then the judge thought twice and said: "Well, let us eliminate the word 'advance'; they were just another step?" and again Greenglass agreed. (R.466) Actually exhibits 6 and 7 were neither an advance nor a step. They represented two different aspects of the same thing.

Suddenly Greenglass was temporarily excused from the witness stand and one Dr. Walter S. Koski was sworn in. Koski had worked on the implosion lenses at Los Alamos as an engineer. He elaborated on the research that was going on there; he told the jury what an implosion was, in clear terms, as one would expect from someone in his position. He was not a technical illiterate. (In an explosion the waves move outward from a common center and the energy becomes dissipated, whereas in an implosion the waves move inward toward the center, and the energy becomes more concentrated.)

Koski told about the high explosive lenses, such as Greenglass was supposed to have testified about. Koski said that, "a high explosive lens is a combination of explosives . . . which produce a converging detonating wave." (R.470) But Greenglass nowhere testified about a *combination of explosives,* and furthermore, while his sketch, exhibit 6, does have a line which might be interpreted as a boundary between two different explosives, there is absolutely nothing in his explanation to indicate this, which raises certain questions. What Koski was doing was reading into Greenglass's testimony and sketches what should have been there but was missing. While presumably authenticating the sketches and testimony of Greenglass, he was really giving it substance. But I was oblivious to all this at the time of the trial.

And so Koski's testimony went unchallenged, and the fraud moved on, with the jury lapping it up. Greenglass, who was supposed to have committed the espionage, but really didn't know anything about the implosion lens he was supposed to have drawn, was not asked all these technical questions. Instead Dr. Koski expounded to the jury all the ramifications of the implosion lens, leading them to believe that Greenglass had in fact supplied all that information for the Soviet Union.

Koski testified that exhibit 2 was a sketch of the lens mold, developed at Los Alamos, which he had submitted for machining, and nobody disputed that this crude drawing of a clover-leaf pattern represented, "with substantial accuracy," that lens mold. A more aggressive defense might have attempted to subpoena the records from Los Alamos, to see if this were in fact so. Exhibit 2 could not possibly have been the entire lens mold; the central part was missing. Koski apparently forgot this, as he forgot to indicate a lot of other things that were wrong with Greenglass's testimony. He then testified that there was no information in texts on implosive lenses, that this was a new and original field. The prosecutor asked:

Q. And up to that point and continuing right up until this trial has the information relating to the lens mold and the lens and the experimentation to which you have testified continued to be secret information?
A. It still is.
Q. Except as divulged at this trial?
A. Correct.
The Court. As far as you know, only for purposes of the trial?
The Witness. Correct.
Mr. Saypol. Will Your Honor allow a statement for the record in that respect? The Atomic Energy Committee has declassified this information under the Atomic Energy Act and has made a ruling as authorized by Congress that subsequent to the trial it is to be reclassified.

The Court. Counsel doesn't take issue with that statement?

Mr. E. H. Bloch. No, not at all. I read about it in the newspapers before Mr. Saypol stated it. (R.479)

Amazingly Bloch uttered these words without a trace of irony; quite matter of factly, as though it were proper for a prosecutor to call a press conference while a trial was going on, as Saypol had done, and announce exactly what he was going to do at the trial the following day. But beyond that, Saypol's statement about the material being reclassified after the trial was a brazen lie. The plain fact that the trial record is a public document, and exhibits 2, 6, and 7 were a part of the record, made it farcical to speak of reclassifing the material. In addition the AEC did not have the authority to reclassify material once it had been declassified.*

Koski was another willing witness who always gave the prosecution the answers it sought. He wasn't even working for the government at this time and had absolutely no independent knowledge about whether the material had been declassified for purposes of the trial. Bloch's attempt to cross-examine Koski was pathetic. Koski kept insisting that the dimensions of the sketch were unimportant, because the sketch demonstrated "the principal is the use of a combination of high explosives of appropriate shape to produce a symmetrical converging detonation wave." The sketches 2 and 7 showed no combination of explosives, and while sketch 6 was ambiguous, Greenglass's explanation does not support this hypothesis.

The government had put on a good show. Koski, the sophisticated engineer, had interpreted Green-

* See proceedings, 1966, 66 Civ. 1328, U.S. Southern District.

glass's sketches for the jury so they could more fully understand it. This is what it must have looked like. The jury had no way of knowing the fraud that had been perpetrated, any more than our lawyers, or the defendants, for that matter. When Koski was through, Greenglass resumed his testimony where he had left off. The worst was yet to come.

The prosecution now offered exhibit 8, a replica of a sketch of the cross section of the atom bomb, which Greenglass testified he had given to Julius, together with some twelve pages of descriptive material, on September 1945. He said he had drawn the replica shortly after his arrest. Without any warning whatsoever, Manny Bloch requested the court "to impound this exhibit so that it remains a secret to the court, the jury and the counsel." Even Saypol was forced to remark: "That is a strange request coming from the defendants." (R.499) Obviously Bloch knew that Saypol was going to offer this exhibit in evidence at this time, and made a decision to ask that it be impounded well ahead of the actual offering. He had probably discussed it with my attorneys who must have agreed. Even in a technical matter like this, my defense attorneys did not consult with me. This move by Bloch was one of the most controversial aspects of his role as a defense attorney during the trial. The court openly acknowledged that it was pleased with Bloch's request, because it was the very move that the prosecution would have made, had it not been afraid that that would be sufficient grounds for overturning its case on appeal. Now, happily, Bloch had saved the government all this concern. Later, at a bench conference, Bloch explained to the court that even though the Atomic Energy Commission had declassified the sketch; "I am not at all sure in my own mind, and I am speaking privately, whether or not even at this late date, this information may not be used to the advantage of a foreign power. Remember, I am talking personally." (R.500) The flaw in Bloch's position was that, as a defense attorney he had no right to speak either "personally" or "privately," because whatever he said could subsequently be used by the government against his clients. It is unbelievable that Bloch did not understand this. It was a big, grandstand play, undoubtedly meant to demonstrate his patriotism, but it sacrificed not only the legal rights of his clients, but also their lives. Whatever Bloch might subsequently do to help Ethel and Julius could never make amends for this betrayal.

The question of clearing the courtroom of all spectators was taken up at the bench, and the court suggested: "Let me ask this. Perhaps we can even avoid this matter of clearing the courtroom if counsel stipulate right now that the matters that were described, as he [Greenglass] is about to describe were of a secret and confidential nature." (R.501) While Bloch probably cleared the impounding of the testimony with my attorneys, this was something new, and he asked the court for time to consult with them. But after consultation he told the court that there was no concurrence amongst counsel, making it clear that while he was willing to stipulate the secret nature of what Greenglass had *not yet testified to*, my counsel would not agree to this. And Alex Bloch gratuitously told the court: "I would like to stipulate it as an American citizen, and as a person who owes his allegiance to this country. I would like to stipulate it first to save the expense; I understand it would save quite an expense for the government to bring all these people here." Alex Bloch might as well have stipulated that Ethel and Julius were guilty and have saved the government the expense of the whole trial.

But this didn't end the matter. The court interjected: "May I ask you gentlemen, Mr. Phillips and Mr. Kuntz, why aren't you stipulating this?" The only thing Kaufman left unsaid was, aren't you patriotic enough to do this for the government, and the hell with *your* client. And here Phillips spoke up like a lawyer who knew that his first duty was to his client, but since all this took place at the bench I didn't hear it. He told the judge:

> *Mr. Phillips.* For the reason that I do not feel that an attorney for defendant in a criminal case should make concessions which will save the People from the necessity of proving things, which in the course of the proof we may be able to refute.

Then the judge, astute as he was, committed a grand faux pas.

> *The Court.* Particularly as to your client, where do you come in on this phase? (R.502)

Evidently the judge was so annoyed that my attorneys were interfering with his plans, he forgot that this was a single conspiracy trial, and that I was held to account for *everything* that took place, whether or not I was directly involved. (Later when my attorneys would argue that I was not shown to be involved "in this phase" as he put it, and had been prejudiced by it, he would lecture them on the single conspiracy theory.)

The court was really trying to pressure my attorneys into making the concession that the Blochs made, but they were unyielding. Finally after more discussion the whole matter was brought into open court, and the jury was able to hear Saypol expound on the fact that Greenglass's testimony had had the grave consideration of the Atomic Energy Commission, the Joint Congressional Committee of Congress, and numerous other arms of the government—all of which was meant to impress upon the jury how important and how authentic the Greenglass testimony-to-come was. Then he continued that the Constitution required the defendants to be confronted with all the evidence against them, and that "solely for the purposes of this trial, the Atomic Energy Commission had authorized the release of this information . . ." and the court joined in the refrain and finally told the spectators to leave. (R.505)

But when the press protested the court sought the opinion of the lawyers. Manny Bloch, after some confusion, said he thought they should be excluded also, unless they were enjoined to secrecy. But the court decided that it would be sufficient if "they will be enjoined in good taste." (R.508)

(The official trial record omitted what then took place and it wasn't until 1966, after a furious court battle, during which the government kept insisting that the material was still classified as secret, that the impounded portion of the trial transcript, together with exhibit 8, the "cross section of the atom bomb," was finally made public; even then the judge urged my lawyers to be cautious about how they utilized the material.)

Despite Greenglass's claims to have given Julius some twelve pages of material, his description of the atom bomb at the trial was scarcely a page long. After this Greenglass went into a lot of peripheral material such as Julius's having told him that he had received, late in 1947, information on a "sky platform" project. (It was at this time that the popular science magazines had written about this subject.) Greenglass said Julius had told him that many of his contacts were attending school, and that he was supporting them with money from the Russians, and had urged him to enroll at the University of Chicago, where he could contact some of the scientists he had met at Los Alamos.

Greenglass told of gifts which Julius was supposed to have received from the Russians, including a console table. With this teaser the court was adjourned until the following day.

March 13, Helen's birthday. She was thirty-three, and for a month, until my birthday, we would both be the same age. Greenglass began his testimony that morning with a description of more gifts which he said Julius had received from the Russians. After this he discussed the arrest of Klaus Fuchs in England, and of Harry Gold, here in the United States. He said Julius had told him on each occasion that he [Greenglass] would have to leave the country because the trial would inevitably lead to him. Greenglass then recounted the instructions he said Julius had given him about getting to Europe. The first step was to go to Mexico City, where he would pick up a passport from the Russians. From there he was to go to Vera Cruz, and thence to Switzerland or Sweden. (Later the jury could logically conclude that I, too, had been given the very same instructions.) I wondered why Greenglass was supposed to go to Sweden from Vera Cruz, when it would have been much easier and more practical to fly there from Mexico City, once he had the passport. Although it didn't occur to me at the trial, it later became obvious that Greenglass's story was tailored to fit my own expedition. After this no one would believe that I had gone to Mexico and on to Vera Cruz without directions from Julius. Part way through the cross-examination Bloch asked David if he was aware that he was smiling, and he responded with an inane "not very." (R.540) It was more of a grin than a smile.

After lunch when Bloch resumed the cross-examination, Kaufman bawled him out for going into minute detail, and for going over the material previously covered. Bloch was desperately trying to find something in Greenglass's testimony to attack, but Greenglass had a conveniently poor memory and things got hazy at every point where Bloch tried to pin him down on statements he had made to the FBI the night he was picked up, and afterwards. Bloch was trying to lay a foundation for getting the statements, but Greenglass simply couldn't remember anything about those statements.

For a brief moment events took a humorous turn when Bloch tried to elicit Greenglass's scholastic record at Brooklyn Polytechnic Institute. Roy Cohn objected, saying he didn't see what difference it made. Of course Bloch was trying to tell the jury that someone who had failed all his courses at school was ill-equipped to draw pictures of the atom bomb and the implosion lenses. Cohn, well aware of the danger this represented to his witness, was quite persistent in his objections. Finally Greenglass was permitted to answer the questions and he explained that, since he was young, he had cut classes too much and thus had failed his courses. But when Bloch tried to show how little Greenglass knew of science, by asking him what an isotope was, he goofed. Greenglass's answer was only vaguely correct, but Bloch was in no position to evaluate it. Bloch questioned Greenglass about the lens mold but since he didn't know the difference between the mold and the lens he got nowhere.

The trial recessed around four and I went back to my cell at the Tombs. Even though nothing much had happened, I felt exhausted. I just tried to relax, my mind a complete blank.

Next morning Bloch renewed the cross-examination, scrutinizing the details of the business dealings between Greenglass and Julius. Manny finally finished his cross-examination, and after a few brief questions by Cohn, Greenglass was dismissed. The government had presented the heart of its case, and Manny, I felt, had been wholly ineffective in rebutting it, though it wasn't entirely his fault.

The next government witness was Ruth Greenglass, David's wife. I was surprised, since I had expected a scientist would be called to authenticate the sketch of the atom bomb, exhibit 8, as Koski had been called earlier, to authenticate the exhibits concerned with the flat implosion lens. Had my lawyers gone along with the Blochs, and had Kaufman had his way, the government would not have been required to authenticate exhibit 8, but I thought they would nonetheless have wanted to do so, for the added mileage. Eight intervening government witnesses took the stand before the prosecution brought a witness to testify about exhibit 8. More astute lawyers would have suspected something strange in this behavior of the prosecution.

The courtroom was cleared as before and John A. Derry, an electrical engineer with a bachelor's degree from Rose Polytechnic Institute, a little-known school, took the stand to testify. He had worked on the electrification of the Pennsylvania Railroad before entering the army where he was assigned to the Manhattan Project as liaison officer for General Leslie Groves, the army man who had been responsible for the administrative aspects of the atom bomb project. After leaving the army in 1947, he was still "associated with the Atomic Energy Commission."

He told the jury that he "was to keep General Groves informed of the technical progress of the research, development and production phases of the atomic bomb project at Los Alamos." (R.906) Even at the time it struck me as rather strange that an electrical engineer with only an undergraduate degree, rather than a physicist, should have such wide-ranging responsibility. Derry went into detail about his planning to expedite the atom bomb project. Of course defense attorneys did not have access to Derry's record, so they were not in a position to evaluate his truthfulness, but the representatives of the AEC and the prosecution surely knew that Derry had no connection with the atom bomb per se.*

The judge had Greenglass's testimony relative to the atom bomb read to Derry, who was given the sketch of the bomb, exhibit 8, and asked if it all related to the

* In the January 1973 issue of the *IEEE Spectrum*, the journal of the engineering society, a small item appeared, headed: *"John A. Derry retires; A.E.C. construction director."* The body of the article spoke of his handling liaison on "the construction of the Los Alamos laboratory." There was absolutely nothing in the article connecting Derry with the atom bomb itself.

I should have guessed that. How could anyone with Derry's credentials be even remotely connected with the construction of the atom bomb? But the prosecution was bold, knowing we had no way of checking Derry's story. He was able to commit perjury with their blessing, if not at their instigation.

atomic weapon of 1945. After Derry had affirmed that it did, the court asked him:

> *The Court.* I believe you told us that you knew each and every detail of the construction of that weapon, that was your job.

Derry agreed with the judge's formulation and the court went on:

> *The Court.* And you understood the entire subject matter?
> *The Witness.* Yes sir, I did, It was my task that General Groves gave to me. (R.910)

He wasn't at all a modest witness. No physicist would have dared make this claim, because anyone who really understood the bomb at all would also have understood that he couldn't possibly know "the entire subject matter." Then Saypol asked:

> Q. Does the knowledge as disclosed by the material read by Mr. Slavin [stenog.], in conjunction with the sketch before you, government exhibit 8, demonstrate substantially and with substantial accuracy *the* principle involved in the operation of the atomic bomb?
> A. It does.
> Q. From that testimony and from the exhibit you perceive clearly the structure of the weapon as it actually was?
> A. You can.
> Q. To a substantial degree?
> A. You can.
> Q. Does the information that has been read to you,

together with the sketch concern a type of atomic bomb that was actually used by the United States of America?

A. It does. It is the bomb we dropped at Nagasaki, similar to it.

When Bloch tried to cross-examine Derry he got nowhere. It was absurd for Bloch to try to play the role of physicist as well as lawyer. He asked Derry if there was at Los Alamos a sketch similar to the one Greenglass had drawn and Derry answered affirmatively. When he asked:

Q. Would you say that the Government's Exhibit 8 reflects a sketch of the atomic bomb when it had already been perfected?

A. Substantially.

Bloch tried unsuccessfully to pin Derry down on exactly when the bomb had reached the stage of development indicated by the Greenglass sketch. When Bloch asked him whether the bomb could be described in twelve pages, as Greenglass had claimed, Derry responded:

A. You could give substantially *the principle* involved. (R.915)

and later on:

A. This substantially is *the principle* involved. (R.916)

When Bloch tried to get Derry's opinion as to whether a machinist like Greenglass, without any training in atomic physics, could describe the functioning of the bomb, the court did not let him finish the question, but shouted, "Objection sustained," although the prosecutor had not even raised an objection. The judge explained it was up to the jury to decide whether Greenglass had the capacity to convey the information he said he had. I wondered, what guidelines the jury would use in deciding this question. Experiences from everyday life?

For fifteen years the Greenglass testimony and sketch of the atom bomb remained impounded. Even though Greenglass's testimony did not impress me, I thought that the sketch, exhibit 8 which I hadn't seen, must have been drawn with the aid of an expert. I never dreamed it might be the outright fraud it proved to be. The whole episode with the sketches of the implosion lens mold and the experimental set-up, exhibits 2, 6, and 7, was very confusing. Saypol said it was being declassified solely for the trial, but didn't bother to have the spectators barred, nor did Bloch suggest that. Yet in November of 1952, when Bloch filed a motion for a hearing, using affidavits from foreign scientists to attest to Greenglass's inherent incapacity to draw meaningful scientific sketches of any kind, Bloch didn't even submit the *unimpounded sketches*, 2, 6, and 7 to the scientists. Thus their comments had to be general. They could only point out that even though Koski had claimed the idea of an implosion was new and original, much work had previously been done with shaped charges, which is what the lens essentially was.

It wasn't until Miriam and Walter Schneir published their book, *Invitation to an Inquest*, in 1965, that exhibits 2, 6, and 7 were first revealed to the public, and to the attorneys, and to myself. Since Greenglass's sketch, exhibit 8, was reported in the press, despite Kaufman's admonition to the reporters to be discreet, Bloch could easily have questioned the same scientists on this testimony, even if he didn't want to try to have exhibit 8 unimpounded.

On April 14, 1966, my attorneys obtained a court order to have government exhibit 8 and the Greenglass testimony unsealed, with the stipulation, however, that it not be made public. My attorneys had agreed to submit in advance the name of anyone to whom they wanted to show the material to the United States Attorney, for approval.

On April 29 the unsealing ceremony took place in Room 318 at Foley Square. The judge made it plain that after the unsealing had served its purpose the material would be re-impounded, since the government maintained it was still secret. It turned out that the material had never been reclassified by the AEC; the prosecution had really been trying to keep it impounded so as not to reveal the fraud that had been perpetrated at the time of the trial. In fact a book which had already appeared in print, *Day of Trinity*, by Lansing Lamont, contained a much more accurate description of the atom bomb than Greenglass had drawn. After bitter argument, when Marshall Perlin, my lawyer, demanded that the United States Attorney produce some documentation to back up his persistent claim that "similar material" was still classified, the government backed down, and on August 3 Greenglass's sketch and testimony were released without restriction.

In 1966, when we finally had a chance to see the material, we realized that the description that Greenglass gave of the atom bomb was probably what he picked up outside rather than at work. He even included incorrect newspaper accounts of the bomb's being dropped over Hiroshima by parachute. His drawing and account demonstrated that he had absolutely no idea of what the bomb was about, except that it worked by implosion. As the physicists made clear, if any knowledgeable physicist were given the problem of devising a bomb, this was one of the three methods he would choose to work on. But having chosen the implosion method, there were still a number of different options which the Greenglass sketch didn't attempt to examine.

Professor Henry Linschitz, who participated in the design of the bomb, pointed out in his affidavit filed in 1966 that Greenglass's lack of comprehension of the function of some of the components of the bomb led him to meaningless garbled pseudo-scientific explanations on the operation of the bomb, and his ignorance of the physical problems involved and his preoccupation with the implosion lenses, resulted in an ambiguous drawing, insofar as the "principle" of the bomb and its detonation were concerned.

One of the major components of the bomb, the tamper shell, was omitted in Greenglass's sketch. The tamper shell was critical in that it had three separate functions in the operation of the bomb. Linschitz analogized Greenglass's drawing of the implosion lens to a drawing of a rocket with a box marked "fuel and engine." The most important omission on the drawing was the polonium, which rendered inoperative the central initiator. The *Life* magazine sketch, published the following week, ostensibly on the basis of Greenglass's testimony, did, mysteriously, include the polonium.

In addition to the implosion lens, there were a host

of other problems that had to be solved before a bomb could be constructed, and there was no single "principle" as the government witnesses had testified. Professor Morrison, who also worked on the design of the bomb, said in his affidavit of 1966 that Derry should have answered, when asked about the sketch of the bomb, that it was a caricature of that bomb.

Why the government chose an electrical engineer to testify about the bomb is now answered. No self-respecting physicist could have testified, as Derry did, that Greenglass's sketch demonstrated the principle of the atom bomb after it had been perfected. The prosecution undoubtedly showed Greenglass's sketch and description to several physicists, and were turned down, before they chose Derry. It would be interesting to know who these physicists were—even at this late date.

Ruth, his wife, followed David Greenglass on the witness stand. She corroborated his testimony in all of the myriad details of their relationships with the Rosenbergs. It was quite boring; like seeing a re-run of an uninteresting play. She did, however, elaborate on the Rosenbergs's console table, which was supposed to have been a gift from the Russians. She said that Julius had told her "it was a special kind of a table, and he turned it on its side to show us why it was so special. . . . There was a portion of the table that was hollowed out for a lamp to fit underneath it so that the table could be used for photographic purposes, and he said that when he used the table he darkened the room so that there would be no other light and he wouldn't be obvious to anyone looking in. . . . He took microfilm of typewritten notes." (R.707)

I found her explanation no less confusing than David's explanation of the atom bomb. It appeared to me that darkening a room while microfilming was going on would be more apt to attract attention than if the room were normally lighted; and drawn window-shades would have sufficed to keep out any prying eyes. Oddly enough, even though the government went to a lot of trouble to produce all sorts of replicas of the various sketches, apparently no effort was made to produce this one bit of *real* evidence—the hollowed-out console table. If it existed it must certainly have been in the Rosenbergs's apartment when the FBI arrested Julius. They found other "evidence," which was revealed when they cross-examined Julius.

The elder Bloch, Alexander, was given the task of cross-examining Ruth. He was able to draw her out on the friction that had developed between the two families because of the differences over the operation of their mutual enterprise, the Pitt Machine Company. It was supposed to explain, at least in part, why David had involved Julius and Ethel in the conspiracy, but it didn't seem very convincing. It was evidently an act of desperation, since there was really little else Bloch could do to attack Ruth's testimony. She had said that Julius had asked her to talk to David about espionage down in Albuquerque. Who could contradict her . . . but Julius? It would be simply her word against his— when he took the witness stand.

The court recessed for the day with Ruth still on the stand, and I returned to my home in the Tombs. It hadn't been a particularly wearing day for me and that evening I was able to write Helen a letter. I hadn't written her very much during the trial. I just hadn't felt like it; my feelings, my thoughts; they hardly mattered to me any more.

I noted that contrary to our expectations, it seemed I would not be accused of having participated in atomic espionage. I also observed that Saypol was saving his biggest guns until the Kefauver Committee (which had Frank Costello on the witness stand) cleared out of New York City, so that he wouldn't have competition for newspaper headlines each evening.

4 The Prosecution Finishes

THE next morning, March 15th, I was taken to the courthouse as usual. However when I got to the tank, upstairs, in front of the courtroom, I was surprised to find Manny Bloch there, quite agitated and talking to Ethel and Julius, with a copy of the *New York Times* in his hand. On the front page was a headline: "Columbia Teacher Arrested, Linked to Two on Trial as Spies." The Columbia teacher referred to was none other than my friend and former classmate, William Mutterperl (who had shortened his name to Perl). Saypol had held a press conference, following Perl's arrest the previous evening, and it was reported, "Mr. Saypol said that Perl had been listed by the Government as a prosecution witness in the current espionage trial. His special role on the stand, Mr. Saypol added, was to corroborate certain statements made by David Greenglass and the latter's wife, who are key government witnesses at the trial."

Perl's arrest was based on his appearance before the grand jury in August and September of the previous year, when he denied knowing Julius and myself. He had recently obtained his Ph.D and must have been terrified by the possibility of having his career smashed. It was foolish of him to tell such an easily exposed lie, but there was some ambiguity in the question. I suppose that he wished that he didn't know us. None of us knew it at the time, but shortly before our trial began Perl had been interrogated by the FBI and the prosecution in a last-ditch effort to frighten him into becoming a government witness against us. He was warned that he would be indicted for perjury, and he was—more than half a year after the ostensible perjury. The indictment, arrest, and Saypol's press conference were clearly synchronized with our trial, and most of the jurors probably read about it, or heard about it over the radio or TV.

I had only a couple of minutes to try to digest what had taken place before I had to go to court. I didn't see Eddie Kuntz until I was seated at the defendants' table, and then we had time for only a few words before the session began. Kuntz assured me that he would take care of this outrageous misconduct by Saypol and he and the other lawyers went up for a bench conference. They returned a relatively short time later and I assumed that everything was taken care of. (I didn't find out what had taken place until over a year later when I was able to read it in the trial record. Kuntz told the judge, "I saw the front page of the *New York Times* this morning in the courtroom for the first time . . ." and Kaufman interrupted him, "Will you keep your voice down." Was Kaufman afraid the jury might learn something through Kuntz? Then Kuntz suggested a conference on the matter—in chambers but on the record. He also said, "I have never tried a case in my life in the newspapers," and Saypol responded, "Well, I don't care for the implication, and I have had experience with this kind of defendants before." Kaufman then said the matter would be taken up later, and the lawyers all dutifully came back to their assigned places. (R.756) Why the lawyers allowed the resolution of the matter to be put off is still puzzling.)

That afternoon, when court resumed, the lawyers again went up to the bench, to conclude the morning's business. Again I had no idea what was taking place. I had assumed it was all taken care of at the morning's conference. (R.816) (The trial record indicates that our lawyers did not even try to make any sort of motion, either to have the jury polled, to see if any had read Saypol's extra-judicial statement, or to have a mistrial declared on the ground of misconduct by the prosecution. Whatever exchange took place was off the record.)

If the lawyers had never taken the matter up at all we would have been in a stronger position, legally, to complain about it after the trial. But having once taken it up, our lawyers had effectively waived any rights we might have had in the matter. My firm belief in the good faith of our attorneys, whatever other defects they may have had, prevents me from feeling that they meant to hurt us. They were not betrayers, but they were miserably understaffed and at times, frightened, harried, and incompetent. Against these lone practitioners was arrayed the full might and the unlimited resources of the government bent on obtaining a conviction, and the huge weight of a manipulated "public opinion." "Great" criminal lawyers have many skilled assistants and investigators to do their research. No such eminent lawyer would touch this case in 1951. In fact many left-wing lawyers who were far more competent than ours shunned this case as if it were the plague; such were the times.

(The Perl matter was however subsequently raised

on a 2255 appeal, after the Supreme Court had turned down our direct appeal. In its opinion, the Court of Appeals wrote, concerning Saypol's press conference; "Such a statement to the press, in the course of a trial we regard as wholly reprehensible. Nevertheless we are not prepared to hold that it vitiates the jury's verdict when there is no allegation or evidence that any juror read the newspaper story and the defendants deliberately elected not to ask for a mistrial.") *

Since the jury was not sequestered, it was highly probable that some members did read the Saypol statement. But the courts nonetheless held that Julius and Ethel would have to die, because their lawyers had not made the proper motions at the time of the trial.

After Ruth Greenglass two minor witnesses appeared; Dorothy, Ruth's sister, and her husband, Louis Abel. They confirmed some of the peripheral details of the Greenglass story. The prosecution also used Dorothy to tell how Julius had on one occasion called Russia the ideal form of government—a damning accusation in 1951.

Harry Gold was the next witness. He had rehearsed his role at the Brothman-Moskowitz trial some months earlier. In fact the whole prosecution team was the same as at that trial, even the judge. The earlier trial had been a sort of warmup for the government. Gold made a most convincing witness, and I am sure that his pregnant pauses must have made a strong impression on the jury.

He described a trip he took to New Mexico in June 1945 where he first met Klaus Fuchs in Santa Fé and

* Transcript of record, Supreme Court, October Term, 1952 #687 and 719, page 334.

then went on by bus to Albuquerque where he arrived on Saturday, June 2, and "finally managed to obtain a room in the hallway of a rooming house and then on Sunday morning I registered at the Hotel Hilton." (R.824) He testified that he met with David Greenglass that Sunday afternoon, received information from him, and took the train back to New York, where he met Yakovlev and gave him all the material. Gold also testified to another meeting he had with Fuchs, in Santa Fé, in September 1945.

At the end of the court session that day the judge told the jury, ". . . and I want to admonish you that you should not read the newspapers in connection with this case on trial, or anything related to it [how could the jurors know if a news item was related to the case until after they had read it?]; or listen to the radio, watch television, read any magazines which in any way deal with this case or anything related to it, and I assume that you are following my admonition right along in this case." With this ritualistic formula pronounced after the horse was stolen, the judge tried to protect the government's case, just in case the question of Saypol's statement about Perl arose in the future. This was the only time during the trial that Kaufman talked to the jury this way; it was obvious what he had in mind.

That night I wrote Helen two letters. The first was a conventional letter in which I complained about my "unknowing state." I also noted that I didn't think about Helen or Mark or anything for that matter—except the rocky road ahead. This letter I sent through regular channels.

A second letter, however, was never intended for the censor's eyes. In it I made love to Helen, as if I were verbalizing my fantasies. This letter I simply took with me when I went to Court the following morning and gave Helen when I had lunch with her in the tiny fingerprint cubicle. We were permitted this luncheon date twice each week, and I decided I might as well take advantage of the fact that I was never searched going to the courthouse. In fact I was given only a cursory examination even when I came back from the courthouse, and I took advantage of this as well.

The following morning, when court resumed, Gold still occupied the witness stand. The government announced that it had no further questions, and when the judge asked, "Any cross?" both Manny Bloch and Harold Phillips announced that they had no cross-examination. Obviously my lawyers had discussed this with the Blochs beforehand. As with so much else during the trial, it came as a complete surprise to me. I have no idea whether Ethel and Julius were told ahead of time. I suppose I didn't ask Julius about it because I didn't want to appear critical of his lawyer.

Later, when others criticized Manny for not cross-examining Gold, he explained that his strategy was based on Gold's not having *directly* implicated Julius in any way; therefore Gold's testimony could stand unimpugned without damaging Julius. In summation Manny said of Gold, "He got his thirty-year bit and he told the truth. That is why I didn't cross-examine him . . . he was telling the absolute truth." (R.1479) While this strategy *may* have been legally tenable, it flew in the face of all common sense. The jury heard Gold tell how he had met Greenglass with the code phrase, "I come from Julius." (R.825) Did Bloch think the jury would forget this? Or that the prosecution would let them forget it? For the prosecution this meeting was crucial since it provided the direct link between Yakovlev and Julius. It is interesting to note that if a code name had been used, the jury might very well have asked itself if in fact the individual from whom it came was Julius. My own lawyers couldn't very well have cross-examined Gold because he didn't even remotely connect me with his doings. The question must then remain—why did Bloch avoid cross-examining Gold? It was surely a golden opportunity missed.

While Gold was on the stand the government introduced several exhibits, much like the previous ones, replicas of pieces of paper which were supposed to have been passed between Gold and Yakovlev (R.823 and 832), but which only served to dramatize the testimony. The jury must have been impressed with all this manufactured evidence. Yet when it came to the one real piece of documentary evidence that was available to help confirm Gold's story of the June 3 meeting with Greenglass, the Hotel Hilton registration card, the government waited until Gold had left the stand before bringing it up. Saypol then told the court that he wanted a stipulation from the defense, that he was presenting a photostat of the hotel registration card, but said he had the original on the way, together with witnesses, if required. Neither Bloch nor my attorneys objected to the introduction of the photostat, nor did they ask for witnesses to attest to the authenticity of the registration card. Again Bloch probably rationalized that this had no bearing on his clients, and again he made a serious mistake, as later findings proved. (R.867)

Exhibit 16, the photostat of Gold's June 3 Hotel Hilton registration card, which the lawyers so readily accepted in place of the original (to save the government expense and trouble?) was the subject of a 2255 appeal in 1966 when investigation demonstrated that it was a fraud. The whole hotel registration episode becomes bizarre when one realizes that Gold said he had registered at the Hilton on the morning of the day he expected to *leave* Albuquerque and return to New York; and that he registered in his own name, as though to facilitate the prosecution's production of the required evidence.

When the Schneirs began work on their book, they investigated each of the exhibits, which were all kept at Foley Square (somehow the exhibits were never made a part of the printed record), and they discovered that while the written date on the face of the card read June 3, when Gold claimed to have registered, the time stamp date on the reverse was June 4. In 1955, John Wexley, author of *The Judgment of Julius and Ethel Rosenberg*, discovered that Gold had registered at the same hotel on September 19, 1945, when he was supposed to have met Klaus Fuchs at Santa Fé. A comparison of the two cards is revealing.

The September 19 card contains the initials of several FBI agents who were presumably responsible for the discovery of the card, but the June card contains no initials of any agents although it is standard FBI procedure to initial any potential evidence for identification. It was learned that the FBI agents had spent several days in the hotel attic, shortly after Gold's arrest, searching the files for Gold's registration card, despite the fact that guest records were so cross-indexed it would have taken only a few minutes to find any registration cards with Gold's name. Yet the FBI did not find the June card during that intensive search! The government acknowledged that the June card was found at a different time, but gave no hints as to when it was found, or by whom.

The prosecution was forced to acknowledge that it had returned the *original* of the June 3 card (which was never introduced at the trial) to the hotel on August 4, 1951, only four months after sentencing, and while the case was still being appealed, although they knew that the card would immediately be destroyed under the hotel policy of keeping cards for only five years. Oddly enough the Government saved the September 19, 1950 registration card, which did not figure in any prosecution, until 1960, before destroying it.

We were totally unsuccessful in 1966 in obtaining an evidentiary hearing, the judge ruling that we had not really offered any evidence that warranted holding such a hearing. In effect the judge asked us to *prove* our allegations before he would grant us a hearing, which was completely at variance with the Section 2255 law. Even at this late date the court recognized two kinds of law: one for ordinary criminal cases and the other for political cases, and for good reason. To have held a hearing at which the conviction of Ethel and Julius Rosenberg was put in question was unthinkable. Our legal system did not have the means for rehabilitating dead people.

After Gold came Dr. George Bernhardt, the Rosenbergs' family physician, who testified that Julius had asked him about inoculations required for Mexico. I found the whole thing confusing since we had gone down to Mexico without any inoculations whereas Bernhardt testified that he told Julius that one would need typhoid injections and a smallpox vaccination. (R.851)

After Bernhardt came Bill Danziger, an old class-mate and friend. Bill was as different from Elitcher as day from night. I had always found him bright and alive, and if he hadn't already been married when I got down to Washington, I would probably have shared an apartment with him instead of with Elitcher. It was a bit of bad luck that got Bill involved in this mess. We had been corresponding for years, but hadn't seen each other between 1943, when he moved to the West Coast, and May 1950 when he returned East and visited us al-most at once. It was the day we left for Mexico that Bill had borrowed my electric drill. As I have written pre-viously we used Bill's business address as a mail drop when we wrote our parents from Mexico. He testified to all of this. I felt sorry for him when I heard him testify because I knew the FBI must have given him a hard time, especially in questions about my request in an enclosed note, to give my Uncle Morris my address. I thought someone in the family should know where we were, and I had been much closer to Morris than to anyone else. (Bill was so nervous on the stand, he called him Max.) My lawyers didn't cross-examine Bill, and for once I agreed.

After Danziger left the stand Saypol started to ex-plain that he really wasn't going to call any more of the witnesses on the long list we had been given before the trial, and the judge interrupted him:

The Court. What you are saying is that in your good judgment you are going to exercise your good judg-ment to do away with calling certain witnesses whom you consider to be merely cumulative—is that stating your position accurately?

Suddenly the prosecution decided that there was no need to examine the remainder of the one hundred–odd witnesses in order to present their case properly, and the court wasn't far behind, explaining the rationale. As if the prosecution hadn't known from the very beginning who was on the witness list for real, who was on to confuse the defense, who was on to intimidate the defense, and who was on for purposes of publicity. Is it conceivable that the prosection would have thought of putting on any of the eminent scientists they named without questioning them beforehand? Many years later we discovered that was the fact. An honest judge would have found that the prosecution had abused and misinformed the defense with its long list of prospective witnesses, but instead the court said it didn't approve of putting on cumulative evidence. Before the trial was over the prosecution would put on so much cumulative evidence in cross-examining Ethel, as to make a mockery of the judge's words.

I didn't write Helen that week-end. I felt depressed—the way things were going. It was apparent that our lawyers were highly ineffective and that we were needlessly taking a beating.

Since court was not in session, I was able to visit with Helen at the Tombs on Monday. The contrast between this visit and the ones we had been having at Foley Square, where we could talk in normal tones and hold hands, placed the Tombs visit in proper perspective. After so many months of Tombs-style visits, Helen and I had begun to accept them as "normal." Anything that happens for a long enough period of time becomes the new norm, and is accepted as such, unless one is aware of what is happening and consciously fights against such passive acceptance. This, I would learn, was the key to remaining alive, while doing a long bit: refusal to accept new norms that offend one's sensibilities—at least at the beginning.

Next the prosecution presented a group of five witnesses from Mexico. These were undoubtedly the ones Saypol had referred to when he spoke previously of witnesses from distant places. Four of the five testified that I had used aliases in traveling to Vera Cruz and Tampico. The hotel registration cards—originals, not photostats—under the names of M. Sand and Marvin Salt were introduced as evidence. What a contrast between this parade of witnesses, hotel clerks who were brought up from Mexico for the sole purpose of authenticating the various cards I had signed—and the complete lack of witnesses to authenticate the photostatic copy of Gold's Hotel Hilton registration card.

The fifth Mexican witness was Manuel de Los Rios, my friendly neighbor in Mexico City. I was somewhat stunned when Cohn, who examined him, told the court that de Los Rios would need an interpreter because "Mr. Rios speaks a little bit of English, but not enough." (R.918) The Rios I knew spoke better than adequate English and, as I noted elsewhere, taught Spanish at the DeWitt Clinton High School when he first arrived from Spain. I told Kuntz about it, thinking he would expose the farce right then and there, but he did nothing. I assumed he was waiting until cross-examination before taking it up.

De Los Rios was one of the very cooperative government witnesses who had tailored his testimony *ex-*

actly to fit the prosecution's needs. He was very wary about letting it appear that our relationship was close. He testified that he saw us going from time to time to the terrace without indicating that, *pursuant to his invitation*, we were going to the terrace of *his* apartment for sunshine. He testified that I had approached him to ask how I could leave Mexico without the proper papers, and that he had said he didn't know. He also testified: "He [Sobell] told me that he was worried because . . . he said he was afraid to return to the army, the U.S. army since he has already seen a war, has experienced a war. . . . He was afraid that they were looking for him so that he would have to go to the army," and that I told him that the military police were looking for me. He testified that he told me that there was nothing he could do for me.

I had of course asked de Los Rios about leaving Mexico, after I had read of Julius's arrest, but the remainder of the conversation was false, both with respect to what I had said and what he had told me. I hadn't told him anything about fleeing the army. This must have been the prosecution's brainchild, since it allowed them to get into evidence my selective service record, showing that I had never served in the army. Saypol must have figured that this—when coupled with his treason charge—was scoring a point against me.

After Roy Cohn had almost finished his examination of de Los Rios, he asked him:

Q. Do you know approximately what date Sobell was deported to the United States by the authorities?

Cohn of course knew that the question was totally inadmissible but used it nonetheless to convince the jury that I had been deported from Mexico, when in fact that was not the case. Kuntz objected that de Los Rios was not a proper person from whom to elicit such information. He was only a private citizen, and had no information of such a nature. The lawyers knew that deportation is a formal legal proceeding, even in Mexico, whereas Helen and I had been brutally kidnapped, quite obviously by direction of the United States Government. Thus, their objection to Cohn's question to de Los Rios didn't even go to the point of the kidnapping. However, when Cohn told the court that he had "other proof" of deportation coming, the judge thought it proper to have de Los Rios answer the question, criticizing Phillips for further objection. But in the end, having made his point to the jury, Cohn withdrew the question. He was a superb tactician.

Then, as was their custom, without even consulting me, my lawyers told the court that they had no cross-examination. I was mad, only I didn't have the sense to do anything. What fertile ground for destroying a prosecution witness! But my lawyers had long since decided that they weren't going to get involved with anything that smacked of Mexico. They should have realized, after Cohn's statement, that Cohn would present "other proof" of deportation and that they wouldn't be able to avoid the issue any longer, as they had been doing ever since I came to New York. But they didn't see it. They didn't want to see it! It was not unlike Bloch's decision not to cross-examine Gold.

Soon after, Roy Cohn sought to introduce into evidence the card I had signed at the American immigration office at the border. The prosecution had just brought up four witnesses from Mexico to authenticate the various hotel registrations; yet they now sought to introduce this record "concerning the circumstances of the departure of Sobell from Mexico to the United States," without a single witness to attest to its authenticity, and even more important, without permitting any questions on the matter, thus avoiding any cross-examination. (R.938) My lawyers objected to this procedure, but when Phillips pointed out that he would have to have the author of the document for purposes of cross-examination, the court baited him:

The Court. I thought you're anxious to make concessions.

The court was referring to the previous episodes, where the Mexican hotel clerks had testified, and Phillips had indicated that he would have been willing to concede I had used pseudonyms for registration, and that the appearance of the clerks was superfluous. Now the judge pretended that if Phillips were willing to concede that, he should be willing to concede that I had been "deported from Mexico":

The Court. Here is your opportunity to make one [concession], now they have to call a representative of the Department of Justice. (R.939)

Then Kuntz made the real objection to the card, that the notation "deported from Mexico" was purely hearsay, as far as the United States Immigration Department was concerned. Kaufman said that, in law, if such a card were made in the *ordinary course of business* it was admissible, even though it contained hearsay. My lawyers kept arguing the point with Kaufman, and he kept taunting them about their previous willingness to make concessions, but Phillips was adamant;

Mr. Phillips. I insist on having the man who made the card so I can examine him, wherefrom he got the information contained on the card; otherwise we are helpless. They could put anything on the card and we wouldn't be in a position to contradict it. It is very clear.

Cohn objected to this, claiming that, under the law, the prosecution was not compelled to produce the author of the card, but the court apparently felt forced to uphold the defense, and ordered the prosecution to produce the witness.

The next afternoon the government had James S. Huggins on the witness stand. He had evidently been well-briefed. He steadfastly maintained that everything on the card had been prepared in my presence, on the basis of information I furnished him, stoutly denying that the Mexicans who had brought us there had told him anything. Not even the words he had written on the bottom of the card *"deported from Mexico."*

Mr. Huggins. That is something I put on there myself from my own observation.
The Court. Do you usually do that in the regular course of business?
Mr. Huggins. I do. (R.1027)

That clinched it: whatever a government official testified he did in the regular course of business became kosher in a court of law.

The card itself was strange. My name was typed, but next to it, the phrase, "accompanied by wife" was hand-written. Yet Huggins insisted that he had prepared it all in my presence (R.1031)

Other parts of the card also had the strange mixture of typed and hand-written, but Huggins couldn't admit that the entire card had not been prepared in my presence as the typed/hand-written indicated. To admit that material had been added after I had signed the card would have invalidated it. Of course the really crucial part, added after I had signed, was the fateful words "deported from Mexico." This was certainly not on the card that I had signed when Huggins told me that the manifest was required of *all citizens* returning to this country. When Kuntz asked Huggins:

Q. And will you tell the jury what occasioned you to stop the typewriting, pick up your pen and put the word "wife" instead of typing it out?
Mr. Huggins. I didn't know it. Mr. Sobell's wife was not present during that time . . . I didn't know that she was out there after that—after that manifest—after the part that is typed there, the rest of it was completed, I still maintained the rest of it was completed during the presence in the office of Mr. Sobell.

Kuntz then began on a different tack, trying to show that Huggins had had foreknowledge of my coming there:

Q. Did you know anything about Sobell's coming there?
A. I read it in the newspapers, certainly. . . . We had a look-out on him to prevent his departure from the United States. (R.1034)

Kuntz was apparently thinking only of his next question to the witness, and completely failed to hear what Huggins actually said about reading about me in the newspapers, *before I was arrested.* I hurriedly scribbled a note, which Phillips took up to Kuntz. Unfortunately several questions had intervened, and so the sharpness of the contradiction was dissipated. Significantly, our astute judge had done nothing to clarify the matter of Huggins's obviously incorrect answer. When Kuntz finally asked Huggins about his having read of me in the newspapers, the court quickly came to his rescue, before he could get himself more entangled,

The Court. He says he knew about the name.

This was beside the point, and only served to confuse the question, as the judge obviously intended.

It was essential that the immigration inspector not admit that he was expecting me at the time I arrived, otherwise the United States Government would be involved in the "deportation." When Kuntz pursued the way in which Huggins happened to type part of the card and write the other part, the witness developed a conveniently forgetful memory. (R.1035) Now it was evident why the government had not been anxious to put Huggins on the stand in the first place. It seemed to me that a more skillful cross-examiner could have torn Huggins apart—that is, if the court hadn't intervened to rehabilitate him.

The previous day Saypol had announced that he would conclude the government's case the next day. This caught Bloch by surprise since Saypol had indicated on Friday that he would take a whole week. Bloch protested that he hadn't had sufficient time to consult with his clients, since they were not available to him on Saturday or Sunday. As a result the judge ordered that Bloch's clients be made available for consultation with him that evening, for as long as they were needed. (How many hours are there in a day?) The marshals also allowed me to remain behind in the courthouse that night, but evidently my lawyers didn't find it at all necessary to consult with their client. I fumed, in the holding cell, until about nine o'clock, when a single marshal came to take me back to the Tombs (there were always two marshals before this). I had never before seen him, and I got the impression that he was one of the wheels. He slipped one band of the handcuffs around my wrist and held the other on one finger as he walked me out the front way, down the long flight of courthouse steps, for the first time. It was quite dark as we walked through the streets of lower Manhattan. Had I wanted to escape, it would not have been too difficult. But the idea never even entered my consciousness. I hadn't reached that stage of development, as a convict. Later I wondered if it had been a set-up.

The last major prosecution witness was Elizabeth Bentley. Like the Greenglasses and Gold, she did not know me, nor I her. Nevertheless, by the peculiarities of the conspiracy laws I was held accountable for anything she said about any of the defendants—all on the basis of having been tangentially inserted into the "spy ring" through a single interested witness, Max Elitcher. Bentley was by then a famous personality; she had been widely publicized by the media as the "Red Spy Queen," she had appeared as a witness at a number of trials prior to ours, and at numerous congressional hearings. She had also been making money lecturing as an expert on communism. She could undoubtedly qualify as a professional in this area.

Saypol first presented her as an expert on communism, to demonstrate that there was a close connection between Communist Party membership and our alleged crimes. She gave quite a detailed description of her activities in the Communist Party, dating back to 1935, in the course of which she hopelessly prejudiced our case—as the prosecution had of course intended. She told how she had made a real high power connection with a Jacob Golos, whom she described as "one of a three-man control commission" of the Communist Party of the United States. He became her espionage boss, as well as her lover. Golos had died in 1943, and there was no one to contradict her.

She testified as if lecturing the jury; "The Communist Party being a part of the Communist International only served the interests of Moscow, whether it be propaganda, or espionage or sabotage." (R.978) (Was it on this basis that the *World Almanac*'s article about the trial said we had been convicted of sabotage?) She had been so informed, she said, by none other than Earl Browder, the secretary of the American Communist Party. Then she added modestly: "My basic knowledge was that I gave orders to Earl Browder after the death of Mr. Golos, transmitted the orders from Moscow to him, and he had to accept them. Sometimes he would fight against them, but he ended up by accepting them." (R.978) I could see the jury eating it all up. She had told her fantastic story countless times, before congressional committees and on lecture tours, and it rolled out smoothly. Yet with all her stories, involving over one hundred people, in the O.S.S. and the Treasury Department with whom she was avowedly in contact in one capacity or another, the government had so far been able to procure only a couple of minor indictments.

Bentley then testified that once while she was riding with Golos, he told her that he had to get material from an engineer living in Knickerbocker Village. (R.986) The noose was now placed around Julius's neck. She then testified that she had received a telephone call from someone who identified himself as "Julius" (R.991), and now the noose was drawn tight. Julius was always identified by his real name, whenever the identification became crucial to the prosecution's case. This bit of testimony was then linked up with the conversation Elitcher reported in which he said that I had told him Julius had once talked to Bentley. The trap door was now sprung.

On cross-examination, Bentley admitted that she had first gone to the FBI with her stories in August of 1945 (R.996), but continued her espionage activities, until 1947, and met with some thirty contacts personally, until 1947. (R.998) When Bloch tried to develop the relationship that existed between Golos and Bentley, Saypol made, what seemed to me, a humorous speech:

"I think throughout this trial the Court has been patient with counsel; has frequently suggested to counsel that cross-examination be cut off because of its extensive repetition, and I think on this subject it would be more advisable for counsel to proceed with the points in issue." (R.1001)

To me it was funny that Saypol was lecturing Bloch on repetition—in the name of the court. But I wondered if the jury also saw it this way.

When Bloch tried to ascertain how much Bentley had made from her lecturing as an expert on communism, her memory failed her, and with an assist from the court Bloch was effectively stymied. (R.1008)

The fatal defect of Bentley's testimony was so obvious that I didn't understand the government's daring to put her on the witness stand. She testified that back in 1945 she had told the FBI about a Julius, an engineer in Knickerbocker Village, supplying the Soviet Union with secret information, and yet for more than five years the FBI had done nothing about it; how many Juliuses, engineers, lived in Knickerbocker Village?

At the conclusion of the government's case, the defense made the usual legal motions for dismissal to protect the record. The court however made it plain that it didn't want any extensive argument: "Very brief" Kaufman said. Bloch first made several motions for a mistrial, because of the government's linking the case to the American Communist Party, and then gave several constitutional arguments attacking the statute. Phillips followed, offering additional constitutional arguments, and then presented his two-conspiracy argument saying, in effect, that if one believed all the witnesses, the government's case proved the existence of two conspiracies, not one, as charged: and that the conspiracy between Rosenberg and myself did not encompass the one involving Greenglass and the atom bomb.

Unfortunately Phillips wasn't really able to articulate his two-conspiracy theory adequately, yet it was enough that he raised the point, because under the law, my appeals lawyers would then be able to appeal this question. It was on this two-conspiracy theory that Judge Jerome Frank dissented on appeal, saying that I should be given a new trial. Unfortunately he was in the minority of one. Phillips failed, however, to take up the matter of our having been misled by the government's tactics into believing that I would in fact be accused of a direct involvement in the atomic bomb conspiracy, which would have bolstered his two-conspiracy argument.

5　Julius's Dilemma

LEGAL MOTIONS finished, Julius took the stand, the first defense witness. Bloch reviewed Julius's history: his schooling, his marriage, his apartment rental; then he asked about the console table, which the government claimed was a gift from the Russians, to be used for microfilming. Julius said he had bought it at Macy's for twenty-one dollars. In response to Block's questions, Julius told the jury that the crucial console table was in his home when the FBI arrested him there and conducted a search. I wondered if the jury asked itself why, if it was so incriminatory, the FBI did not take the console table at that time. To me it seemed evident that the story about the table was really an after-thought. Manny then went over Julius's work history, ending with the surplus hardware business and finally the machine shop, organized with David Greenglass and others. Bloch spent considerable time on the organization of the machine shop venture. I found all of this quite dull, and more important, pointless.

　When Manny finally reached the matter of Greenglass and the atom bomb, all he could do was to elicit denials from Julius that he had asked Ruth or David to get any information for him. Point by point, as was presumably required, Bloch took Julius over the

Greenglass testimony. I knew that later denials never had quite the same impact as the initial detailing of charges—"No I didn't" didn't sound quite as convincing as the story that Greenglass had told—a defect, unfortunately, of our trial system. Julius was very straightforward, his own self. There was nothing colorful about him or the way he spoke. One would hardly have thought he and his wife were on trial for their lives. I wondered if a little emotion wouldn't have made his testimony more effective.

The next morning the trial continued with Julius still on the stand. He was being questioned by Bloch when the cross-examinaton on the question of Communist Party membership began—not by the prosecution but by the judge!

There has been a great deal written about the question of Julius's having taken the Fifth Amendment in refusing to answer questions about Communist Party membership. Many have said that it was his own decision, but there is no evidence available as to how that decision was reached. I had no special information on the matter. Julius and I never discussed trial tactics or strategy. We hardly ever saw each other, except for brief moments before the court session began, or at recess, and we certainly couldn't discuss such questions on the fly. Kuntz never discussed it with me either. In any event the decision to take the Fifth Amendment on this question was legally unsound. Once Julius had elected to take the witness stand, he had no legal basis for refusing to testify about possible Communist Party membership—except possibly for some very specific questions, under the *Johnson* decision. The prosecution was undoubtedly well aware of that, but it never pressed the matter to conclusion, preferring instead to get mileage out of Julius's taking the Fifth each time the question arose. And the prosecution and the judge made sure that it arose very frequently during the trial. They exploited the issue tirelessly, and the jury probably reacted as was intended, each time the question was asked. Legalities aside, those were difficult times, and to admit Communist Party membership would probably have been disastrous. Whether it would have been quite as disastrous as repeatedly taking the Fifth Amendment is another question, a highly academic one at that.

Even after the court had interrupted Manny's examination and interjected the Communist issue on its own, Manny was still deferential, and before he continued he asked the court, "all right, may I then continue, Your Honor?" Nor was there any trace of sarcasm. He went through each of the Greenglass sketches, showing it to Julius, asking him if he had ever seen it before, and getting a denial. When he came to exhibit 8, the "atom bomb," he faced a problem, since it was impounded. But instead of having it unimpounded, he asked Julius, "Did you ever see that sketch, even here in Court?" Neither of us saw the sketch in court. I because my attorneys wanted to disassociate me from the atom bomb, in the eyes of the jury, and Julius probably because Manny felt it might be compromising, inasmuch as Julius wasn't cleared to see classified material.

When Saypol began to cross-examine Julius, he immediately asked him whether or not he knew Perl. Julius objected, saying he had read about Perl's arrest in the newspaper, and Saypol did not press the question.* Every time Julius was asked about the Commu-

* Louis Nizer, in *The Implosion Conspiracy*, described this incorrectly, assuming that the jury was sequestered during the trial.

nist Party and pleaded the Fifth Amendment, Saypol seemed satisfied that he had achieved his objective. Saypol then asked about City College campus organizations, meaning of course left-wing organizations. It all became rather confused, as Julius objected and refused to name the organizations involved. Saypol then questioned Julius about the high points of the Elitcher and Greenglass testimony. Much of it concerned Julius's "political preferences," as related by Greenglass. Julius hedged on this. In 1951 it would have been fool-hardy to admit having said anything good about the Soviet Union. On the other hand, hedging one's answers wasn't good either. Julius was always caught on the horns of this dilemma, and the prosecutor exploited it to the utmost. Questions of the second front during World War II, questions about the Russian system of justice as compared with the American system . . . Then Saypol asked Julius if he had ever contributed to the Joint Anti-Fascist Refugee Committee, and when Julius answered affirmatively, Saypol asked (?) "That is known to be an organization deemed subversive by the Attorney General." (R.1176)

What did it matter that the judge then sustained Bloch's objection to this "question." The jury had heard it; Julius had contributed to a subversive organization. Saypol followed up, asking Julius if he had ever gone out and collected money for the Joint Committee, and when Julius said no, Saypol waved a Committee collection can aloft, asking Julius if he had ever before seen it. The can became government's exhibit 27, seized by the agents when Julius was arrested. (R.1177) Saypol read from the label on the can, "Save A Spanish Republican Child, Volvermos, We Will Return." Julius explained how he had received the can. The International Workers' Order, of which he was a member, had sent it to him back in 1948. But he denied ever soliciting funds for the Joint Committee. That Julius found it necessary to make such a denial! I knew that it was purely by chance that he hadn't solicited the funds. We were both of the generation to whom the Spanish Civil War represented the watershed for anti-fascism. We both knew that it was there that the Western democracies had sold out their birthright, and received World War II in return. Our hearts and souls had gone into this war; many of our friends were buried in Spain, and now Saypol was making Julius deny that he had ever solicited funds to save a Spanish Republican child. I felt sick.

International Workers' Order? Saypol leaped on this, asking Julius if it wasn't a fact that the IWO was a Communist organization. And now Julius took a beating on this issue, with Saypol repeatedly asking him about the Communist membership of the IWO, how he had joined it, when he had joined it, how it first came to his knowledge, to whom he sent the premiums, and finally Saypol wanted to see the insurance policy. (R.1180)

Saypol then explored Julius's separation from his job with the Signal Corps in 1945, because he was allegedly a Communist. Bloch had gone into this matter to some extent since he knew that Saypol wouldn't overlook it. Saypol went on to ask Julius whether or not he had been a member of the Communist Party and Julius again took the constitutional privilege. It was sheer murder. Saypol kept on questioning him along this line and Julius kept refusing to answer. If Julius had ever had a chance, it was now gone. Saypol, with the help of the judge, had played his cards well, and impaled Julius on the horns of the Communist dilemma.

Since the following day was Good Friday there was no court. It seemed a long weekend. I had entertained the remnant of a hope that I might take the stand, but by this time I knew that this wouldn't be. I simply folded up when Kuntz threatened to quit if I insisted on testifying. I don't know why I let him intimidate me. I suppose he had frightened me into thinking I really would get murdered over Mexico if I took the stand, and he was probably right. (This was Sobell's dilemma which Kuntz resolved for him.) Besides, the government attorneys had indicated to him that they had some secret evidence which they were waiting to spring on me if I took the stand.* This was a standard tactic, but Kuntz fell for it like a novice. But I wonder if my own Communist Party membership didn't exercise some weight in Kuntz's decision; we had never discussed the question, and it was much much too late to start now.

Saypol began his cross-examination on Monday morning by asking Julius what he knew about a dozen different people, some friends and others strangers, but in such a way that it was clearly provocative. Bloch objected that this was all improper examination, but the judge allowed it on the basis that it went to credibility. (This was catch-22, at the trial, for allowing many otherwise impermissible questions on cross-examination.) When Julius responded that he thought that Al Saurent, one of those mentioned, was in Ithaca, Saypol asked: "Don't you know that he is in Mexico?" By now Mexico was a loaded word—like Communist. Saypol wanted to know if Julius had ever seen Joel Barr's sweetheart at Communist clubs. (R.1194) Saypol wanted to know if

---

* Perusal of the B. Pollack report in 1974, written for internal Justice Department use in 1956, revealed no additional evidence.

Julius knew "a girl or lady by the name of Carol Dayton?" When Julius said he didn't recall the name Saypol dropped it. He was playing games with Julius.

Then Saypol wanted to know what Julius thought when he saw that he was under surveillance by the FBI, between the time he was questioned after Greenglass's arrest, and his own arrest. Julius played it too cool. When the court asked him what he thought about the FBI agents who were outside of his place of business, he said it didn't enter his mind. I don't know why he felt it necessary to deny that he was disturbed by this outward harassment. Did he think disturbance would be interpreted as a sign of guilt? This is one of the problems of taking the stand; how to project the image of innocence. Merely being innocent is not enough, one also has to project the image of innocence. People have certain stereotyped notions and one has to conform. I would have made a terrible witness; I don't think I could have sat on my emotions, not even if my life depended upon it.

Saypol generally annoyed me, but never as much as when he said to Julius: "Let us have a little talk about this console table." (R.1205)

By this time I had learned that this was the approach of the cops when they had you by the balls. Saypol wanted to know on what day of the week Julius bought the table, where the table was kept in the house, what color it was, and many other seemingly irrelevant details. Bloch should certainly have asked the prosecution why they hadn't picked up the table at the same time they took the "Save A Spanish Republican Child" collection can. Later, in a last minute appeal, in 1953, Bloch did raise this point, but the court responded, "I certainly don't see that it [the government] was under any duty to produce a table which it had never reduced to its possession." *

During the trial the defendants and the lawyers all thought the console table had been disposed of and sold to a junk dealer when Manny had given up the Rosenberg apartment. Later a newspaper reporter discovered that Julius's mother had the table in her apartment, after it had been stored in Julius's sister's basement. Poor communications all around. I know that even between Helen and myself, we had equally poor communication during the trial.

Once the defense found the table, they had it photographed and obtained an affidavit from a Macy's employee which established that the table was indeed purchased from Macy's at the time and at the price Julius had indicated, and that it didn't cost eighty-five dollars as Saypol had "testified." (R.1211) In rebuttal the prosecution obtained two affidavits from Macy's employees which pointed out that Macy's had marked tables of that type with colored crayon and not white chalk. How the employees could have known that the table was marked with chalk from the black and white photographs is not clear (subsequently it was ascertained that the table was indeed marked with crayon, not chalk). Needless to say, neither Kaufman nor the appeals courts deemed it worthy of having a hearing.

* Transcript of record, Supreme Court, October Term, 1953, #497, page 106.

6

The Crucifixion of Ethel

ETHEL Rosenberg was subpoenaed to appear before the grand jury on August 7, 1951, three weeks after Julius had been arrested. A wife would not normally be called to testify against her husband, but this was not a normal case. As I previously noted, when Helen appeared before the grand jury a federal judge instructed Saypol not to question Helen about anything concerning me, and told my attorneys that they should instruct Helen properly: answer nothing but your name. The United States Attorney can always bring a witness before a judge, who will then decide whether or not the witness is required to answer the questions. In court one can at least have a lawyer, but before the grand jury one is alone, without friends or counsel. If instructed by the judge to answer the question, one does not run the risk of having inadvertently waived one's Fifth Amendment rights to remain silent on subsequent questions. Behind the closed doors of the grand jury room the prosecutor plays games with his helpless prey. He can ask questions which one would not ordinarily hesitate to answer and then throw in an apparently innocent question designed to trap. For if it is answered the courts will hold that one has effectively waived all his rights under the Fifth Amendment and is thereafter compelled to answer all questions on the subject matter, or else be cited for contempt.

Therefore lawyers almost always tell their clients to play it safe, if they suspect they may be subject to indictment, and not to answer anything other than give their name. This was undoubtedly what Manny Bloch told Ethel. He could however have made her position legally safer if he had acted as my attorneys did.

Several days after her first appearance, on August 11, Ethel was again called before the grand jury. On the face of it this didn't make sense, since nothing had changed since her first appearance and she would undoubtedly invoke the protection of the Fifth Amendment again, but the prosecution had something else in mind. Ethel was arrested as she emerged from the grand jury room. She had obviously been marked for arrest before she went in. It was with this background that Ethel was cross-examined by Saypol. After some brief preliminary questioning he got to the point:

> Q. Well, at the time that you appeared before the Grand Jury as a witness your husband had been arrested, had he not?
> A. Yes.
> Q. You had not been indicted?
> A. That is right.
> Q. At that time you disclosed to Mr. Bloch everything that you knew about the matter of the theft of atomic materials or defense secrets?
> A. I didn't know anything about the theft of atomic secrets. So how could I discuss it?

Ethel had responded simply and plainly, without becoming upset over the tricky question. This was only the prelude.

Q. Now, you came before the Grand Jury on August
7th; do you remember that?
A. Yes, about that time.
Q. And everything that you told the Grand Jury was
the truth?
A. Right.
Q. Do you remember having been asked this question and giving this answer: "Q." When did you consult with your attorney for the first time in connection
with this matter? A. I refuse to answer on the ground
that this may tend to incriminate me."
Q. Was that the truth?

Was it the truth, Saypol asked, that it would tend to
incriminate her if she told the grand jury when she first
consulted with her attorney? Answer that one—you're
damned either way. What good the Fifth, if a defendant
ends up in this position? For Ethel the Fifth Amendment turned out to be a trap, as Saypol used it. But actually she hadn't said that it might tend to incriminate
her at all. She had only responded to the grand jury
using the approved form, telling them that she wouldn't
answer questions for the prosecutor while her husband
was in prison awaiting trial because anything she told
them might be used against her and her husband. But
when a trial jury hears "tend to incriminate" it immediately conjures up visions of guilt. Who else but a guilty
person would be fearful of incriminating himself? This
is what a jury thinks, never having been faced with
prosecution. The jury doesn't really understand how
our adversary trial system works; it doesn't understand
that it is a game, where the prosecutor is always ready
to jump on anything you say and use it to your disadvantage. They don't understand that a prosecutor is

after only one thing, a conviction, since that's the only way he is going to be promoted. A prosecutor who fails to convict is a failure, and failures are not promoted. (Saypol, for instance, became a judge shortly after this trial.)

After Bloch had objected to the question Judge Kaufman ruled that Ethel had to answer it, and that it was for the jury to consider on the question of her credibility. In other words, the jury was told, it is inconsistent for a person to plead the Fifth Amendment before a grand jury and then to answer the question in a manner consistent with innocence before a trial jury. Kaufman advised the jury that an innocent person suspected of having committed a crime could not honestly assert the privilege before the grand jury. And Saypol pressed on with more questions about what had transpired before the grand jury, but "carelessly" misstated the wording of the Fifth Amendment.

> Q. That you answered that to disclose whether you had consulted with your lawyer about this matter *would* [emphasis added] incriminate you?

No longer was it "might tend to incriminate you," but now it became categorically "would incriminate you." Saypol was telling the jury that Ethel had admitted that answering that question *would* in fact incriminate her. Unfortunately Bloch stood by and did nothing while this legal mayhem was going on, except to mildly object from time to time, in a tentative sort of way. Then the court joined in the pursuit, adding its authority to the persecution.

> Q. And today you feel there is nothing incriminating about that answer?

A. No.
Q. But at that time, before the grand jury, you did?
A. I must have had some reason for feeling that way.

What could she say? They were both playing with her as two cats might play with a mouse.

Q. Now, what was the reason?
A. I couldn't say at this time.

The judge continued:

Q. In your own interest, I think you ought to think about it and see if you can give us some reason.
A. I really couldn't say.

"In your own interest," the judge told Ethel in his most paternal tone. But this was still only the beginning. I don't know how Julius stood it, watching his wife torn apart by this one-two combination of judge and prosecutor, working in tandem; I think I would have screamed—"stop it, you jackals."

Saypol continued with more questions about David Greenglass which she had been asked before the grand jury, and with the same, "was it true," that answering the question "might tend to incriminate." Then came the blockbuster.

Q. How would that incriminate you, if you are innocent?

Could Saypol have told the jury any more clearly that only guilty people find it necessary to resort to the constitutional privilege? Ethel did quite well with that one.

A. It wouldn't necessarily incriminate me, but it might . . .

Saypol tried to interrupt her, as the trial record indicates. Nonetheless she went on and concluded her explanation,

A. . . . and as long as I had any idea that there might be some chance for me to be incriminated I had the right to use that privilege.

It was good, but did the jury understand it? They had all undoubtedly studied American history in school, about the Revolutionary War and the colonies, but how many had learned about our Bill of Rights? I hadn't. I had to pick up that bit of history from nonorthodox sources, to which not many were exposed. Then our judge tried again to trap her.

Q. At any rate, you don't feel that way about that question today, do you?

And without waiting for a response to his purported question, he continued:

Q. You answered when you talked to your brother, Dave, right here in this courtroom, haven't you?

Ethel wasn't caught; she shot right back.

A. But I didn't talk to my brother David!

Did the judge stop to apologize? Instead he tried to confuse the matter, having presumably read the original question from the grand jury minutes, and continued:

Q. You had no objection to answering that question here in the courtroom?

A. I have already answered that question, that I did not discuss it.

Q. And you don't feel that giving that answer will in any way incriminate you here today; is that right?

Then without even waiting for a response he answered his own question:

Q. That is why you have answered it today.

Saypol promply picked up in this one-two attack:

Q. As a matter of fact, a truthful answer at that time would have been that you hadn't talked to him, would it not?

Poor Manny, he had given up objecting to the legal mayhem that was taking place, so he plaintively told the court, "Wait. I just want to record my objection," as if he had given up hope that his objection would actually be sustained. Kaufman finally must have thought that unless he put a damper on Saypol, the Appeals Court might have difficulty in sustaining the verdict, and upheld Manny's desire to record an objection. Saypol had already made it amply clear to the jury that Ethel had been untruthful when she appeared before the grand jury. Having restrained Saypol, Kaufman nonetheless picked up the same theme himself:

Q. Now let me ask you a question. If you had answered at that time that you had not spoken to David, for reasons best known to you, you felt that that would incriminate you?

The judge also joined in the switching "might tend to" to the more damning "would."

There was one way out of the impasse; to educate the jury so it understood all of the ramifications of the Fifth Amendment, why this provision against possible self-incrimination was included in the Bill of Rights. Beyond that the Fifth Amendment had become highly technical—as our courts had interpreted it—and Ethel was no lawyer. She did not know how far she could go in answering Saypol's questions without waiving her Fifth Amendment rights. Even lawyers had difficulties in following the guidelines set by the courts. (Frank Costello's lawyers got him in trouble here.) But this was the wrong time and the wrong forum for such jury education, and so the unfair struggle continued, with Saypol asking:

Q. As a matter of fact, at that time you didn't know how much the FBI knew about you and so you weren't taking any chances; isn't that it?

Bloch in very dignified tones said merely, "I object to the form of the question."

Saypol persisted: "May that question be answered yes or no?" and the court said helpfully:

The Court. Yes, first answer it yes or no, then you can explain.

Fortunately Ethel was not cowed by her tormentors:

A. I don't know what the FBI knew or didn't know.

Without waiting for her explanation Saypol said:

Q. Of course you didn't so you weren't taking any chances in implicating yourself or your husband?

The official trial transcript actually contains a question mark at the end of that accusation, as if to legally make it a question. Finally Bloch spoke up:

I object to this entire line of questions as incompetent, irrelevant, and immaterial and I now move for a mistrial upon the ground that Mr. Saypol is persisting in asking questions, the import of which can only prejudice this defendant in the eyes of the jury, and it has no probative value whatsoever.

The court of course denied Bloch's motion for a mistrial, with a lecture:

They don't expect a witness to volunteer, and the cross-examiner has to phrase his questions in such a way as he thinks, with propriety, he can elicit the information which he thinks should be elicited. I think it is proper cross-examination.

Again Saypol asked Ethel to explain "how the fact of whether or not you had talked with David Greenglass regarding this matter applied to possible incrimination, if you had nothing to do with his activities?"

In 1956, Judge Jerome Frank, of the Second Circuit Court of Appeals, wrote: "No one who legitimately exercises the constitutional privilege ought to be so placed that he must subsequently justify it to a jury." But that wouldn't be said for another five years, and in the meantime judge and prosecutor were both telling Ethel that in her own best interest she must justify having exercised her constitutional privilege.

It was a wonder that through it all Ethel remained calm and collected, never once becoming emotional. (A famous actress who portrayed her in the Broadway production of *Inquest* became melodramatic at this point, but the truth was stranger than the reconstructed drama.) The cross-examination of Ethel in that courtroom was the most dramatic episode I had ever seen— on stage or off: a confrontation between a victim and two inquisitors of the Establishment, rather like a modern Greek tragedy. Manny Bloch who should have helped balance the struggle was mostly ineffective. Only occasionally did he raise a dignified objection, mainly, it seemed, as a matter of record. Manny was really Julius's lawyer; Alex Bloch was supposed to be Ethel's lawyer. But that was a farce; could it have been that he was the restraint that Manny felt, when he should have screamed about what was being done to Ethel?

From time to time Kaufman would uphold one of Bloch's all too infrequent objections, but that was strictly for show. At the very next question Saypol would be at it again, as if the judge had never overruled him, and this time he would be allowed to proceed unhindered. At one point Saypol appeared to be outraged at Bloch's objections:

> Of course there has been interspersed here without deviation to every question an objection on every imaginable unsupported ground.

Kaufman himself told Bloch, in front of the jury, "What, you have thought of another ground for objecting?"

Manny was now getting it from all sides, though he wasn't in fact objecting nearly as much as the situation warranted.

The court's questioning took a different tack when Kaufman asked Ethel:

> Q. Has something transpired between the time you were questioned before the Grand Jury and the date of this trial, which makes you feel that your answers at this time, at the trial, to those particular questions are not incriminating, and if so what is it?

But the object of the questions was the same: to demonstrate a supposed inconsistency between Ethel's behavior before the grand jury and her behavior here.

I suppose Manny must have been thinking hard, while sitting there quietly. Finally he came up with a formulation of the basic objection to the cross-examination.

> *Mr. E. H. Bloch.* I just want to interpose an objection, Your Honor.

Kaufman responded in unkind terms to this timidity.

> *The Court.* Have you thought of another ground for objection?
>
> *Mr. E. H. Bloch.* I think, Your Honor, that the method of trying to import an unlawful act to a person who has asserted the privilege against self-incrimination destroys the privilege and undermines and takes away the person's right under the Fifth Amendment, and I object to this entire line of inquiry because inferences may be drawn which are not warranted under the law or under the facts.

In essence this was what Judge Jerome Frank wrote in his dissent in *United States vs. Grunewald*, 233 F. 2d 556, but only four Supreme Court judges, in *Grunewald vs. U.S.*, 77 S.Ct. 963 p.984, agreed with him.

The Court refused to see Bloch's point and replied:

The Court. However, when a witness freely answers questions at a trial. The answers to which, the answers to the very same questions to which the witness had refused to answer previously on the ground assigned by that witness, I ask you, is that not a question then for the jury to consider on the question of credibility? Nobody is seeking to destroy any privilege.

How could a smart judge not see what was plainly obvious, that the privilege was, in fact, destroyed, by asking Ethel to *explain* why she had utilized it before the grand jury. Bloch continued coming still closer to the crux of the matter.

Mr. E. H. Bloch. There is a failure here to distinguish between the circumstances where a witness involuntarily appears before tribunal and is sworn to testify in response to a subpoena, as in the case of a Grand Jury proceeding, and a case where the witness willingly comes and takes the stand and testifies.

The Court. Where the witness willingly . . .

Mr. E. H. Bloch. Here. This witness has voluntarily taken the stand here. There was no obligation on her part to take the stand, Your Honor.

But his Honor didn't give Bloch the courtesy of a response, since he knew that Bloch was right, and merely ordered him to proceed. Saypol again demanded of Ethel the categorical yes or no, and the court added:

> *The Court.* And I have given the witness every opportunity to explain, indeed I have sought an explanation if she could give it to me as to anything that occurred that caused this change.

Of course he was not giving Ethel an opportunity, but was pillorying her with his demand that she explain that which did not require an explanation. "No one who legitimately exercises the constitutional privilege ought to be so placed that he must subsequently justify it to a jury," said Justice Jerome Frank. In the meantime Ethel told them:

> My brother had been arrested, my husband had been arrested, and I had been subpoenaed to come before the Grand Jury. It was not for me to state what I thought or didn't think the Government might or might not have in the way of an accusation against me. I didn't have to state my reason, but I did feel that with answering certain questions I might be incriminating myself until I exercised my privilege.
> *Saypol.* What you are saying is that you were under no compulsion to confess your guilt in respect to this conspiracy?

Again the trial record contains a question mark after this accusation. Nor did Kaufman censure the prosecutor. Ethel shot back, before her lawyer could even object:

> *A.* I had no guilt to confess.

On and on it continued. How much more could Ethel take before she threw up her hands and began to scream at these two beasts who were tormenting her with their repetition? Or was I only imagining that they were torturing her? She sat in the witness chair so calmly that one might have thought she really didn't understand what was going on. But she understood, as her responses attested. Then how could she take it, blow upon blow upon blow, first from Saypol in front of her, and then from the judge at her right. Back and forth they alternated, spelling each other, while it went on and on. Finally Ethel really began to counter attack.

Q. Was it truthful?
A. I have already answered it.
Q. Truthful?
A. I explained the reasons for my answering it that way.
Q. Do you care to answer it yes or no?
A. It can't be answered yes or no.
Q. You mean he might have shown you the sketches [of the atom bomb]?
A. I didn't say that.
Q. Was it truthful? Yes or no.
A. I have already answered. It can't be answered yes or no.
Q. . . . . was that testimony given by you at the time?
A. You have the record. Of course that is the testimony.
Q. Was it the truth?
A. I have already answered that.

Question after question which Ethel had refused to answer before the grand jury were now fired at her with record speed as she shot back her replies in the same pace.

Finally the court said: "I don't think this serves any purpose, Mr. Saypol." But when Saypol responded that he needed two or three more minutes, the court told him to go ahead. Nor did Kaufman chide Saypol when he took many times two or three more minutes, as he had Bloch under similar circumstances. Why Saypol felt it necessary to get in every last question which Ethel had been asked before the grand jury was not clear. Perhaps he was simply compulsive about completing a task he had begun. Ethel was long past suffering under his blows, the jury was no longer being impressed by the rapid exchange and the new questions were certainly no more "incriminating" than the ones he had asked her earlier.

Even though the court had urged Saypol to end it, Kaufman couldn't resist getting in his own last licks, demonstrating once again the "contradiction" between Ethel's unwillingness to respond to the questions before the grand jury and her testifying here, in open court. Was it possible that she might have discussed the atom bomb with David Greenglass? Did she know Anatoli Yakovlev? Would she care to identify his picture?

Q. Why didn't you want to care or attempt to identify Yakovlev if you never saw him before or had never seen him before?

Manny Bloch sprang to life;

Mr. E. H. Bloch. I object to the question on the ground that if the witness purported to answer this question it would vitiate her privilege.

The Court. I want the jury to understand that I am permitting this question, as I said before in answer to counsel's objection, on the question of credibility of the witness. The witness has answered the question here in court and on previous occasion had asserted privilege. As I said before, there is no interest [*sic*] to be drawn from the assertion of the privilege against self-incrimination, but it is something the jury may weigh and consider on the question of the truthfulness of the witness and on credibility, and in the charge proper. In my main charge, I will have more to say about how you judge the credibility of witnesses.

That was quite a speech the judge managed. When he had repeated it for the nth time the jury was sure to understand, even those who might not know how to judge credibility. When Saypol began all over again, after the judge had given his final speech, Kaufman got angry and said:

The Court. I think we have had enough on this subject, Mr. Saypol, and for this particular purpose, and the purpose for which it is limited [*sic*], I don't see anything would be added by constant questioning and more assertion of the privilege. So I am going to ask you to go to another topic.

I wondered why this speech hadn't been made a hundred or so questions earlier, instead of after all the questions had been asked and interest was waning. But Saypol would not give up. He asked: "May I ask an omnibus question?"

The trial record does not show that Kaufman responded, but consent was apparently understood, and Saypol proceeded.

Q. Is it not a fact Mrs. Greenglass, that before the Grand Jury . . .
A. Mrs. Rosenberg.
Q. Excuse me, I'm sorry. You are the defendant here. Is it not a fact that after consultation with your lawyer, in the course of your two appearances before the Grand Jury you refused to answer any questions asserting your privilege against self-incrimination insofar as you're asked questions relating to the employment, the activities of your brother David at Los Alamos in 1944 and 1945, insofar as concerned his wife, insofar as concerned Harry Gold and insofar as concerned Yakovlev, and insofar as concerned your association and your husband's assocation in connection with these people whom I have mentioned relating to the theft from Los Alamos of material relating to the development and production of the atom bomb and the objective of delivery to the Soviet Union?

When Bloch objected to this question, Kaufman explained that since he had cut Saypol off he would permit this "general question." Ethel gave a short but exact answer.

A. It is a fact that I exercised my privilege against self-incrimination whenever I felt the need to do so.

With such an answer no one could argue. So the court, forgetting its admonition to Saypol to cut it short, again picked up the theme:

Q. But you did not exercise that privilege here in Court with respect to that same subject?

Could Kaufman really have not understood? It wasn't over, not even after the omnibus question had been asked and answered. But then this wasn't Bloch, who had been slapped down when he had asked two questions after receiving permission to ask only one. Manny Bloch and Saypol stood as equals before the court, only Saypol was a little more equal.

After the court had again clarified the issue of the contradiction in Ethel's behavior, Saypol went on, asking a rather ill-formulated question:

Q. That need you felt was necessary for assertion by you so that you would not incriminate yourself, is that right?

The meaning was quite clear; he asked Ethel if she found it necessary to assert her privilege so that she would not incriminate herself. Then after getting Ethel to acknowledge that when he asked her if she cared to make any statement for the grand jury, she declined, Saypol went on:

Q. You knew by that time that your husband was under arrest in connection with this crime?
A. Yes, he was under arrest.
Q. You knew at that time that you were suspect, did you not?

That took gall—to acknowledge that he had brought Ethel before the grand jury when she was already suspect.

Saypol went on; still with this *one* omnibus question, and again brought out that she had asserted her privilege when asked about "membership of activity or participation by your [*sic*] or your husband, the defendant, David Greenglass, the defendant, or Ruth Greenglass in the Communist Party, you similarly asserted your privilege against incrimination, is that so?"

After some exchanges between the court and Saypol the cross-examination was at last over.

Manny Bloch then asked the court for permission to take over Ethel's re-direct examination, even though Alex Bloch was nominally her lawyer. Manny hadn't completed two questions before Kaufman interfered picking up the theme of Ethel's inconsistency:

The Court. The point is you answered these questions at the trial and refused to on the ground that it *would* [emphasis added] tend to incriminate you before the Grand Jury.

Here even the court reporter did not put a question mark.

Manny was able to show that when Ethel was subpoenaed to testify before the grand jury, she was already aware that David had tried to implicate her and Julius. Then he showed that Saypol was not really serious about getting Ethel to testify, since he had never brought her before a judge who might have directed her to answer some particular questions—or not. In either case, had Saypol done this, he wouldn't have been able to conduct his cross-examination as he had. This was crucial, but I was sure the jury didn't get its full significance, and Manny, unlike Saypol, would certainly not have been permitted to expound repeatedly on this to the trial jury—if he had tried. But he didn't try. Then there was re-cross examination by Saypol.

Q. If you had the fear that you told Mr. Bloch about, why didn't you at that time tell the same story to the Grand Jury that you have told to this jury rather than take refuge in your constitutional privilege?

Saypol would rather there had been no Fifth Amendment, or any other of the amendments to the Bill of Rights. It would have made his job as prosecutor much easier, like a prosecutor during colonial days. Refuge he termed it; and many think of the Fifth Amendment as a refuge for the guilty, rather than a right for all citizens, including the innocent.*

Mrs. Evelyn Cox was the government's first rebuttal witness. She had worked for the Rosenbergs for about a year during 1945, helping Ethel with her house chores during a period when she was having trouble with her back. Mrs. Cox testified that Ethel had told her that the console table was a gift from a friend. (R.1410) Since Mrs. Cox was obviously a disinterested party her testimony was most damaging.

* In appeal my lawyers argued that the improper cross-examination of Ethel had prejudiced my case, since, according to the government's theory it was all one conspiracy. During argument Justice Thurgood Marshall asked the United States Attorney how he thought the bench would rule if the case were being argued for Ethel Rosenberg, not Morton Sobell. Without any equivocation or hesitancy the United States Attorney admitted that the Court would have to overturn the conviction of Ethel—if she were still alive. (United States v. Morton Sobell, 151 U.S. 27, 558 [2d Cir. 7 December 1962].)

Manny couldn't press too hard in cross-examination because it would look as if he were taking advantage of a poor defenseless black woman, and yet it was evident that Mrs. Cox had been well-coached by the government.

(In 1953, after the console table had been found, Mrs. Cox refused to help identify the table as the one that had been in the Rosenberg apartment, though she admitted it looked like it. She said she had become sick and tired of the case and didn't want to become involved again. [See affidavit of Leon Summit, transcript of record, Supreme Court, October Term, 1953, #497, page 46.] One can only suspect that the government had put the fear of God in her. Why else would Mrs. Cox refuse to testify, when the lives of two people were at stake?) Ben Schneider, a commercial photographer, was the last government witness. He was a "surprise witness," whose name did not appear on the prosecution's list of witnesses. Saypol claimed that the FBI hadn't located him until the previous day when two FBI agents came into his shop and showed him photographs of Julius and Ethel. Schneider testified that he identified them as customers who had come to his shop to have passport pictures taken, with their children, around May or June of the previous year.

It seemed a little strange that the FBI had not been able to locate Schneider until the very last hour, when his shop was in the shadow of the FBI headquarters, and only a stone's throw from where Julius and Ethel lived. The question was whether the photographs he took of the Rosenbergs were passport pictures, or ordinary family photos, as Julius and Ethel testified they took from time to time.

On cross-examination Schneider maintained that

he hadn't recognized Julius from pictures of him which he had seen in the newspaper some weeks ago, and that he had never seen Ethel's picture in the newspaper, despite the fact that he read all the tabloids. When Manny asked him if he had ever seen the Rosenbergs from the time he said he took their pictures until the time he walked into the courtroom, the Court spontaneously intervened:

The Court: He answered that question.

And then Saypol objected. (R.1437)

The Court: I understood he answered. He said "No."

It was true that on direct examination Schneider had answered thusly, but it seemed strange for the judge to become so exercised over such a simple question as not to allow any cross-examination. Subsequently a reporter revealed that he had seen Schneider brought into the courtroom the previous day, while Ethel was still on the stand, to have a good look at her and Julius, in obvious contradiction to his testimony. Saypol knew this, and in view of the judge's haste in shutting off cross-examination in this area it seems reasonable to conclude that he too was aware of the perjury that Schneider had committed. (On appeal the court pooh-poohed the whole thing as unimportant, but the question remains: why if it was so unimportant, did the government suborn this perjury by Schneider?) First the prosecution commits perjury, and then, when caught, says it is unimportant. They have their cake and they eat it as well.

When Schneider stepped down our lawyers made

the usual legal motions for acquittal and for the dismissal of the indictment, but then Manny made a surprise motion: "I move for a mistrial upon the ground that the frequent questioning by the Court, not intending harm, of course, of witnesses, especially of the defendants, had the tendency of unduly influencing the jury to the prejudice of the defendants and depriving them of their constitutional right to a fair and impartial trial." (R.1442) I think that Manny really believed that the court meant no harm, and was not merely trying to be politic. The court accused Manny of making the motion in bad faith, merely so that he should have a point upon which to appeal.

Manny went on to tell the court, "I, for one, and I think all my co-counsel feel, that you have been extremely courteous to us and you have afforded us lawyers every privilege that a lawyer should expect in a criminal case." I don't know if Manny did get the consent of my lawyers before he spoke for them; they couldn't very well disagree, once he had spoken. In any event there is no question but that Manny really believed what he said, and it is equally true that Manny hurt his clients as much as any defense lawyer can. If now, on appeal, we said that the judge had deliberately prejudiced our case, the government could always point to Manny's words to refute us, as they indeed did. Why did Manny do this to us? What did he hope to gain?

Phillips spoke for me. He renewed his argument about the vagueness of the indictment, and how this affected the defense. Unfortunately Phillips never seemed to find it necessary to cite any legal precedents to uphold his arguments. He hadn't done any homework since the first time I met him. So much the worse for me.

The following morning, before court began, the

lawyers and the government had a conference in the judge's chambers where they went over their requests to the judge concerning his intended charge to the jury. Afterwards, Manny Bloch began summation in open court.

He started out telling the jury how fairly the court had treated us, and then went on to similarly praise the prosecution for its behavior. (R.1453) Manny may have thought he was being slick, but the government never let us forget those words of Manny whenever we brought up the misconduct of the judge and prosecution, on the appeals. He did a good job of pointing up the hollowness of the government's exhibits, but when he began to theorize that the Greenglasses had put one over on the FBI I shuddered. (R.1475) Again he conveniently forgot about Gold's crucial testimony, "I come from Julius." It is impossible to know at this distance in time if he really believed it—or if it was only a desperate attempt to turn aside the Greenglasses' testimony. Was Manny aware that it was truly a frameup? And was he afraid to say so for fear of incurring the displeasure of the judge—in order to ameliorate the sentence in the event of a guilty verdict? One can only speculate.

From his cross-examination of Bentley we know that Manny read the record of the Brothman case of a few months earlier. In view of the clear demonstration at that trial that Gold was a sick liar, how could he now tell the jury that Gold was telling the "absolute truth" (R.1479), and then try to convince them that Gold was in no way connected with Julius? The fact that he never questioned the introduction of the photostatic copy of Gold's Hotel Hilton registration card might lead one to conclude that Block was not really thinking in terms of a frameup.

Manny could have made a telling point by demonstrating the paucity of the evidence against Ethel, and comparing it with the case against Ruth Greenglass, who never spent a day behind bars. He didn't.

I had been unsuccessful when I queried Kuntz about his intended summation. He told me he worked by inspiration. He wasn't in court while Manny was giving his summation; he was going over the trial record, he told me, getting some last-minute ideas.

Kuntz's summation sounded all mixed up to me. He spoke about the three indictments that had been handed down, about his lengthy experience as a trial lawyer, and about Elitcher being a liar. I felt very uncomfortable during the whole thing—as if I were ashamed of him. He attacked Saypol with vigor, but it was on a person-to-person level—not on the issues involved. He warned the jury that if they countenanced the methods of Saypol our country would be in danger. But I doubt that the jury understood what he meant; they had no standards by which to judge. Of my Communist Party affiliations Kuntz said nothing—as if it would go away and be forgotten.

After lunch Saypol began his summation. He didn't depend upon inspiration—he had it down on paper. (Kuntz hadn't even referred to any notes when he spoke.) All well calculated to produce a maximum effect on the jury. But first he counterattacked, telling the jury that where a lawyer has neither the facts nor the law on his side, he indulges in a game known as "kicking the prosecutor around." I was afraid that that is what it must have sounded like to the jury. One shot we had and Kuntz muffed it badly. I felt sick.

Then Saypol began the actual summation in a low key, quoting from various eminent legal authorities.

After a cool beginning on the law of conspiracy

Saypol got right to the point—the devotion of the defendants to communism and the Soviet Union. Saypol had a profound disregard for the facts. He told the jury, "[W]e know of Rosenberg's dealings with Bentley from the statements made by Rosenberg himself to Max Elitcher and David Greenglass." (R.1517) The entire record is devoid of any testimony to support this statement, but Saypol went unchallenged.

Saypol then went into his traitor oratory, brought in the sky platform, the atomic powered airplane (still not in the realizability stage, more than twenty-five years after the supposed espionage), and then got into full swing, ". . . to deliver the safeguards to our security into the hands of a power that would wipe us off the face of the earth and destroy its peace." (R.1518) And a little later he told the jury, "We know that these conspirators stole the most important scientific secrets ever known to mankind from this country and delivered them to the Soviet Union." * Nothing that Kuntz could ever have been inspired to say could possibly match Saypol's magnificent hyperbole. We were sunk.

Saypol didn't let up on the Communist bit. "It was Sobell who was chairman of the cell, who imparted orders from the Communist Party to the Government employees who belonged to the cell, the doctrine of worship and service of the Soviet Union." (R.1531) "These defendants before you are parties to an agreement to spy and steal from their own country, to serve the interests of a foreign power which today seeks to

* In 1966, the U.S. Attorney sang an entirely different tune, after the fraud of exhibit 8 had been exposed. He told the court that the government took no position with respect to the value of exhibit 8. But the jury that convicted us wasn't present to hear this, and Julius and Ethel were long since dead.

wipe us off the face of the earth. It would use the produce of these defendants, the information received
through them, from these traitors, to destroy the Americans and the people of the United Nations." (R.1535) At
no point during the trial did I sweat as I did while
Saypol spoke.

When he was finished Kaufman began his charge to
the jury. It is truly amazing how the law assumes that
the jury will understand the judge's charge after listening to it but once. In any other field, the understanding
of anything as complicated as a judge's charge would
call for a course of study. Here the most abstruse questions are thrown to the jury as if they are part of one's
everyday experience. Another one of the many myths
surrounding our legal system. I found the charge quite
complicated and beyond assimilation.

7 Awaiting Sentencing

AT five o'clock the formalities were concluded and the jury retired to deliberate. It had been a heavy day, listening to the speeches and trying to follow all the legal nuances in which the judge instructed the jury. *I couldn't always understand what Kaufman was saying* and I wondered how much the jury understood. The lives of three people hung on these instructions. I supposed no one had ever proposed testing a jury to see whether they were capable of following a judge's legal theorizing.

Julius, Ethel, and I were taken downstairs to separate bullpens. The time passed slowly. During the evening Helen and I were allowed to be together for half an hour. Several times the defendants were taken back upstairs, when the jury requested answers to some questions. At one time Ethel, Julius, and I were locked in the upstairs bullpen for more than half an hour. Manny came in to talk; we talked about everything but the trial. Mostly about our families . . .

When we returned to the downstairs bullpen Ethel began to sing. I had never heard her sing before; she had a lovely voice, and it made the waiting a little easier for me, and I suppose for Julius.

We went back up to the courtroom about eleven.

One of the jurors wanted to know whether or not he could recommend leniency for one of the defendants. Kaufman's response was to re-read that part of the initial charge that dealt with punishment being the responsibility of the judge. He said it was his prerogative to follow or disregard any recommendations the jurors cared to make. I assumed that the defendant the juror had in mind was Ethel. After all, the evidence against her had been so minimal. It wasn't until years later, when I read John Wexley's book on the case, that I learned that I was the subject of the juror's inquiry. The thought had never occurred to me, and after the trial this question—one of many—never arose in my letters and conversations with Helen. What was, was.

At 12:30 A.M. the jurors sent a note to the judge asking that they be allowed to retire for the night. Kaufman responded that if they had reached a verdict on any of us, they should return it immediately. When the elder Bloch objected to this procedure, Kaufman asked "why prolong the agony?" and sent the jurors the note.

I felt no sense of agony; I could remember experiencing a far greater anxiety while waiting to learn the results of my French comprehensive examination. Presumably my life was hanging in the balance, and yet I didn't feel as fearful as one might expect. I was aware of this anomaly and it puzzled me, but I assumed that I was simply too tired from the whole trial to respond normally.

The jury was obstinate. They told Kaufman, "We have reached our verdict on two of the defendants, and we prefer to reserve rendering our verdict on all of these defendants until we have complete unanimity."

When I got back to my cell at the Tombs, the officer took away my eyeglasses, my belt, and my shoelaces. I almost laughed at him—he had no idea how much I wanted to live, no matter what the verdict. I fell asleep as soon as I put my head on that straw pillow. The following morning the jury handed down its "unanimous" verdict: guilty! Afterwards everyone began congratulating everyone else—while the defendants looked on helplessly. The court congratulated all our lawyers on the way they had "demeaned themselves as attorneys should" during the difficult trial, and I wondered if the lawyers felt proud. The contempt sentences that had been imposed on the attorneys in an earlier trial of the "Communist eleven" had had its intended effect. Our lawyers had behaved themselves, and now Kaufman awarded them their gold stars for good conduct. Not once during the whole trial did any of the lawyers ever come close to challenging any of Kaufman's outrageous rulings. They knew that as long as they had objected properly, the Appeals Court would examine Kaufman's conduct, and rule accordingly. At least that was the way the law books said it was supposed to be.

Kaufman was even more effusive with praise for J. Edgar Hoover and the FBI, as was only proper. And then Saypol delivered his piece, praising everyone. When it came to Eddie Kuntz's turn I could have hit the ceiling: "I want to say to Mr. Saypol, as an officer of the court, as one officer of the court to another, I am willing to shake his hand after a job we both had to do." That was my lawyer talking—after all of Saypol's dirty tricks before the trial and during the trial. Manny Bloch was only a little less obsequious. It was all a part of the game theory under which our legal system operates. The trial was a game, and the officers of the courts the contestants. In this case the lives of the defendants were the stakes. Our friendly lawyers had been so long and so well indoctrinated that they hadn't even realized their Judas roles.

Julius, Ethel, and I were taken downstairs, but instead of being locked up in a tank we were taken to one of the conference rooms, where we found all our lawyers. A short time later Helen joined us for a last reunion. The lawyers sent out for lunch and we sat around the long table and talked. We talked about the trial, but in a lighthearted way, joking about Kaufman's raw rulings and ridiculing Saypol's uncouth behavior. There were no recriminations—not even for the performance the lawyers had just before put on. Lunch arrived and each of the attorneys fumbled in his pocket. Manny Bloch finally won the race. We all knew that this was to be *our* last supper, and we enjoyed eating sandwiches so thickly laden with succulent meat.

But in spite of the good fellowship, it was apparent that the lawyers were depressed, and so we, the convicted, made a valiant effort to cheer them up. We didn't want the occasion to be spoiled. It felt good to be sitting next to Helen in such natural conditions, eating and talking. I wanted very much to be able to recall this get-together as a joyful occasion. We wouldn't have another such opportunity for a long time. Julius and Ethel must have felt much the same.

Phillips passed around a recent newspaper clipping which referred to his chess triumphs at the turn of the century. Manny told us how much weight he had lost during the trial, and we all joined in a discussion of hot pastrami *vs.* corned beef. Oh how we wanted this to continue, but at two Helen and the lawyers left, and we were taken back to our tanks to await return to our respective jails. The sentencing was yet to come, and this none of us had talked about.

Now that I was a legally convicted felon I rated something better than bums row. Accordingly I was shifted to the eighth floor—murderer's row. My new home was much quieter, which was a relief, and I found I could talk to some of the men. The days passed easily. In fact, I felt more relaxed than at any time since the beginning of the trial, and I wasn't anxious about the sentence; I told Helen my guess was twenty years. I didn't want to think about what Julius and Ethel might get.

I was caught by surprise when Phillips came to see me, on April 4, with an affidavit purporting to detail all the events of the kidnapping. This, he explained, was to be filed the next day, before I was to be sentenced, in the form of a motion in arrest of judgment. The lawyers had questioned Helen on what had happened to me during the kidnapping, and from this they had drawn up *my* affidavit. Even now they didn't consider their client a responsible human being.

As was to be expected I found my affidavit unacceptable, mostly because of what had been omitted. After we had been taken from our Mexican apartment, Helen and I had not been together, except for the brief episode at Monterrey, so she could not have told the lawyers what had happened to *me*.

Working under the miserable visiting room conditions, and with very limited time available, I tried to correct this last-minute effort so that Phillips could take it back and get it retyped and returned to me for signing before the four o'clock deadline. I was disgusted with the sloppy and haphazard way in which the document had been drawn up and wrote Helen that we definitely would have to find another lawyer for the appeal.

The next morning, April 5, 1951, I was taken to Foley Square for sentencing. Manny Bloch first made a legal motion covering the objections that had been raised previously. Phillips joined in this motion and then made the motion in arrest of judgment, based on my kidnapping affidavit. Kaufman kept asking why I had not taken the stand to counter exhibit 25, the card on which the immigration inspector, Huggins, had written "Deported from Mexico." Phillips kept evading the question and Kaufman pointed out: "You can't have your cake and eat it, you know. You had an opportunity to put him on the stand." Phillips read the affidavit describing the kidnapping, whereupon Kaufman renewed his queries as to why this information was being submitted after the trial.

> *Kaufman:* Why didn't you submit that to the jury?
> *Phillips:* Now, just a moment. I will answer that, of course.
> *Kaufman:* Answer it right now.
> *Phillips:* I am coming to that.
> *Kaufman:* Would you answer it right now?

Finally, Phillips told Kaufman that he had thought that I should have been put on the witness stand, while Kuntz took a contrary position, and he had "yielded to the superior experience in criminal trials of my colleague."

Kaufman listened to Phillips a while longer and then ruled: "I don't think there is any merit whatsoever to the motion and I shall deny it."

Phillips could have told him that I was under no

obligation to rebut the perjury which the prosecution had knowingly introduced, because such perjury made the entire trial a nullity. But he didn't! Phillips again pointed out that even if the government's case were accepted as true, it proved the existence of two separate conspiracies, rather than a single all-inclusive one, as charged. Kaufman also ruled against this. This proved to be Phillips' one contribution to the case, since it laid the basis for Justice Jerome Frank's dissent on the appeal.

Then Saypol offered some "observations" (instead of the usual recommendations) before the judge pronounced sentence, with comments such as, "In terms of human life, these defendants have affected the lives, and perhaps the freedom, of whole generations of mankind." Bloch followed with a plea aimed at mitigating the sentences, which he prefaced with the remark that "Julius Rosenberg and Ethel Rosenberg have always maintained their innocence; they still maintain their innocence. And they have informed me no matter what, they will always maintain their innocence."

Kaufman's extraordinary speech sentencing the Rosenbergs, contained such incredible statements as: "I believe your conduct in putting into the hands of the Russians the A-bomb years before our best scientists predicted Russia would perfect the bomb has already caused, in my opinion, the Communist aggression in Korea, with the resultant casualties exceeding 50,000 and who knows but that millions more of innocent people may pay the price of your treason. Indeed, by your betrayal you undoubtedly have altered the course of history to the disadvantage of our country."

Neither Julius nor Ethel moved or manifested any reaction when Kaufman pronounced the death sentences. I think they probably had expected it. And as if timed to add to the drama, a nearby clock tolled the noon hour.

Immediately afterwards the judge declared a brief recess and I was taken to the bullpen next to the courtroom. Julius and Ethel were taken downstairs where they are said to have kept up their courage by singing. I never saw them again.

When the court convened a short time later, Phillips informed Kaufman that the statute under which I was convicted did not provide a minimum sentence, thereby allowing the judge the widest leeway. To this day I do not understand the reason for Phillips's action. In sentencing me, Kaufman said, "[T]he evidence in the case did not point to any activity on your part in connection with the atom bomb project. I cannot be moved by hysteria or motivated by a desire to do the popular thing. I must do justice according to the evidence in the case . . . I, therefore, sentence you to the maximum prison term provided by statute, to wit, thirty years." And then he added: "While it may be gratuitous on my part, I at this point note my recommendation against parole."

As I listened, my heart did not change pace. I had told Helen I'd probably get twenty years. Instead it was thirty. Really not much different. Both are eternities and equally impossible to visualize. I turned around and looked at Helen, seated where she had been during the whole trial, barely fifteen feet from where I was standing. She looked exquisitely pretty and sad.

I had never experienced such an overwhelming desire to see and speak with Helen as while waiting alone in the bullpen in the basement after sentencing. I wasn't frightened by the long sentence, but was concerned that Helen might be overwhelmed by what lay ahead for both of us. Helen did try to see me, but was not permitted, so we had to think our thoughts of the day apart.

It was around five o'clock when I was finally returned to the Tombs, where I was told that the next day I would be taken to the Federal Detention House on West Street. I had no feelings on the matter, since it was completely out of my hands. The thought that it was only because Julius had been taken to the death-house at Sing Sing that I would be permitted to go to West Street made for certain conflicts in my emotions. I hated the idea that I might somehow profit, even this way, by Julius's misfortune. In any event I was not taken there. And that night in my letter to Helen, a letter which took the place of the visit we never had, I wrote her that I didn't know which made me feel worse, my sentence, or the death sentences of Ethel and Julius.

The next morning I saw Helen in our familiar setting, the Tombs visiting room booth. It was a somber visit, filled with anxiety. I didn't know when or where I would be shipped away, and this uncertainty weighed more heavily on my mind than the thirty years. I was concerned with the here and now: how much longer would I continue to see Helen five times a week—even under these conditions? Ten, twenty, or thirty years are such long periods of time as to be all but meaningless when viewed as the future. If I had received one year, or even five, where I could have seen daylight at the other end of the tunnel, then the period would have had some significance; but sentencing a man to thirty years is sentencing him to the distant unknown.

I suppose it was a measure of my anxiety that I suddenly became preoccupied with the question of bail. It was highly unreasonable of me to think that the amount previously set would be lowered, now that I was convicted, but this is what I did think. However, Kuntz argued against making any application on the grounds that a denial would prejudice the appeal. His view prevailed and my anxiety continued. (Almost twenty years later, when we were arguing in court that I should be given credit for time I had "elected not to commence service of sentence," which I signed after being shipped to Atlanta, the government used the fact that I had not applied for bail as an argument against granting me the credit.)

The following day, April 7, to add to my anxiety, I read a piece by two columnists in the *New York Mirror*, saying that when I got to the penitentiary I would wish that I too had been given the death penalty instead of a mere thirty years; that the other convicts were patriotic and would make life miserable for me. Subsequent events proved the assertions of these two miserable journalists absolutely untrue. The item was undoubtedly planted by the FBI to exert additional pressure on me. The authors had no special expertise in the area of convict relations in penitentiaries.

The preparation of an appeal was perhaps most responsible for my anxiety during this period. Kuntz told me that in case I was moved a considerable distance from New York, he would come to see me before submitting our appeal. This was hardly sufficient. I felt I had to participate in the formulation of the briefs. I knew that once the briefs were written, my reviewing them would be meaningless because it would be too late to change them. Besides, in view of their record, I had little faith in the ability of Kuntz and Phillips to write a good appeal brief. Kuntz talked of the "weak case" the government had made, insofar as I was concerned, but I wasn't impressed. Weak or strong, I stood convicted.

I knew I needed another lawyer for the appeal and I pressed Helen to find one, somehow. She didn't tell me the details of her efforts and I didn't want to know. I only wanted a capable lawyer so I would at least have the chance on the appeal that I felt I had missed at the trial. In addition, probably because of my anxiety, I made severe sexual demands on Helen. All of this led Helen to confess that she felt inadequate. This saddened me. I knew that she was far more capable of the task at hand than anyone else, but I felt she could always do more than she was doing. For me there was never a *best* effort. One could always exceed the *best*.

April 11, 1951: I was thirty-four years old. My first birthday behind bars. How many more? Each year I repeated the question. Helen sent me a card, wishing me a "happy birthday," fully cognizant of the peril of this. She was concerned lest I be bitter. I told her I understood, and that as long as she spoke from the heart I would never misunderstand; that I wanted her to act toward me without exercising any special caution and to treat me as a normal person.

That year Passover began on the evening of April 20, and as a token gesture to the Jews, a special "Passover meal" was served in a small mess hall on the third floor. About one hundred of us gathered to partake of the rubbery chicken (layers, killed after serving out *their* time) with the omnipresent Spanish sauce and a piece of "sponge cake." After the meal we were each given a five pound box of Matzohs and a small kosher salami. The latter went well with the baked beans we had several times a week.

The outside world seemed as ludicrous as ever. In October I read the transcript of the conversation between Truman and MacArthur on Wake Island, and was amused that such important figures would express such pedestrian thoughts. One newspaper commented that democracy was alive because MacArthur could disagree with his commander-in-chief. It seemed to be the time of the children.

After a while the days really started to drag. Unlike the period prior to the trial, I had nothing to look forward to. The appeal? My lawyers made it appear so remote by their total inaction that it lost all meaning. If I was shipped to the Federal Detention House, where I would only be permitted to see Helen once a week, she would move to Virginia to stay with her mother. It would be cheaper to travel up to New York once a week than to continue living here. Also I had dreaded the thought that she and Mark would remain in the city during the summer solely for our daily visits in the Tombs. It would have been a difficult decision for both of us to make, but fortunately the choice as to whether I was to remain in the Tombs or not, was not ours to make.

On the eighth floor I learned for the first time that each floor was supposed to have a weekly two-hour exercise period on the roof. The first time I went to the roof I got a headache, because I was so unused to fresh air and sunshine in such large doses. We didn't go up every week. Some weeks they said the weather wasn't good enough, other times they were short of guards.

Seldom did we get the full two hours of the precious outdoors, but then it was so much better than the fourth floor. It seemed as though the men on the fourth floor were discriminated against in every way—because the officials knew they wouldn't get any static there.

Having been convicted and sentenced I got bolder in my correspondence and wrote much bitter criticism—without repercussion. In a letter of April 25, I wrote, "Coming to think of it—even in the stinky Laredo jail they knew how to prepare rice. It's almost as if they delight in preparing it so as to make it almost unpalatable for humans. Chances are a dog would reject it and he wouldn't have to be a finicky dog either. I wonder what the dietician puts down on the menu each time they dish out that concoction of rice and ground up frankfurters." Occasionally I would come up from my visit at eleven when the runners were dishing out the food. I'd see them pick up the meatballs with their hands (thumb and forefinger) and the mashed potatoes with a spoon and a thumb. Nobody asked the men to wash up before they began these chores, and even if they had been asked, it was doubtful they would comply. The New York City Department of Health had no jurisdiction here.

One day we even had a fire drill; this consisted of our lining up at the fire exit door on our floor. I wondered who had the key, where it was kept, and whether we should really be let out in the event of a fire? Where would we all go? To the street? In the thirties over three hundred inmates burned to death in their cells in the Ohio State penitentiary, when the guards would not let them out during a fire; and they had a yard from which escape was not possible. I wondered if prisons have set policies on such matters, or was it always a spur of the moment decision. Of course the Tombs was supposed to be a fireproof building.

While my range was reserved for such serious offenders as murderers, the range above was for homosexuals. This was my first verbal contact with them, and I was quite disturbed by their effeminate mannerisms, which seemed to me to be highly exaggerated. My puritan ethic revolted when they referred to each other as "she." But before I had finished my bit I learned to accept this and more as "natural."

Kuntz had been visiting me from time to time, but not Phillips. Finally on May 8 he came—too late. I got down to the lawyers' visiting room exactly at four when visits were terminated. All the lawyers liked to come between three and four because, they said, they were usually busy in court earlier. The next day Phillips returned after three, and before I even sat down said that he could only stay twenty minutes. Of course it was an unsatisfactory visit. I had the impression that Phillips was hypnotized with what he conceived to be his own cleverness. A whole month had passed and no research directed toward the appeal had been done by either of my lawyers. Phillips claimed he had done some reading on the kidnapping point, but when I questioned him his answers were vague. Kuntz came on May 18 after three, as usual, and told me I would probably be sent to the correctional institution in Danbury, Connecticut, since he *thought* the law required that pending appeal, I be kept in the Southern District of New York, of which this was a part. Otherwise it would be the Detention House on West Street. Kuntz was as confused here as he was on so many other aspects of the law, but

I didn't learn this until I was already on the bus on my way to Atlanta.

On the eighth floor I met prisoners from upstate, who had come from Attica or Dannemora for a hearing in court, usually in efforts to get their sentences reduced. Having been sentenced to outlandishly long terms as third or fourth offenders, they were trying to show that one of their previous convictions was illegal—usually for want of counsel. If they succeeded in reversing a previous conviction, their maximum term of sentence was necessarily lowered. From these men I learned how they had had to fight the prison authorities in order to file their appeals in the courts. The prison authorities felt it was part of their job to cut down the work load of the courts. Frequently when prisoners returned from a court hearing, they would be beaten up and put in the "hole" on bread and water for thirty days. It wasn't until many years later that the Supreme Court, in a landmark decision, held this practice unconstitutional.

After my conviction I began to have a new type of anxiety-dream. I was taking a number of college courses, but somehow I completely forgot about one of them and stopped going to the class until about a week before exam time, when I became painfully aware of the situation. I definitely did not need such dreams and I wasn't going to take any college courses in the near future.

On Tuesday morning, May 22, Helen and I had our last visit at the Tombs, although we didn't know at the time it was the last. It was a very good visit, Helen came beautifully dressed and my eyes dwelt on her irresistible being as we talked lightly of everything that was unimportant. She had given herself a haircut the previous evening and wore a becoming pair of earrings to offset it. It was an unusual visit—but then we were always having unusual visits. In the end I felt filled with Helen.

Part Three

THE APPEALS

1 A Brief Stay at the Atlanta Penitentiary

THERE was no warning: I was told to pack my things and get ready to move. Where? I'd find out in due time. And when Helen would arrive for our visit that Wednesday morning she would be told that I had gone.

My possessions were few. Some books, a hat I had worn while walking to Foley Square, Helen's letters, and some odds and ends. I had them packed in a moment.

At nine I was taken downstairs where I was picked up and driven to the Federal House of Detention. There I was told to get into a bus, with twenty-three others, a bus specially built to transport prisoners. The windows were barred; a heavy screen mesh divider with a locked door separated the driver and another guard from us. To the rear was a small caged cubicle with a third guard, who entered the bus through his own side door. In the back of the bus was an open toilet and a large coffee container. All the guards were well armed, but I was surprised to note that there was no radio communication apparatus on board. We were handcuffed in pairs, which made it difficult to do anything, including escape. From my fellow passengers I learned our destination was the federal penitentiary in Lewisburg, Pennsylvania, and also, to my dismay, that I could have remained in New York pending the appeal, if I had signed an "election not to commence service of sentence." Kuntz evidently didn't know about this procedure. I wondered: was it too late now?

The trip should have taken about six to seven hours but the timing chain on the engine broke and it took twice as long. Charles Best, one of two American correspondents convicted after the war of treason for his German broadcasts, was seated behind me. I found his conversation sparkling, especially after the long siege I had just been through; at this moment I was not troubled that he had been a Nazi.

We arrived at Lewisburg shortly after midnight, but before entering the prison we each had to pass through a metal detector. I repeatedly set off the alarm until it was discovered that my shoes contained large metal arch supports. Once inside, we each had to be processed. This included a mandatory hygienic shower, after which we were given ill-fitting white coveralls and canvas sandals. During the processing one of the guards asked me my eventual destination. When I told him I didn't know, he accused me of trying to be "smart," and warned me that this was not the way to start my bit. I felt terrible, being so unjustly accused— as though I had never before been unjustly accused! Even though it was three in the morning and I was worn out before I got to bed, the pleasant contrast between my present cell and the one at the Tombs didn't escape me.

When I awoke in the morning to the chirping of the birds I was doubly impressed by my quarters. The cell was about eleven by six feet, with a relatively high ceiling. I had slept on a full-sized cot between two white sheets with a real mattress and pillow. We also had hot and cold water.

We went to breakfast single file, marching military style. The dining hall overwhelmed me. It was huge and Gothic in style, reminding one of a church, with its arches, columns, and the wrought iron work on the windows. The food too was impressive: fresh milk for breakfast, liver for lunch, and lettuce salad for supper, none of which I had tasted since I had been confined.

Best of all was the large well-filled library to which we were taken several times. It was a civilized feeling to be browsing in a library for half an hour, even though the latest technical works had been published in the twenties. I took some O'Neill and Shaw back to the cell. We were also taken outdoors for an hour each day.

But I learned that this good life would soon end, since I was to be sent to Atlanta on the next bus, though I didn't know when that would be. Thus I was suspended between two points. I wasn't receiving mail from Helen or my lawyers, but was allowed to write Helen three letters a week, and in each of my letters I tried to make it clear to her that it would be impossible for me to stay in Atlanta while the appeal was being written, and that she should get Kuntz to take whatever action was necessary to have me returned to New York.

Despite the fact that my way of life had been disturbed, I was able to relax and enjoy the new surroundings. My confreres, trying to cheer me up, pointed out that with the "Good Time" I could earn, I should be behind bars only about sixteen years. I didn't know how accurate they were, and I didn't really care. Sixteen or thirty was all the same to me.

I found the guards at Lewisburg much less coarse

than those at the Tombs; they didn't curse the inmates, nor did they spit on the floor. They were definitely high class. An amusing note was that the matches that were passed out had a printed warning against venereal disease!

On Wednesday morning, a week later, the bus left Lewisburg for Atlanta, with a stop-over at Petersburg, Virginia, where the Bureau of Prisons maintained a youth reformatory. We traveled by way of Washington, D.C., passing within a couple of miles of Helen's mother's home, where I had courted her during the war, and where she would now be living when she moved from New York.

After the overnight stop in Petersburg we were awakened before the sun rose and given breakfast. A real southern breakfast, consisting mainly of grits and fat drippings. Evidently the policy of the Bureau was "when in the South . . ." We were on our way with the break of day. It was so hot and we all sweated so much that our drinking water ran out halfway through the journey. Replenishing the ten-gallon container proved quite an exercise in security. One guard stood off at a distance with a drawn gun while another unarmed guard unlocked the front gate and withdrew. Then an inmate was instructed to push the water container through the gate, and close it. The unarmed guard then came up and relocked the gate, the object being to prevent a guard from being seized as hostage. When the container had been filled the operation was repeated in reverse. It was quite a show. We had two meals: spam sandwiches for lunch and spam sandwiches for supper. Uppermost in my mind was my return to New York. I was angry, since if my lawyers had advised me properly on the procedure I would never have been taken away.

We arrived at Atlanta at two in the morning, having ridden for more than twenty hours in a hot bus, hand-cuffed and miserable. Even from the outside, Atlanta, which was much older, had a lot more of a prison look than Lewisburg. I could see the main cell house from where we disembarked and it looked uninviting. All the cells were stretched out and stacked one upon the other, like boxes many, many tiers high. Everyone was asleep and only the night lights were on, giving the whole scene a grayish, muted, forbidding cast.

My first letter from Atlanta was dated June 2, 1951.

Sweetheart, dearest, I'm here. Got in about 2 A.M. (today), but it was 5:30 before I was processed, so I missed one night's sleep. But I feel OK. (June 3d). I really didn't feel like writing last night (It's Sunday afternoon now) My letter might have sounded too pessimistic had I continued. It's lucky I got that first letter of yours, (addressed to Lewisburg). I'm enclos-ing the institution instructions (after thirty days when I am out of orientation, they become more lib-eral). I listed both you and Mom as my corre-spondents. You may send me two letters per week, if Mom doesn't write. The trip was fairly tiring, what with Spam for lunch and Spam for dinner. I'm in a cell for two. It's unlocked at 7:30 A.M. and lock-up is at 4:30 P.M. We're free to roam about the "orienta-tion" building—play chess or talk or go outside for recreation on occasion. The mess hall here is a let-down after Lewisburg. This is a prison mess. Sweet-heart, would you get me a one month's subscription to the New York Times, *addressed as on the sheet. I am wondering how Kuntz is making out with my return to New York—in July. When I see my parole officer here, I'll see if he has anything to say. It's so hard to realize that I haven't seen you for two weeks almost and I almost forgot about our Sunday night date—until now. You'll also send me a couple of the pictures, darling. One hears so much from the other men that one hardly knows what to believe. I'll just have to wait and see. I'm wondering how you are proceeding with the moving down to Virginia. I can only imagine with what little enthusiasm you are moving. But at least it's not into a void. On the trip down here we went through Washington, down Wisconsin Avenue and across the 14th Street bridge. We eat supper at 3:15. This means it's sixteen hours to go to breakfast at 7:15. Tomorrow my roommate goes out into the regular prison, so I'll have the cell to myself—for how long I don't know. I must confess during the past few days I've hardly thought about you or Pips [Mark]. I don't quite know what I've been thinking about. Everything is in a whirl. But I really feel quite well dearest. But to think that you won't be able to visit me until thirty days after I've been here. I don't know why I find it so difficult to write you sweetest Helen. Tonight I know I'll think about you and that will ease the vise that seems to grip me. It's almost as much as if I have too much to say to you darling and am unable to start saying it. I find myself going in cycles. Historical perspective is, I find, the best way. But it doesn't help in solving our personal problems. I'll finish tomorrow morning. Good night darling. It's A.M. now, Monday. I fell asleep so fast that I hardly had begun to think of you, darling, before I was asleep. With only one more letter to write you until Saturday, I don't quite know how I'll make it. It's quite hot here, these days, but I don't mind it too much. I hope you're not delaying your going down to Virginia, darling. You know how miserable it gets in New York. I have a couple of books here, One—The DeKruif and Waugh. They have a library annex of about 100 books in this building; Mann, France, a few others and a lot of junk. I hope Kuntz is working on getting me back to New York darling. Please tell me all that is happening here [sic]. Be brave and strong and good. I tell that to you and to myself. Morton Sobell, 71342.*

It didn't take long for me to realize that the whole orientation program was a farce, and in fact the five weeks were spent in almost complete idleness. There was a non-verbal I.Q. examination; a cursory physical examination; a meeting with the psychiatrist (this was purely fortuitous, since the psychologist whom I would ordinarily have met was on a leave of absence); a lecture by a priest and a visit to the vocational training school. We also had to attend a half-dozen movies, which bore no relationship to the ostensible purpose of the whole period, consisting of propaganda about oil wells and steel mills and some travelogues. I was given a job polishing the proverbial brass in the hallway.

The program must have looked good on paper. The main games in the day room were checkers, dominoes, and chess, but most of the men spent the time in conversation, largely talking about their crimes. Oddly enough card playing was strictly forbidden at this time, though when I returned in 1958 it was an approved activity. When I went out to our small play yard I usually participated in the volley ball game. From here I could see the six clay tennis courts that were a part of the main recreation yard. Initially I was amused at the thought of coddling penitentiary inmates with tennis courts. However, when I returned to Atlanta in 1958 I made good use of those courts.

The advertising for the education department's Dale Carnegie courses also amused me, for different reasons. I had always thought that these courses were designed to produce better confidence men, rather than to change the character of the individual. And I thought the last thing the prison authorities would want was better confidence men. The touted purpose of these courses was to give the men more confidence so that they could speak in public, but I was never able to understand how this fitted into the rehabilitation program of the prison system.

Early in my orientation period I discovered the *New York Mirror's* prediction that in the penitentiary the other inmates would give me a rough time was completely wrong. As a matter of fact I was welcomed by all the inmates, without exception. The two most important reasons for this were that I had been "socked with a thirty year bit," and that I had withstood all the pressures of the authorities. The latter seemed to be common knowledge among the inmates, and the nature of the crime of which I had been convicted did not seem to matter to them in any way. That our trial had been well publicized added to my prestige, and I was relieved when I found that I had no difficulty getting along with the other men.

The cells in the A and O building were the same size as those at the Tombs, except that they were more like rooms than cells, having solid wooden doors that opened on hinges instead of sliding iron-bar gates. However, there was a double bunk, which meant double occupancy, except when the population was down.

I was locked in from four-thirty in the afternoon until seven-fifteen the following morning, which meant that the three meals were compressed into a period of less than eight hours. This, I learned, was for administrative reasons. And for the same reason we were marched to the mess hall in a group and isolated from the rest of the population during the meal.

The Atlanta mess hall was as ugly as the Lewisburg was beautiful. The penitentiary had been constructed in 1905, and the mess reflected this. Sitting on hinged seats, barely a half square foot in area, we all faced the front of the hall, jammed together elbow to elbow, eating from a long, narrow, enameled metal table barely a foot wide, with the back of the man in front less than a foot away. It felt crowded. And with the flimsy design of the whole structure, any time a man in front shifted himself on his seat, the whole table of the men behind him rocked.

Despite all the precautions of the authorities, the men did double up on some of the meals like Sunday dinner, the best meal of the week. No one was permitted to leave the mess hall until the last man was seated. However, some of the men who occupied aisle seats would duck down and lose themselves in the lines filing by, and go past the steam tables for a second helping. Only occasionally would they get caught.

By Tombs standards the meals were quite good. All of the meats and the fresh vegetables came from the prison farm, but starches predominated, and most of the food was prepared southern style. Here one had to eat everything he took on his tray or suffer punishment. Yet, I discovered later, there was a tremendous wastage of food in the kitchen itself. When, as frequently occurred, the hamburgers were too outrageous to eat, everyone simply threw them on the floor; as we filed out it was quite a sight to see the litter of rejected hamburgers.

Once a week the men of A and O were taken to the commissary to spend up to ten dollars a month, if they had that much in their accounts. There were the usual commissary items: candy, cookies, cigarettes and cigars, toilet articles, ice cream. There was also supposed to be fresh fruit, but they were always out of it. The commissary ordered only a minimal amount of fruit, which was usually sold out by the first day of the week.

Since I was no longer seeing Helen I could easily have written her several pages daily. Instead I had to figure out how to space my two letters optimumly. The first letter was generally written over the weekend, to relieve some of the emptiness, and posted Sunday evening. Then when a letter came from Helen Monday, I would often find something in it to which I felt I had to respond immediately; if I succumbed I would be left letterless for the remainder of the week. An intolerable situation.

My total receiving allowance was two single sheet letters a week from all my correspondents, that is, my mother and Helen. However, Helen used closely lined three-hole notebook paper and was able to write a great deal more than I could on the official compulsory stationery.

After I had been in A and O a week I requested permission to write Edie, my sister-in-law, but when I discovered that this entailed a local police investigation to verify that she had no criminal record, I withdrew the request. This was one way the authorities discouraged correspondence with friends and relatives.

During my third week in A and O, while I was in

the day room, an officer I didn't know came up to me and told me to follow him to my cell, which a lieutenant and two other officers were searching. I was told to strip and given a body search, including a rectal examination. Lieutenant Brown, who had an odd sense of humor, explained that this was standard procedure. In the circumstances I didn't ask him to define his terms.

The search was completed without a single word of explanation; they took away Helen's letters and some photographs, and I knew it would be wasted breath to ask them what they were looking for. If they wanted to play games there was little I could do to stop them. A week later I was called into the office of the associate warden who had been nicknamed "Mophead," a smallish character with a huge head of white hair. As I sat down he told me he was recording everything that was said (evidently to impress me with his fairness). He then questioned me about everything he could think of, without giving me an inkling of the reason. A short while later my letters and photos were returned. More than two years later I learned what had triggered this incident. An inmate in population (as differentiated from A and O) had sent me a *Life* magazine article on some electrical apparatus with some questions about it; he sent it via the A and O runner, a stool pigeon. Fortunately I had disregarded the query, not knowing the inmate who sent it. When I met him on the Rock the mystery was unraveled.

The hacks, the lieutenants, the associate wardens; they all fancied themselves psychologists, in addition to being penologists. It was not difficult for the cleverer inmates to outwit the officials in this game of amateur psychologist.

Ever since my arrival here, I was in a state of constant turmoil. Uppermost in my mind was the thought of getting back to New York so I could be in touch with the legal situation, whatever good that might do. Helen wrote that Kuntz was working on my return, but a month had gone by with no direct word from Kuntz himself. In the meantime he had apparently convinced Helen that I could not help if I did get back, and she too was trying to discourage me, bringing up such irrelevancies as the terrible heat of the New York summer. That Helen didn't understand what was involved infuriated me, since by then it should have been obvious.

On July 2 I got a letter from Kuntz saying that if I signed an "election not to serve" I would have to remain in New York until the Supreme Court decision. I had wanted to go back for about six weeks, during which the Appeals Court brief would be written, and then return here, as time spent in New York would be "dead time," not counting toward my sentence. This was the pound of flesh the state exacted for the privilege of consulting with one's attorney. However, other inmates told me that I could withdraw my "election" anytime I chose and would be returned forthwith. Whether Kuntz had fabricated his information, or someone in the United States Attorney's office had misinformed him, I never found out. Since this was urgent, and strictly a legal matter, I wrote my parole officer requesting permission to send Kuntz a telegram (at my expense) telling him to go ahead with the "election."

As we had planned, Helen moved to her mother's house in Arlington, Virginia at the end of June. Even if I did return to New York, there was no reason for her to remain there. After all she had undergone the last year she was tired, physically and spiritually, and Arlington, where she had lived for many years, would be a resting place where she could recoup.

I spent five weeks in orientation, doing almost nothing. My agitation over the appeal was such that I found it difficult to read. When I was out of my cell during the day I generally managed to pass the time talking with my confreres, but once locked up I would brood, and without anyone to talk to my mind became confused and fixed until I was turning the same thoughts over and over again, cursing my lawyers for permitting me to be removed from New York and angry with Helen because she did not understand. What had not happened at the Tombs happened here. For the first time since my arrest I felt lost. Bad as conditions at the Tombs had been, the daily visits and letters had sustained me. Now, suddenly cut off from Helen, I no longer recognized myself. "Am I Morton Sobell, electrical engineer, husband of Helen Sobell?" Or only inmate, number 71342? Doomed to this non-existence for the next twenty years? The idea of twenty years of imprisonment did not bother me most; having to do it without an opportunity to fight back disturbed me, as nothing else did.

At last July 9 arrived, my last day in orientation. In the morning I met the classification board, composed presumably of experts: the associate warden, the captain, the Catholic priest, the Protestant minister, the chief medical officer, and other functionaries. Though the associate warden and the captain carried most of the weight they had no professional training for the job. If questioned they would have explained that *experience* mattered most, and since many years ago they had both started out as hacks they had years of experience between them, which qualified them to evaluate men. The most immediate function of the board was to make a job assignment, and they decided I was best suited for the book bindery in the library. It was evident that my appearance was merely pro forma, that they had clearly made their decision before I entered the room. I was also assigned quarters in A cellhouse, on the third range.

No sooner had I transferred my belongings when I was called out to report for a visit. After six torturous weeks I would again see my Helen. How many nights had I dreamed of this reunion? How many days had I daydreamed of this moment? It would last two hours and we had to make the most of it.

The visiting room was fairly small, with a long table in the middle and a guard at one end. On one side of the table sat the inmates, shoulder to shoulder; on the other side the visitors, similarly crowded. In the center of the table, running down the length, was a wooden barrier about eight inches high. Helen was already seated when I came into the room. I took my place opposite her and we were allowed one awkward kiss before the visit began. We each had to lean across the table which was about three feet wide, and without any other contact, manage a kiss.

This was the *white* visiting room. There was another one for blacks. A couple of years later when Bumpy Johnson had a visit from his white wife, it created consternation. They neatly solved the problem by sending him to the Rock, where I met him. All other facilities in Atlanta were equally segregated, the mess hall, the showers, the cellhouses, federal government notwithstanding. We were in the South.

After the kiss we both sat down and tried to talk,

but separated by three feet of table, with visitors and inmates on each side trying to do the same, it was not easy. Each prison seems to have its own special way of making visiting difficult. After an all-night ride sitting up in the train Helen looked tired, but she was beautiful. And I so much wanted to hug her, even for one moment. We looked at each other and we talked of the light and the familiar, nothing of tremendous importance. I didn't want to spoil the visit by getting into the questions about the lawyers, since I knew I had to make these two hours last—for a month at the very least. And Helen and I did manage to achieve the ecstasy we both hoped for. Love—or whatever it was called—we both experienced it to the extreme. Such unimaginable joy; such a feeling of oneness—as few experience even when together during sexual intercourse. It was a memorable visit for both of us, one which I can still recall more than twenty years later. The visiting room wasn't filled, and it wouldn't have hurt anyone to let us be together for two times two hours or three times two hours. But by the rules husband and wife could only spend two hours together, separated by a table with a guard peering down to make sure that propriety was observed by all—southern propriety.

After the visit I barely had a chance to settle in my new quarters in A cell house before the supper call sounded. Afterwards (it was only five o'clock) all the inmates went to the recreation yard, which was a gigantic field with many sports taking place, rather like a field day at school. But a field day every day of the week? And twice on Saturday? I walked around observing all the activity and people losing themselves completely in the games, as I was to do years later.

I didn't get off to a good start in my new quarters.

The first evening I committed a tremendous faux pas, by brushing my teeth in the sink reserved for face washing. The other men looked at me as though I were a barbarian, violating the civilities of A cell house.

The cell house was even more depressing than the mess hall. A and O had been a recent addition to the penitentiary; A cell house was pre-World War I. It was a huge shell of a building, about fifty or sixty feet high, with the cell blocks running down the middle of the shell, five cells high, and no less than fifteen feet from any window. This was a standard high-security design. The cell house had originally been built for a maximum of four hundred inmates, but now, almost forty years later, the capacity was up to eight hundred. Progress.

The cell itself was about nine by eighteen feet with a ceiling about seven feet high. In here were fitted four double bunks, four floor lockers, a kitchen table and four wooden chairs, as well as the toilet, unshielded for security reasons, in the middle of the cell next to the wall. There was a small and large wash basin. It was crowded and in the July Atlanta heat we all stripped to our shorts. Almost all of my seven cell mates were southerners; I didn't play dominoes, and since I hadn't whored or gone on drinking binges, the range of my conversation was somewhat limited.

That night, trying to sleep in my upper bunk barely two feet from the ceiling, it seemed as though the cell lights were turned on and off every hour. Actually it was only three or four times during the night—each time the cell house officer made his rounds. It was easier for him to count the men with the lights on, but to me it seemed like a form of deliberate harassment.

In the morning all sorts of bugle calls came over the amplifier system. Everyone seemed to know what each of the various bugle calls meant, but they served only to remind me of Walt Whitman's poem, "blow bugles blow, through the windows, through the doors, burst like a ruthless force . . ."

The work in the bindery was mildly interesting, even though the equipment and methods seemed primitive. There were three other men besides myself, none of us was paid a penny and the quality of the work reflected this. The civilian librarian didn't seem to care how the books were bound.

The place was a haven for the two weeks I remained in Atlanta. No one bothered you there, you set your own pace, you were your own boss, and compared with the crowded cell, the bindery was spacious. Even the huge athletic field was crowded. We were permitted to lie on the grass at one end of the baseball outfield, not too close to the wall which was constructed of concrete over six feet thick at the base and over thirty feet high. Five towers, high above the walls, overlooked the athletic field, and in each a guard with a high-powered rifle was plainly visible. The guards also had binoculars with which they often scanned the crowd.

The intimacy of living with seven strangers in a small cell was devastating. The five weeks I had spent in A and O in no way prepared me for what was to come, and if it hadn't been that I saw others somehow managing I don't think I could have retained my sanity.

Each evening at seven-thirty we returned to the cell house from the athletic field, and I had to suffer the sociability of cell life. I couldn't read or even be with myself and daydream. Despite an antiquated ventilating system, the air was stifling. The whole atmosphere was stifling. Most of the time the chairs were occupied by inmates playing dominoes, so I climbed up to my bunk. We had a choice of two radio programs on our earphones—usually a ball game and country music. Lights went out at ten-thirty, but the radio remained on until eleven fifteen, and I would usually listen to the local news broadcast the last fifteen minutes.

I held my breath wondering if I would get back to New York, not allowing myself to think of what would happen if I didn't. On Friday, July 20, the librarian, my boss, told me to report to my parole officer, who handed me a form marked "An election not to commence service of sentence," and told me that if I signed it I would shortly be sent back to New York. (I had already begun my sentence so it didn't make sense signing an election not to *commence,* but I didn't question it.) As soon as I had signed the form I was handed an opened letter from Eddie Kuntz in which he had enclosed an identical election form and a letter asking me to sign and return it to him.

Apparently the authorities had decided that I should sign *their* election form rather than my attorney's, and had managed the sequence of events. I didn't know why they felt it would be to their advantage, but from experience I had learned that they didn't do anything they thought would in any way benefit the inmate.

On Sunday I got a letter from Kuntz telling me he was doing "preliminary work" on the Appeals Court brief. After more than three months! Helen was still writing me about the terrible August heat in New York and I was still trying to explain that no heat could deter me from returning to where I would at least be close to the scene of action—or inaction.

Now that I was certain of returning a tremendous weight was lifted from my shoulders, and nothing about the prison bothered me anymore. In fact I began to feel so lighthearted that I once more dreamed about Helen, as I had been unsuccessfully trying to do these past weeks.

On Monday, shortly before noon, a busload of prisoners arrived after traveling all night. One of the prisoners was Eugene Dennis, the chairman of the Communist Party, who had been convicted under the Smith Act. I saw him in the mess hall, but we never had an opportunity to meet. After lunch I was told to pack my things for the trip. There were eight of us; we were stripped and searched in a small room off the main corridor, given a new set of clothes for traveling, and then fed. Once we had been searched we were not permitted to make contact with the other prisoners. Late that afternoon we started the first leg of the journey, riding all night. The weather was not unpleasantly hot and I experienced sensual delight as I dozed and dreamed while the rhythmic motion of the bus engulfed me like slowly undulating waves at the sea shore. I was handcuffed only to myself.

We arrived at the Petersburg reformatory early the following morning, not unpleasantly tired, and started the next leg of the trip that afternoon. Again we traversed the familiar streets of the nation's capital, passing so close to where Helen was now staying that the thought was agonizing. We arrived in Lewisburg late that night and on Friday I was on board the prison stationwagon bound for New York.

The two-month stay in Atlanta was the roughest short period I experienced in the more than eighteen years I was imprisoned. I was in constant inner turmoil from the moment I arrived until I knew I was leaving. Though one would have thought that the initial shock of imprisonment would have made the greatest impact, this simply was not so. What threw me for a loop was my sudden removal from the scene of action, and the abrupt cessation of almost daily communication with Helen.

(below left) Radio Club, Stuyvesant High School, 1933, Sobell, second from right, front row—President and Chief Operator of Radio Station W2CLE. (below right) Graduation photo, Stuyvesant High School, 1933.

Dr. Luis Sanchez Ponton, former Minister of Education of Mexico and eminent Mexican attorney, in New York in 1957 to argue the case of Morton Sobell before the Appeals Court. He and his wife being greeted by Mrs. Rose Sobell, mother of Morton Sobell.

Lord Bertrand Russell greeting Helen Sobell at his residence when she toured Europe in 1963 to gain support for the release of Morton Sobell.

The Rock with lighthouse and burned out Warden's residence in foreground. *Photo by Phiz Mezey.*

Alcatraz recreation yard, overgrown since abandonment.
Photo by Phiz Mezey.

Water tank used to supply fresh water to the Rock with slogans painted by Indians during their occupation in 1972.

Photo by Phiz Mezey.

Cell number C-156, located on corner. It was a convenient stopping place for the Warden's tour. Here he pointed out the "notorious atom spy" to the group on tour. Yard entrance at far end of "flats." *Photo by Phiz Mezey.*

Cell interior. Steel bed, now removed, was on right, eight inches in front of toilet. Ventilator hole is below sink. Seat and table on left. *Photo by Phiz Mezey.*

View of library—minus books and stacks—as seen from Sobell's cell, C-346. No one but library workers were allowed inside. *Photo by Phiz Mezey.*

"Broadway," on which blacks and kitchen workers lived. (It was as dark as this photograph suggests.) *Photo by Phiz Mezey.*

Helen and Mark were then denied permission to visit when they reached the Rock—without explanation.

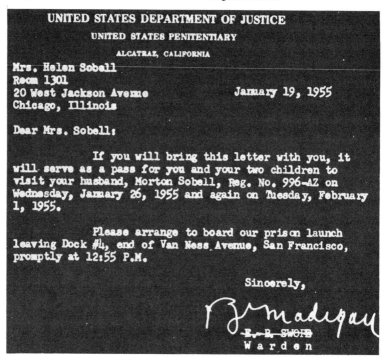

UNITED STATES DEPARTMENT OF JUSTICE

UNITED STATES PENITENTIARY

ALCATRAZ, CALIFORNIA

Mrs. Helen Sobell
Room 1301
20 West Jackson Avenue   January 19, 1955
Chicago, Illinois

Dear Mrs. Sobell:

      If you will bring this letter with you, it will serve as a pass for you and your two children to visit your husband, Morton Sobell, Reg. No. 996-AZ on Wednesday, January 26, 1955 and again on Tuesday, February 1, 1955.

      Please arrange to board our prison launch leaving Dock #4, end of Van Ness Avenue, San Francisco, promptly at 12:55 P.M.

                    Sincerely,

                    E. B. SWOPE
                    W a r d e n

Morton and Helen with their daughter Sydney and her husband, Ron, at Lewisburg Penitentiary in 1967, a much happier time.

Poster in Rome, Italy, prior to electrocution of Julius and Ethel Rosenberg.

(below left) Sobell family with friends picketing the White House in 1961. (below right) Rose Sobell, mother of Morton, being escorted from the White House in 1962.

Atlanta Penitentiary 1961. Tie and dress jacket were not part of prisoner's wardrobe.

Helen and Morton in Lewisburg, 1967, when photos of visitors and companions were permitted to give the Jay Cee prison group a source of income.

(below left) Morton and son Mark at Lewisburg. (below right) Morton and mother Rose at Lewisburg.

2 Good to Be Back in New York

I WAS taken to the Federal House of Detention. Julius had long since been taken upstate to the death house at Sing Sing so there was no further danger that I might conspire with him. The next day, Saturday morning, my mother visited, and Tuesday, July 31, Eddie Kuntz came (with inconclusive results), and on the following day Helen came from Washington, for a disastrous visit.

The visit was only thirty minutes, and I spent the whole time trying to make her understand the absolute need for getting another attorney. In the process I relieved all the pent-up emotions I had suppressed during the last months. Although Helen was on the brink of tears several times I was not deterred, feeling the situation too critical and the time too short to allow myself the luxury of concern for her. After the visit I had a feeling of utter emptiness and unbearable anxiety; I knew I had torn Helen apart. Thirty minutes was of course much too short a period to accomplish what I had set out to do.

In a letter Helen wrote right after the visit, she tried to make the point that our meetings should serve to reestablish the feelings that had at one time existed between us, and to reinforce our love, not to tear us apart. I couldn't bear to read these lines because I recognized their validity, but I did feel that at that moment other considerations had priority in what I saw as a life and death situation.

In a subsequent letter she said that I had seemed frightened. I may have acted frightened, but not in the way she meant. I was frightened to find myself "doing" twenty years for trying to be a "nice guy," and not offend my lawyers or hurt Helen's feelings. That was why I was really frightened—that I might be unwilling to risk the blowup that might occur if I pressed too hard. I realized that my good upbringing was a trap, a trap out of which it would take a lot of energy to extricate myself. No one would encourage me in this direction, least of all Helen.

The following Sunday Helen came back to New York, and we tried again. As soon as I saw her I realized I should have to let up this time. This was then a positively joyous visit, and we even arranged a date that evening, when Helen was to be back in Washington. But after that I was sometimes frightened by the thought that if I so chose I could make our visits traumatic; I rarely flew off the handle, except quite deliberately. Wanting to have a good visit didn't guarantee one, but at least it made it possible.

West Street, as it was usually called, was a jail, not a penitentiary, and the atmosphere reflected this. The building had been a garage, said to have been sold to the government by Governor Alfred E. Smith. Everything was obviously make-shift, as though meant for temporary service. All of the accommodations were tanks, with bars on four sides as well as the top; it was a cage such as one might find in the zoo. There were small tanks, with tiny built-in cells, which held twelve people, and larger tanks, like dormitories, meant for forty men. In all there were three floors and a caged-in recreation roof. The jail had a nominal capacity of two hundred and twenty-five men, but there were times when more than three hundred were crowded in. While West Street housed some sentenced prisoners, who were doing their time, few had more than two years and none over five. Everyone else was either awaiting trial, or, like myself, was on an "election" pending appeal.

My first job was with the mop detail, a demotion from the book binding job, but since this entailed my working only about fifteen minutes daily I could make the afternoon roof period, as well as the one in the evening, a considerable summertime advantage. Everyone was given some kind of a job, mostly of the make-work type.

Life was a little more normal there than it had been at the Tombs. I was not locked in my cell during the day; and while the ventilating system was far from adequate, it was much better than it had been there. At West Street the guards would open up the windows at night so that we could get some fresh air after going to sleep—winter as well as summer. The guards were more civil, and I neither saw nor heard of any brutality. Visiting room facilities were also superior to those in the Tombs, even though visits were conducted through a telephone. The long, narrow visiting room was divided from floor to ceiling into two sections, along its length. Inmates and visitors faced one another across a fairly narrow table, with a solid curtain of glass about three feet high immediately above the table. Glass wings about a foot deep partitioned off each place. Inmates and visitors sat on stools, one to one, while additional visitors sat on chairs lined up along the wall about five feet back, visible to the inmate. One of the favorite topics of speculation for inmates was whether the visiting room telephones were bugged. After examining the way the telephone cords came through the partition (it was quite thin at this point) I concluded that the phones were probably not bugged. And if they were?

My relationship with Kuntz was a continual frustration. I kept pressing him to let me see the results of his research, or the legal opinions upon which he intended to base the appeal, but without an actual refusal he put me off. In addition he never seemed to be able to make up his mind, disconcerting me with his constantly shifting positions. After one discussion I wrote him a memo outlining what I thought we had agreed on, but to no avail.

I didn't see Phillips until August 18, and then he expounded some very abstruse legal theories. When I asked him to cite the decisions upon which the theories were based I got a lot of double-talk. I had learned from jailhouse lawyers that legal theories are only as good as the case law upon which they are based. Without any legal opinions to back it up a theory was so much hot air, and Phillips, despite his many years of lawyering, didn't seem to recognize this truism.

The legal opinions were seldom as clear-cut as I had naively expected, and were written with technical jargon which it would take some months properly to learn to interpret. But more important, at least to this legally untutored engineer, the opinions frequently appeared self-contradictory.

After the conference with Phillips I wrote Helen a strong letter asking her to be less trusting and more critical of our lawyers. I had recently discovered a certain selective fatalism in my wife's outlook, which, when combined with an unwarranted optimism, made me quite angry.

Finally Helen and I agreed on the *absolute* need for a third lawyer in the case, but getting one was not simple. Lawyers apparently do not like to take on other lawyers' clients, and even though Kuntz had agreed to join in the search, his lack of enthusiasm seemed to be hampering his efforts. The alternative, firing our lawyers, took more courage than was mine at the time. Despite my frustrations and my occasional anger with Helen that nothing seemed to be happening, I felt more alive and more at peace than at any time since my arrest: I was *working* at getting things moving, and for the first time I was becoming educated in the ways of the law. From other inmates I had learned that legal opinions of all appeals could be purchased for sixty cents each and I began to order them. Over the next year I bought more than one hundred opinions covering a broad range of the hallmark decisions pertaining to our conviction and studied them until I knew a considerable number by heart. It wasn't difficult for an inmate to know the law in a particular area much better than his attorneys, because the inmate had much more time to devote himself to the one area of the law which affected him personally and because law was not basically a very difficult subject. The state prisons were not so liberal; there the prisoners were not permitted to accumulate legal opinions.

After a month in New York I decided to remain until the Supreme Court handed down its ultimate decision. The real stakes were so high, it would be silly even to consider this "dead time" here not well spent. Twenty years later, when I would be due for release, I might regret this, but I decided to let twenty years take care of itself. I was aware that this thinking represented a considerable change in my character.

The food was tolerable, certainly compared with the Tombs. There were fresh vegetables, salads, eggs, small portions of meat and fish, all fairly well prepared, though the Sunday pork chops were cut so thin they were referred to as "pork chop wafers." We ate at long wooden tables, seated on long benches, and on Sundays there were even bed sheet tablecloths!

At first, despite the fact that I had quite a bit of free time, I didn't read much. The library was small, stocked with cast-off volumes from other government libraries, and had no budget for buying books. It did have the daily newspapers. The medical facilities were also superior to those of the Tombs, with a staff of five Medical Technical Assistants (MTA's) who were well below the registered nurse level in training, and a consultant M.D. who visited for less than an hour each week day. The hospital, partitioned off from the rest of the prison, had a dispensary and a ward with half a dozen beds. There was also a dental clinic and an x-ray room. An outside civilian dentist visited once a week, and I was pleasantly surprised when I was able to get a couple of cavities filled. Later I realized the seamier aspects of the medical care there. It was only by contrast with the Tombs that I was so impressed at the beginning.

August was hot, and we were officially allowed only one clothing exchange a week, even though the jail had its own laundry. After I had been there a short time I learned how to scrounge around for additional clothing. There was also only one linen exchange a week but this represented an improvement on the

Tombs, where there was no linen at all. The laundry at West Street was used mainly to supply clean towels to the United States post offices.

After a stifling day the evening roof period was a joy, my main recreation breathing fresh air with an occasional game of Ping Pong. The games were limited because of the small space; in an area no larger than twenty by forty feet the men managed to play an abbreviated form of punch ball (a variation of baseball), though when one hundred and fifty men came to the roof there was little space even to walk, let alone play games.

We returned to our tanks at seven-thirty where the usual recreation was card playing. On each floor, all evening long, a loudspeaker system carried the ball games, the fights, or music. I found this noise disturbing.

One of the reasons that I found the prison loudspeaker so annoying was because it had so much distortion. I was able to locate the wiring diagram of the system and examination revealed several obvious sources of the distortion. The official in charge of the system, Captain Soares, agreed to let me work on it and in a few days I had considerably reduced the distortion. This accomplishment was an ego booster, and it was good to work again. I had also noticed that one of the two 35mm. film projectors used in the auditorium cast considerably less light on the screen than the other. It was a simple matter of aligning the light optics, once I got the permission to work on it. After that I cleared up a hum problem in the sound system of the projectors. This was the beginning of many projects I carried out during my stay at West Street. I was unusually fortunate in the cooperation of Captain Soares, who provided all of the equipment I needed, since captains were usually obstructionist.

The only other thing that interested me at this time was my appeal brief. I hardly thought of the past and never of the future; I zipped through the *New York Times* in record speed, but buried myself in reading the legal opinions of the various federal appeals courts as well as the Supreme Court.

In the latter part of August the Court of Appeals unanimously reversed the conviction of William Remington.* This momentarily bolstered my hope for reversal in our case until I realized the tremendous difference between the two cases. In referring to the reversal the media constantly used the term "technical," to imply that Remington was guilty and had had his conviction reversed only because of a "technicality" in the law. The same press never called a conviction "technical," although the conspiracy law did provide "technical" loopholes for the prosecution to obtain unjust convictions. A jury's verdict was treated by the press as the voice of God—no matter how fraudulently the conviction was obtained.

Labor Day weekend was a big holiday and we had an inmate review followed by cola and social tea biscuits, courtesy of the summer intern chaplain. The winter movie season began with *Harvey,* which I resented because a psychiatrist was chosen as the butt of the humor. I still revered psychiatrists.

I was told by other inmates that family bench visits (visiting across a table in the attorneys' visiting room)

* Remington had been convicted for perjury for denying under oath that he had been a member of the Communist Party. (U.S. vs Remington 191 F.2d 246)

were frequently permitted where there was an unusual situation. Not having seen the children since the trial, this seemed to me the best way to get reunited, but the authorities denied that bench visits were ever allowed for social purposes; I later found this to be untrue.

Helen brought the children up from Washington the weekend after Labor Day. I didn't recognize Mark—he had grown so much during the short months since we had last met—and Sydney was now a young lady, almost twelve. Trying to talk with children over the phone was very frustrating, but I knew we had to have this visit, to start somewhere. It would have been so much more meaningful across a table, where we could have all talked together.

About the middle of September I learned that a young man being considered as our third lawyer had been out of law school only five years, but had been working in the office of a busy firm writing many briefs. Helen had met him and told me she was impressed with his qualifications, and on September 27, Kuntz brought him to me. Skeptic that I was by this time, Howard Meyer nevertheless impressed me most favorably. I questioned him in great detail about a number of legal points which had been bothering me and he cleared these up masterfully. I saw that he had a solid background in federal law, something neither of my two other lawyers had. When I met him he had already been working on the brief several weeks and expected to have a first draft ready shortly. Phillips wanted to draft the section relating to the kidnapping himself and Meyer agreed; I would have to wait and see.

Attorney visits were not limited in duration, except that they could take place only during normal business hours. There were two separate facilities for attorney visits. The first was located in the regular visiting room, where, toward the end closest to the guard, about five visiting places had glass doors which could be unlocked to permit the attorney and his client to talk directly instead of having to use the telephone. The courts frowned on a facility where an attorney had to consult with his client through a telephone—for obvious reasons. The guard could easily keep a close watch to see that nothing was passed between the attorney and his client. The second visiting facility was located upstairs, in the office of the warden's assistant, Kenton. Here there were several tiny cubby holes, each with a small table and a couple of chairs where an attorney could consult with his client tête-à-tête in full view of Kenton. This was the so-called bench visit.

My attorney was permitted to pass me material to read, but only after Kenton had inspected it. Going to and coming from such a visit I was given a superficial shakedown, thorough enough in one instance to detect diamonds a smuggler was taking out to his lawyer.

As he had promised, on October 6th Howard sent a draft copy of his brief, which I spent all that day reading and re-reading. My initial impression of Howard's legal abilities was upheld, and I knew that if I hadn't returned to New York and applied pressure to Helen and the lawyers, Meyer would never have been employed. It wasn't until a year later that I learned from Howard that he hadn't wanted to undertake this appeal, but that Helen had persuaded him to change his mind and accept a case that so many other, older, progressive lawyers shunned.

On October 10, the Court of Appeals granted my lawyers an extension of time to file the brief; the new date was November 5. We were also given permission to submit a maximum of seventy-five pages instead of the usual maximum of fifty pages.

It wasn't until October 25 that Phillips brought me the draft of the kidnapping section on which he had so diligently been working. It substituted Phillips's logic for case law, in addition to being turgid; for example, "and they rendered him unconscious with blows over the head, with blackjacks, until he lost consciousness." Many years earlier Oliver Wendell Holmes had pointed out that the law was not logical; the law was based on *stare decisis*—past judicial decisions—except in those rare instances when the Supreme Court decided to make a switch, as in the separate but equal doctrine. But I knew Howard would revise Phillips's draft. My own contributions had been minimal, but Howard had taken the time to explain to me everything that I had questioned. I had ordered sixteen of the most important opinions that Howard had cited because I wanted to read the entire thing, not simply the quotations he had selected. I wanted to make absolutely sure that these opinions were as strong as they seemed, and not quotations out of context. When I studied them I saw that Howard had been scrupulously honest in not claiming that a decision represented more than it in fact did. When I read the government's brief I couldn't say as much for it.

Ever since I could recall I had followed the decisions of the Supreme Court in the *New York Times*, but from then on I paid far greater attention to them, and began to understand some of the finer points of law. This made me forget that in a political case the ordinary rules did not apply. Through the years I would be taught this lesson over and over—forgetting it between lessons. People forget what they wish to forget.

The evening roof recreation period had ended in September but while I was still on mop detail I could always make the afternoon roof period. Those who worked full time during the day could now only enjoy fresh air on weekends. With the cooler evenings I would occasionally make myself a "hot chocolate" using the standard prison recipe: a Milky Way dissolved in hot water. The temperature of the hot water regulator was turned up each evening at nine with official approval, and now that the baseball broadcasts were over, the cell house was a lot quieter in the evenings. With the prolonged evening cell house periods I found myself studying once more. Helen had brought me one of her physics texts on light, together with a slide rule for working the problems. It was a fairly elementary text, but just what I needed at the time.

The visiting room also became more crowded on weekends with the onset of fall, and especially when the weekend weather happened to be bad. I could never ascertain why bad weather increased visiting, but the result was that the usual forty-five-minute visit was curtailed to thirty minutes, the official allowance. This happened when my parents were visiting on one weekend, and I dreaded the thought that it might also happen when Helen came up from Washington. My parents and Helen alternated weekends. Of course I wanted to see Helen every weekend, but the expense and energy involved in the trip ruled that out.

After Howard had brought me the first draft of his brief and I was satisfied that I at last had a lawyer who could write an appeal brief, my visits with Helen began markedly to improve. Now that the lawyer problem was solved Helen and I could go back to being as one. I looked forward to our bi-weekly visits with delightful anticipation.

To avoid the possibility of an abbreviated Sunday visit Helen came Monday mornings, when there were at most only a few other visitors, and she wore her sheer nylon blouse so that I could feast my eyes on her. Toward the end of October the visiting room guard allowed her to stay a full hour, which seemed a great plenitude, and Helen's bright and shining Monday morning face, full of life, was like a transfusion for me. After such a visit I would always go back to my cell and write her a letter, trying to maintain the visiting ambience a little while longer. The visiting room officer who had extended the time was a rare creature, a "good hack." If he got to know you and felt you wouldn't make trouble, he would oblige you. Officers with such good hearts were few in the prison system; the sadists were far more numerous.

I had unearthed some classical recordings buried in some junk, so after finishing an amplifier I had built for the auditorium I suggested to Captain Soares that I be allowed to hold a music appreciation session one night a week. Nine men showed up for the first concert and twenty the following week! But the day after the second concert the captain called me into his office to let me know that my project hadn't been cleared with the "proper authorities," that is, the inmates who were closest to the authorities and whose province was extracurricular activities; who chose what movies were shown and what ball games were broadcast. These were the key men, who occupied positions like head butcher, baker, or cook, all sentenced prisoners doing at least three years. They were jealous that an "outsider" had been able to promote a successful activity. I had had my first lesson in prison politics, but there were to be many more before I qualified as prison-wise. Captain Soares was a good man, but didn't want needless trouble, and since I had reasonably good relations with these wheels I acceded to their wishes and there was no more music appreciation.

I then acquired the job of movie projectionist. This involved running two old 35 mm. projection machines, which had to be switched manually. I took inordinate pride in my reel-switching technique, almost never missing the cue marks at the end of the reel. It was a simple operation, but in the circumstances, an accomplishment. Only when I was actually projecting the film for the inmates was there an officer with me; when I worked on the projector or the amplifier I was alone, and it would have been easy to acquire some hack saw blades and cut through the mild-steel-reinforced windows in the projection booth. From there it was only a three story drop to the street, and there was plenty of stout cord to facilitate that. But the thought of escaping never once occurred to me. One had to be attuned to such wave lengths. Years later, after I had become more of a con, I thought of all these missed opportunities.

Good as the West Street food was, there was almost never any fresh fruit. Thus it was something of a minor miracle that in October the commissary carried fresh oranges. For four weeks I indulged myself, eating several oranges a day, until, just as mysteriously as it had started, it stopped. The commissary usually carried cakes, cookies, candy, ice cream and toilet articles—including razor blades, which had been forbidden at the Tombs. But it didn't carry milk or sandwiches because these were considered foods, and under Washington rules were forbidden. Nor at West Street did we carry money. The "store" had a card with an ID picture, for keeping a record accounts.

Every prison was run on entirely different philosophies, and what was accepted as a matter of course at one was absolutely forbidden in another—with explanations about why any particular practice would be detrimental to the inmates' welfare. In this sense prisons differed markedly from the outside world, where the rules and regulations had far greater uniformity.

I began to read fiction again, though much of it was political fiction like *Never Call Retreat,* by Joseph Freeman. Written during World War II, it was a psychiatrist's account for laymen of an analysis of a former Nazi concentration camp inmate. I blushed inwardly when I found that I was identifying myself with Condorcet (a leading figure during the French Revolution), even though I hadn't written revolutionary leaflets, while the revolutionists were hunting for me, as in his case. Condorcet looked at the revolution impersonally, and his being hunted in no way changed his views of the French revolution. He saw it in its historical perspective—and it was in this sense that I felt a kinship, for I too had historical perspective insofar as this case was concerned, as I was sure Ethel and Julius did. I felt this was the only reason they could withstand the pressures to "confess." While I was reading this book I saw a sickening movie of Rommel's exploits. Only six years since Hitler had been vanquished, and Rommel, who had fought to preserve Nazism, was lauded for being a gentleman. I suppose Freeman's book sensitized me to such movies, but I wondered about the short memory of the public.

A silly item in the press, "Anti-semitism reduced forty percent in five years." If one attaches numbers to something, it automatically becomes scientific. As though anti-semitism could be measured by numbers.

Kuntz visited toward the end of November, bringing a bound copy of our brief, as well as a copy of Manny Bloch's brief for Julius and Ethel. Theirs leaned heavily on constitutional arguments. Originally, when Kuntz and Phillips had spoken to me about their intended brief, they talked a lot about a constitutional attack on the espionage statutes. This frightened me because I felt that after they had withstood such attacks for more than thirty years the courts were unlikely to find the statutes unconstitutional in a hot political case like ours. And now when I saw that Manny Bloch had evidently adopted this line in his brief, I wondered whether he had consulted his clients on the matter, or whether they had simply trusted him to make the decision.

At the time I did not know that Manny had had considerable help in writing the brief from attorneys who, in view of the political temper, preferred to remain anonymous, and that he refused the proffered help from other attorneys who also wished to remain anonymous. It would be interesting to know how he chose those whose help he accepted and those whom he rejected.

My parents had visited me every other Sunday until November 11 when my mother appeared alone. She explained that my father had become ill after doing a small paint job around the house, probably from the effects of having inhaled the paint fumes. At the time I didn't think much about it, even though it didn't seem plausible. Actually he had had the first of a series of cerebral strokes. I enjoyed seeing my parents at West Street more than at the Tombs, where I had been permitted to see one of them at a time. Together we found enough to talk about to make the visits interesting.

Several weeks later, I received a letter supposedly from my father. It was typewritten, which was not in itself very unusual, but the phrases and expressions were definitely not his, though the ideas may have been. I felt terrible because I felt that they were lying to me as though I were a child. This was something Helen would never have done. But my mother in her own way, while trying to spare me a hurt, hurt more deeply than if I had known the extent of my father's illness in the first place. When I questioned her about it she became evasive. I didn't ask Helen because I knew she would have felt herself torn. It was enough that I knew my father was seriously ill.

A month before Christmas Helen lost her job as telephone solicitor for a health insurance company. Since her wages averaged about eighty-nine cents an hour I thought it was probably for the best, but I knew she didn't want to feel a burden on her family.

The period prior to the Appeals Court decision could be called my optimistic period. I was actually thinking in terms of a possible reversal of the conviction for Julius and Ethel, as well as for myself. I also began to think about who would make the oral argument before the Court of Appeals.

It turned out that this was entirely academic; I did not know that Phillips insisted he be allowed to argue the case, threatening to pull out otherwise. I suppose Howard, as a junior, didn't want to assume the responsiblity and acquiesced. I don't know whether I would have had the courage to tell Phillips to leave, but having heard him on several occasions, I knew I wanted Howard to make the argument.

Phillips visited me on December 11, coming late, and promising to come back earlier the next week. He told me that he was trying to arrange for me to be taken to the court to hear him argue. From what I had learned from the other prisoners I knew this to be complete nonsense, but I concentrated on trying to find out what was to be the tenor of his argument. I got the same response from him which Kuntz had given, "I work by inspiration, not by recipe." This really frightened me. However, when Kuntz visited the following week, he assured me that Howard had briefed Phillips thoroughly, and that Phillips would go along. I believed it, though by this time I should really have known better.

When the weather turned colder we were issued pea coats made of reprocessed wool. A penetrating wind whipped off the Hudson River, and for the first time I became aware that our prison, née garage, was not insulated. The bare concrete walls were always cold and all winter long the place never felt warm, though it never emanated the hardness of the Tombs.

Around the middle of December I was given a real full-time job: inmate photographer, an inmate who took photographs of other inmates on their arrival. It was a "twenty-four-hour a day job" which I enjoyed, since I could now utilize some of my technical knowledge, closing my eyes to the implications of the work. To compound the evil, in addition to photographing the men, I finger-printed them. I didn't even bother to rationalize my position. I pictured myself as a technician who tried to carry out his assignment to the best of his ability.

Full awareness of the collaborationist nature of the job came to me when I had to photograph and finger-print the five lawyers who had defended the Communist eleven. They were given between thirty days and six months, the sentences varying with the degree of contempt manifested in Justice Medina's courtroom. Feeling as guilty as though I had been "caught in the act" by friends, I apologized to each of them, but continued on the job.

During the next thirty days I got to know them all well. Harry Sacher, the smallest of them, was the most dynamic; Abe Isserman, who was subsequently disbarred for the duration of the McCarthy era, got to know Helen and extended her considerable help over the years; Louis McCabe made the deepest impression on me. He was the oldest, and we had many heart to heart chats; the genuine warmth he emanated quieted the most disturbed people who came in contact with him. When he was released, a delegation was awaiting him on the street, to take him to breakfast at a nearby hotel where there were still others to welcome him and to honor him for his courage in the courtroom. I dreamed of the time when I would finish my thirty years, wondering if I too would be honored with a breakfast, and blushed.

The photo darkroom where I worked was located next to the "inside" office, on a sub-floor somewhat isolated from the mainstream of the prison movement. The surroundings were fairly pleasant and the officer I worked for was quite human. He was a black man, with some college education, who had been sent down to the Atlanta penitentiary shortly after the war as the first black officer. He didn't even last two weeks; the other officers, hacks and lieutenants alike, drove him off. As a sop the Bureau gave him this office job in New York.

It was stupid of the Bureau to have sent a black man down to Atlanta without first making sure of the reception he would get from the other hacks. This was only another example of the many I would see over the years, where the Washington bureaucracy acted with a total lack of sensitivity. Yet I was also to see where The Bureau of Prisons sometimes took the side of the angels (Integration), just because they were far removed from the scene and more subject to pressure from those who were closer to the seats of power.

Sometimes when I complained to Helen about the food she would jokingly tell me the story of the boy writing home to his mother from summer camp; that the food was poisonous and vile—and the portions too small. I had no complaint at Christmas: half a fried chicken, french fries, candied carrots, pickled onions and cauliflower, and mince pie à la mode. We also received the traditional (only I didn't know it yet) Federal Prison Industries' Christmas gift package of nuts, candy, cookies, and cigarettes. It was overwhelming.

As a special movie we saw *Kim*, that old British myth about the Englishman's innate superiority to the native, which was really not so different from Hitler's myth of the super-race. That weekend there was also an amateur night show with prizes awarded on the basis of the loudness of the applause. I had built a rudimentary sound level meter which a committee of judges used to measure the applause. And the prison took on a different appearance with four or five Christmas trees around. We all forgot for a moment where we were. On New Year's Eve we stayed up until past midnight and were treated to doughnuts and coffee—another Federal

Prisons tradition; we also had another feast; steak with many side dishes. I would have complained about the steak at home, but not here!

Helen brought Sydney up from Washington for a visit and we talked lightheartedly, covering many different topics. She said a word, I said a word, a few more words—we understood each other. This Christmas was so different from the last.

The following week I saw my father for the first time since his stroke. He seemed bewildered, but he was back at work. When he told me he had difficulty compounding prescriptions I felt a twinge of anxiety and wondered what part my imprisonment had played in his illness. I wanted so much to sit down and talk with him for the whole day, slowly and gently, but those few minutes over the phone had to serve instead. There would be none other, ever.

On January 3, government agents conducted widespread narcotics raids and arrested some sixty-odd men they claimed were the major pushers around New York. But the pushers who were brought in that evening were all users—every single one of them. Anyone at all familiar with the narcotics racket knew that the big pushers were not users; users who sold narcotics were either making an accommodation sale, or were selling a few bags to support their habit. I worked all through the night as they came in because I knew that the following morning they would not be in any condition to be photographed; they were all overdue for their next shots. The following morning all these bigtime pushers were sprawled on the floor in front of the hospital waiting for their fixes. Under federal prison rules narcotic addicts were allowed three shots, spaced one day apart, to help them while they kicked the habit. It wasn't very much, but an improvement on the Tombs, where they were cut off cold turkey.

In the years that followed, whenever I read press reports about the big narcotics raids that netted big pushers, I knew how to interpret them. I was also told by many first-hand sources that the big pushers were never rounded up because of the thorough corruption of the Narcotics Bureau, which was said to be the biggest importer of narcotics.

Argument in the Court of Appeals, set for Monday, January 7, was at the last moment postponed, at the request of the government, until the tenth. Kuntz brought me a copy of the government's reply brief just before argument, which I read with trepidation. I was afraid that somehow the government attorneys would destroy some of our most important arguments with one resounding stroke. When I finished reading their brief and found our arguments intact, I breathed a long sigh of relief. I was thoroughly acquainted with the weaknesses of our brief but had feared that beyond these Howard and I might have overlooked something important.

Helen came into New York for the argument and visited me immediately afterward. She looked tired and wasn't very informative about what had transpired. That Sunday the *Times* carried a full column devoted to the government's side and three lines to ours. Phillips visited me on Tuesday to tell me what had happened, but I knew that his account could not be objective. Now all that remained was to wait. Decisions generally took from six weeks to three months, so I set my sights on two months, March 10.

During this waiting period everything went flat. I

kept reading and re-reading the opinions on various cases which were cited in our brief and in the government's, having bound them into one volume, complete with index. But they were growing stale, and so was I. I dreamed a little of possible forms for reversal of the conviction. On the one hand the court might denounce the trial for what it truly was—a mockery of justice, and on the other, they might select a trivial "technicality" upon which to base their reversal, to avoid the real issues. Such dreamy dreams.

Although I had been refused a bench visit with the children I made another request in January and got another definitive refusal. I mentioned this to Captain Soares, and much to my surprise he told me to let him know the next time Helen came with the children and he would see if he could do something for me. I wrote Helen about it, and the next time she came I went down to see the captain, who escorted me past the high security gate out the "front," where the visitors registered. Here Helen, Mark, my mother and I all sat down on a real bench for a "bench visit," while the captain stood by at a distance. It was a thrill to sit and talk, with nothing between us. After about fifteen minutes the captain approached and asked if I wanted to get Mark something from the vending machine, giving me a coin. He knew that going over to the candy machine with Mark would be something meaningful for us to do together—more at that age than just talk.

Toward the end of the visit my mother took Mark aside so that Helen and I might be alone for a moment. There were visitors coming and going, but we were oblivious to them all as we sat on the bench, holding hands and looking into each other's eyes, only inches apart. It was a visit to be remembered.

By this time, I had so many different jobs and projects going that I was hardly ever in my cell, except to sleep. My letters to Helen were generally written in installments, whenever I had a spare moment. In addition to the 35 mm. film projector I also ran the 16 mm. projector which was used to show "fight films" to the inmates on rainy days. These were films of the historical boxing matches of years gone by. The men had seen them many times but I suppose to them it was no different than listening to a symphony was for me. I also showed training movies to the personnel, almost all of which were nonsense, completely unrelated to their jobs. I had uncovered an ancient Einthoven galvanometer electrocardiograph machine in the hospital and put it in working order; I installed a thermocouple temperature gauge in the smokestack of the boiler room, and got a flue gas analyzer for monitoring the operation of the oil burners. I didn't allow myself free time to brood about the Court of Appeals decision, but I learned that nine out of ten requests for *certiorari* (the technical term for the first stage of the appeal) to the Supreme Court were denied, and that almost every capital case was granted *certiorari*.

One day I solved a big mystery about the odd taste of the cream of wheat. It was really hominy grits, and corn does not taste like wheat. Later I discovered that grits instead of wheat was universal in the federal prisons, one aspect of their southern orientation. I began to receive the periodicals *Electronics* and *Scientific American,* each of which took me more than ten hours to read. I knew that if I remained imprisoned my engineering knowledge would be dated in a few years.

3

The Dice
Were Loaded

SIX weeks had passed since the oral argument, and I knew that the decision might be forthcoming any day but didn't think it likely for a few more weeks. I was wrong. The following Monday, as I passed the boiler room where a radio was playing, I heard that the conviction had been upheld, albeit with a dissent by Judge Jerome Frank. With the noise in the boiler room I couldn't hear very clearly. On the next news broadcast I learned that Frank had dissented only on my conviction; that Julius and Ethel's conviction had been unanimously upheld.

Late that afternoon I wrote Helen:

[T]he dice were loaded darling, from the moment we got Chase [the most reactionary of the three judges on our bench]. Having a dissent from Frank means that we are almost certain to have certiorari granted—sometime in June. Then it should be argued in November—and perhaps in January a decision will be forthcoming. Yes there would be a motion for a rehearing in the Court of Appeals. Guess it will be granted [a Freudian slip—I meant denied] What thoughts??? Well, that Pips [Mark] will be almost four before the Supreme Court hands down its deci-

sion; that if we were together now we'd cry and we'd feel better . . . it was good that the decision came down so soon, for the next weeks would have been difficult. Naturally, in all of this it becomes important to keep the historical perspective always in sight—otherwise it degenerates into a personal tragedy—which it isn't—or must not be allowed to become. But how can Pips understand that? Having passed one and a half years in prison, the prospect of another year isn't too frightening. I am a little worried about how Mama and Papa are taking it . . . what torment must be in the hearts of others [Ethel and Julius]. If you were here sweetheart, I'd know I'd just keep talking to you endlessly. We'd fall asleep in each other's warmth and rest—undisturbed by all. As is, we'll fall asleep knowing the depth of each other's love and the certainty that the well will never dry up—that its supply is almost infinite, to draw upon whenever we are thirsty—wherever we may be. Good night my sweet Helen, sleep softly tonight. Time goes on and we'll go on with it, as best we know. I love you.

The following day Helen came up from Washington. I was never so impressed with her strength and determination as during that visit, and she seemed more full of life than ever. She told me she planned to return to New York to participate in the growing movement to save Julius and Ethel from the electric chair; it was already quite late and there was no time to lose. Of course I agreed that that was the only thing she could do, even though I didn't see how she would support herself and the kids. We also discussed what I should do while the appeal was pending in the Supreme

Court; remain in New York or return to Atlanta. But in the end I wrote James V. Bennett, director of the Federal Bureau of Prisons, asking that, to facilitate visits with my father, I be sent to the penitentiary in Lewisburg; Helen promised to try to see Bennett when she returned to Washington. Several months later she sent me a poem she had written on the question of my returning to Atlanta or remaining in New York. It was one of the many poems she was to write over the years.

Atlanta

You ask me, my Morty,
What I think, and how I feel
About Atlanta.

I set my judgment to one side.
I answer full and free.

My darling, Atlanta is a jagged flint stone
Catapulted in soft flesh.
It is a napalm bomb adhering
Burning to my breast.
It is a hair shirt, a bed of nails,
The concentrated essence of the "wailing wall,"
The horror of the bridge of sighs,
And all this threatens you, my life,
And all this menaces you, my love.

Almost my psyche cannot bear it,
I exorcise it from my mind,
I hide it deep in unfrequented places.
I deny it.
If it should come to be
As once its shadow darkened through our lives,
I will not let it touch itself to me or mine.

This I know forever
Having probed each tender spot.

Choose our destiny, decide Atlanta now,
I shall find within, uncharted seas of courage,
Vast new fields of fortitude and strength.

But to me the crumb of here and now
Tenfold outweighs the bread of yet to be.
Monday after Monday makes a rosary
As we go from bead to prayered bead,
Telling visits for our living,
Absences for dying.

The passion of your unattenuated love
Melts the glass between our hands,
I need your spoken word, your smile.
As worlds crash to their dooms,
Yet let me love you here awhile.

Phillips came the following day with an advance copy of the opinion, which had cost him five dollars, and which he wanted to take back with him. I had to shame him into leaving it with me. It was an odd opinion, because even though Jerome Frank had written it for the majority, he dissented on the matter of my conviction. It was odd in still another respect. Toward the end there was a lengthy dissertation on the power of the Appeals Court to upset the death penalty; even though Frank came to the conclusion that the court could not overturn the death sentence, the other two judges did not want to be associated with this rather critical examination. (Less than ten years later the Appeals Court in Washington, D.C. sent back a case to the lower court for resentencing because they thought the sentence was too harsh.)

Frank thought I was entitled to a new trial because the government had failed to show that I was involved in any aspect of the atomic conspiracy, and was thus prejudiced. He felt that the jury could not properly weigh my alleged involvement in the smaller conspiracy (Julius and myself) because the atomic conspiracy was so overwhelming. Thus Phillips was vindicated for having pointed out to Kaufman in his bumbling way that the government's case had shown two conspiracies, not one, and that my case should have been severed from the "atomic conspiracy"; the two-conspiracy theory as it was called.

Frank was one of the most progressive judges, but all judges knew that they had to be conservative in political cases. Hadn't the trial judge in the first Alger Hiss trial (also a Kaufman) been attacked in Congress because the jury had failed to convict? After analyzing the opinion and seeing how the court had upheld the most blatant injustices perpetrated during the trial, I was brought back to an awareness of the completely political nature of the trial. Never again would I be as calm and optimistic as I had been for the three months before the appeal.

In less than two weeks Helen had moved to New York with Mark and gone to work for the newly formed National Committee to Secure Justice in the Rosenberg Case. During our next visit she told me of the efforts being made to get some of the underlying facts before the people—in the United States as well as abroad. However my attention was so firmly focused on the legal aspects of the case that I wasn't very responsive. I couldn't imagine a mass movement being built around the case in these frightening times. I knew Helen felt she had to do all in her power to promote such a movement, but I felt it was a lost cause. Most important, the legal aspect interested me more than the extra-legal because I could participate in the former struggle, helping in the formulation of the briefs, while I could do nothing in the other activity.

On Tuesday, April 8, as was expected, the Court of Appeals denied our motion for a re-hearing and the date for filing the petition for *certiorari* in the Supreme Court was set for June 7, sixty days later. Again I first learned about this from the radio. The Court of Appeals had stayed the mandates, which meant that the execution date for Ethel and Julius was stayed, and that until the Supreme Court handed down its decision, my "election" was still in force.

4　Only One Vote Out of Nine

THE next weeks were rough. April 11, 1952, I was thirty-five years old, and I received no birthday card from Helen. Usually I scoffed at Helen's sending me a card, but under these circumstances I was deeply hurt. She had apparently forgotten about me, her husband. She had become so involved with her committee work that she had forgotten what it was about—Julius, Ethel, and myself. The case had overshadowed the individuals. At least so I reasoned. I wrote her many letters and tore them up realizing they would be misconstrued; I had no desire to hurt Helen needlessly.

The next couple of times Helen visited, I unburdened myself to her; we were able to work things out—more or less—and the feeling of depression lessened. I was beginning to feel human. Then Helen came for a visit on the twenty-second of May. Even today I recall how she looked, dressed in a smart black suit. She looked dynamic, and most desirable. I hadn't planned it, it came out spontaneously: suddenly I asked "Helen, have you been sleeping with anyone?" Without a moment's hesitation she responded "I have." The shock was unlike anything I had ever before experienced. I was completely unprepared. Never, in my most despairing moments, did I dream that Helen would ever have sex with anyone while I was in prison—while I was still fighting to get out. In one single moment my sense of security was totally destroyed. For me her action represented hopelessness: I felt she must surely have thought I wouldn't get out of prison in the near future. I wished the earth would swallow me up; I didn't exist anymore.

I had been able to satisfy my own sex needs by masturbating, and it hadn't occurred to me that Helen wasn't able to do likewise. I was so completely smashed that I couldn't write her until the following day:

What can I say in this letter: that all—everything has seemed changed since yesterday. When I came upstairs it seemed to me that I was trying so hard to justify your conduct, too hard—darling. Basically I guess it was this wonderful sense of security I felt. I had heard others talking [about the infidelities of their wives]—and I smiled inwardly—smug-like. But it served to keep me aloft, riding as easily as one can ride these waves. Is it merely that it destroyed my sense of being different from the others? No! What then? Oh darling–what avails it to analyze–when the feelings are there . . . do you really think that one can intellectualize over the feelings? I asked myself— what are you seeking? You said, "to feel alive." What can I say to that? Look at the price! Why did I ask you sweet Helen? Because I expected to be reassured of course. Can't you see that your course is defeatism? . . . Where before I was fairly content to go down to Atlanta and to leave you, now the thought strikes terror through my being. Oh darling, I don't know what we can do now. What am I expecting of

you—the impossible? You know I love you more than
ever, and you know why I do—I guess. What else?

That evening I received the letter which Helen
had written after the visit, and it was strange, because
although I disagreed with most of it, it had the effect of
partly relieving the terrible anxiety which had pursued
me since we parted. And what was more I was relieved
that Helen's letter could still have such an effect on me,
that her magic still worked. I began to sob, and by late
evening, for the first time in my adult life, I was really
crying. The night guard must have observed me, because the next morning Kenton called me into his office, with an air of concern for my well-being. I knew
that he must know what it was about because he, not
the regular mail censor, was censoring our letters
(wherever I went I had a special censor; they evidently
felt they could not rely on the regular one). I gave him
no information, since I knew it would only be used
against me at an opportune moment, but responded
courteously to his questions and indicated he need
have no concern that I might commit suicide.

After several days passed my primary complaint to
Helen became that she hadn't discussed the whole
question with me before entering into sexual relations
with another man. Her response was that she sought to
save me the pain, and I was certain that she never
thought to lie to me. The days dragged, one by one, and
my heart ached as never before. I tried to bury myself
in work or sleep and for the first time I understood
some of Dostoevski's characters: I felt like them.

After the Court of Appeals handed down its opinion, Howard worked on the petition to the Supreme
Court. His initial draft was terrible; rambling, without a

viewpoint, and what was worse, it treated Frank's dissent in an off-hand fashion, and Frank's dissent was the
strongest thing I had going for me. Of course it didn't
help Ethel and Julius, but that was no reason not to
utilize it to the fullest. I learned later that the first drafts
are only working papers, nothing more. On May 26,
when I got the final version of the petition I was glad to
see a ten-fold improvement. By this time my sugges-
tions had much more substance, and I was gratified to
see that some of them had been incorporated. The following day Howard visited and we had a long conference, discussing the petition and the question of how to
go about getting an eminent lawyer to argue the case in
the unlikely event *certiorari* were granted. I also
brought up the question of bail, to which Howard
reacted negatively, albeit with restraint. Actually the
idea of getting out on bail now was silly, because it certainly would have been set above the previous one
hundred thousand dollars, if granted. All I knew was
that I wanted to be out, so that Helen didn't have to
feel that she had to go elsewhere for sustenance, so that
we could talk together—endlessly. I was astonished,
when, later, Helen told me that she had interpreted my
first reaction as one of rejection. How dreadfully wrong
she had been. By this time I had managed to calm my
letters, but my heartache was as painful as ever: it
ached worse than any physical pain I had ever experienced.

As legal paupers, Ethel, Julius, and I could have
gone to the Supreme Court with several typewritten
copies of the trial transcript, but then not all nine
judges would have had ready access to the material.
The Committee decided to print the record with enough copies to go around. Since the complete record

was more than seventeen hundred pages long it cost more than ten thousand dollars. Initially the money was raised by loans from a few friends, which was repaid when the Committee began to receive money from many people concerned that a grave injustice had been perpetrated.

The final date I now had to look forward to was October 13, when the Supreme Court would reconvene after the summer recess and hand down decisions on all the accumulated cases. In the meantime I felt it was imperative to find a good prominent attorney who would be willing to argue the case. Helen had put a lot of energy into the search, with little to show for it. All those she had approached had turned her down without even discussing the question of the fee, which we knew would be considerable. They didn't want any part of an "atomic" conspiracy. However, she did find one attorney in Philadelphia, Thomas McBride, who after hearing her told her to come back if *certiorari* were granted. We took this to be a commitment, even if it wasn't absolute. It was better than the rejections Helen had been getting.

When Helen first told me that she had had sexual intercourse with another man she had refused to tell me who he was. As the weeks went by I found this intolerable, since it indicated that she didn't trust me. She promised me that she would not continue—at least not until we reached some sort of understanding. She felt that, in the circumstances, I should offer her *carte blanche.*

I should have liked to be noble, to tell Helen I had faith in her, that she had *carte blanche,* but I didn't have the strength. Actually it was not primarily the idea of Helen's having sexual intercourse with another man that disturbed me, so much as the danger I felt it posed for our future relationship. This might be the first step away from me. Another disturbing thought was that Helen might have another child by someone else. I knew it was irrational to be frightened by this, and yet I felt powerless to see it in proper perspective. It was as though having a child by another man would somehow put Mark in danger, or at least diminish him as a human being. After about a month we began to have some meaningful communication on the subject, and after I spent most of one visit demonstrating that her reluctance to reveal the name was absolutely untenable, she wrote me in her next letter that she would tell me who it was at the following visit. The relief I felt when I received this letter was almost mystical. I wept tears of relief and joy. It was an anti-climax, when during the next visit she told me it was R. The most difficult part of the crisis was over.

I would frequently awaken before dawn, mind hyperactive, and think about all manner of things, some connected with Helen and some on a more general plane. One morning, after about two hours of such furious mental activity, I became frightened. It seemed to me that everything I thought about had become arbitrary; I could justify any position I took on any question, even contradictory positions. I no longer knew what was right and what was wrong. How could I possibly go on, I asked myself, if I could not find a sound basis for the position I took. I knew that as soon as I got up and started moving about, everything would straighten itself out, but I wondered if this happened while I was in Atlanta, should I then be able to straighten things out? With one visit a month, at most, and three letters a week? Letters that took about ten days to make a round trip? Here I was writing Helen a letter a day, getting a response within four or five days at most, and seeing her every week. Without such communication I knew I would find it difficult to keep my equilibrium.

I knew I wasn't on a level keel because from time to time, for no apparent reason, small irrationalities threw me off balance, such as Helen's beginning to call me "pal," during one visit. It offended me deeply. On another occasion she began to sign her letters "your wife," to me a term of estrangement. However when she explained that she was trying to convey just the opposite, a sense of closeness, I accepted the explanation. I recognized the delicacy involved and tried, unsucessfully, to determine what was taking place within me. When Helen spoke of *carte blanche,* I asked her to bare her soul to me: I sensed that she was withholding much that she had felt when she had taken that fateful step. Such was the tension.

When Kenton took a two-week vacation in June, Franciscus, who was much more of a human being, took his place, so I told Helen to be freer in what she wrote me during this period. I expanded my own letters from the officially limited two pages to four, knowing they would be passed. It wasn't so much that I needed four pages to say what I had to say, rather it was the satisfaction I got while actually writing the letter; it was the next best thing to talking with Helen. I also began to read and re-read Helen's letters of the past. The past month, two months, the past year. This helped to put the present situation in better perspective. If I couldn't go off at a distance to see the present, at least I could look at the past from a distance; the present. And suddenly I became aware of an enormous truth: "the future determines the past." I found it remarkable that I had never before encountered this. Of course, since then I found it expressed by others, Jean-Paul Sartre, for one. It was obvious to me that one can only understand a period by looking at it from the vantage point of the future—after time has had its chance. Heroes can become villains, and good, evil, with the passage of time. The present was only a transient phase of history, so loaded with "noise" as to be undecipherable. When events are looked at from a distance in time, the noise smooths out and the important events stand out. I was amazed at my discovery, and how I had made it. If only we were aware of it, we would waste less effort interpreting present events.

During this period I frequently asked myself if trying to live on both sides of the bars was not impossible. On the one hand I had told Helen to tell me everything that went on outside, big and small things. I wanted to be able to evaluate them all. I wanted to feel that I was still Helen's husband, in more than name. And yet I knew that I could not fulfill the responsibilities. And I also had my own life within prison, a separate existence which I had to make sure would not become intolerable. If it did, then everything else would be meaningless. The question that plagued me was whether this double existence was in fact possible without tearing myself and Helen apart. For the moment I found no clear answer. But this was the beginning of a long dialogue with myself which never ceased the whole time I was in prison, and always came down to the question of the double life: was it possible? Was it desirable? I decided in the affirmative, even when it created turmoil within me. So many times it would have been easier for me to withdraw from the outside world, saving Helen and me much suffering.

It wasn't rational, but this was my style: the way I wanted to live. To have lived more than eighteen years *inside* prison would have meant the death of Morton Sobell as a human being.

I began to realize that there might be little time left for such close contact between Helen and me. If I was shipped to Atlanta after the Supreme Court decision visits would be sparse, and even letter writing would not have the same fluency. With this in mind I appealed to Helen to make this period an idyll, one we could both look back at with satisfaction: we had to extract every last ounce we could out of the situation, while it lasted. In a way it was strange, trying to turn the present situation into one I could look back at and dream about as a happiness for both of us. But I was always a relativist and didn't feel it was as ludicrous as it might have appeared. And Helen understood. Yet each time Helen was due for a visit I was filled with terrifying, all but unbearable anxiety, as the hour of her visit approached, as though she might not come, ever, though these thoughts never entered my consciousness. When I heard my name called to report to the visiting room, the relief was not unlike an orgasm.

When I wrote Helen about my feelings (which I didn't want to bring up during visits because I feared they might prevent a free exchange of emotion) she replied, "Don't worry Morty, I will always be waiting." I cried when I read these words, yet the thought of such self-sacrifice revolted me. Life had become so filled with contradictions that I could no longer reason. Time and again we reached the same conclusion, that it was a mistake to look ahead, that we had to live in the present.

As I said, our next meaningful date was October 13 when the Supreme Court reconvened. From now on we would live from crisis to crisis to crisis, yet we both really began to enjoy our visits as never before. Once I was in the visiting room, my anxiety relieved, we soared skyward, achieving heights of ecstasy that properly should not have been ours. This state of affairs was quickly cut short when toward the end of June the FBI came to see how I was doing. They didn't ask *me*, but instead examined all the records and questioned the guards. When they saw in the log book of the visiting room that my visits were running an hour or even longer, they issued strict orders that I was not to have a second more than thirty minutes a week. Thus when Helen came on June 23 the visiting room officer, who had evidently been frightened by the FBI, tearfully explained what had happened making sure that I understood that this was not his doing.

But cutting down on the visit was only the beginning. On July 10 I received the first of the letters signed "a friend." Although my list of approved correspondents did not include anyone by that name, Kenton had passed the letter. "A friend" told me Helen was being "unfaithful" to me. It was at once obvious that since the letter had passed Kenton, it could only have originated from an official source, like the FBI. It was also apparent that the letter was not referring to the affair Helen had had, since it was couched in general terms. Knowing all this, and being rational, I wish I could say that the letter had absolutely no effect. But it did affect me deeply—although not as deeply as the perpetrators might have wished. I knew that Helen was not having an affair at this time; she had assured me of this. And yet the letter filled me with generalized anxiety. At our next visit Helen and I both laughed at the letter. It was so clumsily done. A week later I received a second similar letter from "a friend," with added elaboration. Again it affected me and I felt the shame of reacting so deeply, to such an obvious provocation. But I showed nothing of this in my letters to Helen because I knew my mail would be closely examined for such a reaction.

Within a week there was a third letter. This one was different: it contained details of Helen's infidelity. The previous week she had gone to speak about the case at a summer camp. Helen had told me about it at our visit. "A friend" told me Helen had been driven there by a black man, they had gone into a cabin together and hadn't emerged for several hours.

It was grossly overplayed. The letter was obviously written by a racist who also took me for one. I felt insulted, and this time not at all anxious—which made me very happy. Howard happened to be visiting me the following day and I took the letter out with my legal papers and showed it to him. We both had a good laugh, dissecting the FBI's racist mentality.

The following week when a fourth letter came, Kenton had the effrontery to try to hand it to me personally, and I enjoyed handing it back unopened saying he could keep it. Of course I should have liked to say more, but while he could hand me a poison-pen letter with impunity, I couldn't call him a son of a bitch—not without being punished for it one way or another.

The letters from "a friend" were not the first attempt by the authorities to split Helen and me. Beginning around March or April, a fellow inmate, John D.

Walker, who was called John D. for short, began to work on me, though it wasn't apparent at that time. In almost every conversation he pursued a general misogynistic line. I thought nothing of it at the time, since it was true that a woman had put him in prison so to speak. He married wealthy widows and made off with their fortunes, assuming that they would be too embarrassed to testify against him. However he now stood convicted under a federal statute making it a felony to transport illegally acquired money across state lines. The widow had testified against him in New York, well away from her home town.

I would listen politely, thinking he was simply relieving his feelings. But then he became more specific: all women were unfaithful—without exception. Even then, I still didn't grasp immediately that his talk was aimed at me. John D. had been assigned to the library, which gave him much spare time to work on his legal writs. He was a fairly competent prison lawyer, and was working hard on his appeal. However when he ran out of money and couldn't buy any more legal opinions, he got a paying job as an inmate clerk in the kitchen and frequently brought me such food as canned tuna or meat. I looked at it as an act of friendship, although I couldn't see why he should have chosen to bestow his largesse on me. I certainly couldn't give him anything in return, and despite his name I knew he wasn't a philanthropist. Then one day toward the end of July I heard him called to report to the front office. About half an hour later I was also called to the front office. Kenton had some papers for me from my lawyer. While with Kenton I glanced at the warden's office and saw John D. there with two men whom I recognized as FBI agents I had seen there before.

Later, when I told John D. that I had seen him out in the warden's office, he said he had been speaking with some men from the United States Attorney's office, who had come to talk over some matters concerning his conviction. I didn't say anything, but it became obvious to me that John D.'s fulminations against women were directed from above. There were other indications that he had been given this special assignment. I learned that on one occasion when he had been shaken down and caught with a can of tuna and some tomatoes, no action had been taken against him—nor did he cease bringing me food as would have seemed prudent. It seemed to me as though this too was a part of the scheme. I didn't let my knowledge change our relationship, but in the end I couldn't resist playing a prank on him. One of the officers who liked to play the good-guy thought he had my confidence, so I "confided" in him that John D. was working with the FBI. And about three days later an agitated John D. told me exactly what I had told the officer. I looked him straight in the eye and asked, "John, you don't think I'd say a thing like that. Can't you see, they're trying to make enemies out of us?" After that we remained on the best of terms, but he dropped his unfaithfulness line. I think he understood.

I don't know exactly what the authorities hoped to achieve by cutting my visits with Helen to thirty minutes, but evidently they were disappointed with the lack of results, and on Wednesday, July 16 the axe really fell. I was working in the darkroom, when my supervisor called me out. After putting the prints I was developing into the fixer, so they wouldn't be spoiled, I opened the door and another officer, Zeiss, told me to follow him downstairs to the captain's office. Here

Zeiss told me that I was no longer to be a photographer. I was told to return to my cell at once!

I wasn't shocked, because I had been expecting additional pressures. Besides, I rationalized, it was all to the good. Psychologically I might previously have needed such a job, but now I could use the time to my own advantage. That evening I was transferred to a high security cell, so called because it was located next to the desk of the night guard, with an all-night lamp hanging close by. This was a nuisance.

Several days later, when I asked Kenton why I had been removed from my job, he said that I had been insulating myself, living in a "dream world," and he thought it would be best to bring me back to reality. He was doing his part, he said. The rest was now up to me. There was an element of truth in what he said, by keeping busy at my job I had had less time to think about my situation. This was, of course what he wanted me to do, think about my situation.

To make certain that I didn't lose myself in any of my minor jobs, these were also taken away—all of them—and I was back mopping the floor for fifteen minutes a day. However, after several weeks in the high security cell I was moved back to a regular cell. I concluded that someone in Washington had issued some kind of general directive, to bear down on me, which the local people were trying very hard to interpret.

On Monday, Helen and I responded with a joyous visit. We always drew closer together in the face of additional pressure, as if to show we could not be split asunder by such tactics. We were aware that only we ourselves would be responsible for any split. It was a fast thirty minutes, superficially traversing much territory, leaving the digestion for later, when we were alone and had more time. Helen had visited Sydney at summer camp that weekend, and had gone to a parents' social in the evening, but had had to walk out. Seeing all the other married couples together was more than she could bear.

About a week later I was told to report to the warden's office. Here I was invited to sit down and listen to the warden himself tell me that I would be shipped to Alcatraz as soon as the Supreme Court had denied our petition. After the stick came the carrot: if I cooperated with the FBI, he said, I might avoid Alcatraz.

Howard happened to visit the following day; when I told him what had taken place he had no response. It was a measure of the times, that none of my lawyers suggested going to court to attack the government for its blatantly illegal threats. This is not to say that the courts would have done anything, but acquiescence was absolutely defeatist, and it never even occurred to me that anything could or should be done.

A short while later James V. Bennett came up to New York, to attend the funeral of an FBI agent who had been shot, and when I heard that he was going to stop by West Street I put in a request slip for an interview. It was granted. When I asked him about the Alcatraz threat he told me "Surely they wouldn't send a man like you to Alcatraz." What could I say to this? But during the following weeks I kept hearing about Alcatraz from officials as well as inmates. It was all vague, usually "I heard . . ." Where had he heard? Just a rumor. Obviously someone was at work spreading the rumor. For the next month nothing more happened, except for the continuing rumors.

Thompson, the warden, was a queer duck. Once

when Howard was with me, he burst into our visit waving a wrist watch, telling Howard he had just received it from the Bureau for twenty-five years meritorious service. As if Howard gave a damn. Thompson had a sick wife in an institution, and a severely retarded son who was also institutionalized. Thompson himself lived in the bachelor's officer's quarters—wooden housing erected on the roof of the prison (it would have been illegal if this had not been federal property).

That summer Warden Thompson brought his son to live with him, entrusting him twelve hours daily to the care of John D. The boy was about twelve or thirteen. No one seemed to think it strange that a warden should treat his son in this manner, but his behavior was also strange in other ways. One Sunday night he brought his girl friend to the prison to watch the Sunday night inmate movie instead of taking her to a movie outside the prison where he would have had to pay for the tickets. I was amazed that he had risked possible censure from higher quarters, to save a few pennies. Or was it perhaps that he was only trying to impress his date with his position? Whatever the reason I didn't think it was a responsible act.

Jack Friedus was the first engineer I encountered in prison. He was returned from Lewisburg Penitentiary, where he was doing time for income tax evasion, in connection with another charge against him. Although he was a chemical engineer we found we had a great deal of common engineering interest. I found our association stimulating, and was able to resume study. I began with a text he had, *Applied Engineering Math,* and lost myself in it, spending whole mornings working on the problems. The authorities tried to take advantage of our relationship and approached Jack to use his influence to get me to cooperate. He promptly reported this to me. Had he been as stupid or unscrupulous as John D. he might have tried to con me, hoping to be rewarded with an early parole. I missed his company when he went back to Lewisburg.

Even though with no job I had a lot of free time, I wasn't able to read much. Somehow I couldn't get interested in books. I tried Rachel Carson's much praised best seller, *The Sea Around Us,* but found it too dry, crammed with undigested facts. *A Tree Grows in Brooklyn* proved moderately interesting, but I couldn't understand the wide acclaim. I tried reading something by Pierre Van Passen, but found I couldn't stomach him. I enjoyed Erich Marie Remarque's *The Arch of Triumph* with its World War II European background. Perhaps it was the empathy I felt for his characters, refugees of all kinds trying to flee Europe before Hitler could seize them. I had always thought of Remarque as a one novel author, *All Quiet On The Western Front, the* anti-war novel of my generation. Later I read his other novels and enjoyed them equally, but wondered how authentic they were. He made even the grimiest aspects of existence seem romantic.

Even though it was the middle of the summer, when everything usually slowed down in New York, Helen was working harder than ever. Meetings, meetings, meetings, day and night, trying to organize a large protest movement to head off the scheduled execution of the Rosenbergs. Morton Sobell of course was in the background, since his life was not in immediate jeopardy. But his wife had special standing in the organizing efforts, since he had been tried with Julius and Ethel. I couldn't help Helen in her activities, but tried to participate vicariously. When she told me that she was up to four and five night meetings a week, I asked her to slow down. Not only was I concerned that her health might suffer, but I was also worried about Mark's reactions, with no father and almost no mother. I asked Helen to give me an outline of her activities at the start of each week, telling myself and her that this was so I could better follow her schedule. But I wasn't entirely sure of my own reasons. I derived a certain satisfaction from knowing that tonight she was speaking in the upper Bronx around Mosholu Parkway and that the next night she would be speaking in lower Manhattan near where I had once lived as a child.

Frequently Helen didn't have time to sit down and write a letter. Instead she would dash off a note while on the subway or the bus. These notes pleased me greatly for somehow they transmitted a feeling of her hectic pace. On the other hand, when Helen was too busy to write a full length letter, and substituted a brief note, I would feel cheated—unless she specifically mentioned that this was only a short note. I realized that my own reactions were illogical and gradually became more and more aware of the limits of reason. The same pattern appeared when Helen did not write me for several days. If she noted the lapse in a subsequent letter I was satisfied, but if she seemed oblivious to the hiatus I would become greatly upset. I knew this was silly—and yet . . .

I had been urging Helen all summer to take a vacation. She finally agreed to go away with Mark for two weeks, but not until I had assured her that I could maintain my equilibrium even though we would have to forgo one weekly visit. When she visited me on August 18 we both felt we had to cram enough to last for the two weeks we would be apart. A good visit, like a work of art, had several elements. We could have a good visit even if Helen were tired from overwork or lack of sleep, but it wouldn't have the same quality as when she was vibrantly alive. During a good visit Helen related the "battle front" highlights of the previous week, as well as a couple of stories about Mark, Sydney, and herself. Then she told me the plans for the following week, the scheduled meetings and conferences. Then we would discuss any legal problems which had arisen since our last visit, things we had discussed in our letters, which required clarification. Sometimes we might get into one of those unending discussions on faith versus reason, or other abstract philosophical subjects. And last of all was our love making. Helen would tell me about our last "date," which we tried to schedule for the night before the visit so it would still be fresh in her mind's eye. And while she related to me all that had transpired, going into minute details, I would gaze as she slowly unbuttoned her blouse. The various forms we invented for love making over the telephone and through the glass pane were endless. We treated the situation as a challenge to our ingenuity. Without the love making the visit was terribly unsatisfying, as I had found out on several occasions.

The August 18 visit was good. The object was to rush through the visit, touching all bases, and yet make it seem like a leisurely stroll with all the time in the world. Of course it was self-deception, as we both knew. I had given Helen detailed instructions on how I wanted her to pose for photographs she was to take during her vacation. In one I asked her to stand feet apart, arms akimbo, in the classic stance of defiance. She carried this off to perfection, and I kept the resulting photograph until the day of my release.

My parents visited while Helen was away and it pained me to see my father in such a condition without being able to do anything for him. He was like the shadow of the father I had once known; he just didn't seem to be all there. I would have given anything to spend a day with him.

August 22, 1952 was the twenty-fifth anniversary of the culmination of another political trial. On that 1927 August day, a shoemaker and a fish peddler had been executed. I was unable to find a single word about the Sacco-Vanzetti case in any newspaper—and I wondered how history would treat us.

There was a joyous reunion when Helen and the children visited me on Monday, September 1. I was glad to see Helen looking well tanned and rested. Of course a family visit didn't allow us time for our usual formula, but it had its own satisfying quality. I seemed to detect an improvement in Mark's diction since our last visit, but felt it had been too short a time for any change.

The cycle was about to begin all over again. It was Labor Day and the inmate movie season started with *A Streetcar Named Desire.* In the summer of 1947, when we moved to New York, Helen and I had seen the play. I was deeply moved at the time, perhaps because it reminded of my cousin Rose who was then in a mental institution. Now the movie hardly touched me. In fact I found it dull.

I had been trying without success to get a copy of the trial transcript. Only a dozen "extra" copies were printed and I hadn't rated high on the list. Finally I received one that someone else must have given up; it was annoyingly and sloppily underlined. The record was handsomely printed in two huge volumes totalling over seventeen-hundred pages. I began with Elitcher's testimony. Since it was still fresh in my mind I had only to scan it. It didn't raise my blood pressure one milli-meter, but reading the inane and ineffective cross-ex-amination conducted by my counsel disturbed me anew. It confirmed my impression of what had taken place. It was at this time that I discovered what had happened at those bench conferences, which were held out of the hearing of the jury, but which also tuned out the defendants. The testimony of Greenglass and his wife bored me. It didn't add up to the story it was sup-posed to tell. I skimmed most of the testimony the first time I went through it, until I came to Saypol's cross-examination of Ethel—poor Ethel. And I suffered again over her crucifixion.

For more than ten years, wherever I went, I kept these two volumes with me. I wasn't always permitted to keep them in my cell but they were always available. They were the basic text for all the subsequent appeals, and there were parts of the testimony that I must have read and re-read hundreds of times, trying to find a subtle point I might have missed, or trying to clear up some ambiguity. It was the testimony of the physicist Walter S. Koski and of General Grove's messenger boy, John A. Derry, which intrigued me the most, because here lay the heart of the government's case, open for ex-amination.

With October 13 rapidly approaching I found my-self ever more desperately trying to experience life, which meant visits and letters. Thirty minutes of visit-ing a week and one two-page letter daily, as the rules permitted. In my letters I no longer talked about the place or the food or the people. I had told Helen all there was to tell; the characters and the situation remained the same, only the actors changed. As the new men arrived, the old ones were shipped off to the various prisons around the country.

Then on September 10 Kenton called me into his office and informed me that I was writing too many letters, that henceforth he would restrict me to four letters a week. But he didn't say he was doing this for my own good; he said this was the rule. When I told him that I knew of many men who were writing more than seven letters a week, he denied it and challenged me to name someone. I was on the spot: to name an individual might result in his letter writing being curtailed. Fortunately I remembered an inmate who had been writing over fifteen letters a week (we had all joked about it) and who had been shipped out a few days earlier. When I named this inmate Kenton didn't even bother referring to the letter log, but denied it out of hand. The whole situation was straight out of Kafka whom I hadn't yet read.

Kenton must have been reading stories about medieval torture; eight days later he again called me in to say that the new limit was three letters a week. This time I didn't say a word. Why give him the satisfaction of seeing me squirm? And the following day he told me that Helen's letters were "too erotic for your own good." This was strange. He wasn't complaining about my letters, but about Helen's. And yet he was complaining to me. It was of course true that Helen's letters were, in part, erotic. She was trying to please me, but he couldn't direct the complaint to her, because she was free. I dutifully relayed the message to her in my letters, but privately told her not to let it disturb her style.

Kenton's efforts to put pressure on me were only

partly successful. Initially, when I lost my photography job, as well as all the other odd jobs, my movements around the prison were restricted: I wasn't allowed to leave the third floor, except for meals. But with the passage of time I managed to get back many of my small jobs, and my movements were no longer restricted. In general I didn't feel the pressure from the hacks which had been manifested initially. This was the way West Street operated: a directive would come down from on high, but time eroded it. Only machines could maintain a steady alert, not human beings.

I don't remember how I passed the few weeks before October 13 but I know I spent the evenings playing bridge, a game for which I had a marked ineptitude. At least I lost myself while I was playing. Quinn, a chemist who had been convicted for illegally exporting controlled commodities, had just come up from Atlanta, and was usually my partner. He must have had a lot of patience to suffer me.

Kenton never lost an opportunity to needle me. He called me into his office to inform me that I had received Rosh Hashanah greeting cards from friends, but that since none of the friends were on my approved list he wouldn't let me see the greetings. I didn't point out his lack of consistency in having given me those letters from "a friend" who wasn't on my list of approved correspondents. Several days afterwards he again called me in to explain that I would be shipped out immediately after *certiorari* was denied. There was no if. He must have had an inside wire to the Supreme Court.

With all the tension of the approaching deadline Helen and I remained fairly stable. Yet on several occasions things went awry, as when she visited me the week before the decision, chewing gum. This had never happened before and it annoyed me. The more it annoyed me, the more vigorously Helen chewed. Part of the conflict lay in my lack of interest in the Committee's efforts. To Helen the Committee was everything, personally and otherwise. She was putting countless hours and energy into the death and life fight, but when she tried to tell me about it I told her not to consume precious minutes giving me all the details. I recognized my absurdity even as I told her this, but I wasn't going to feign an interest where it didn't exist. I knew that the Committee was paying Howard's fees as well as the printing bill: we had long since run out of money. In fact after the trial we had had to rely on relatives for the twenty-five hundred dollars to pay Howard for his work on the Court of Appeals brief. But the essential work of the Committee, trying to stave off the execution, hadn't really gotten through to me. I never even considered the possibility that the Committee might also help cut my thirty years.

Two days after the chewing gum visit Helen got permission for a special ten minute visit, ostensibly to discuss a brief for a subsequent motion, which she had left for me. It was the most wonderful ten minutes we had ever spent together. All the tensions of the previous visit were dissolved.

Four votes are needed to get *certiorari* in the Supreme Court. This means that at least four of the nine judges think that, for whatever reason, the case merits their examination. We got exactly one vote—Justice Douglas's. Despite Justice Jerome Frank's previous dissent the other eight judges apparently did not feel that there was any question about the conviction; they could hardly have granted me *certiorari* and denied Julius and Ethel. It was all one case.

Almost immediately after the news, I had a bench visit with Helen and Howard. Howard was good that way; he told the officials there were essential legal questions which we *all* had to discuss. When I first greeted Helen I kissed her, but stiffly and without emotion since this was supposed to be a business visit and I was afraid that Kenton might reprimand me if my kiss was too emotional. I disliked giving him any opportunity for a reprimand. At first I thought Helen looked unwell, but as we began to talk, her face lighted up until it radiated a strong beauty I had never before seen. We talked, almost casually, about what the denial meant, for me and for Julius and for Ethel. Howard told me he had fifteen days in which to submit a petition for rehearing, a meaningless formality, after which, within a couple of weeks, the Court would hand down its ultimate denial.

The only thing I felt about the decision was a mild, smoldering anger that we had gotten only *one* vote. That evening I played bridge as usual. None of the men around me made any reference to the denial, but it was there. When I went to bed I thought of Helen—and I cried a little before I fell asleep.

Howard came again on Wednesday and told me that the mandate had been stayed, which meant that the execution was put off until the Court had its final word. We also discussed the material which would be included in the section 2255 motion that would be filed after the Supreme Court had had its final say.

Title 28 of the United States Code, Section 2255 was the federal equivalent of the old habeas corpus. In it one was not limited, as on the direct appeal, to those things which had been taken up at the trial; on the other hand, the burden of proof on the defendant was much more severe than on the direct appeal. Before I would be free my lawyers would file seven or eight such 2255 motions, each of which would be unsuccessfully appealed to the Court of Appeals and then to the Supreme Court.

There was no mystery in the Court's decision not to hear the case. Had they heard it they would have been compelled to write an opinion, which would have taken time and further delayed the execution. The public clamor might well have been too great to go ahead with the execution. Vinson, the chief justice, undoubtedly saw that the validation of the cold war policy required the immediate execution of Julius and Ethel; he was more noted as a politician than a judge. And as Justice Frankfurter was so fond of saying, by denying *certiorari,* the court did not pass on the merits of the case.

With the death sentence for Julius and Ethel closer in time and probability, the Committee's tempo increased, which meant that Helen's limit of four nightly meetings a week fell by the wayside. How could one explain that the only reason Ethel was tried, and sentenced to death, was to put added pressure on Julius? I don't think one person in a thousand really understood the flimsiness of the evidence brought against her. Surely it was not enough to warrant the death penalty.

As *we* were suffering the full measure of American justice, John Provoo, a United States army sergeant in World War II, accused of having collaborated with the Japanese, was tried for treason. The courtesy and consideration he received contrasted amazingly with our treatment. The court provided him with the two best attorneys available, attorneys who had participated in the Japanese War Crimes trials; they gave him a list of prosecution witnesses well enough ahead of trial time to allow his attorneys to interview them. The jury convicted him, but the Court of Appeals reversed the verdict on a "technicality." In his case there was no fear of political repercussions from Congress. We had both received equal justice under the law only his justice was a little more equal.

Our next visit was filled with sadness—but not a hopeless sadness. We knew we had arrived at the crucial point. But we were there—together and alove [*sic*]. I told Helen that if there were any way, I would willingly take Ethel's place. For me the greatest horror of the case was that our government was about to orphan two children.

A couple of days later I had still another bench conference with Helen and Howard on the projected 2255 motion. I thought I detected a certain hardening in Helen's demeanor since our previous conference. She seemed to be more sure of herself and had an almost executive attitude. It was at this conference that we both agreed on one of the basic premises which was to guide us for the duration of the struggle: one doesn't only fight battles, one expects to win—there are matters of principle which must also be fought for, no matter how hopeless the outlook. Helen told me that with the denial of *certiorari*, it was now easier to gather support for Julius and Ethel, for there were many who thought the death sentence savage, guilty or not. But when she told me she wouldn't have time to write very much that week, I became angry, despite the fact that I knew how busy she would be. I was annoyed with myself, that I found it difficult to keep a balanced viewpoint.

Kuntz came to discuss a motion for the reduction of sentence, which would have to be filed within sixty days of the Supreme Court's final word. I thought the whole thing silly; it was inconceivable that Kaufman would lessen my sentence, when he had plainly said he wished he could have given me more time than the thirty years the law allowed. Anyway I did not want to beg Kaufman for anything. But I sat on my feelings, as I had done so many other times, and let Kuntz draw up the motion.

As a result of my law reading I had developed a theory under which I could only have been sentenced to twenty years, not thirty. When I outlined this to Kuntz he pooh-poohed the idea. Ten years later another lawyer filed a 2255 motion based on my theory— whether the evidence the government presented against me was so unambiguous that the jury must have concluded that my participation in the conspiracy took place in time of war. The statute under which we were convicted allowed a twenty year maximum if the espionage did not take place during war time. We lost the motion, but not because the theory was bad: the Court was hard pressed to justify its denial. Anway it was a good fight which I enjoyed.

The Alcatraz rumors suddenly started again. I began to hear them from all sides; inmates, hacks, and lieutenants. Captain Soares told me he couldn't understand why they would want to send me to Alcatraz, and I knew he was being sincere, and I told him that not everyone was like him.

The next time Kuntz visited, I broached the question of my protesting their threat of Alcatraz by undertaking a hunger strike. Of my three lawyers he was supposed to be the political one. I hadn't raised the question with Helen because I didn't want to subject her to the conflicts which such a question would most certainly give rise to. Eddie was non-committal and told me he would consult with others.

At the next visit he reported that everyone he had discussed it with felt it would not be useful for me to undertake such action, and I acquiesced. Many years later on the Rock, during one of my sleepless nights, I suddenly realized what must have taken place. Kuntz had probably consulted Manny Bloch, who must have felt that any action I took might de-focus attention from Julius and Ethel, and thus hinder the struggle to save their lives. It hadn't occurred to me to undertake a hunger strike against Eddie's judgment because I felt I would need the whole-hearted support of everyone outside. I had no illusions about my own strength, and always sought to avoid any action which I did not feel I could carry through to a creditable conclusion.

Our visit on Monday, October 27 was not one of our happiest, but it left me with a very solid, secure feeling. However I wished I could better appreciate the work that Helen was doing for the Committee. Ironically, when the movement to halt the execution really started to burgeon, I was already on the Rock and could hear nothing about it, cut off as I was from all newspapers and the radio, and with the weekly news magazines heavily censored.

On Tuesday Kenton again called me into his office to "promise" that I would be shipped away from West Street "sooner than you think." Ordinarily prison officials try to keep intended inmate movements secret, and in this case the notice that was given me was obviously not designed merely to keep me informed.

On Sunday, November 2, I had a forty-five minute visit with the whole family: Helen, the children, and my parents; as much time as the other men had. Perhaps the discrimination would have been too obvious if I had been asked to leave before another inmate who had come down earlier than I. Or perhaps sufficient time had elapsed since the FBI's visit, so that the visiting room officer no longer felt their pressure. But the visit left me unsatisfied, as did all big family visits, when I had to spend a few minutes with everyone instead of seeing Helen alone. It was a sacrifice, not one that I was happy about, and one that I probably shouldn't have made.

Meanwhile I half-believed that I would be shipped away before the mandate came down. I had met an inmate from Boston who had been illegally sent to Lewisburg while his "election" was still supposed to be in force. I knew the prison authorities would try anything they thought they could get away with.

Friday, November 14 was a memorable day. The commissary finally had apples, and I bought a dozen nice red juicy delicious apples for which I had been hungering a very long time.

I learned from the radio, shortly after noon on Monday, November 17, that the Supreme Court had denied our petition for a rehearing. This was hardly unexpected. Within an hour I was called to report to the front office. Kenton told me to take a seat and got right to the point: I would be shipped to Alcatraz "at once." I don't know what sort of reaction he expected, but I simply laughed at him. Something in his manner amused me, and there was no longer any reason for me to restrain myself. He dismissed me at once.

That evening, after supper, I received another call to the front office. This was highly unusual, since everyone in the front office had presumably gone home by this time. Everyone but the warden, it turned out.

He was there with a telegram in his hand, which he shoved under my nose. It read "Send Sobell to Alcatraz as soon as is expeditiously possible," Signed, James V. Bennett. Evidently Kenton, when I laughed at him, must have thought that I thought he was bluffing. Now the warden himself was showing me the written word from the chief to prove that it was no empty threat. Again I responded with laughter, but this time consciously and deliberately. The warden made a feeble and inept attempt to convince me they weren't fooling, and dismissed me. As I was leaving the front office I wondered whether I would be the first political prisoner on America's Devils' Island. That night I wrote Helen, "I don't feel at all apprehensive about being shipped to Alcatraz at this point." And I meant it.

The following morning both Helen and my mother visited. My mother wept bitter tears, and I was sure that Helen must have felt like weeping every bit as much, and for better reason. But she didn't. Almost everything which had previously seemed important now faded into the background. We both knew what we faced. We both knew what Ethel and Julius faced, and we were prepared for it. That night I made a package of my personal possessions to send to Helen when I was shipped off; some of my legal material, the back copies of *Scientific American* and other things I had accumulated. Somehow I didn't feel that it was hopeless, but I was acutely aware that we were in for a long siege. I knew that I had to take the long view if I were to survive. I remembered Edgar Snow's account of the Long March and the long view of the Chinese Communists.

On Wednesday I was called into the hospital, ostensibly to be given a medical examination "to see if I was fit to travel by air" Kenton said. Their tactical "psychologists" were obviously working overtime. Evidently they still thought I didn't believe them. Late that afternoon I was told that the mandate had arrived and that I would be shipped out the following morning. This was fast! Usually, when the Supreme Court handed down a decision, the mandate would be returned to the lower court by mail, and the notice to that effect would be mailed to the prison authorities, all of which would certainly take more than the two days that had elapsed in this case. Obviously someone had personally delivered the mandate and the notice. They were in a great hurry.

In the meantime Howard was not twiddling his thumbs. While Kenton was telling me I would be shipped to Alcatraz, Howard went before Judge Weinfeld to ask for a temporary stay of my removal on the grounds that we were in the midst of preparing a 2255 motion for which he needed to consult with me. Weinfeld granted the stay, and for the time being I was saved. But when Saypol learned of the stay, he ran to the judge to try to get it withdrawn and Howard got a phone call to come to court at five, well past the usual court hours, to re-argue the motion. Surely Weinfeld must have been puzzled at the importance placed on my transfer to the Rock. During that argument Saypol mysteriously alluded to complex plans for my transfer. This didn't impress Weinfeld who continued the stay until Friday when the motion would be re-argued at greater length. Even though I had never heard Howard argue, I had no uneasiness when I heard what was taking place. In fact at no point in our relationship—even when we disagreed—did I lack trust in Howard. I knew that he was doing as well as anyone could do, and better than most, and what was even more important, that he wasn't afraid.

On Friday after the argument we were no more enlightened as to the nature of the complex arrangements for my transfer to Alcatraz, even though Saypol kept insisting that it was imperative that I be shipped at once. Weinfeld, who must have come under considerable outside pressure by this time, decided to continue the stay only until the following Wednesday morning, no doubt thinking that I would surely not be transferred the day before Thanksgiving.

That Sunday Helen and I really had a wonderful visit. While it lasted only forty-five minutes, it seemed so all-embracing, and so full of love, that when we parted we were completely at peace with ourselves and with each other. The children were also there, but they stayed in the background. Again Helen reiterated that she would be fighting for me until the day of my release—no matter how long it took. I knew she meant it, and I accepted it. We were both putting up a good front; underneath it our hearts were weary, and I was saddened by the thought that Helen was going to waste her life fighting for my release. Of course at the moment I was in the background, and she was fighting, literally, for the lives of Ethel and Julius. But I was looking beyond. I cautioned Helen to always be frank with me; "heartache is easier than uncertainty," and for the remainder of the time I was imprisoned I kept repeating it, no matter how much I was hurting.

Howard came to see me on Monday and Tuesday, and we discussed the projected 2255, which for the first time attacked the basic idea that "the secret of the atom bomb" could be stolen, and then we said our goodbyes. I had hoped to visit with Helen on Thanksgiving Day, but early Wednesday morning, right after breakfast, I was given the usual body search and dressed out in a set of street clothes. I was then told to go to the small isolated cubicle in front of the control desk usually used by the chaplains for interviews with prisoners. Apparently the chaplains were not considered completely trustworthy, since the cubicle was located to always be under the eyes of the control desk officer. As soon as I had made myself comfortable the warden came in to talk in what he must have assumed was a fatherly tone. "Why don't you cooperate with us? Just write the judge a letter, tell him only that you are willing to speak to him. That's all. That's all you have to say and we'll stop your transfer to Alcatraz immediately." That was all I had to say. That wasn't really anything. But I was stubborn. The warden never spelled things out the whole time he talked to me, and I didn't say a word to him. I simply listened. He went on in this vein for about fifteen or twenty minutes and then left, but I wasn't alone for very long.

Kenton came and sang the same refrain, but with more style. After all, he was a college graduate, while Thompson had come up from the ranks. But no matter how varied, it was still an appeal that I perjure myself to save my own skin. They were so uncomprehending that they didn't realize they never came within a light year of influencing me, that I wasn't tuned into their wave length. Finally in came Captain Soares. I was amused that they had started at the top of the hierarchy and gone down. I liked the captain who had always treated me fairly. The warden must have sent him to talk with me, but the captain's heart simply wasn't in it. We talked a little. He told me about his son who was studying for the priesthood in Rome, and then he left. I was glad he hadn't really tried to get me to cooperate.

I was momentarily amazed when John D. walked into the cubicle. Under the rules, it was strictly forbidden for any inmate to come into contact with another inmate who had been dressed out for shipment. But John D. was evidently not an ordinary inmate, and the rules did not apply to him. Yet how blatant it was! He opened up with his faithlessness-of-women-line, how Helen would leave me the moment I was transferred, and went on and on even though it should have been obvious that I wasn't listening. When he got tired he left, and the parade of visitors started again, with the warden first.

This time the warden lowered the price for my not being shipped to Alcatraz: if I would get Helen to stop agitating for the Committee, I would be saved. Now they were bargaining, and I learned that Helen was a thorn in their sides. Good! I said to myself, good for her!

Kenton was the last one to talk to me, and when he finally saw he wasn't getting anywhere and that the time had run out, he became vicious and picked up the John D. refrain, shouting, "your wife will drop you like a hot potato the moment you leave New York." I didn't say a thing but stared back at him and he understood me better than any words I might have uttered.

Not once during the whole morning of haranguing did it occur to me to consider their offers, nor did I think of asking them for clarification. Once one began to negotiate, there would be no end. That was the way it worked, first minimal demands and then, when you were involved, more and more. I knew what was meant by cooperation, and no threats could have succeeded in getting me to sink to the depths of the Greenglasses, Gold, and Elitcher.

I had been dressed out early only to give them this last chance to work on me. It wasn't until after eleven that the marshals came to pick me up. I knew one of them, Fitz, from the times he had taken me to the court-house, and as he handcuffed me he explained that the cuffs would be removed before we boarded the plane. I suppose that this was because the airline didn't want the other passengers frightened. A prison guard drove us to La Guardia, where we boarded a DC-6 and went up front to a small compartment next to the cockpit. On each side of the compartment were two pairs of seats facing each other. We occupied the four seats on one side, and a young woman with her two small children, bound for Australia, were on the other side of the aisle. I had a whole double seat for myself while Fitz, a small-ish Irishman, probably weighing not much over one hundred pounds, and the other marshal, who would have made a linesman for a pro football team, occupied the opposite seats. I was no little surprised when the big marshal took off his holster and stowed it away on the rack above his seat. Fitz didn't seem to have a gun, at least I didn't see his shoulder holster.

Before the plane took off I kept looking at the visitors' pavilion, hoping that by some miracle Helen might appear. I kept calling to her softly, "Helen, Helen," as if I could evoke her presence. I had such a need to see her. We took off bound for Chicago, since the DC-6 couldn't make it across the continent non-stop. I made small talk with the marshals. They did not hide their annoyance at having to be away from home at Thanks-giving, but neither expressed sympathy for me in this regard. From time to time men would poke their heads into our compartment which was separated from the rest of the plane by a curtain, glance around and quickly withdraw. It didn't take me long to realize that these were FBI agents. How many were aboard the plane? I must have seen at least a half dozen different men look in. What were they looking for? That I might try to grab the marshal's gun and shoot my way to freedom? Was this a part of the preparations for my transfer to which Saypol had referred in court?

Flight has universally been associated with freedom, so that the irony of this flight didn't escape me. I knew I was headed for a small cell on a rocky barren island, where I would experience the greatest deprivation of freedom. But I meant to enjoy every moment of this flight of freedom, because I knew that it would be a long time before I would again experience the richness of sights spread out below.

The flight to Chicago took three or four hours, and when we landed the marshals told me we were getting off the plane to stretch our legs. I wondered why, if I needed such a large escort of FBI agents to guarantee my safe arrival, the marshals risked leaving the plane. As we walked toward the waiting room no particular effort was made to guard me. It was all very loose and very strange. We were standing around the waiting room when the woman bound for Australia came by, and our big linesman marshal took off to give her a hand with the two children as if it were the most natural thing to do, leaving me alone with unarmed little Fitz. We stood there next to the candy stand for a few moments when Fitz leaned over and whispered into my ear, "be careful, there are FBI agents all around us." I looked around and there must have been at least four pairs of men standing with their newspapers narrowly folded. This, I thought was part of the complex plan to which Saypol had alluded, a plan to get me killed. The marshals must have been instructed to take me into the airport lobby and set me up for an escape attempt, but Fitz double-crossed them and warned me. Did they really think I might take off? How could they possibly have misread my state of mind so badly, except that they were so eager to shoot me. Later, on the Rock, I learned that such escape-baiting was not as rare as one might suppose. Others told me of similar incidents.

Our big marshal finally came back and after Fitz bought me some candy we returned to the plane for a rather uneventful flight to San Francisco. I carefully noted my last meal: duck in wine sauce and much fresh fruit.

It was late when we landed at San Francisco, and once more I was taken from the plane without handcuffs. The marshals searched everywhere for the man from the Rock who was supposed to meet them. In the meantime a reporter from the *San Francisco Chronicle* approached me. I don't know how he knew who we were, because I still wasn't wearing my cuffs. He started to interview me. The marshals protested, telling him, not too convincingly, to go away. I was much too surprised to take advantage of the golden opportunity, and only made a few inane comments, until the man from the Rock finally found us. He explained that he had had a telegram saying we would land at Hamilton Field, an Air Force base, which had confused him. As he led us to his auto, he suggested to the marshals that they first handcuff me. He must have been surprised to see me so free. Men who came to Alcatraz were not usually treated this way.

We were driven to a pier where we all boarded the

Alcatraz launch. The launch normally ran on a schedule, but for me it made a special trip. I couldn't see much as I looked out of the launch; perhaps I was too conscious of what this last leg of the trip meant, to take in the scene. I saw a cell house high up on the island, surrounded by nothingness.

After we landed there was a bus trip up a winding road, but first our big marshal had to surrender his gun to a guard who lowered a rope from a tower above the dock. No one was permitted to have a weapon on the island except the guards in towers or equally inaccessible places.

Did I realize that I would not return to the mainland until more than five years had elapsed? I didn't know if it would be one year or five or ten. However long it was going to be, I felt prepared for it.

Once I was inside the prison itself, the marshals removed my cuffs and I was taken to be outfitted with a nondescript pair of largish coveralls, which replaced my civilian suit. I was also given a new number—996: the nine hundred and ninety-sixth prisoner on the Rock since 1934 when the Federal Bureau of Prisons had taken it over.

Formalities taken care of, I was led to my cell. Everyone was asleep in this most gloomy of all the gloomy cell houses I had seen.

Part Four

ALCATRAZ

1 Getting Acquainted

AS THEY would be for the next five years, the cell lights were turned on at seven, and after a rather restless night I saw my new abode. It was much like the Tombs cell, the same five-by-eight-foot floor, with the same high security cold water sink, the same toilet without a seat, the same sleeping cot, the same steel folding seat and table and the same iron bars on the front of the cage. By now I knew it well. Although it was morning it was dark outside my cell, with not a window anywhere in sight.

I was grateful for the seventy-five watt bare electric light bulb in the middle of the ceiling. It cast much more light than the forty-watt Tombs bulb recessed in the high security fixture. This, I later learned was B cell block, which faced A, an unused cell block whose toilets stank.

It was quiet in the cell house, and when the door slid open at seven-thirty I walked out and marched single file with all the others to the dining hall, as though I had been doing it all my life. I found myself the subject of much curiosity, and the other inmates at the table appeared most solicitous. I felt almost at ease, despite the strangeness of the place and its reputation.

Filing back from breakfast I got a little out of line

to have a better look at the ranges above; a guard let me know, in courteous but authoritative terms, that such deviations from a straight line were absolutely forbidden. It upset me somewhat that I had been caught in the act. Later that morning I was taken to the clothing room and given a complete wardrobe: a raincoat, a short sleazey outercoat made of re-used wool, a cotton sport jacket, trousers, shirt, and underwear. I was already wearing the coveralls, obligatory dress for the dining hall since it had no pockets in which food could surreptitiously be taken out. I was then told I could go to the yard, where I was immediately invited to join in a bridge game.

At first it felt strange, playing bridge with dominoes instead of with cards, but it took only a couple of games to get used to it.* It also seemed strange to be playing cards here, whereas it had been absolutely forbidden at Atlanta. I would learn that such inconsistencies were common throughout the prison systems. I spent the morning seated on a small square stool, playing with three friendly strangers, in a decrepit-looking prison yard, almost freezing to death in the foggy bay weather. We said little; somehow the cold seemed to inhibit speech. It was a strange introduction to the Rock.

Our Thanksgiving dinner was nothing much; small portions of dried-out turkey served on ancient, deeply eroded, aluminum saucers. The dining hall itself was another matter; spacious for the population, it contained about twenty ten-man, long wooden tables, with double that number of wooden benches. We sat facing each other, as in a boarding house. Coffee and water pitchers were on the tables. After we finished eating a

* The dots were colored to denote the suit, with one dot for an ace, up to thirteen for a king.

guard counted the cutlery (no knives, only forks and soup spoons), then motioned us all to rise, rather like a conductor leading an orchestra. We filed out under the watchful eyes of at least a half a dozen guards and a lieutenant. I had noticed a guard with a large ugly rifle walking up and down an exterior enclosed catwalk right outside the dining hall, and peering into the windows as he passed. He wasn't the only one with a rifle. On another catwalk inside the cell house there was another guard similarly armed. And there were portholes all around the cell house, obviously to facilitate shooting into the cell house. Very impressive.

After dinner we all went to the movies. Here again we had to wear our coveralls, and before entering we were expertly frisked by five or six hacks. Evidently the authorities were afraid a weapon might be taken into the movies which could be used in the dark against another inmate or an officer. Once inside I was too occupied observing the surroundings and the men to follow the movie; it wasn't as dark as usual. Two hundred of the most "hardened" criminals, jammed tightly together . . .

That night I was thankful to be alone in my cell even though I had not encountered a single hostile inmate, and the guards were uniformly courteous. In fact some of them inadvertently addressed me as Mister Sobell. For the moment they still thought of me as a human being—not something inferior, with a number. In due time this error was corrected. Lying on my cot after supper I felt the inner tension slowly ooze away. It was heaven, simply to lie there, momentarily without a care in the world.

In the time I had spent in the Tombs, Atlanta, and West Street, I had never encountered such a population. All the men seemed so subdued that it was frightening, like a tomb of living souls. That night I told myself, "Morty, you mustn't begin to live your life here—for that would be certain death."

After I had rested I tried to write Helen, but the letter didn't turn out as I had intended. I wanted so to write her a warm letter (probably to warm myself in the writing) but it just wouldn't come out. I asked her not to transfer my subscription to *Scientific American* until I had received the proper authorization from my keepers, feeling that such matters had to be handled properly.

I had no job, and wouldn't have one until I met the Board and came off orientation status. Nor was there any sort of pretense concerning orientation. Here it meant absolute idleness. Except for going to meals, I remained in my cell all day Friday. However inmates who worked in the library were very helpful and brought me a number of books, as well as the standard mimeographed library catalogue. Thus it was that Stefan Zweig's *Sergeant Grisha* was the first volume I read on the Rock. I found I had to keep reading almost continuously, otherwise my thoughts went wild. I'd start thinking about everything that had gone wrong since I was arrested, and before, and I'd feel I couldn't stand it any more. Reading was my only escape from this inner turmoil which would otherwise have overtaken me.

Saturday after breakfast we all went to the basement for showers, clothing, and linen exchange. Afterwards, those who wanted to went out into the yard. It was foggy and windy, the usual weather for this time of year, and the cold penetrated through the cotton clothes and the cheap coat. I had to keep moving; some brave souls huddled inside their raincoats were playing bridge. At this moment warm surplus Navy peacoats were lying in the prison warehouse, unused. Warden Swope, never noted for humanitarianism, evidently didn't believe that his prisoners should be too comfortable. At the end of the yard a number of men were playing handball against one of the higher walls. It was an odd game, with no far boundary; a wearing game. Every once in a while a ball was hit above the wall and lost. I was told that these were later recovered by one of the inmates and restored to the pool of balls.

The yard itself was only about a hundred and twenty feet long and varied in width from forty to sixty feet. Along one half of the long side were concrete seats, which served as steps for getting up to the cell house. Two of the walls were surprisingly low, with reinforced concrete crumbling so as to expose the iron rods within. In three corners of the yard there were towers, manned by guards armed with carbines and rifles. In the middle of the long wall opposite the steps was an iron door, which was opened for men to go to and from Industries. The wall did not represent much of an obstacle to escape: the problem was what one could do, once over the wall. No indoor recreational facilities were available, although there was plenty of space in the basement; I suppose they didn't believe in pampering. When it was cold outside it was also cold in the large cell house, with its few antiquated steam radiators scattered around on the flats. But perhaps the cold was more than a matter of the temperature of the air.

Saturday afternoon was more of that foggy yard. I wouldn't have missed it for anything, but once having chosen to go out, one couldn't go back in until the end of the yard period, which in the afternoon ran for almost three hours. I don't think I missed a single yard period during the first three years—rain or shine, fog or drizzle, I was out there as though my life depended on fresh air. Sunday the fog lifted for the first time, and standing on top of the steps leading down to the yard I saw the Golden Gate in all its splendor. It was magnificent, and as I absorbed the view I thought to myself, "I will never have such a magnificent view in any other prison." Prison notwithstanding, I enjoyed it until the day I left. The distant green hills, and the soaring towers of the bridge, with the graceful catenary suspended between them, always lifted my spirits. When viewed against a setting sun it had the appearance of a picture postcard.

I was in the yard all day on Sunday, listening to the other inmates while we walked. They told somewhat different stories from those I had been hearing; these involved more daring than the usual run-of-the-mill escapades. I managed to get a heavy undershirt in the clothing room Monday morning. Everything here was much more informal than at Atlanta, the population considerably smaller—only two hundred twenty-five inmates and one hundred fifty civilian personnel. I read all day long and when the lights were turned off at nine-thirty, I welcomed the end of the day. Nine-thirty to seven—nine and one half hours of sleep for adults?

The meals were adequate, including vegetables and salads. I had learned not to expect too much in the way of meat, but the other men said that whenever one moved to a new institution the change to a new menu seemed to have a salutary effect. Again I noticed that the noon meal and the evening meal seemed to be of equal weight, a pattern in federal prisons. I thought it had some connection with the high proportion of southerners working within the prison system. The mailman made his rounds after supper, but it wasn't until Tuesday evening that he stopped at my cell with a letter from Helen. She had written me only a few lines Saturday morning. What a blow! I had expected an outpouring, written on the day I left. I was aware that my expectations were based on desire, not on the realities of Helen's situation, but this did not help. For Helen, my transfer here meant a redoubling of her efforts with the Committee; I did not see that at that time.

Books, books, books. I never read so many books in such a short time. The news weeklies were available, but no newspapers. And of course no radio. As with everything else, the reason for the edict forbidding newspapers was the universal term "security." Exactly how security might be breached by permitting newspapers was never spelled out. As a matter of fact, for the first several months we did get the Green Sheet, the late-edition sport sheet, of the *San Francisco Chronicle.* The *Chronicle* actually delivered, gratis, ten newspapers to the Rock; the Green Sheet was extracted and circulated amongst the inmates—the hacks appropriated the remainder of the newspapers—apparently representing no threat to the security of the prison. However when the *Chronicle* had a retrenchment drive the ten papers were stopped and that was the end of the Green Sheet for Alcatraz.

The lack of radio disturbed me most, since I knew it meant I would not be able to hear proper English as long as I remained here. Neither inmates nor prison guards were noted for their English usage. This was only one additional step in isolation from the outside world.

Except for a near-accident the second weekend I was in the yard, nothing very much happened that first month. I hadn't planned my bowel movements very carefully; it was a new place, with a new schedule, new food, and I found myself in the yard with stomach cramps after only the first hour of the three hour period. There was a urinal, and that was all! I asked the guard if I could be re-admitted to the cell house, since it was an emergency. He called up inside and then gave an incomprehensible answer which I took to be negative. My cramps became worse and I again approached the guard, with no better results. I wondered what they would do if I went to a corner and defecated. But I was chicken and waited out the two hours like a good boy. My abdomen hurt for the next three or four days.

One of the early books I read was Jawaharlal Nehru's *Towards Freedom*, written while he was doing a three-year bit for political agitation, when India was still under British rule. Unlike Nehru, I couldn't write a book while I was in federal custody; in fact I couldn't even write an essay. One had to get official written permission from Washington in order legitimately to write almost anything. This involved submitting an outline of the subject, as well as giving the purpose. Poetry was not excluded from this requirement which was absolute. Of course many men wrote without the required permission, but it was one of those rules which could selectively be enforced if the authorities were so disposed. In my own case I knew there was no question what they would do.

In his book Nehru noted that he missed most the soft voices of women and the laughter of children. I never forgot that, because with the passage of years I found this lack painful even to think about. And I wondered at such cruelty when I realized that some of my new found compatriots had not heard the live voice of a child or a woman for almost twenty years. There were movies, which had only started after World War II, and popular songs played over the yard amplifier, but these could not compare with listening to a woman in person.

Nehru's book described the technique of passive resistance perfected by Mahatma Gandhi in India, and I wondered that it had never been tried by prisoners. It would have been an ideal weapon for them, but alas, it would have also required tremendous self-discipline under the extreme provocation which would undoubtedly come from the guards.

In my desire for cultural dialogue I sought out the Catholic chaplain, Father Richard Scannell. There was something soul-satisfying in talking with another college man even if our conversation mainly concerned theology. It was a relief from the usual pattern of inmate talk. Father Scannell was a Jesuit; I had many discussions with him over the years.

It didn't take long to realize that the first days I spent on Alcatraz were not what they seemed. I must have been in a trance, going through the motions like a person in shock. It was only as I became acclimatized that I understood how far off the ground I had been those first days. After a longer period I was able to recognize the trance-like qualities of the first week, but only in retrospect.

Almost everything I read served to recall some past association. G. B. Shaw's *Pygmalion* reminded me of the movie with Leslie Howard and that superb British actress, Wendy Hiller, which I had seen in Washington, about 1940; a period with very many good memories, which would now have to serve me instead of real life.

In one of his briefs written just before my transfer, Howard Meyer spoke of the Rock as a "living death." I passed it off as lawyer's hyperbole. But I slowly became aware that he was right, and when this realization dawned, I warned Helen that I would demand much from her in an effort to compensate for what I was missing. Even as I told her this I knew that it was unfair to shoulder her with such an onerous burden. What could I give in return? Where would she get the energy she would need? A thousand such questions plagued my mind. But I kept reading: Joyce, Gogol, Ibsen, a critical biography of Jack London by one of his daughters, a novel by Albert Maltz (one of the Hollywood ten) which had missed the censor. Reading was really the only "activity" I could carry on in my cell.

More than ten days elapsed before I was given my personal possessions, which included the last three letters Helen had sent to West Street. Kenton had withheld them until they became history. I also received the photographs I had accumulated, my pen and my personal books. And then, two weeks after I had arrived, I was given a cursory physical exam; my blood pressure, my heart, and a check for hernia. I was pronounced healthy; that is, healthy enough to do my sentence. The following day I met the classification board. Usually thirty days elapsed before one met the board; I had no idea why my period of orientation was mercifully shortened.

If the men had not prepared me for the farce I might have been taken in by the seriousness of the proceedings, but the story current at this time was that when an old-timer appearing before the board was asked, "What can we do for you?" he answered, "You can get me a ham and cheese on rye." At Atlanta the board took up the question of education, but this did not arise here since there was no school on the Rock. I was prepared, and I asked one question, "Why was I sent to Alcatraz?" Obviously they couldn't tell me the real reason, that I hadn't cooperated. And they couldn't even come up with an excuse of a reason. I was shocked when they simply said that they didn't know. That a board, supposed to be looking into my behavior, and whatever else they were charged with, would not know why I had been sent there in the first place, did not strike them as ludicrous, only demonstrated their complete insensitivity to the situation. Each succeeding year, when I met the board, I repeated my question, and each year they told me they did not know. The next obvious question was, how could they know when I was fit to leave the Rock, if they didn't know why I had been sent here? But I never got to that; I decided it would be too difficult a question for them to understand, let alone answer. I got my amusement each year by repeating the question and watching their unembarrassed faces as they gave the same answer. I found it significant they they could not be embarrassed. Not everyone was capable of such behavior.

After some expert penological deliberation, the board found the proper job for me; waxing and buffing the dining room floor. Each morning after the men who worked in Industries had left, and things had settled into their place in the cell house, a guard "racked" my cell door open, and I came out, picked up the buffing machine which was stored in A block and wheeled it into the dining hall—but not before I was shaken down and the machine searched for hidden contraband. It didn't take long to become an expert floor buffer; in fact, after one week I had learned how to guide the machine with a single finger. As with all safety devices on machines in prison, the dead man's switch had been taken out of the circuit. Thus if the machine ever got away from me it would not automatically shut off, as was originally intended. It took about an hour to do the floors, and this left me with an enormous amount of cell time on my hands. One hour a day, five days a week. I wasn't overworked to be sure, but neither was I paid.

It wasn't long before the censor returned the first of many letters; my writing was too small for him to read. Too small? It was certainly smaller than most people's, and I suppose if everyone wrote two letters a week— the maximum allowed—as closely as I, the censor might have had some difficulty in doing his job. But I tried to make my letters neat and legible to compensate for the crowding of the words. I suppose I should have been happy that letter writing had eased up on the Rock; in the Thirties, pencils and paper were passed out for letter writing, and collected afterwards. For security reasons they said. Anyway it was fortunate that I didn't get my letter back on Friday, because then I would not have been able to rewrite it and post on that same week's quota—so complicated.

What a place this was. Desperate and hardened criminals, even the nineteen and twenty year olds, doomed to a life of crime, having been tagged for life with the Alcatraz label which would follow them wherever they went. In the words of James V. Bennett, these were all "tough hombres" and beyond rehabilitation. And if they weren't already the Rock would make them so.

About the middle of December I was greatly disturbed when Helen wrote that she was coming to the Coast to visit me over the holidays. I was afraid that we might be permitted only a single visit, as in Atlanta, which here would be only ninety minutes long. To travel across the country for such a short visit was, I felt, highly irrational. And I would not be permitted to see the children, in case Helen thought of bringing Mark, or Sydney, or both. At least this was how I explained my strong reaction against Helen's idea. But the very strength of my objections should have warned me that these were probably not the real reasons. No doubt I was afraid that the visit(s) might end in disaster for Helen and myself. And in each of my letters I told Helen that under no circumstances should she come.

Christmas Eve we were given the traditional Christmas bag, courtesy of the Federal Prison Industries. The way the guards rushed around from cell to cell, throwing in the bags, with a "Merry Christmas" for each of us, one would have thought they were racing each other. Actually they were doing this on their own time, while the launch which was to take them back to the mainland was being held up. Whatever the reason for their haste, it did not seem approrpriate to the occasion. Each bag contained seven nickel bars of candy and one pound of cheap hard Christmas candy. The warden was actually allowed one dollar per bag, but for Warden Swope, fifty cents was enough to spend on his tough hombres, and he returned the other fifty cents to Industries, feeling virtuous no doubt. It was easy for the inmates to discover these financial details since the office which handled purchases was staffed by inmates with only a single civilian at the top.

That night, to lend authenticity to the festivities, the hitherto silent speakers, located on the ceiling of the cell house, filled the place with festive tunes—Bing Crosby singing *O Holy Night* and *White Christmas*. It was just what we needed! I couldn't remember ever having felt more depressed. The combination of the grey dimly lighted cell house, the knowledge that it was Christmas out there, and the recordings to remind us of the occasion—all created the terrible ungay mood which must have filled every soul in that cell house.

Some of the men ate all seven candy bars that night. Virtuous Sobell merely sampled the hard candy (which tasted like some vile medicine) and put the bag away to be eaten gradually and at leisure. Some gambled with their bags, and lost. And then, in an effort to recoup, gambled for another bag, losing again. After that they went wild, ending up owing five or six bags to different inmates, at which point they usually had themselves checked into the segregation unit, emerging after two or three months had elapsed—long enough for their debtors to have cooled off. Whenever anyone asked to be checked in around Christmas time, the officials knew the reason, and usually complied without even asking for an explanation. They knew there was a chance of a fight, or even a stabbing, if they didn't honor the debtor's request. It didn't look good on the warden's record to have stabbings at Christmas.

I spent Christmas morning in the yard, walking and talking. Some of the old-timers must have felt that this was how Christmas was meant to be spent. Then the Christmas dinner, which was no improvement over Thanksgiving, and finally the movie. The holiday movie was not an extra movie. Ordinarily we saw two movies each month, on alternate Sundays, and occasionally three weeks elapsed between movies. The holiday movie was simply one which had been rescheduled from Sunday. There were exactly twenty-four movies each year. The old-timers remembered that before 1945 there hadn't been any movies. Now they felt they were being pampered.

The cell doors were not shut after we left the cells for the movies, to conserve the guards' energy, I suppose. Presumably no inmates were at large in the cell house during this time. Those who hadn't gone to the movies were supposed to remain locked in their cells. Anyway, when I got back my Christmas bag was missing. There wasn't very much I could do. The most important thing *not to do* was to complain to the authorities. But I did mention it to my confreres. The next day, when I returned after supper, I found a small bag of candy in my cell. I learned from other inmates that Red Lovett had "passed the hat" around for me. I followed Red first to Atlanta and then to Lewisburg, and we always chuckled on Christmas when I thanked him for his noble gesture. More than a year later I learned that the inmate who had taken my bag was most appropriately nicknamed Dog.

Despite my intense objections Helen was adamant in insisting that she would come, and on December 31 she and my mother arrived. Helen had to get written permission for the visit. Without this she would not even have been allowed aboard the launch. After debarking she and my mother took the bus up the hill, the same bus which had brought me.

Alcatraz was the only federal prison where visitors had to pass through a metal detector before being permitted to enter the visiting room. There was a story that Al Capone's mother kept setting off the alarm, until the officials concluded that it must have been the metal stays in her corset. But that had been many years earlier.

The final insult came when my mother and Helen were locked in a cell, one wall of which was the cell house wall itself. The officials on the Rock were not interested in fostering good public relations. There were five visiting positions in all, each one consisting of a cut-out in the common wall, about six inches by ten inches in area, with a thick slab of bullet proof glass. Since the wall was almost a foot thick, one seemed to be looking through a tunnel to the opposite side. In addition, there was very little light, and when Helen and I sat down it became obvious that the small window was much too high, making it difficult for us to see each other. Consequently Helen sat on the arm of her chair to gain altitude. It wasn't too comfortable, but at least that way we could see each other. Communication was by phone, and I was forewarned by my confreres that our conversation would be monitored by the guard in the armory who ordinarily had little to do. I was the only inmate who had a visitor that day.

There was only one visiting period a day, from one-thirty to three (if the bus wasn't delayed.) I was usually there alone. Most days saw no visitors at all. Only about one tenth of the population had visitors, a very low percentage compared with other prisons. The officials did everything in their power to discourage visiting and succeeded all too well.

As I talked with Helen I also saw my mother sitting in a chair directly behind her. All my fears proved groundless. For ninety minutes I escaped from my prison as I talked alternately with Helen and my mother. Helen looked more beautiful than ever, and despite my instability of the past weeks all went well.

The next day I walked in the yard in the rain, humming to myself and thinking of my beloved. I no longer felt cold within. Such was the magic of the visit, which would never evaporate during all the years Helen visited me.

On New Year's Day I also acquired a wooden board, about eighteen by thirty-six inches, which I was able to fasten to the top of my small metal table, to use as a desk. An inmate who worked around the cell house had found the board buried in a pile of discarded material, and had offered it to me. I had no hesitation about accepting it because I had noticed that quite a number of other inmates had similar make-shift desks. In fact some had a gadget whereby they could slide the board out toward the bed, which could then be used as a seat. After I had been there several months I too acquired such a slide. Of course the board was not official issue and was not listed on my property card, but it seemed to be one of those variances to which officials closed their eyes.

January was a new month and Helen received permission to visit again on the fourth. This visit was even better than the first. We did reach some kind of understanding on legal actions, and we agreed that Helen would in the future tell me if she wanted to engage in sex with another; after which we would discuss it before she took any action. I had been dissatisfied with her previous promise simply to abstain; in these new circumstances I felt this was manifestly unfair to her.

The aura of the encounter had always remained with me after a good visit, but nothing like after this. The emptiness of my existence contrasted with the richness of my encounter with Helen to a degree I had never before experienced; and this in turn magnified the after-effects. It was as though I spent that whole evening, even when I went to supper, with her. I floated in clouds of ecstasy. I never would have believed that a visit could have filled me so full of good spirits. Helen told me she really liked San Francisco. She had found warm friends there, and, even though it was the place of my imprisonment, from her descriptions I too began to like the city.

When the motion for reduction of sentence was turned down by Kaufman it didn't really bother me. I hadn't been expecting anything in the first place, but I was annoyed with myself for having allowed the lawyers to file. This was only the first of many similar motions which lawyers would file for me against my better judgment.

Because the population was so much smaller than at Atlanta the relationships between men were much closer. I was always getting advice from others on various aspects of the place. Thus when some of the men told me that I could get a cell change simply by putting in a cop-out, I took their advice since I didn't like the constant darkness of my cell. (Some of the men liked it dark.) It took only a couple of days before the request slip was returned with the notation "denied" written across it. So either my informants hadn't proved accurate, or I was being given special treatment.

Four days after having received the denial I was transferred to a new, bright, airy cell, C-156, on the flats, with a western exposure, but I could see nothing from my cell except the sky. The windows began about ten feet above floor level, and I faced a blank wall. Nevertheless, the bright light streaming in, and the absence of the A-block odors, made it much more pleasant. Why the authorities had chosen this curious transfer procedure was their secret. Some of the mystery of the move was cleared up when I found myself, several times a week, the star subject of the standard guided prison tour conducted by the warden or associate warden. C-

156 was a corner cell, and a convenient stopping place. The warden always pointed me out to the visitors as the "notorious atom spy," though I couldn't hear what else he said. I didn't like the idea of being placed on exhibition, but there was nothing I could do about it, and I certainly didn't try to point out to him that I had not been convicted of being an atom spy.

Just when I began congratulating myself on my new found stability everything seemed to fall apart. The understandings I thought I had reached with Helen blew up, and I found myself once more on the roller coaster. I couldn't put my finger on anything which might have explained the sudden shift; it just happened. In addition, for the first time since I had been imprisoned I began to have nightmares. In one, I was lying in my bed, face down, and I knew that a cop was right above me, ready to swing his night stick down on my skull the moment I made a move. Thus I had to lie there absolutely still until I felt I was suffocating. Then slowly and fearfully I turned my head, and I realized that it was only a dream.

Whatever had precipitated the instability, it didn't last long. Before the end of January I was able to write Helen that I felt so good, I didn't think I would ever again ride the roller coaster. But even as I wrote, I knew it was more wish than reality. For so long as I tried to lead the dual existence I had set for myself, I knew I would again experience heights of ecstasy and depths of despair. Of course I was always aware that I could get off this psychic energy-consuming journey by divorcing myself from the outside world, anytime it became too painful, and living my life circumscribed by the prison walls as so many of those around me did.

Then life would move along on an even keel; too even. This, I felt, would be the equivalent of death, and I was not yet ready to give up.

As in all prisons, or in other institutions for that matter, the basic routine never varied, and there were no unexpected happenings. The lights were turned on in the cells each morning at 7:00. I shaved, washed up, and the doors were racked open about 7:30. By 8:15 breakfast was over and I was back in my cell. Shortly afterwards the Industries men were let out to go to work. When they were gone the other prison workers were let out: library, hospital, clothing room, and cell house orderlies. I was let out around 9:00 for my one-hour stint with the floor buffing machine and then I was back in my cell, my day's work done. There were many such one-hour jobs around the cell house. The Industries men returned around 11:40 and five minutes later we started to go to lunch. Back in the cell by 12:15, and then sick call. And again the Industries men went to work. Supper was at 4:00, and we were locked in our cells from 4:45 until the following morning. Lights went out at 9:30, though we had the option of turning them out earlier.

Wednesday afternoon the schedule had a slight variation. Immediately before the evening meal we showered and exchanged our clothing. There was another clothing exchange Saturday morning after breakfast. Saturday and Sunday, morning and afternoon, we had yard for a total of about five hours each day (exception on movie days). However many men never went out except when the weather was ideal and some never at all. One aspect of the yard I found most annoying, was the loudspeaker continuously blaring out *country music.* I suppose most of the men liked it, but I found it hard to take since there was never a moment of silence in the yard.

I found it too cold to play much bridge in the yard during this time of the year since a commitment to play was for the whole day, morning and afternoon, and frequently for the whole weekend (my first game was special). So I walked with one or two inmates, talking, but with all the time in the world, I found it diverting.

Outside of my work schedule I had no real routine. I had begun to study, and frequently spent the whole day working at problems in the vector analysis text—a relatively painless way of passing time. I spent a total of one hundred and forty-five hours in my cell each week, and could sleep for only some fifty of those. That left ninety-five at my disposal. Many of the men simply slept the time away; I dreaded being reduced to this state.

After having gone through several dozen books, my fictional reading slackened, and I began more thoroughly to read news weeklies, trying to keep abreast of world events. I would frequently go through *Time* and *Newsweek* without skipping a single word, although I knew this was only a killer of time, and not a stimulant to mental activity. In all my reading I never ran across a single word about the case. The censor, under a rule forbidding any news in the prison concerning an inmate, or notorious criminal, tore from all magazines any pages touching on the case. It wasn't unusual to find ten pages torn out of an issue of *Life* when it had a feature article on crime. Usually the index was also missing, to conceal the nature of the missing article. But sometimes these articles would be smuggled into prison, probably by a guard, and circulated surreptitiously, usually concealed in the pages of another magazine.

There were so many things I missed in prison about which I could do nothing that whenever an opportunity to compensate presented itself I seized it. The weekly periodicals did, on occasion, reproduce the art of popular painters. I culled them and built up my own personal art collection. Surprisingly, we were permitted to hang a limited number of pictures on the walls of our cell, provided they were not obscene. This had been forbidden in Atlanta, for reasons of security (pictures could conceal a hole in the wall).

I would hang four or five pictures from my collection, rotating them whenever the mood seized me. Before I left the Rock my collection had grown to well over one hundred works. Van Gogh was easily my favorite, and fortunately he was also the favorite of many of the periodicals. But as with all rules, various guards interpreted the picture hanging differently, and, on occasion, I would come back to my cell to find my pictures crumpled, and in the toilet. A guard who had shaken down my cell must have been annoyed that he could not find any contraband, and reacted in a way that he knew would disturb me. There was nothing I could do; I should have been laughed at if I had complained.

It was here that I first became aware of the prison artist. His paintings, generally oils, were like no other amateur art I had ever seen. They were hopelessly two-dimensional. The flesh tones of the portraits reminded me of the heavily made-up clowns of the circus, devoid of feeling. Quite a number of men on the Rock painted, since unlike other federal penitentiaries here it was permitted in the cells.

Many of the men who had worked in Industries over the years had accumulated large savings and thought nothing of buying expensive oil paint sets. With a pantograph they would copy the outlines of a picture from one of the magazines and then try to fill it in. There was no one around to criticize or to help them.

Some men however did have an aptitude for art, like Hayman who did protraits in pastels. He was an exception. Coincidentally, he was the subject of a famous decision by the Supreme Court, in which they reversed a Ninth Circuit decision holding that Section 2255 of Title 28 was unconstitutional, because, in effect, it did away with federal habeas corpus. Hayman, a black, said that he had been sent to the Rock solely because he had fought his case vigorously, giving the Justice Department some anxiety.

The men were allowed to send their art work home, and this led to a considerable amount of commerce in portrait painting. The artists would paint portraits from photographs for other inmates. Then, through complicated negotiations, the oils would reach the proper parties and the monies would be transferred to pay for the work. All done through the mails, despite the censorship.

Although I was only beginning my bit, I was intensely interested in finding out what it was like to come out of prison after doing a long stretch. I asked some of the long-timers who were doing their second or third sentences, and learned that it was not instant joy. Long prison terms having dulled their senses, even the pleasures of sex had to be relearned. Of course to most of these men the outside world represented a hostile environment: they had no close family ties or real friends. I didn't go into the question again until a short time before my release.

March—I recalled the previous March, when Helen moved back to New York, and began to work for the Committee. It had come a long way since then, but in my isolation I had no feeling for its activities. Helen would write me about the large meetings but this meant very little to me personally. I recognized its worth de facto, but could not relate to it. Yet, at times I would allow myself to fantasize about achieving freedom. I knew it was beyond the realm of possibility, but it was such a pleasant luxury, and I had so few. After everything had been taken from me I felt victorious in still being able to dream of freedom, but I wasn't unaware of the dangers of such fantasies.

With all the cell time I was doing I wasn't surprised to find myself rethinking long forgotten episodes, re-examining them from the vantage point of my ivory tower. Suddenly I found it incomprehensible that I should have allowed Helen to deliver Mark in a hospital where I couldn't be present while she was in labor; how could I have taken her to the hospital early one evening, then checked with a phone call around midnight and gone off to sleep. I wondered that I had accepted this without protest. Only here and now it became obvious that the doctors were essentially uncivilized to impose their own dictates on husband and wife.

My recollections of the past were not restricted to purely personal matters. One day, while I was expertly buffing the dining room hall floor, I suddenly realized that my approach to the solution of an engineering problem some ten years earlier at General Electric had been topsy-turvy. The problem had involved the design of an electron gun for which I had had to find the shape of the electrodes, by the use of an electrolytic tank. I had used a trial and error approach, which I now saw had not been necessary. The strange thing was that I hadn't really been thinking about the matter—at least not consciously. I was tremendously pleased by this incident, as revealing a certain activity taking place in my otherwise dormant brain, and excused the ten-year-old technical lapse by noting that my superior should have caught it.

Man is doomed to repeat. Having weathered the previous visits how could I possibly have allowed myself to get upset when Helen wrote me that she was coming to visit at the end of March? I found all sorts of reasons to manifest concern over the success of any visits at this time, and even while I recognized that they were rationalizations, I felt terrified. And again my fears proved totally baseless.

We had one visit at the end of March and two at the beginning of April. The warden allowed us to accumulate the February visit we had missed. Why? Why in this area had he stretched the rules for us? Another mystery, added to the long list. Only for once this was a pleasant mystery.

It was wonderful to see Helen three days. By the end of the third visit I was really riding high on my roller coaster. I knew I would have to come down, and that it would be painful, but it was so wonderful while I was up there that I wouldn't have traded the feeling for anything.

When I left New York, the question of my having a liaison attorney in San Francisco was discussed. However it wasn't until I had arrived that the matter was settled. Benjamin Dreyfus, a progressive local attorney, volunteered to serve as a link between myself and my East Coast attorneys. He had already visited me on several occasions when legal questions needing discussion arose. I liked him from the start. He was a genuinely concerned person, and a good lawyer to boot. I thought to myself, if only I could have had him for my trial it might have been different. How different? A tantalizing question.

Since the courts had ruled that attorney visits were privileged, even where prisoners were concerned, we did not have to talk through the monitored telephone. Instead we sat on opposite sides of a small table in the cell where Helen had sat while visiting me. Since Dreyfus usually came in the morning, we never had any problem with social visitors in the same room. However his visit had to be scheduled to the launch time-table. This meant that we could have somewhat less than one hour (from nine to ten), or about three and one half hours (from nine to twelve-thirty), with nothing in between. In these conditions we naturally tried to get all our business transacted in the shorter period.

The prison authorities didn't trust attorneys and I was subjected to a strict shakedown, including rectal examination, each time I went out to visit Dreyfus and when I returned. However, different guards manifested different degrees of responsibility in carrying out this task. Some were absurdly thorough, while others waived the whole procedure since no one was around to monitor them.

During the entire period that I spent in Alcatraz, Dreyfus regularly came to visit me about once a month, even when there were no legal matters to discuss. In the legal arena he frequently served as mediator between my New York attorneys and myself, which in some instances became extremely difficult. He was one of the most wonderful people I have ever met, and helped me immeasurably to do the Alcatraz portion of the bit without my becoming bitter or going crazy.

The Alcatraz library was unlike any other library I had ever seen—in or out of prison. The library itself was located in a large alcove of the cell house, separated by a heavy wire mesh screen, and inaccessible to all except those who worked there. Each inmate had a two hundred page mimeographed book catalogue listing some twenty thousand volumes. If I wanted a book I entered the call number on my library card, which I then deposited on the library table, on the way to breakfast. The men who worked on the library squad were supposed to fill out the orders for books and throw them into the proper cells during a brief tightly supervised period in the morning. (Ever since the 1946 attempted break all movements in the cell house were very rigidly monitored.) Actually it didn't quite work that way. I generally listed between five and ten books on my card, and I would get one or two at most. If there was a particular book I urgently wanted I'd speak to one of the men I knew in the library, and he would make a determined effort to find it. Many of the books were misfiled and would remain unavailable for years, until they were found. I don't believe the library had ever purchased any books. From time to time we'd get a shipment from a government facility that had closed down. Thus it was a completely haphazard collection.

Nor was there a civilian librarian. Sometime after I arrived the parole officer made his office in the library and nominally supervised the inmates who worked there, but by and large it was a self-run establishment.

Since no funds were available for the library, inmates had to purchase their own magazines. Actually this was not a hardship since anyone could earn money by going down to Industries (at this time I, of course, was the exception). The magazines were then circulated either by passing them on directly, if the recipient happened to live close by, or else dropping them off on the library table, with a routing slip appended. The library squad would then deliver the magazine to the first cell noted on the slip. Some of the periodicals would be circulated to more than twenty cells, taking several months to complete their rounds. But almost everyone had plenty of time and no one appeared to be in any great rush.

The inmates read magazines that covered a broad range, though the tendency was to the lightweight. High on the list were movie star magazines, as well as *House Beautiful;* the inmates were no different from the square johns on the outside. I chose to live vicariously in Helen's real world, but not everyone was so fortunate as to have this option. These men chose the make-believe world of the movie stars, and I don't suppose their thoughts, contrary to popular notions, differed from those of people on the outside.

Not all magazines were permitted on the Rock. Washington's approved list did not include crime magazines or politically unpopular periodicals. Thus, while the *American Mercury,* a far right publication, was included, *The Nation,* which I had always thought a mildly liberal magazine, was forbidden. I put in a cop-out to the warden to be permitted to subscribe to *The Nation,* and six months later received a denial; probably after due consultation with Washington. However I was able to circumvent this ruling to some degree.

Helen had a subscription sent to the parole-officer/librarian. When he went out front to get his mail he would bring it back and place it on his desk, and it wasn't too difficult for an inmate to filch the magazine before he even saw it. After I got it I put it into circulation quite openly amongst the inmates, since none of the officers were aware that it was on Washington's proscribed list. However from time to time the system fouled up and I wouldn't see a copy for months; and then it would start coming again. Under these conditions it was difficult to ascertain where the difficulty lay. It became another exercise in patience.

As soon as I arrived I put in a request to get my *Electronics* magazine subscription approved (understandably it wasn't on the general approved list), but it was almost a whole year before Washington assented. I couldn't imagine what considerations had entered into this. Then when Helen tried to enter my subscription with McGraw-Hill, the publishers turned it down on the grounds that the magazine was meant only for those *actively* engaged in the field; obviously I was not. However, after two years of effort, with the help of Professor Harold Urey whose publisher was McGraw-Hill, I finally managed to get the magazine. It proved a life saver for me, allowing me at least to acquire a reading knowledge of what was going on in my former engineering world.

When inmates tried to take the prison officials to court for denying them access to certain magazines the courts refused to even look into the question, holding that it was the warden's right to censor the reading material of inmates; holding, in effect, that an inmate could be denied his constitutional rights, without reason. Of course the courts never even began to consider that the warden himself might be only semi-literate, which was frequently the case.

However, I began to get *Scientific American* almost from the beginning, since it was on the approved list. I would read it from cover to cover, skipping nothing, not even articles on archeology, in which I had very little prior interest. However, after about three years of this sort of indiscriminate reading, I became a little more selective. I would have given my right arm if I could have discussed the articles with someone—anyone; or if I could even have discussed some of the articles by correspondence. Unfortunately since the rules limited correspondence to personal matters, this proved impossible.

We also had a legal library, set up in accordance with several court decisions in the area of prisoners' legal rights. After many years of bowing to the theory of the warden's prerogatives, the courts had finally decided that in this area a prisoner still retained some of his constitutional rights. The library was located in A-block, in one of the cells, and consisted of a couple of well-used and abused volumes of the United States Legal Code, a couple of old battered typewriters that barely worked, a small table and a chair: all together a far cry from the intent of the courts' mandate that the prison set up a law library so that the inmates could research their own appeals. (This was to correct the obvious imbalance between those who could afford lawyers for appeals and those who could not.) Another couple of cells were set aside to store inmates' legal materials, since many worked on their cases for several years on and off. The question of what legal material one could keep in his cell was never definitively answered. In Atlanta, the *Federal Reporter* and the *Supreme Court Reporter* were both restricted to law library use, whereas these journals, reporting current federal cases, were permitted free circulation on the Rock. One was also allowed to keep the various briefs of his own case in his cell. The restrictions on the legal material that one could keep in his cell was justified by the prison officials on the grounds that otherwise the inmate-lawyers would write writs for others and inundate the courts. Even with the restrictions some inmates did write legal writs for others.

At the end of April I re-read all of Helen's first letters to me, and, as I should have known by then, they read much more warmly than when I had first received them. I was amazed, but the explanation was simple. The problems that had been raised in those first letters were by now more or less resolved, and I didn't have to agonize from letter to letter while awaiting the development. I could re-read Helen's letters for sheer pleasure when things got rough and I needed a little more faith to sustain me. This the letters provided. They were like a reserve, which I hoarded and used only at times of extreme need, or when I wanted to indulge myself.

The Jews were permitted to celebrate Passover. Chaplain Coffee came over on the one-thirty o'clock boat, and the entire Jewish population, consisting of three born Jews and three converts, assembled in the movie hall—after a thorough shakedown. There, while a guard looked on, Coffee conducted services. Somehow he managed to tell us a great deal about his wife, what a fine playwright she was and much else, but he didn't ask a single soul a question. He left to catch the three o'clock boat, apparently satisfied with his performance. On leaving the services we were each given a couple of pounds of matzohs. That was it for Passover.

From other inmates I learned that this was a standard performance for Coffee. In addition to his once-a-year duties as Alcatraz chaplain, he held the same office at California's San Quentin prison, and at the San Francisco Fire Department, which explained in part his institutionalized approach. But I don't think he could have been much of a human being even when he first started. Human beings do not turn into cold-blooded bastards.

After a couple of weeks on my floor-buffing job, I began attempts to be transferred to Industries, where, under a complicated formula, I would earn "Industrial Good Time." I.G.T. would mean that if I had to do the whole bit, that is, not be paroled, I should be released sooner; and I knew that that probability was quite high. After five months I was finally transferred to Industries.

I was assigned to the furniture factory, which didn't really make furniture; wooden clothing stands and letter trays were the chief products. These were sold to other governmental agencies by the General Services Administration (GSA), which ran a large mail order department store. I now worked a full day, which was still only a little over six hours, and I also earned money—ten cents an hour. Compared to some state prisons this was high.

Aside from the Good Time and the money, I was glad to get out of my cell and expand my horizons, even if it meant only sanding wooden poles all day. But the best part was the going to and coming from work, twice each day. It was so lovely to go up and down the hillside where I could smell and see the shrubbery and not be continually faced with hard, cold concrete. Five months of nothing but the cell and the yard had really been imprisoning. Oh lovely freedom—be it ever so slight.

2

A Strike

BUT this new-found joy didn't last long. Industries was struck, appropriately enough on May Day, and I didn't go back to work for over a month. The May 1 date was coincidental: I doubt that any of my confreres were aware of its historical significance. So far as I knew the strike had not been planned. For some weeks prior to the strike there had been a great deal of agitation, but this was not unusual. The old-timers were always "signifying," and nothing much usually came of it. However, a certain amount of tension had been building up amongst the inmates, ostensibly over several issues. While the food had initially appeared good to me, after a few months I thought otherwise. It was difficult to say exactly what irked the men most about the food. Probably the sameness from day to day and from week to week. All prisons put filler in the hamburgers and Alcatraz was certainly not unique in that respect. But I think that a tight prison like Alcatraz couldn't get away with the same low quality food as other prisons. There was so little there that food played a much more important role in the daily lives of the men (I became acutely aware of this only after several years). During the week or so preceding the strike a great deal of food had been scattered over the floor in the dining hall; the officials apparently took no measures to correct the situation, or even to find out what it was all about. They closed their eyes to it, probably hoping it would blow away. But food was only one part of the story, and if that had been the only issue nothing might have happened.

The main part of the prison consisted of two long parallel cell blocks facing each other, with cells on both sides of each block. Thus there were the outer cells, which had an outside view, and the inner cells of each block, which faced each other. The corridor between the two blocks was known as "Broadway."

Daylight never reached Broadway, where the air was always heavy. Originally there had been some sort of ventilating system, but it had been destroyed by the hand grenades dropped through the roof during the 1946 escape attempt. There was no question but that the cells along Broadway were in all ways the least desirable.

Three categories of prisoners lived on Broadway. First, the kitchen workers, who lived on flats: the rationale being that when they were let out of their cells very early in the morning, they would not disturb the other men who were still asleep. This seemed to me a pretty thin excuse. I think it was just more convenient for the guards to have all the kitchen workers together where they were more readily accessible.

On the second tier on Broadway were the black prisoners. A federal prison in 1952, located in a progressive state, practiced such open discrimination. I could see only one explanation for this: that the Federal Bureau of Prisons was top heavy with southerners whose brand of racism permeated all its national policies.

The third category of prisoners on Broadway, who figured in the strike in a very direct way even though they were not working in Industries, were some twenty-five new arrivals who were almost finished doing their one-month orientation farce. It had been a rather large shipment, most of the men coming from Atlanta and Leavenworth penitentiaries. A number had been accused of attempting to escape and had lost all their Good Time after a prison "trial." These men felt they had nothing to lose, consequently the agitational efforts of some of the Alcatraz old-timers hit the mark. Most of the agitation revolved around the question of Broadway. The new men felt that they were being kept there too long.

No amount of agitation would have succeeded in starting the blowup if there hadn't been a real basis for the men's grievances. It was the coming together of all these factors that precipitated what followed on the night of April 30.

Things began to happen soon after lock-up. At first it was nothing much, the usual bed pounding where some men lifted up one corner of their beds, bringing it down hard on the concrete floor. Others joined in unison, making a loud racket, but still that was nothing unusual. Actually anyone caught pounding his bed post this way was sent to the hole, but the one cell house officer on duty at night had a difficult time catching anyone in the act. The men were usually able to warn everyone along the line that the officer was on that range. Bed pounding was such a common after-supper activity that most of the cells had deep holes gouged into the concrete floors where the bed posts came down as the result of many years of such activity. I had never engaged in bed pounding, or in the cat-calling which sometimes followed. Some officers were more subject to cat-calls than others, depending on their unpopularity.

Usually this activity would go on for about a half an hour, rising and falling in intensity several times, and then cease, as if by mutual consent, but this night was different. It kept growing in intensity, with practically the whole cell house demonstrating, but still I didn't join. This wasn't my style, and I was probably also afraid of the consequences if caught. I wanted to get off the Rock and I knew that were I found bed pounding, it would serve the authorities as a ready made excuse to keep me here. I didn't want to give them such an *easy* excuse.

While all this was going on I thought it strange no officers had passed my cell. With things so out of hand I thought the warden would have tried to regain control one way or another. As it was, the pace of the disturbance was accelerating while authority appeared unwilling to show its face. I was puzzled and not a little frightened: I wondered where it would end.

Finally, around nine o'clock one of the men threw the wooden shelf out of his cell onto the flats. The shelf, a board about a foot wide by five feet long, which rested on steel rods imbedded in the back concrete wall of the cell, was easily torn off its supports. It was strange that the officials had not foreseen this possibility. They were always so security conscious about everything around the prison, and everything was usually designed to be indestructible.

This first shelf was a cue for the others to follow, and shelves as well as library books, rolls of toilet paper, bedding, and other miscellaneous objects were hurled out. And then bottles of ink were thrown against the walls, where they made beautiful impressions, not to be easily erased. The final blow was struck against the half-dozen clocks hung around the cell house walls. With accurate pitches the men hit these with the ink bottles—halting the flow of time. I wondered if they realized what they were doing. For one doing time to stop time was tantamount to extending his sentence. Only one clock was not hit that night, and that only because it hung in the library, behind a wire mesh screen.

The next escalation occurred when some of the men hurled out torches made from toilet paper, igniting everything that would burn: books, boards, toilet paper, pillows and mattresses; all smoking as the merry bonfires burned. Finally someone got a really good idea: "burn the coveralls" the cry went up, and out went the coveralls, into the fires. Morton Sobell however wasn't brave that night, and he, with about half the men, thought it more prudent not to destroy his coveralls.

I had heard all the stories of 1946, when the cell house had been bombarded with mortar shells and hand grenades dropped through the roof, and wondered if this would end up the same way. Of course back in 1946 there had been an escape attempt, and several guards held hostage, but I knew that authorities sometimes didn't believe in using a minimum of counterforce to regain control of a run-away situation. There were guards who were only itching to shoot their rifles, given any sort of pretext. So, watching the scene unfold, I was nervous. In one sense I remained a spectator yet at the same time I was enmeshed in what was happening. It wasn't a question of my not believing in violence; it didn't come naturally to me. I had to overcome my middle class scruples if I were to accept violence as an answer to wrongs, and I remembered Gandhi's non-violent resistance, which would have been ideal for this situation. I wasn't a pacifist, but I couldn't see the point to "senseless" destruction. The coveralls, yes, how I hated those demeaning coveralls; I had nothing against the clocks, but I lacked the courage to participate. During all the uproar no hack was to be seen, and had one dared show himself, he would have had to walk under the upper walk, to avoid the likelihood of being hit by some hurled object. But I didn't see or hear a single one all evening. Finally officialdom made its presence felt by water, which began to accumulate on the floor, reaching into my cell so that I had to get up on my cot. When the water reached the burning debris, a huge volume of smoke began to erupt and it wasn't long before the men on the top ranges began choking and pleading for air. Pretty soon the whole cell house was filled with smoke and even those of us on the flats began to experience difficulty in breathing. It may have been a desperate response to the smoke, which led some of the men to pick their cots off the wall, where they were hung from two hooks, and use them as battering rams to break up their washbasins and toilets, then use the broken pieces of vitreous to break the window panes in order to get some fresh air.

It got to be midnight (the men who could see the one clock in the library called out the time), there was a mess of smoldering wreckage on the flats, and about two or three inches of water covered the whole floor. Suddenly, a voice cried, "no work!" and very quickly the cry was taken up around the cell house "no work, no work, no work." And so it went, until about three o'clock when there was nothing left to throw out, in the cells of those so disposed, and the cell house became quiet enough so that I could get a couple of hours of sleep.

What was going to happen in the morning? Would the cell doors be racked open? Would there be armed guards? All around, on the outside? These were the questions that weighed most, even while I was fitfully sleeping. It had been an anxiety-producing experience thus far, and I couldn't begin to guess what lay ahead.

I awoke at dawn. There was still an inch or so of water on the floor, but it was being drained off. As the breakfast hour approached the tension rose to an unbearable level, until finally the gates were opened and we all stepped out, stopping for only a moment to survey the awful mess, and then moving single file to the mess hall as though nothing were amiss; except that nobody was wearing coveralls. It looked strange, that first time, to see ourselves in the dining hall dressed in ordinary prison blues, trousers, and shirts. There were usually quite a number of guards around at breakfast time, since a new shift which included the Industries guards had just come on duty. There didn't appear to be any extra, or at least none who were visible.

At breakfast not a thing was said about what would happen later, as though it was understood. "No work." It was wild. Here we were, eating breakfast, as if nothing had happened, or was going to happen. It was May 1, a meaningful date for me. For how many others? I recalled the May Day parades, when half our engineering class turned out to celebrate this workers holiday, marching as a contingent from City College. May 1, what better date to choose to strike?

We returned to our cells, and when the time came the guards opened up the doors on each of the ranges in turn, calling out the familiar "Industries workers report to work." But no one stepped out of his cell, that is, no one except the blacks on Broadway. It would have been odd if they had gone on strike to support the grievances of whites who complained that they were being kept on Broadway too long, when the blacks had to live there all the time.

We remained in our cells that morning, except for the inmates who worked around the cell house and in the mess hall. They all went to work. This was going to be strictly an Industries strike, though I don't know when this strike policy was formulated, or by whom. Oddly enough I didn't hear any ill words directed against the blacks who had gone to work in Industries. Either the whites recognized the justice of their action, or they simply didn't care. At noon the routine was repeated, and again everyone stood firm. Not a solitary soul went to work, except for the blacks. The lack of rancor against the blacks surprised me, because I was more or less used to the whites (at least some of them) using the blacks as scapegoats whenever opportunity arose. Surely the opportunity was now present.

We heard that the hacks were trying to keep the Industries laundry going, since it did the linens for many of the military installations around the Bay area, and if these contracts were lost the laundry, which employed more inmates and civilians than any other part of Industries, might have to close. This would in turn mean that the civilians who supervised the operations might have to be transferred to some other prison. We heard that the civilian supervisors were actually doing the manual work as though their lives depended on it. The other shops, like the glove and clothing shops, were not as critically situated, since their output was based on long-range production schedules.

The next day the routine was repeated, as though we were taking part in a well-rehearsed play. We all remained in our cells, leaving only for meals. For most of the men who had been working in Industries steadily for years, this was like a vacation. It didn't make any difference that they couldn't leave their cells. And we were all pleasantly surprised that first weekend when the usual weekend routine was maintained and we were permitted to go to the yard; almost as though the officials were being extra-nice, trying not to give us reason for complaint.

Around the third or fourth day a curious incident took place. Alvin Karpis, also known as (a.k.a.) Creepy Karpis, a real old-timer who had been captured by none other than J. Edgar himself, *in person*, went up to the captain (a.k.a. "Grandma," because he didn't look like an authority figure) and tried to explain the men's grievances. He committed the horrendous faux pas of trying to make himself the middle man in the strike. This was really odd behavior for one who had spent as many years as he had behind bars. Anyone who had been around even a couple of years could have predicted the outcome. He was thrown into Special Treatment Unit (S.T.U.), a euphemism for the hole, also known as "solitary." Later I learned that the Nazis used the exact same euphemism for one of their death houses. There seemed a certain similarity between *all* prison keepers.

After about a week the officials decided to try to break the strike. In the morning, when the cell doors were opened for work call, certain inmates were singled out and "personally" requested by the captain to go back to work. When they refused, the "goon squad" entered their cells and dragged them off to the Treatment Unit (T.U.), otherwise known as segregation, located in B cell block, a cell block very much like the unused A, but located on the other side of the cell house and walled off from the rest of the cell house. S.T.U. was also located there. The goon squad was the unofficial name given to a group of officers given assignments that might involve them in violence. They were frequently the initiators of the violence. They were usually well built, heavy set, and with distinctly brutish casts, looking remarkably like their roles.

Every morning and every afternoon more men were dragged off to T.U., until it was filled to its capacity of thirty-two men, there being thirty-two cells in which the men were kept twenty-four hours a day, well isolated from the general population. While the Prison Bureau rules prescribed a minimum diet of twelve hundred calories a day for all men in T.U., every one knew this to be a fiction. For the duration of the strike the men in T.U. were given even smaller rations than those usually prescribed there. An ice-cold mixture of ground-up vegetables of various kinds, dished out with an ice-cream scoop was a main part of their diet. This and similar deliberate inedibles were the foods served in T.U. and S.T.U.

After all the T.U. cells were filled, the men were doubled up, and before the strike was finished they were tripled—with only one bed in a cell. Toward the end some eighty men were locked up in B-block, fully one half the white population. Normally T.U. had a population of about twenty men. The S.T.U. cells (I think there were three or four) were also over-filled. These were dark, completely enclosed cells, with only a hole in the floor for natural functions. A guard supplied rationed water. In the evening a mattress was thrown in for sleeping, and in the morning it was taken away, which meant that the men had to sit or stand on the cold steel floor sixteen hours a day.

Some of the men in S.T.U. began to clamor and pound on the walls during the night. We could all hear the resonant steel panels boom as they were hit with bare hands. These men were already in the lowest depths, being systematically starved to death, there was little more the officials could do to them. It was heartbreaking to hear their protests go on for hours, night after night. All the men sympathized with them, and we wondered if the sound of their futile protests carried across the water to the mainland in the stillness of the night.

I suppose the example set by the men in S.T.U. must have spurred on the T.U. inhabitants to start their own rumpus. First they began yelling and rattling the bars. In response to this the officials opened up all the windows during the night. With only a couple of blankets in each cell the men froze, even though they huddled together. To up the ante, the men burned toilet paper and other inflammables in the sinks and toilet bowls, and the heat cracked them (the beds could not be taken off the wall in T.U.) and then they pulled out the wires from the electric conduits. It was a savage battle, with no holds barred on either side.

T.U. was patrolled at night by a guard within a wire mesh enclosed cat-walk like in the main cell house, and the men began to taunt him, telling him that his wife was sleeping with a whole list of other officers who lived on the island. Their taunting was so effective that they had him in tears and he had to be withdrawn from this particular duty. Every night we heard T.U. and S.T.U. raising hell. How they were able to do it on their meager rations, I don't know, for each of the men was losing about a pound a day (at the end of a month each man had lost thirty pounds). I suppose one could say the community spirit at Alcatraz was strong.

I had been at work less than a week when the strike began, so it meant going back to my previous schedule, only I no longer had my hour of floor buffing each day. I had ordered a couple of mathematical texts more than four months earlier, and fortunately I received them less than a week before the strike began. Very good timing. Sometimes it took more than a half a year to get books.

One book was an advanced calculus text, and the other covered complex function theory, one of my favorite subjects. I literally buried myself in these books for the duration of the strike, especially the function theory. The problems were thought-provoking, and satisfying, and I spent from six to eight hours each day studying and working problems. If I had deliberately planned it I couldn't have found a better way of doing cell time during the strike. It helped relieve the tension better than any sedative and it made me feel good to find that I could still study, especially under these conditions.

When the goon squad began to pull inmates from their cells I waited for my turn, but it never came. They left me alone. At the time I didn't know why, since this seemed a ready-made opportunity to get me. What I didn't know was that the strike had been successfully kept out of the newspapers. The authorities didn't want publicity. Had I been placed in segregation I still could have written Dreyfus, my attorney, and asked him to visit me, and that would have meant an end to the secrecy. Had I realized the true situation it would have saved me a great deal of needless worry. I wasn't afraid of segregation, as much as of what it would do to my health. I had seen prisoners on the Rock whose health had broken down. It was very difficult to recover in circumstances where medical care was nonexistent, the diet hardly adequate for one in good health, and every other amenity for health missing. Each morning when they dragged more men out from their cells I waited— as one doomed—for the axe to fall. When I was saved for that day I went back to my studies.

In the evening I generally read lighter books. I read Scott Fitzgerald for the first time, and found it difficult to understand why he was rated so highly. *The Caine Mutiny* was such an obviously synthetic novel that it amused me. The author must have studied popularized Freud to produce his characters, instead of creating them from life. It was a formula novel, calculated to yield a best seller.

There was a great deal of chess-playing during the strike. Each of the players had a chess set in his cell and called out the moves to his opponent. After a day of study I would play one or two games this way. It was under such conditions of sameness that the timelessness of prison became even more accentuated. Every day was exactly like every other day. And when the fog descended on the Bay for several days, and the two fog horns on the island, one in the lighthouse and one at the other end of the Rock, started wailing, I felt like a Kafka character. It was eerie to hear the cacophony of the fog horns going on for days, without stopping even for a moment to catch their breaths.

I didn't write Helen a word about the strike. I knew that the censor was on the lookout for any message, and decided not to try to outsmart him. Besides, it would have been difficult to tell Helen what was taking place, since we had not previously discussed the possibility of an event such as a strike. I didn't write to Dreyfus to ask him to come because I didn't want to bother him with unimportant matters; after all, while all this was going on the death date of Ethel and Julius was fast approaching. And yet I had no feeling of their approaching doom. For instance, on the weekend of the 23 of May I knew that the Supreme Court *might* be meeting on the following Monday to rule on a motion to delay the execution, but not actually knowing for certain that the Court was going to sit then, it was difficult for me to react as I felt I should. In effect, here on the Rock I was out in limbo.

On Monday I did learn from another inmate, who had been told by a guard, that the Supreme Court had handed down a ruling denying our last motion, thus dooming Ethel and Julius to death, unless some unforeseen miracle occurred. That night I wrote Helen, "I know that you will be working hard and long, my love, while I luxuriate in idleness." And this was precisely how I viewed the situation.

I never missed the newspapers as much as during this period. Not a written word about the case penetrated the walls. The censor saw to that. Every news magazine was carefully scanned and properly expurgated.

Finally, on June 4, the strike was broken by a relatively simple technique. The authorities called in a half a dozen long timers who had less than a year to go to complete their sentences, and warned them that if they didn't return to work *all* their statutory good time, as well as their Industrial Good Time, would be taken away. In some cases this meant more than ten years of Good Time! Faced with the alternatives of doing one more year, or twelve more years, these men quite understandably chose to return to work and no one uttered a word against them. Once they went back to work it was a simple matter to get the other inmates to capitulate. That night I wrote Helen, "Today I returned to work," but doubted that she would get the import of this simple statement. One of the official reports to Washington on the strike, phrased it, "the men declined to work."

Among the more tangible results of the strike was an end to the coveralls. We were never given new ones to replace those that had been burned, and anyone who still had his coveralls was asked to turn them in. The authorities must have concluded that this little bit of humiliation had outlived its usefulness. Even while the strike was going on the food became progressively better, and it continued to improve over the next year: during the next five years this lesson was not forgotten. From the men in the kitchen we heard that the warden would bear down on the steward (the title for the head of the kitchen, at this time) every now and then, literally frightening him to do his best to keep the men from complaining about the food.

The improvement was most obvious in the formerly lowly hamburger. We used to get baked hamburger made with about 50 percent soy beans, and other adulterates, so that the meat taste was completely lacking. Now the hamburgers were made from pure meat, grilled instead of baked. Of course it meant more work, making them this way, but it was obvious to everyone that the kitchen staff was trying to please the inmates. Now we all looked forward to the hamburger, instead of cursing and flinging it on the floor. The most remarkable aspect was that the meat allowance remained the same, six ounces, gross weight, per man, per day. And yet it seemed as though we were now getting more meat.

Before the strike we got two fried eggs a week— eggs that had been prepared well in advance and kept warm in the oven until they had hardened. Now we were served two fried eggs, three times a week, and they were prepared as the men filed into the dining room. We also had a choice of sunny-side up or turned-over. In addition, once a week we had three small link sausages with the eggs. Many improvements and innovations were gradually introduced into the diet during the next couple of months, until the meals actually became something to write home about. Unfortunately under the correspondence rules this was forbidden; it was fifteen more years before the Bureau of Prisons realized that the rules actually kept the inmates from writing about the good as well as the bad, and to rectify this situation.

The smashed clocks were removed and never replaced, but the cell house walls were given a new coat of paint to hide the ink splotches. Among the less tangible results, the atmosphere became more relaxed and the guards didn't push quite as hard. However in T.U. there was no more smoking after the initial fires, and the twice-weekly one hour fresh air periods, which had been routine before the strike, were effectively abolished. The men were now subjected to a rectal examination going to and coming from yard, and few chose to go out.

Ironically, those who were "convicted" of having broken toilet bowls or causing some other destruction of government property were the first ones taken out of T.U. and sent to Industries, so that they could earn money to pay the cost of their destruction. Incidentally they were charged three times the actual cost of the article (the difference going to pay for the officer supervision of the installation—they said). The actual installation itself was done by inmates.

I have heard the authorities say many times that inmates never gained a thing by violence. I had witnessed one illustration disproving this bit of mythology.

Immediately after the strike there was lot of "signifying" amongst the men: some of the old-timers spoke about burning down the Industries building. The authorities took measures to contain the situation in case of trouble in the cell house. They moved all potential "troublemakers" down to the flats, where I was celling, so they could be under closer scrutiny. As a result I was moved to a new cell on the topmost range, C-342. Now instead of looking at bare concrete I had a magnificent view of the Golden Gate, and I didn't get any more cold drafts on my feet. One other advantage was that I could see the only clock left in the cell house, the one in the library. This was most important to me; I liked to schedule my time in the evening.

I knew that no matter how long I remained in prison, or where I might be transferred, I would never have another view as beautiful as the one from this cell. Each evening, when it wasn't foggy, I saw the sun descend over the Golden Gate and enjoyed it beyond measure.

3

The FBI
Never Gives Up

IN A way, the timing of the strike was unfortunate, since it diverted my thoughts from the struggle to save the lives of Ethel and Julius. I was caught up in my very personal maelstrom, and found it impossible to relate to what was going on out there. I was quite aware of the contradiction (even while it was happening), but powerless to rectify it, and it pained me deeply.

Everything about my situation made it difficult to keep a proper focus on the case. My news sources were so poor as to be nonexistent. Dreyfus visited me twice the month before the execution. Since I had explicitly told Helen I felt that our personal dialogue had top priority in her letters, she didn't have the time or energy to keep me posted on the current events. In fact she sent Mark to her mother's in Washington to minimize all personal responsibilities during this crucial period so she could devote all her energies to the single most pressing task—saving their lives, or at least postponing the execution date. Of course the news periodicals were expurgated of all references to the case, and since this was 1953, the thought of going to court to make an issue of the absolutely illegal denial of my First Amendment rights did not occur to me, or to anyone else. In the first place I would have lost (a warden is king in his dominion, is how the courts would have put it). But even more important, all the available lawyers were too busy with other cases where the stakes were far more crucial than my merely wanting to know.

Thus, even after the strike ended on June 4, I still couldn't switch my thinking to the impending doom of Ethel and Julius. How could I think about that concerning which I had nothing to think with? No facts, no theories. I had absolutely no idea of the pace of events. Had I had even an inkling of the crescendo of mounting protests—domestic and foreign—against the execution, it would have helped me immeasurably. Of course, Helen wrote me bits about it, but it is one thing to read about world-shaking happenings in a personal letter and quite a different matter to read about it in the national press.

Thus it wasn't until the next shipment of men arrived from other penitentiaries (about five or six months later) that I began to appreciate the extent of the public protest. The new arrivals were always glad to tell me about what had taken place; at least what they knew from the Establishment press. Unlike times when Dreyfus or Helen visited, my confreres and I had all the time in the world to talk about the past. Hearing about it from their lips half a year later brought it home to me with an unbelievable delayed immediacy.

On June 17, the eve of the execution, a friendly guard dropped me a word that Justice Douglas had just issued a stay; I learned about the execution similarly two days later. But such bits of information were quite insufficient to form a basis for any emotions. A few drops of water have no meaning to one thirsting as I was. But the picture of our last meal together, with the lawyers, in the basement of the courthouse, after the jury had come back with the verdict, had become so indelibly impressed on my mind that I could hardly think of anything else except of how Julius and Ethel and I had tried to buoy up our downcast lawyers and had joked about the thickly loaded corned beef sandwiches we were eating, knowing this was the last of such fare for all of us—at least for sometime. Were we brave, or were we foolish? Who is to say? I also recalled how, at West Street, I had told Helen I wished there could be a way for me to exchange places with Ethel. I felt that it was terribly important not to make orphans of their children, Michael and Robert; besides, thirty years was such a long long time. I had wondered if death was not preferable. But now, faced with the reality, the answer was all too obvious—while one lives there are always possibilities, while death is so damned final.

Dreyfus would have come the following day but it had been too late to arrange for a visit after the execution. Rules were applied strictly, especially when Morton Sobell and his attorneys were concerned: an attorney visit had to be approved on the prior day. Thus it wasn't until Monday that Dreyfus was finally able to see me and tell me a little of what had transpired during those last critical moments. Chief Justice Vinson had recalled the Court from vacation—an act almost unprecedented in the history of the Court. After a few hours argument, the Court had vacated Douglas's stay and the execution had been expedited for 8:00 P.M. Friday—so as not to desecrate the Jewish Sabbath!

Howard Meyer had also sent me a telegram immediately after the execution, but I didn't get it until Monday evening, with no explanation offered for its delay. It was understood that inmates were never entitled to explanations.

I was most pleasantly surprised by the sensitivity shown by my fellow inmates. They treated me as if Ethel and Julius had been my siblings, not just my "rap-partners." Their air of concern was so at variance with the picture even I had of them that I didn't quite know what to make of it.

I expected a letter from Helen on Monday; when none came on Tuesday I was ready to climb the wall. I don't know why a letter was so crucial then, but I must have surmised that the death of Ethel and Julius marked a turning point in the case, and I may have been fearful that Helen might leave me, as though I too were dead. Of course no such thought occurred consciously, but the intensity of my anxiety could have been accounted for only by something akin to this. As a result I wrote Helen a strong letter, castigating her for forgetting that I was a person, with an identity, and turning me into a symbol. I didn't know how I'd manage until the next day without a letter. I was unaware that Helen had been leading a picket line in front of the White House until the very last minute: after the executions she was drained of all energy—physical and psychological. It was a terrible disaster for her, to have lost the struggle into which she had put all her energy during the past year. It just never occurred to me to put myself in her place, nor could I have done so even if I had tried. Our worlds were too far apart for us to understand each other's position.

Howard Meyer flew to Alcatraz the following week and we met for two whole days. Each day he caught the earliest visitor's boat to the Rock, and left by the last.

We had from nine until three. No one offered us anything to eat at lunch time, and we were too busy to make a point of it.

We had one action pending in the Court at this time, a left-over 2255 motion: from the last appeal of Julius and Ethel. The Court gave them the bums rush so as not to delay the execution. The United States Attorney had originally tried to get my appeal heard at the same time as the Rosenbergs, but was fortunately overruled by Judge Weinfeld, one of the "liberal" District Court judges.

It was silly to expect the Court not to affirm its previous ruling, since all of the points involved in the appeal concerned solely Julius and Ethel. But since ours had been a conspiracy trial, in which I had been held to account for all that transpired, even for the "theft of the atom bomb secret," I could legally bring up any points of the trial, even where they did not concern me directly.

The major point of the appeal concerned the "console table" which the government had claimed was a gift from the Russians and which allegedly contained some special hollowed-out part for use in microphotographing the secrets. A newspaper reporter for *The Guardian* located the table after the trial, and it was conclusively proved that Julius had purchased it from Macy's, as he had claimed at the trial, and that no hollowed out part existed. Clearly Greenglass had lied when he claimed that the table was a gift from the Russians, but the courts held otherwise—despite the available evidence. The courts asked why Bloch had not found the table during the trial, a stupid question when measured against Bloch's available resources at the time. The question might better have been put the

other way. Why hadn't the FBI seized the table at the
time they arrested Julius, since they had a search warrant and presumably knew Greenglass's story about its
being a present from the Russians? It would have made
more convincing evidence than the tin collection can
for the children of the Spanish Republic they had produced at the trial.

Howard and I discussed the 2255 motion, as well
as what action we could take to get the courts to have
me transferred from Alcatraz: "the Alcatraz Point," as
it would be called from now on. I knew it wouldn't be
an easy one, but I wasn't going to let it go by default. It
felt good to be taking part in these contemplated actions, but I thought of what I had missed in not being
permitted to enter into the deliberations concerning the
trial itself.

As a result of our conferences Howard asked
Homer Cummings, a former attorney general under
Roosevelt, now practicing law in Washington, who had
intimate connections with the most highly placed individuals in the Establishment, to look into the Alcatraz
Point. Howard had met Cummings through a Washington case they had in common. Cummings's findings
confirmed what I had suspected—J. Edgar Hoover himself had ordered that I be sent to Alcatraz. (Maybe Bennett hadn't lied when he said I would not be sent to Alcatraz, but had subsequently been over-ruled by
Hoover?) Cummings wasn't willing to get involved in
this aspect of the case because he evidently had a lot
of respect for Hoover's power. Helen went to Washington and spoke with Cummings but couldn't alter his
decision.

I had learned that other inmates had been designated by Hoover to do their time here, usually because

they had in some way placed the FBI in an unfavorable light. Tom Robinson was one such. He had gone around the country for over a year, disguised as a woman, while the G-men were looking for him with their whole apparatus. He had already spent about twenty years on the Rock, and only Hoover knew how many more he would have to spend. Of course Hoover kept his favorite big time gangsters there also, like Basil Banghart, whose exploits went back to the prohibition era. These gangsters were all has-beens, but Hoover couldn't destroy his own myth by having them transferred to an ordinary penitentiary.

As a result of these conferences with Howard I drew up a memorandum on the question of my so-called flight to Mexico and my not having taken the stand at the trial, because at every turn of the legal proceedings the government kept harping on these points, even though they had absolutely nothing to do with the pending actions. The memorandum was then filed as an affidavit with the 2255 appeal, although it had no connection with it.

Here, for the first time, I told how I had wanted to testify at my trial, but had been held back by my attorneys (Phillips had never told me that he thought I should testify, even though he told the court that he differed with Kuntz on the question). I didn't go into the details of the story; it wasn't the place. I then related all the events which led up to our trip to Mexico, and how I panicked there, but I didn't record my fear of being convicted of perjury. Even though it wouldn't stop the government from bringing up these points, at least this was now a part of the official record.

Helen came to San Francisco for several weeks about the middle of July, and we had time for extended discussions during our spread-out visits. The most important question was what direction the Committee would now take. Previously there had been only one short-term objective—to save Ethel and Julius from the electric chair. But in view of my thirty year sentence, long range planning was now in order.

The campaign to save the lives of Ethel and Julius had been waged on several fronts. There were those who devoutly believed in their innocence, and there were those who simply had grave doubts about their guilt. In addition, many had given their support because they felt that the death penalty was too harsh even if they were guilty. Helen was for continuing my campaign on the same grounds, but I felt quite strongly, as a matter of principle, that I didn't want the support of anyone who didn't think I was innocent. To Helen this was strictly a tactical matter, to gain maximum support, but from the inside I couldn't see it the same way; I had elevated it to a matter of principle.

I also urged Helen to change the name of the Committee from the National Committee to Secure Justice in the Rosenberg Case to the Committee to Secure Justice for Morton Sobell. Julius and Ethel were dead: justice was no longer possible for them. Oddly enough there were some members of the Committee who did not want to change the name to reflect the new reality, and it took a great deal of effort to get their consent. Helen told me she always worked by consensus with the Committee even though she could have done some things on her own.

But I fell into the same error that my trial lawyers had made. I thought that the only way I could gain my freedom was to separate my case from that of Julius and Ethel; that unless I was able to accomplish this, their deaths would be like a millstone around my neck; because to free me would be to acknowledge their wrongful death. Helen understood that it would be wrong to try to separate my conviction from theirs, even though it appeared logically sound. We had many long and difficult discussions on this.

We also differed on the question of the relative emphasis to be placed on the legal fight and the extra-legal fight. Until the day I was freed I constantly insisted that the case be kept before the courts in one form or another, for while I recognized the unique character of the extra-legal efforts, I nonetheless felt that, in the end, it would be up to the courts.

This thinking was not without its contradictions. I wasn't a believer in miracles, and knew that in order to survive the ordeal of a thirty-year sentence I would have to fight it, even if it was hopeless, or perhaps because it was hopeless. Over the years well-meaning prison officials would sometimes counsel me that I might make parole, if only I gave up the fight, and I would always tell them I didn't want to find myself in the position of having done the whole bit quietly in the hope that the parole board might grace me with their benevolence.

Even though I recognized the hopelessness of my own situation I didn't have a true picture of conditions beyond the walls. *Time* and *Life* failed utterly to give me any idea of what it meant to live in America while Senator Joe McCarthy was running rampant. I was truly in the classical ivory tower here on the Rock. Only after I emerged from prison, spoke with some of the victims of McCarthyism, and learned of the firings and intimidations, did I begin to appreciate the meaning of this epoch. I almost felt glad I had been spared the ordeal, but for Helen it was very real and a daily part of her work with the Committee. When she approached people to help the Committee they frequently had to think twice, worrying about possible repercussions.

So while the nation was being torn apart by the Red hunters, I was concerned with such mundane problems as getting hair oil for my scalp, or getting rid of the ants that invaded my cell. Fortunately these two problems were related. Since we had no commissary, the hair oil was dispensed by the hospital, and it irritated my scalp, as I had been warned it would do by others. However, I found it an excellent ant repellent, when applied to the back wall of the cell, where the invading ants entered through the old ventilator opening. The ants were conquered, but my dandruff marched on.

With my educational background I could easily have gotten a clerical job at Industries. However I preferred manual work. It was more meaningful to take a piece of raw wood and shape it into a finished product than to add a column of figures. Others sought clerical jobs because they were easy. Besides they were the status jobs, and usually involved less supervision by guards, an important consideration on the Rock where everything we did was so closely watched. But I liked working with wood.

I started on fourth grade, making approximately ten cents an hour. The pay scale varied with our production, from month to month, since we were all on a pool piece-work basis. For me the Industrial Good Time I earned was far more important than the wages. The Good Time amounted to two days a month for the first year, and rose to five days a month after the fourth year. The Good Time was subtracted from the maximum time (in my case about twenty years, since I would earn approximately ten years statutory Good Time if I didn't fuck up). One did maximum time only if he didn't make parole. In the end I earned more than two years of Good Time working in Industries and elsewhere; two years I didn't have to spend in prison.

The Industries building, sometimes referred to as the New Industries Building, since it had been built after World War II, was a long two-story structure, nestled in the rock of the island above the water's edge. It was separated from the water by two wire fences of moderate height. These were not the main deterrents to escape. Every thirty minutes we were counted by the guard in the shop, who then called in the count to the control tower. One couldn't get far in thirty minutes swimming in the San Francisco Bay. In addition there were extra counts, both before and after the ferry left the island. The prison security lay in the continual monitoring of the inmates.

Going to work was a complicated procedure for the guards. At work call we'd march out into the yard, through the metal detector, and assemble according to our place of work. We were first checked off by the guard from our shop, then, after the lieutenant in charge of operations was satisfied that all men were present, the door in the long wall of the yard was opened, and the lieutenant would station himself there and check off the men as they passed out of the prison proper.

On the way down to Industries we passed through another metal detector, a more sensitive one. And finally when we entered our particular shop, we were again counted by the shop guard. After he was satisfied that we were all present he would call in his count to the control tower. Though each of the shops was located in the same building, there were no interconnections. This was designed presumably to maximize security. To go between shops one had to go outside the building, which involved another complicated procedure, with the control tower again involved.

Returning to the cell house the procedure was reversed, except that this time about half a dozen guards stood waiting to shake us down as we entered the yard. It would have taken too long to search each of us so they only made spot checks. Inmates who wanted to bring up contraband from Industries devised many beautiful schemes for evading the search. One simple method was for the "hot" man to engage services of a dozen confederates, who would precede him to the yard. The confederates had only to act suspiciously, not a very difficult act, and all the guards would be occupied searching the suspicious characters while the man with the contraband went by unnoticed. In another scheme one tall inmate with long arms would wait for a nasty day, when he could wear his raincoat and strap the contraband to his wrist. Because the guards always had the inmates stretch out their arms to be searched, searching in orthodox fashion none could reach his wrists.

Most of the time the contraband was quite harmless, a bottle of glue, or a piece of wood, or perhaps some varnish; more infrequently it was a shiv constructed from scrap iron. I knew one inmate who had sent shivs up the hill inside some pipe. There were countless ways of getting around the vigilance of the police, if one had the desire.

In addition to our shop (in official parlance each shop was called a factory) where we made letter trays, coat racks, and wooden floor mats for the post office, there was also a brush factory which manufactured push brooms. The men inserted the horse hair into the holes of a wooden block by hand, and fastened them with brass wire as they might have several hundred years ago. There was also a glove factory for making leather work gloves, and a clothing factory, which made pants for the armed forces. On the second floor of the building was the large laundry which serviced some of the military installations in the Bay area as well as the prison. All incoming laundry was supposed to be subjected to an x-ray fluoroscopic examination, yet metallic objects like bullets or lipstick cases were frequently found by the inmates in the laundry. The guards who were supposed to conduct the examination would have had to be dark-adapted to find such small objects, and there were probably lapses in this procedure.

In each of the factories there were one or more inmate clerks, and in the main Industries office, four or five inmates and a civilian supervising clerk. More than half of the prison population worked in Industries, with some turnover from month to month.

In September one of two inmate electricians in Industries was discharged and I was asked if I would take the job. I jumped at the opportunity, surprised at the offer. I thought they would be afraid to let me get my hands on their electrical equipment lest I make an atom bomb—or worse.

The electric shop was located in a caged section of the laundry. Bill and I were the only men working there, and we had only nominal supervision. After a while I realized that Bill knew very little about motors and had prevailed upon the Industries supervisor to get me, so that his own shortcomings would not be revealed. The inmate who had left had carried most of the load. Bill could do wiring, or repair motor controllers if he were shown how. He was reputed to have been an Arkansas inmate shot-gun guard.

Alcatraz had an antiquated direct-current electric system, thanks to Thomas A. Edison, its most powerful exponent, and I looked forward to using some of my hitherto useless direct-current theory. I liked the idea that the system was antiquated since it would give me more room for experimentation.

The next period was comparatively my happiest on the Rock. I redesigned and rebuilt many motor controllers; I rewound many types of motors, but mainly those on the sewing machines. These had originally been designed to run at eighteen hundred revolutions per minute, but the men working in the glove and clothing shops were on piece-work schedule, and many pushed themselves to the limit to make more money. It was a simple matter to rewind the motors to run at twenty-four hundred r.p.m., or even faster, which allowed more production. Nor did it bother any of us that the sewing machines would not last quite as long, at this accelerated pace. For me it was a game to outwit the officials. I don't know why the other men pushed themselves so hard when they would have rebelled at working at half the pace outside. After a while I found out that Bill was getting paid off in cigarettes, stale packs of Wings.

I was amazed at the lax security in the electric shop. Hacksaw blades were absolutely forbidden, so we had to improvise when it came to cutting metal, but we had about a dozen files, in addition to scores of other tools, which were handled freely and without any real accounting. We also had a home-made lathe, used for turning down motor commutators. Metal turning lathes were forbidden since they could be used to make "bar-spreaders," to spread the prison bars apart. But this lathe, that a clever inmate had put together some time in the past, wasn't even listed on the books, so the authorities conveniently overlooked it. They knew it was essential to proper motor maintenance.

I enjoyed working in the shop, because in addition to allowing me to use my engineering expertise, it also gave me a degree of responsibility, and there were few things I minded more than being shorn of all responsibilities.

At the end of September, World Series time, I was astonished to learn that all those who could be spared from their jobs were permitted to go to the yard at game time to listen to the baseball broadcast. We were deprived of what I considered essential human contacts, but baseball evidently fell into a different category. Practically everyone from Industries came up on the hill about a half an hour before game time. The men who could be spared from the kitchen, as well as most of the other institution workers, were already in the yard. The Bay area weather was usually ideal during September. Some men sunned themselves, others played bridge, and everyone was relaxed. No one was playing ball, which made the scene different from any other day, even without the radio broadcast.

I joined the ranks of the bridge players, listening to the progress of the game with half an ear. It was, after all, communication from the outside world, something which was otherwise tightly restricted. The game was interrupted for a fast lunch break, after which we again went out. The game over, we all went back to our jobs, hoping that the series would go the full seven games. World Series time was the only time the regular rhythm of the institution was broken. I wondered whether the monotony was calculated, or just happened, and why the World Series?

Alcatraz was full of inconsistencies. I couldn't believe it when I first learned that we could get non-fiction books from the California State library. I suppose I hadn't heard of it sooner because so few men took advantage of the opportunity; in fact this service was used almost exclusively by inmates who faced prosecution in different states after they were due to be released from federal jurisdiction. These men obtained the statutes of the states in which they faced prosecution, and attempted to fight their cases before being transferred. But for me the State library became a gold mine of technical books. I obtained the titles from magazines I was reading, or from the bibliography of other texts, and would generally request three books at a time. I usually received one, and sometimes two. I tried studying some new engineering texts, but found it difficult to get much out of them. Renewal after four weeks was not permitted. The most satisfactory books were in the area of philosophy of science. I started with some of the classics, like Morris R. Cohen's *Reason and Nature* which I found unsatisfactory, but when I got to the moderns like Louis de Broglie, the physicist, I really enjoyed the readings. I thought it a poor reflection on my engineering education that we had never gone into this area of study in school.

After I left the Rock I learned that the State library privileges had been withdrawn, because, the story went, the privilege had been abused. Whenever privileges were withdrawn it was for the same reason. If the same yardstick was applied to people out of prison, they would have hardly any privileges left. The prison officials expected a more sensitive morality from inmates than from people outside the walls.

Though I had been given permission to purchase math texts, when I tried to buy a volume of poetry that Helen had suggested, *The Poetry of Freedom*, by W. R. Bennet and Norman Cousins, permission was denied, with the explanation that poetry was only a pastime and not a serious study.

I did some lighter reading during this period, like Kafka's *Diaries*. What a tortured soul, and how well he was able to communicate his feelings. Of course I identified with him, which heightened my pleasure in his work. I also read *The Castle*, a work I would never have been able to read before imprisonment. Again I made an identification. K's village was not too different from my prison. Both were completely irrational, in the classical sense, but had a special rationality of their own—like that of a dream. My Kafka appetite whetted, I very much wanted to read *The Trial*, but it wasn't in the Alcatraz library; I was lucky I had found the other two volumes.

I discovered the German classic, *The Weavers* by Gerhart Hauptmann, in our unpredictable collection. It described the plight of the textile workers, at a time when few authors thought such subjects suitable for novels. I enjoyed the book so much that I stayed up reading it after lights out, using the illumination from a small night light in the ceiling of the cell house. It was too little light and after a few nights my eyes rebelled. Some men read by this dim illumination night after night with no such repercussions.

A coincidence was finding David Alman's *World Full of Strangers* in our library. Dave was one of the people who worked for the Committee for many years, organizing and writing propaganda.

Since I couldn't get the magazines I would have wanted to read, I read the magazines I could get. Father Scannell brought in both *Commonweal* and *America*, the first a liberal lay-Catholic magazine, and the latter a Jesuit publication. I read them closely and found it interesting to follow the Catholic position from these two viewpoints. Had I been outside I knew I would never have found time for such reading; being imprisoned certainly had its broadening points.

One year passed, Christmas came again, Helen and I visited for the second Christmas on the Rock—some of our best visits. We laughed together, we talked slowly, with many pauses, even while facing the task of compressing so much wantingness into so little time and in so cold an atmosphere. Maybe it was because we knew they were tuned in and wanted to show how little it bothered us.

Suddenly during one visit we heard two other people talking on our circuit. We listened, it was evidently a telephone conversation to which we had been connected. The FBI must have been monitoring our conversation from the mainland over a telephone line, and this particular line was getting cross-talk from another line; that was what we must have been hearing. It couldn't have been anything else. Before this I knew only that the guard in the armory was tuned into our conversations. What did they expect to hear? Some escape plan? Helen telling me the plans of the Committee? Or our making love over the phone?

Although the population of Alcatraz was small, as penitentiaries go (it rose to two hundred and fifty while I was there), it took me a year to get to know most of the men by sight, and about half by name. I knew a lesser number by number. The number was important in that it told when the inmate had arrived. There were approximately fifty arrivals a year, with the number 1,000 occurring at the end of 1952. Those with numbers near 500 had arrived about 1942. I think the earliest number in my time was 151; one of the original shipment to the Rock when it was opened.

When I first got there everyone was part of a big blur, except for the inmates with whom I came in direct contact; but later I had a feeling for the "one big family," and actually felt part of it. I felt the pulse of the place, the tensions rising and falling, from day to day and week to week. More important, I had become accepted by my peers. They still treated me differently, but they accepted me. If I chose to express myself in prison jargon they would smile, knowing it didn't come naturally, and joke about my attempts to play the role of the con.

Though I was well accepted by my confreres on one level, I found I had difficulty relating to them whenever the relationship assumed a slightly more intense form. Ernie Lopez was a good example. He had originally come to prison for stealing O.P.A. food stamps from a government office. He had been socked with ten years for a crime which every con knew called for a year or two at the most. Then he escaped from Mc-Neil Island, the federal penitentiary in the northwest, not an easy feat, and wasn't recaptured until several months later. In talking to Ernie I learned that his mother had sent him out in the morning to steal milk from the milk-man; she had many children, and there wasn't enough money to buy the necessary food. I was attracted to Ernie; I suppose I wanted to learn more about him, and he seemed agreeable to discussing his past. But then came the blowup. I usually had my radar up and could sense static before it developed into a real storm, but this caught me by surprise. It was so silly. We had seen a movie, and Ernie told me he didn't like one of the actors. So I tried to explain that that was merely the role the actor was playing, and did not represent the man himself. But he couldn't understand me and we didn't talk for a couple of years after that.

Shortly after my run-in with Ernie I put in a cop-out to see the consultant psychiatrist. On the Rock no one in his right mind ever put in a cop-out to see the psychiatrist—it was the other way around—but I was still innocent. Even though I hadn't had more than the usual number of clashes they were disturbing, and I suppose I was hoping that the psychiatrist might be able to help me understand why they occurred. I felt I could cope better if I knew why. I suppose I was also looking for dialogue.

The psychiatrist visited the Rock once a month for a couple of hours. His main purpose was to "certify" as psychotic, inmates whom the authorities wanted to transfer to the Springfield Medical Center. A consultant psychiatrist in a prison (and elsewhere, I suppose) occupies a curious position: if he doesn't cooperate with the authorities, a replacement can easily be found. I never heard that this psychiatrist had been unwilling to certify anyone. But then the authorities usually didn't send anyone to Springfield unless he was really far gone.

Two or three months after I put in my cop-out, I got a call to go to the hospital for an interview with the "bug-doctor," as the M.T.A. put it. He was a cold fish, and I couldn't get much dialogue out of him. He explained that his procedure required that I write a detailed autobiography, which he would study before we could have any conferences. He said this was the same procedure he used with his patients on the outside. I spent the next couple of weeks on the autobiography. It wasn't a very frank account, since I wasn't ready to expose my inner self to my enemies. Maybe he would keep it confidential, but I wasn't certain it wouldn't be shown to the FBI. I gave him my seven thousand–word masterpiece which he sent back the following month—without comment. Finis!

I suppose I feared run-ins with others because I had seen some situations develop into nasty confrontations. Inmates lost control over the situation, which then took off, following a course of its own. Most often one could see when a situation was going to get out of hand far enough ahead to shift direction, but frequently the fireworks began without any warning.

Time and again I would see two inmates confronting each other, with neither apparently attaching any particular value to his life, and I felt sick when I saw such a scene. Perhaps I feared that some day I might unwittingly become one of the actors, and then it would be too late; I wouldn't be able to back out. Thus I always imagined that Helen was looking over my shoulder at whatever I did. If I were only considering myself I would frequently have acted far more recklessly, but I felt a greater responsibility toward Helen than toward myself. It was then that I understood what it was like to not have anyone on the outside toward whom one felt such responsibility. Since there is so little of life in prison, prison makes life less valuable.

One of the most remarkable aspects of the Rock was the rhythm of its moods. As a matter of fact it was the psychiatrist who pointed it out to me during that interview. He noted that he could gauge the tension of the Island as soon as he got off the launch and spoke with the first guard. The tension affected everyone, guards and inmates alike.

Once it was called to my attention, I became aware of how the tension cycled up and down several times a year. When it was high there were usually more fights, and the guards were quicker to write up a man for some chicken-shit shot. I never made notes of the exact times of the cycles, so it would be difficult to gauge what caused them.

Later I was surprised to find that no such phenomenon existed in larger prisons. I wondered if the authorities were conscious of these tension cycles, since they could surely have made compensatory efforts. At times it almost seemed as if they were bent on augmenting the tensions, and I would wonder if it was deliberate or plain stupidity. Once they distributed a set of rule books (we hadn't had any before) when the place was at the height of tension. The rule books were burned up that night, and the officials didn't do anything about it.

Ever since I'd entered prison I dreamed a great deal, in addition to my day-dreaming. Some of the dreams were repetitive. A frequent one was a dream in which I would soar gracefully above the populace, without any visible means of propulsion. I would just lift myself off the ground through sheer will-power, and then zoom above the trees and under the bridges, ascending, descending, like a bird without wings. But I did have to expend energy when climbing, and I could feel my energy being drained. But I also had dreams in which I would fall endlessly, until I finally awakened with great relief in a sweat.

Manny Bloch died that February: he was by far the youngest of the four lawyers who had defended us. I never saw him after that last lunch at the courthouse, but I know he must have come to realize what he had done, because he spoke out so strongly against the injustice which had been perpetrated that he was brought up on disbarment charges. The role of the defender of Julius and Ethel called for a hero, but alas, Manny did not have that quality, though it took guts to take on the case at all. Years later, when he came under attack from all quarters, I felt compelled to come to his defense. It was almost twenty years before a new breed of lawyers was born, lawyers who did not automatically bow to all the rulings of the bench; who were not afraid themselves of going to jail; who understood the political nature of the cases they were called upon to fight. How then could one fault Manny for not being ahead of his time? In death he was a pathetic figure, not the evil one his attackers portrayed him.

How strange it is when we sometimes awaken to an obvious truth, and wonder that we were completely unaware of it until that moment. Such was my feeling when I overheard one inmate telling another that he was never really hungry at mealtime. Then it came to me that I never sat down to a meal with the appetite I recalled from my previous life. Thus I never experienced the satisfaction of satisfying that hunger; I ate strictly from habit.

And this was but another manifestation of the lifelessness of my Alcatraz existence. We were fairly well fed, housed, and clothed, but we were treated more like animals in a zoo than human beings. The casual observer would probably not have found anything amiss in the way we were cared for, because a free person doesn't understand what his freedom consists of. While it is true that society decreed that the convicted be deprived of their freedom, nowhere was it spelled out how far this deprivation was to extend. Where was it written that we were to suffer this monotonously deadening existence which the warden meted out? Where was it written that all contact with the mainland was to be cut off, to an extent practiced in no other prison? Who had decreed that education was forbidden (except by correspondence)? Who wrote the decrees making us spend almost three quarters of our time in the cell? Who had formulated these arbitrary rules under which we existed in a form barely resembling human life? It was truly a tribute to the human race that each year only about 3 or 4 percent of the population was certified as insane and shipped to Springfield. But the Bureau of Prisons was never charged with crimes against humanity.

I was very happy when Helen wrote me that Dr. Erwin Gaede, the minister of the Unitarian Church of Los Angeles, wanted to visit me. I immediately wrote her to tell him to ask for a bench visit, as with the attorneys, rather than the bullet proof glass visit. Not too many ministers came to see men on the Rock, but it was a universal practice in the federal prison system to allow the clergy bench visits. As I might have foreseen, Dr. Gaede was denied permission to visit me at a time when his visits might have meant a great deal. Later, when I was in Springfield, I corresponded with him, but when I was transferred to Lewisburg permission to continue this correspondence was denied, on the ground that he "doesn't really know you" (I had never met him, in person). Such were the ways of the federal prison system.

But life moved on despite my frustrations, and new inmates arrived, sometimes individually like myself, and sometimes in a chain of ten or fifteen. In June of 1954 the Yugoslav who had at West Street hit Bob Thompson (one of the Communist eleven convicted under the Smith Act) over the head with a pipe and fractured his skull, arrived at Alcatraz. He had hit Bob only a day before he himself was scheduled to be returned to Yugoslavia, to face a murder trial there, and it was unmistakably an attempted political murder. The Yugoslav correctly calculated that there would be many who would sympathize, and that the appreciation for his "patriotic" act would save him from deportation. He was given a nominal sentence for the crime, was overwhelmed with contributions (which the Bureau of Prisons gave to him on his release, despite rules to the contrary) from assassin-sympathizers and, I was told, was finally released to another country. It was an ugly time in America, when attempted murder was officially and unofficially rewarded by the government, a government that professes to abhor terrorism. I evaluated the danger the Yugoslav represented to me, and decided I could cope. I'd just have to be careful not to give him a chance to "pipe" me. I didn't come into contact with him at work, which was about the only place he could get a pipe. Of course he could still use a baseball bat out in the yard, but I didn't think he would try. Besides a baseball bat is not as deadly as a pipe.

However Helen, on the outside, saw things differently. She asked, why I should take any chance, and swung into action, utilizing the situation to direct a campaign to get me off the Rock, away from the potential danger the Yugoslav represented. In addition she took me to task for what she felt was a violation of our understanding of frankness, in that I hadn't told her of the presence of the Yugoslav. She had learned about it from the press. I had to examine her accusation with great care before I was able to pick up the source of our difference and decided that I had unconsciously accepted the inmate code, not to complain to the authorities about another inmate. This would have been tantamount to snitching. Then I realized that over the years I had unconsciously assumed the attitudes of the other men, so that their ways became an integral part of my thinking. Helen's campaign must have been convincing. The Bureau separated the Yugoslav and myself, by shipping *him* away from the Rock.

For a year before the actual work was begun, we heard rumors that we would get a radio installation. I knew it was doomed to fail as soon as I learned about the plans. The loudspeakers were to be installed in the five foot space between the backs of the cell blocks and the sound was supposed to diffuse through the cell house from there. Even the civilian electrician who was in charge knew it wouldn't work, but the plans had come from Washington, and he was only following orders. I had met the Washington expert when I was in West Street, in connection with a TV system I had proposed. He was a fraud, like most authorities in the federal prison system. His only previous experience was as a radio technician in the Navy, hardly a proper background for his present position as Communications Engineer. I wondered how he had faked his pedigree, to get a civil service appointment. While all technical jobs in the federal prison system were theoretically supposed to be open to all as a civil service position, in practice, as I was to find time and time again, a hack with a smattering of ignorance in the field usually ended up in the position. This was true in the field of education, in vocational training, as well as various maintenance jobs.

I wasn't very gleeful when the installation was completed in July and we received a totally unintelligible fifteen-minute news broadcast. The reverberation in the cell house was much too high, so we all tried to kneel down, and put our ears right next to the hole in the rear wall of the cell, to hear the sound more directly. This way we could catch a few words, or a phrase, from this very advanced acoustical design. Night after night we all knelt down at the five-by-ten-inch opening, listening, and hoping to get a morsel of news. Those in the cells located closer to the loudspeakers heard a little better than the rest of us.

The holes in the wall had served as air vents until the blowup in 1946, when the whole ventilating system was blasted to bits, along with much of the plumbing system. After that the wrecked ducts were removed, and the holes served no purpose except to admit ants into the cells. Now they were serving as a communication medium, but only teasingly so.

After several months of the fifteen-minute news broadcasts, someone got the idea that the radio system might be better used for music; and he was right. The excessive reverberation was not too bad for music. After a year we were getting up to an hour a day of music, and I was glad it wasn't more, since the music played didn't enthrall me.

Finally the Bureau actually acknowledged the error of the loudspeaker system (probably the new warden that came in had something to do with it), and in July of 1955 work was begun on the installation of a standard Bureau two-channel earphone system. Each cell got a box with two jack outlets and a pair of earphones, so the occupant could plug in the program-of-his-choice. The end of September marked the end of the kneeling ordeal and the beginning of the twentieth century earphone era. It was ironic: the earphones we were given were essentially the same as the ones my father had used in 1922, for listening on his crystal set. And the fidelity hadn't improved one iota in that period. I noted that shielded wire was used in the conduit to distribute the program, which from an engineering point of view was sheer idiocy. The telephone company rammed two thousand telephone lines in one cable without shielding, but the Bureau expert must have felt that there was danger of cross-talk between the two programs.

The new installation meant little to me, since I now had only a choice between country music and popular music, both equally obnoxious to me, with an occasional fight or other sporting event. However I was able to listen to the Bell Telephone Hour each Monday evening, so it wasn't a total loss. Furthermore the earphone system had indirect benefits—I no longer had to listen to the loudspeakers. More, the cell house was quiet, now that the programs continued from the time we returned from work until ten in the evening, a half hour past lights out. On weekends we had a new game. The men would bet on some fifty or more football games, "bidding" each of the bets. The whole process might take thirty or forty minutes for the two bettors, and so this would go on all night long the night before the games. Fortunately the football season was short, and I was grateful when it was over. The men bet the stale packs of Wings cigarettes we received. I gave my cigarettes away. Only about half of the men smoked, so there were in fact enough for those who did smoke, especially since no one really liked them. Many of the men smoked George Washington tobacco, from which they rolled their own cigarettes. The G.W. was free for the asking.

Over the years there were several humorous incidents on the radio. On one occasion Helen spoke over the local liberal FM radio station and by a queer coincidence one of the two prison channels was tuned in. Thus I was able to hear Helen for almost ten minutes before the program was switched. I was very popular the next day with all the inmates.

Walter Winchell had been fulminating against me for several weeks, on his Sunday night program, to which everyone listened. Evidently the efforts of the Committee were being felt. On one occasion he solemnly reported that I had had myself checked into the hospital to escape the wrath of my confreres. Of course I was in my cell as usual at the time and the story was completely fabricated. All the men in the cell house heard the broadcast and laughed. But what was depressing was that, having heard him tell one very obvious lie, they still went right on believing everything else he said. It would seem that most people do not learn from experience, as they are supposed to do. It was apparent to me that the unsubtle hand of the FBI was behind this story, although I had no evidence. Who else could have fed this misinformation to Winchell, with any degree of authority?

One afternoon in late August the Industries lieutenant told me I was wanted up on the hill, and escorted me to the cell house. I was puzzled, but assumed it must be an emergency visit from Dreyfus, since it was past the social visiting time. In the cell house I was taken out front, without the usual shakedown, but instead of being shown into the attorneys' visiting room, I was escorted upstairs to the room where the Classification Board met. It happened so fast I didn't even have time to wonder what was happening.

In the room a man got up from his chair and introduced himself as a local G-man. He was there, he said, to arrange for the return of some documents which had been taken from me at the time of my official arrest. More than four years had elapsed, and I was puzzled that they had chosen this particular time to return the various identification papers I had taken to Mexico. If I had been smart I would have told the G-man to see my attorney. But I felt quite cocky and almost welcomed the opportunity to tangle with the FBI. There was one odd aspect to this meeting; he was alone. From what others had told me I knew that the FBI usually came in pairs.

My visitor didn't have the documents with him, only a list. Once he knew that I wanted them, he assured me he would arrange for me to get them. We talked for a while and gradually he began to get to the real purpose of his visit. He assured me, in his most sincere manner, that the efforts of the Committee were hurting my chances for parole. I didn't trouble to dispute this.

I learned several bits of information in the course of the interview. Most surprising was the fact that my erstwhile boss at Reeves had stood foursquare behind me when he was interviewed by the FBI. He told them they were crazy. He might have made a good witness at the trial, but my attorneys had not interviewed him, or anyone else for that matter, prior to the trial.

Several weeks later I went through the same routine finding myself before the same G-man. He must have felt sure of himself, offering me a stick of gum as I sat down, knowing how much I would have liked to take it. I acted aghast as I told him that it would be a breach of prison rules for me to accept the gum. But I didn't tell him that it was a criminal offense for him to try to introduce contraband into the prison; he knew it full well. In a small way this incident epitomized the mind of the FBI; they considered themselves above the law. My lawyer would have been ejected, had he offered me gum. I signed the paper authorizing him to return the material to Dreyfus (he didn't really need my authorization, this was phoney), and I didn't try to play any more games with him. I had found out all I could, and there was no point to going on. Besides, he was boring me with his sincerity.

When Helen visited me afterwards, I told her about the visits from my sincere friend. She wrote his boss in Washington a nasty letter telling him to call off his dogs; whereupon Mr. Sincere came rushing over to the Rock for a brief third and final visit. Somehow because I hadn't cursed him or acted violently, the G-man was under the impression that I had, in fact, considered him my friend, and that Helen's letter to Hoover did not represent my feelings on the matter. I made it clear to him that even if Hitler—I couldn't think of a more extreme example—had come to visit me on the Rock I would probably have sat down and talked with him, as I had in fact done with our G-man. Naturally he left after such an odious comparison. What a fool he was to have thought that Helen would act against my wishes in such a situation. But I had learned that the FBI was not noted for thought; everything was strictly formula.

At that time, nothing very much was happening on

the "legal front" (the term I used in my letters) since I had parted company with Howard Meyer a short time before. He and I had diametrically opposed views as to how the Alcatraz matter should be handled in the courts. (He wanted to file a habeas corpus in the San Francisco District Court, and I wanted to file a Declaratory Judgment in the Washington D.C. District Court.) I had been urging Helen to look for an attorney to take on the Alcatraz point, but attorneys weren't exactly eager to become involved in this case. Senator Joe McCarthy's anti-Communist tirades had had a chilling effect on the legal profession's enthusiasm for taking on unpopular legal cases.

4 I Almost See My Son and I'm Fired

ALL federal penitentiaries except Alcatraz had a three letter a week allowance; here we were restricted to two, and even this was a great improvement over former conditions. Originally the quota was one letter a week, and the letters sent to an inmate were never received by him. Instead, in the name of security, they were "transcribed" on a typewriter to remove any possibility that the letters contained hidden messages. In the process of "transcribing," I was told, the typist-guards shortened them considerably, to lessen their work. Happily that was now over; I received Helen's letters, albeit I never saw the envelopes. The letters came in standard long brown Manila envelopes. This was to foil attempts to smuggle in dope, under the glued flap or the stamps.

To overcome the letter limitation I devised a number of techniques for increasing the density of communication. Since the official letter stationery (printed at the Leavenworth print shop) had some unruled space on the top of both sides, I ruled in the missing lines and wrote on them. In addition to compressing my writing I also eliminated both margins. Thus I managed to get up to twelve hundred words into my letters. In addition I used certain abbreviations, though this was forbidden.

The main method of compressing the letter lay in my writing style. I would first draft the letter on scratch paper (we were only allowed two sheets of letter paper each week), and then tighten it up for the final version. Every once in awhile I would get the letter back from the censor, telling me to expand my writing and to allow a half an inch margin. I dutifully followed his order for the next couple of letters, but then I'd slowly begin to compress the words, and close down the margin, at a rate of about one-sixteenth of an inch per letter. In four weeks I would be back to my marginless letter. I accepted the restrictions on letter writing as a challenge to my ingenuity, and it became a game. Otherwise I would have been totally frustrated.

The game was not entirely without risks. If I wrote my second letter Thursday night and it was returned, I would get it back the following evening, too late to rewrite it for that week's quota. If I wrote some other member of my family, I would only be able to write Helen a single letter that week. This was always painful. Thus I would write Sydney and Mark on the bottom of the letter to Helen, so the children could cut their own letter off from Helen's. On certain occasions, like birthdays, I would write them a full letter. And my mother didn't get as many letters from me as I should have liked.

While the professed purpose of imprisonment was generally to effect a rehabilitation, on Alcatraz it was different. The Bureau of Prisons openly acknowledged that everyone who was sent there was beyond rehabilitation—even the youngsters of twenty and twenty-one. Thus no conflict of principles arose when the officials discouraged correspondence between the prisoners and their families or friends. As a matter of fact it was extremely difficult for an inmate to get a friend on his correspondence list, and as I've noted many men had absolutely no family ties, having been disowned.

Another way that correspondence was discouraged was that unlike any other penitentiary, Alcatraz had a special post office set up so that mail originating from the Island was clearly postmarked with a large Alcatraz stamp, although the return address on the prison envelopes never indicated the true source of the mail. It was a P.O. box number, the same as the other penitentiaries. Many men explained to me that they didn't want to correspond with their families, especially in small towns where everyone knew everyone else's business, because of the embarrassing postmark. Certainly the amount of mail originating from the Rock did not warrant the establishment of a separate post office, and I had to conclude that it was set up deliberately for the chilling effect it would have on correspondence. The mail censor's wife was the post mistress; it was all in the family.

After I had been there about a year I got a letter from Helen with several lines scratched out. It wasn't a good job of obliteration, and I was able to decipher some of the material; it concerned the details of a Committee conference. I didn't protest this because I knew that on matters of visits and correspondence, the prison officials had me by the balls; they could squeeze any time they wanted to, and there was little I could do.

Several months earlier a letter in which I had discussed some political matters was returned to me. When I saw the associate warden about it, he explained that letters were solely for "personal matters," and added gratuitously, "if all you can find to write about to your wife is philosophy and politics, then you and she don't have a close relationship." Skinhead, as he was called, happened to be a particularly stupid man. "Psychology is only horse sense," he opined.

Sometimes I'd get a letter back with some vague warning, and then I'd hold my breath and wait to see if the censor had merely had an argument with his wife that morning or if this presaged a new direction in restricting the scope of my correspondence.

I was always amazed by my own tenseness each evening as the time approached for the mailman to pass. I could hear him making the rounds on the lower ranges and finally coming down my range, stopping along the way. When he arrived at my cell, my tension rose to unbelievable heights. If I got my letter the feeling of relief was tremendous like being bathed in balm; if he passed by without stopping, the tension would evaporate, but be replaced by a hurt.

Friday night was particularly critical, since there was no possibility of further mail until Monday night, fully three days later. Sometimes it would happen that the mailman would pass my cell on a Friday night after I hadn't had mail for two or three days, and the sinking feeling I experienced was coupled with a desire to simply not exist. But a few moments later he would return with a letter in hand, having passed by in error, and the joy was like a re-birth of my being! My whole body would dissolve with relief from the excruciating tension. After a while I learned to steel myself for the non-letter, making up excuses for not getting mail that night. This would work for one or two nights, but when on the third night I still didn't get anything, it would be impossible for me to continue the game.

Why did I subject myself to all this torture? I didn't think I was a masochist. Most of the pain and anxiety could have been avoided if I had asked Helen to write me a brief note each day. But then, with the avoidance of pain, there would be less pleasure in receiving the unbidden letters. Now I knew that each time I received a letter it was because Helen wanted to write and found the time to express her feelings. The letter on demand would have been a matter of duty, rather than of love; I would not have felt the warmth when Helen flooded me with three or four letters in a week. To make letter writing a duty would have destroyed much of our relationship. The love versus duty question arose in many contexts all through the years of my imprisonment, and was never really resolved.

No matter how many times it happened, whenever I didn't hear from Helen for more than three days, I would begin to get frantic. Helen called it lack of faith, and each time there was some explanation. Toward the end of July 1955 I hadn't had a letter from her in over a week, and I went through the routine torture. When it finally arrived, after ten days, she said that a very long letter had been returned by the censor because it was too long. But having returned it, one would think that as a human gesture he would have sent a note telling me (he read my letters, and knew the torture I underwent). Helen typed the letter, which had originally been handwritten, as two separate letters, placed them in separate envelopes and mailed them together. I received both at the same time.

At the end of September Helen and the Committee organized a large Carnegie Hall meeting. In addition to Helen, my mother, Senator William Langer of North Dakota, Dr. Otto Nathan, Waldo Frank, and other notable liberals addressed the gathering.

I felt strange, lying in a cell alone, knowing that

thousands had gathered three thousand miles away, to ask for my freedom, and that I couldn't even get a glimpse of the meeting. But it brought back memories of my early childhood. In 1923 my mother and I had attended my father's graduation in the same Carnegie Hall when he received a pharmacist degree from Columbia. I remembered my mother pointing out my father on the side of the stage, and the impression it made on me. Now I was on center stage, but only figuratively.

I had expected that Helen would write me about the meeting immediately afterwards, but no letter came until eleven days later. In the meantime I suffered a thousand deaths. Everytime a meeting was scheduled I had a terrible fear that it would be a flop; now with no letter for so long I was sure that this had actually occurred. Finally there were two letters from Helen, numbers ninety-five and ninety-six. They had been mailed several days apart. But there was nothing in them about the meeting. Where was letter number ninety-four? I inquired from the mail room officer, and several days later received letter number ninety-four, with a note explaining that it had been "misplaced."

In that letter Helen told me in great detail what had happened at the meeting, and afterwards, when she and the other speakers had coffee together. She also sent me a large eight-by-ten-inch photograph taken at the meeting, showing her standing next to Bill Langer. Ordinarily an eight-by-ten was not allowed inmates on the Rock. But Senator Langer was a wheel on the Senate Judiciary Committee, and the prison authorities were very sensitive in their relations with influential politicians.

After I left the Rock I never experienced the same

degree of anxiety over the mail as there, especially not the intense anxiety which occurred at mail time. There was something about Alcatraz that magnified the problem.

In September I got my first serious cold. After a weekend, nursing it with aspirins in my cell, I landed in the hospital on Sunday with a fever of 102°.

The hospital consisted of four large cells, directly above the mess hall well isolated from the remainder of the prison, as well as an operating room which was used about once a year in emergencies; an x-ray room; a dental office and one or two other small office rooms. There was one other room; a private room for Bob Stroud, the famous bird-man, which didn't even have running water or a toilet. Here in the hospital Bob was more effectively isolated from the rest of the prison than if he had been kept in T.U., since far fewer people came to the hospital. I was placed in one of the cells, each of which contained four beds. In another cell was an inmate who had been operated on for appendicitis two days earlier, by two surgeons who had come over from the Presidio Army Hospital. Regular O.R. nurses were forbidden to assist surgeons, by order of the warden; the MTA's assisted. Instead of a simple appendicitis the surgeons found themselves confronted with multiple perforations of the large intestines, which they could not handle under the miserable conditions of the operating room, and without qualified assistance. They performed a temporary colostomy, with the operation to be continued at a later date in more suitable conditions. Post-operative care on the Rock was absolutely nonexistent. Only two days after the operation the inmate was on main line mess, which that night consisted of corned beef hash.

In another cell lay an inmate I had never before seen. I learned that he had been shipped from the Leavenworth Hospital, five months earlier, being fed intravenously all the time. When he had initially become ill he had been operated on at Leavenworth, but had not been cured. After he refused permission for a second operation, he was labeled non-cooperative and shipped to Alcatraz. He told me he had lived in the tropics and felt he had contracted a tropical disease which the Leavenworth doctors were not competent to diagnose. His present treatment was a result of the combination of a medical bureaucracy and a prison bureaucracy.

I received no medication or treatment of any kind, and when I asked for fruit juice I was told that the fruit juice was locked up in the kitchen, and no one had the key but the head steward, who wouldn't return until the following morning. When supper arrived the only thing I felt I could eat was soup, but unfortunately it was much over-salted. I called this to the attention of the MTA on duty, and received the by now classic response, "where do you think you are? In the Waldorf?"

A minor miracle took place during my short stay in the hospital. I became a convert to non-nail biting. I had been biting my fingernails all my life. On several occasions I had made serious efforts to stop, without success. Sunday night, as I lay on the comfortable hospital bed, I found myself gnawing at my finger nails; I suddenly realized that my heart wasn't in it, I wasn't doing it compulsively, as I had been all my life, but merely playing with my nails from long habit. So I stopped biting them. Whatever force had impelled me to bite my nails up to then was no longer present.

A week later I found my fingernails actually growing out, without effort on my part, and knew I had been right that Sunday. But having achieved this success, I wondered why? and why so easily? I had to conclude that the tensions which existed on the outside were conducive to nail biting, whereas the tensions of prison were of another variety. However I was afraid that not everything about the reduced nail-biting tension was good; I was fearful that it was akin to a death of a part of me.

When I first arrived on the Rock a full-time medical officer was in charge of the hospital, but later a local M.D. visited the hospital for forty-five minutes a day on week-days. As a consequence the MTA's ran the hospital and the M.D. merely counter-signed their orders.

Each day, seven days a week, an MTA would come down from the hospital with his little medicine cabinet and hold sick line. An inmate had a freedom of choice: he could either prescribe his own medicine from what was available in the medicine cabinet, or he could ask the MTA to prescribe for him. If the MTA thought the situation warranted it, he could have the inmate brought to the hospital the following day to see the M.D. Most of the common medicines were freely available and the sick line had its steady clientele: when "Beef Stew" missed sick call one day the MTA inquired if he weren't feeling well.

Everyone knew that if he became really sick he would be in trouble. The MTA's were hopelessly incompetent (one was nick-named "shoemaker"), and were completely lacking in any feeling for the inmates. The contract M.D., Dr. Wolf, didn't seem to be too interested in the men, either. When I had severe stomach pains the following April, he suggested I undergo a G.I. series, which I did. He administered the tests with an ancient x-ray apparatus, even though he had no special qualifications in this area, and pronounced me free of ulcers. It wasn't very reassuring. Everyone knew of the case of W., a bank robber from Chicago, who had been complaining of stomach pains for years, and had had no fewer than five separate G.I. series, until finally he had to undergo emergency surgery for a perforated stomach. The old-timers told stories of inmates who had checked into the hospital with rather minor illnesses and died a short while later. They were convinced that these men had been deliberately killed. Of course there was no way of ascertaining the truth. Everyone felt that the hospital was a good place to avoid, if at all possible.

A civilian dentist visited the Rock one afternoon a week. I tried several times to get work done, and found him highly incompetent. He never looked for cavities, but only acted on the complaint when the decay was usually well advanced. The last time he worked on me he tried to replace a bridge-facing that had cracked. He seemed quite wobbly. I didn't think much of it, but when he finished cementing in the facing and I felt it with my tongue, I knew that something was wrong. Looking in the mirror, I could see that it extended more than an eighth of an inch beyond the adjacent teeth. I had smelled alcohol on our dentist's breath, but I had never suspected he was actually drunk.

A couple of hours later he apparently became even more drunk, and the hospital guard found a bottle of liquor in his bag. He was escorted from the island and fired, not because he had been drunk, but because he had broken a strict rule against bringing liquor to the island.

My elongated facing didn't last a day before it split,

and I had to wait several months, facing-less, before a replacement dentist was found.

The inmates who had been here during the last war told me that there had been no dentist on the Rock for several years. Cavities were not filled and an MTA pulled teeth when necessary, but since he had no training and probably didn't care, the results were disastrous. Years later, when these men had to be fitted for dentures, the dentist had to trim the broken bone left by the MTA. This was in marked contrast with the situation I later found in Atlanta, where an inmate dentist, without formal training, pulled teeth so well that inmates would report on emergency sick call on weekends, which was the only time he was permitted to pull teeth.

Medical care at Alcatraz was poorer than at any other Federal prison, but better than in many State prisons which is not saying much.

I was now earning money hand over fist (eighteen cents an hour in my new job), and felt good to be able to send Helen a hundred and fifty dollars. By ordinary standards it might have been considered blood money, but since I wasn't really working for the money per se, it was more like found-money. Helen knew that she could use a part of it for something "silly," something that she couldn't buy with her fifty dollar weekly salary from the Committee—when there was money to pay her and the secretary.

Another holiday season came, and I enjoyed the resulting change of pace. As usual I carefully chose an entertaining book for my Christmas Eve reading: a substitute for the play or concert I might have attended. This year it was Thomas Mann's *Joseph in Egypt;* a familiar story, told with a great deal of erudition, and skill, and it read easily. There was the familiar bag of candy from Industries, and the holiday meals. Ever since the strike the holiday meals had improved immeasurably. Turkey for Christmas, and a juicy grilled steak for New Year's, with all the trimmings; a far cry from the first Thanksgiving dinner. We also had music. An instrumental quartet was installed in the corner of the mess hall, and entertained us through the meal.

The men who wanted to practice their instruments on the Rock had to undergo an ordeal. The shower room was their practice room. It was a high, cavernous room in the basement, with plenty of reverberation from the concrete walls. The men usually installed themselves in the shower stalls and each tried to concentrate on his own playing. The flutists couldn't really hear themselves when the trombones or large horns played, but they struggled valiantly nonetheless. The only time the men were permitted to practice was during yard time. Thus the musicians had to forgo the outdoors. The string players had an easier time, being permitted to practice each evening in their cells until seven. Of course no music instructors were permitted on the island; each man was his own teacher. Some had an aptitude for music, and others played mechanically. One hillbilly played the fiddle as if he were born with it. He held it against his belly instead of on his collarbone, and could make the instrument sing. I had never before seen anything like it. He would take his fiddle out in the yard even though it was risky since a baseball could come crashing down on it at any time.

I was surprised when I first learned that electric guitars were also allowed here. During practice in the basement these instruments with their powerful amplifiers had an advantage. When I first arrived I learned about MacIntyre and his special electric guitar. He told me that he had a radio receiver built into the instrument, and his cell wired up so he could operate it. I didn't believe him at the time and assumed it was inmate boasting, but about a year later Mac got busted for having the radio receiver and went to segregation for the better part of a year. What amazed me was that the whole joint knew that Mac had the receiver, and yet the officials were apparently not aware of it over such an extended period. If there were any rats on the Rock they certainly weren't tuned in. Some of the men were always griping about how the place was infested with rats (the human variety), but I thought that the incident with Mac proved otherwise.

I continued to work on paper solutions to engineering problems, arriving at many neat answers to some of the problems I encountered with the direct-current equipment in Industries, but none of the solutions had practical value, since almost no one else was still using direct current. However, when I read that the great General Sarnoff ordered his men at R.C.A. to invent a video tape recorder, I accepted it as a challenge to my own engineering skill and began to "invent."

Some very simple calculations demonstrated that one could not make a satisfactory video recorder simply by increasing the tape speed of the audio recorder. The tape would have to go much too fast to reach the required frequency response (there were other problems as well). I concluded that the recording head would have to revolve past the tape to reach the proper tape speed.

The following year I learned that this was indeed the approach Ampex had taken in their successful video recorder, while R.C.A. fell flat on its face trying to speed up the tape. Naturally I felt good when I learned this.

The first Warden on Alcatraz, J. A. Johnston, had retired in 1948, before I got there, but one of the prison launches bore his name. The Bureau was always naming things after their wheels. The athletic field in Atlanta was supposed to be called Bennett Field, after the Bureau director, but no one ever called it that except in official correspondence.

The second Warden here was E.B. Swope. No one liked him, guards and inmates alike. He was a sadist. One afternoon I came back from work and discovered that the sliding board I used for my desk was gone. Inquiry revealed that Swope had passed by my cell and ordered the board removed. Why mine, when any number of other inmates had similar boards? I heard that when he came to the Rock he immediately began to give Bob Stroud, the bird-man, a hard time. He confiscated his whole bird library and ruled that he could keep only two books in his cell. He also stopped Stroud's correspondence with the friends who had an interest in birds. In a word he was the classical sadistic prison keeper. Thus it was with some joy that we greeted the news that he was retiring, and would be replaced by Paul Madigan, more popularly known as Promising Paul.

The first big change Promising Paul introduced was to distribute the new surplus navy peacoats which had been lying in the warehouse for no one knew how many years, replacing our flimsy coats. Only after I wore the peacoat did I realize how miserable I had been in the sleazy coat. It felt good to go out in the yard now, when the wind was blowing and the air was sharp, and walk up and down without feeling the least bit chilly. It was such a luxurious sensation. I didn't have to wonder why I hadn't been aware of how miserable I had been in the other coat. It was the same defense mechanism which operated to prevent my seeing the reality of the whole place. Knowing the nature of the mechanism, and being aware of it, did not prevent it from operating, or rather, did not prevent me from allowing it to operate. This would eventually be verified after I left the Rock, and it would take a while—months, years—before the defensive mechanism which allowed me to survive here was completely obliterated. Not every one chose to erect the defense which allowed me to function at a minimal level. Some inmates slept away the time. They were always in the sack when they weren't eating or working. Others became embittered beyond measure, destroying themselves in the process. Each man made his choice and then lived with it.

Madigan, like Swope, had begun his career as a prison guard, and had worked his way up the ladder. In the federal prison system this was the only way of becoming a warden, at this time. During this climb upward these men also became penologists, even though they had never studied penology, sociology, or psychology.

One of the last things Swope did, as warden, was to send Helen a letter giving her permission to bring Mark and Sydney on the next visit. This was not his decision. It was Washington's. Helen had been writing the Bureau, submitting all kinds of evidence that Mark would not be psychologically injured, as they insisted, if he saw his father in prison; in fact Frederic Wertham, the noted psychiatrist, maintained that not letting Mark visit me would be injurious, because it could lead to harmful fantasies about his father. Helen had also had others write the Bureau on the matter. It was this pressure which brought about the change.

On January 19 I received a notice of approval of the visit for January 26, which gave me a whole week of pleasant anticipation, and on January 26, when I came up from work at noon, I was told to remain in my cell. When visiting time came my cell door remained shut; nor did any guard appear to offer a word of explanation. All I could do was speculate about what might have happened. I didn't ask any of the guards because I knew they wouldn't tell me the truth even if they knew, and I felt uncomfortable whenever they lied to me. They could so easily have told me what was up, instead of letting me sweat it out, but that was how they operated. It was the usual ironic situation; everyone in San Francisco knew why I wasn't seeing Helen and the children, but I didn't. An unstated rule in prison might be stated: a prisoner does not have the right to know— anything.

I suffered all through that night and the next day. In the evening I was handed a notice to remain in the cell in the morning for a visit with Dreyfus. This put my mind somewhat at ease, because I knew that I would soon learn why I hadn't seen my family.

I don't know what part the change of regimes played, but Swope gave Helen the permission, and Madigan revoked it. Helen had appeared at the boat dock with Mark (Sydney was ill and couldn't make it) where some photographers and reporters materialized. This must have offended the warden and he canceled the visit. Apparently he didn't want the visit publicized, unlike the circus the prosecutor put on at our trial—

which we had to accept. It hurt me very deeply not to have seen Mark.

Dreyfus told me that not only did the warden forbid me to see the children, he also refused to allow Helen to visit me. What rule had she broken? The warden didn't need a broken rule; it was sufficient to incur his displeasure. Truly he was the king of his prison. Dreyfus spent the whole weekend drawing up the legal papers for a motion, and went before Judge Goodman of the District Court on Monday to obtain an order allowing Helen to visit me. Goodman ruled against the motion at once, claiming that the courts had no power to interfere with the operation of the penitentiaries (not even where there was a showing of abuse of administrative discretion!).

A few days later, after pressure had been brought to bear in Washington, Madigan relented slightly and agreed to allow Helen one visit.

She came in an evening gown, the one she would shortly be wearing in Chicago at a dinner honoring Professor Harold Urey for his efforts in this case, and it was good to see Helen dressed so splendidly. In the midst of all the drabness it was truly an enriching experience. We talked rapidly for one and a half hours, covering a wide range of subjects, and when the visit was over I felt satisfied that nothing had been left unsaid. This visit was another illustration of the rule that no matter how restricted we might be, we managed somehow.

Dreyfus immediately filed notice of appeal in the Ninth Circuit, since the single visit allowed us was by their grace, which we did not want to rely on. The right of a wife to visit a husband in prison was too basic to lose by default. But Dreyfus told me that he wasn't going to draw up the appeal brief yet, because he felt that the government wouldn't contest the action in the Appeals Court, even though Goodman had ruled against us in the District Court. The government knew that Goodman's decision would never hold up on appeal. They had shown their muscle, but knew just how far it would work.

Three months later, when Helen wrote for permission to visit (the motion was still before the Court of Appeals), the warden acted as though nothing had happened and granted her the visits.

Dreyfus did not think that we could win in the courts in the matter of the children's visit. This was not so obvious an abuse of administrative discretion, and the burden would not be on the warden to show why he should deny me the right to see my children, but on me to demonstrate that his decision was an *abuse* of administrative discretion. Like having to prove oneself innocent. Anything the warden would tell the court would be accepted as the word of an expert. Mythology was not yet dead, in this, the age of "experts."

As a result of investigations by John Wexley, the author of *The Judgment of Julius and Ethel Rosenberg*, which was soon to be published, we became aware that the Mexican Government had not, in fact, sanctioned my kidnapping by the FBI. This meant that the prosecution at our trial had committed perjury when it placed Huggins, the immigration inspector, on the witness stand to testify that I had been deported by the Mexican Government. Under several definitive rulings by the Supreme Court this gave me a solid basis for going back into court and attacking my conviction.

I was frantic about getting back into court on this and the Alcatraz question, and was bombarding Helen with ever more urgent requests that she find a good lawyer. Finally, about the middle of January Helen wrote me that she was going to put her full energy into the matter. Yet I felt no elation when I received this bit of news. Helen had also written me that she was going ahead with the commutation project, which I opposed, and I felt that this may have put a damper on my enthusiasm. Or perhaps it was simply that I had become deadened against any sort of feeling of enthusiasm over anything.

I felt that it was contradictory for me to be filing a plea for commutation of my sentence while at the same time going to court to attack the government for the perjury they had knowingly introduced into the trial. Besides I didn't like the whole idea of asking for commutation, since it would place me in the position of a beggar. But Helen wasn't really a free agent in this matter, and I didn't know this, or, more accurately, I didn't want to know it. Well-meaning friends in high places told her that they had received assurances from administration people that a commutation plea might be looked upon favorably. To have disregarded our friends' well-meaning advice would have certainly estranged them, which Helen felt she could not afford to do. I didn't feel quite the same way.

After some lengthy exchanges I relented and agreed to go ahead with the petition for commutation. Fortunately this project took a long time to get off the ground, and I wasn't troubled with it for almost a year.

Within a month Helen wrote me that she was talking with Frank Donner, a well-known constitutional lawyer. I told her to stress my desire to go back into court on the "knowing use of perjured testimony" point, outlining all the legal arguments. I had been doing a considerable amount of legal research on this point, and testing my conclusions on Dreyfus whenever he visited. I was definitely not working in a vacuum.

In addition I had the help of some of the best inmate-lawyers in the country, like Courtney Taylor. In one year alone Courtney had won three cases in the Supreme Court, with the government confessing error in one of them. (Actually professional lawyers continued the cases he had initiated for some of the Alcatraz men. But he knew enough to lay a good groundwork in the lower courts for the lawyers; an important consideration in any appeal.) In fact Courtney Taylor would very much have liked to have handled my case. That is, I would have filed it in my own name, under his guidance. But Helen had objected to this, feeling that it would not have been in keeping with the image of the case she was trying to project. Only friendless people file their own appeals.

It wasn't until the middle of April that Donner's law firm, Donner, Kinoy and Perlin, finally agreed to take me on. They must have had considerable discussion prior to their decision, sensing that it was going to become a huge undertaking. But even then, with the full knowledge that I at last had some young and sharp lawyers, I felt no emotion; I had lost the capacity for feeling joyful except in the immediate presence of Helen. I could remember a time when such news would have lifted me off my feet. It frightened me to think that I had changed so in such a short time.

In July Marshall Perlin came to visit me, accompanied by Dreyfus who made the introductions. I was somewhat disappointed. I had expected Frank Donner. Fortunately my disappointment didn't last long. Dreyfus stayed for the morning part of the session that day, and the next day Mike came back alone for another full day. For me it was the most stimulating two days. If Mike disagreed with any of my ideas he didn't simply dismiss them out of hand; he made me defend them, until I realized that they weren't quite what I had thought. Other times he played the role of the devil's advocate, to clarify the issues in his own mind.

After the first day I was a little frightened at my becoming giddy when I had to think hard. My mind was no longer used to such intensive give and take. But by the second day I found myself more in the swing of things, and knew that my mind was not deteriorating (a thought that never really left me the whole time I was on the Rock; a thought which I was always searching to disprove).

Mike agreed to file a section 2255 motion, attacking the false "deportation" card and the testimony of Huggins, the immigration inspector. But first he wanted to go down to Mexico to see if he could find more evidence.

I knew I had a competent lawyer, with a great deal of understanding and energy, but I wondered where the money would come from to carry on the investigation and the legal actions. Mike stayed with me through all my subsequent appeals, though several times I was on the verge of firing him, and when I was released from prison and got off the bus, he was there with Helen to welcome me. I wasn't an easy client. I knew that, and Mike knew that I knew it. But we managed—for fourteen years.

The legal profession never moves fast, especially when the immediate situation isn't critical. Mike went down to Mexico and conducted an extensive investigation of the events surrounding my kidnapping. He couldn't have done this if he hadn't had the protection

of former Mexican President Cárdenas; the security police would have hustled him out of the country. He discovered how the FBI operated in Mexico, and how they
had managed my "deportation," without the benefit of
the Mexican Immigration Department. But when he
tried to get documentation to back this up he failed.
Mexico was too loyal an ally of the United States. Then
Mike filed a 2255 motion (but not before we had some
rough arguments over some of the details). And it
wasn't until June of the following year that the case was
finally argued before Judge Kaufman, as required by
the 2255 statute, even though it offended common
sense to require a judge who had sat on a trial to later
pass on the fairness of that trial. It wasn't always this
way. Before 2255 (1948), a prisoner could file a habeas
corpus petition before a judge in his immediate locale.
This put a large load on the federal courts near the penitentiaries.

That February, when I met the Board, I asked them
the usual question and got the usual response of ignorance as to why I had been sent there, but in the course
of our little discussion Associate Warden Lattimore revealed his true ignorance when he indicated that he
thought I was one of the Communist eleven, convicted
under the Smith Act.

That month I also received lots of very warm letters
from Helen, and much enjoyed the luxurious envelop-
ing feeling. Of course it worked both ways, and, once
started, her continuing letters were undoubtedly, par-
tially at least, a response to my response. But even as
this was taking place I knew that it would not last indefinitely. This awareness did not lessen the pleasure;
to the contrary, I strove to enjoy it while it lasted.

I had told Helen about my art collection, and she

got the idea of sending, when she had only time for a little note, picture postcards of my favorite art classics. In this manner I acquired a large collection of Van Gogh's works, which would have been impossible any other way. Luckily the authorities didn't know how much I enjoyed these cards. With my photographs I wasn't so fortunate. I had accumulated a grand total of thirty-four photographs—nine more than the legally prescribed maximum—when one of the officers shook my cell down on a routine search and discovered this violation. He ordered me to select nine of the photographs to send back home. It was like asking a mother to part with some of her children; they had become a part of me. During the shakedowns the officers checked the property card which was kept in the cell against the property card which was kept in the front office, against the actual property in the cell. Every time one purchased something, like a notebook, or a ballpoint pen, or a book, it was carefully entered on both property cards. Of course the duplicate card out front was to prevent the inmates from entering items on their cell cards at will. The twenty-five photo limit was loosely enforced, and the officer had undoubtedly gone after me. After this incident I kept accumulating photos until I had more than fifty before I left the Rock, and no other hack ever bothered me about them.

Until now my mother had only visited with Helen, but at the end of March she came alone. The visit didn't go well. She took me to task for not properly appreciating the work of the Committee. I tried to explain how difficult it was for me to relate to this activity, but saw I couldn't get across. I knew she herself was working hard, speaking at meetings and collecting funds for attorney fees, as well as related activities. I *knew* I should have been more appreciative, but I just couldn't *feel* it. My mother didn't understand the difference between the head and the heart, and why mere knowing did not give her son the necessary impetus.

This was not a new argument. From time to time Helen had also taken me to task on the exact same issue, but when Helen did it she didn't bear down with all her weight. She knew I was in a defenseless position, and that I was fully aware of its irrationality. Helen knew that I was waging an internal struggle, and all her criticism, I felt, was directed toward helping me.

My mother remained on the West Coast and visited me again in April. She felt she had to play the mother role to the hilt. She wanted to know why I didn't play baseball with the others; walking, she thought, was not sufficient exercise. It brought back so many childhood memories, when the exact same scenes had taken place. Why didn't I go play baseball with the other boys? I don't know why I never told her that I just wasn't good enough, and no one wanted me on his team. Was I ashamed to tell her? But when the boys on my cousin's block played hockey on roller skates, in the streets, I got to play. I was the supplier of beautifully round hockey-pucks which I made in the Stuyvesant High School wood shop. You can't play hockey without pucks (before they had been using scraps of wood), and besides I was able to roller skate fairly well.

Tradition was shattered that Passover. Chaplain Coffee did not come over, but several days after the start of the holidays he sent a young rabbi in his place.) Instead of meeting in the relatively large auditorium, where the six of us felt swallowed up by the empty space, we were allowed to meet in the office where the annual reviews took place. For the whole hour we all sat around a table on chairs—and talked. It felt so human that I was at once conscious that in all the time I had been here I had never before had the opportunity of any sort of discussion under such civilized conditions. We had "round-tables" out in the yard, the usual inmate bull-shit, but nothing that could remotely be called cultural even though by this time my standards for culture had dropped to a pretty low plane. We talked about the background of the Jewish people, but I would have been just as happy if we had discussed the Arabs. That Passover I also attended Protestant services, and was rewarded with a fine recorded vocal concert.

The end of April found me again in the hospital. I had been having severe stomach pains and the doctor decided on the usual G.I. series of x-rays. I didn't question his hospitalizing me for two days for the tests. Afterwards he came up with a negative diagnosis, but spoke most knowingly of a spasm of the duodenum. In due time the pains went away. But at the end of my second hospital day I found myself completely disoriented; I had lost my frame of reference, and hadn't yet had a chance to acquire a new one. I was much relieved when I got back to my cramped cell. I suppose it represented a certain security, though I couldn't imagine what was threatening about the large clean hospital cell, with its luxuriously soft beds.

As I got out of the hospital, I received news that Helen was in the hospital. She wrote me something about shoulder trouble, but so vaguely that for a moment I thought she had reneged on our agreement and was trying to protect me. The anxiety I experienced knowing she was hospitalized exceeded all tolerable limits. I felt like screaming or banging on the walls.

Subsequently I learned that her lack of precision was merely a reflection of the doctor's ignorance. The trouble arose from arthritis of the cervical vertebrae, which was an area in which doctors had had little success.

When I received a letter from Helen about a week later, telling me she was 80 percent well, I began to relax. Until then, while she remained in the hospital, all the other problems that had been plaguing me suddenly evaporated. This seemed to occur frequently: a sudden new serious problem would make hitherto important problems appear minor. There always seemed to exist *one* major problem, which if it would only go away would simplify life tremendously. Reality, or an illusion, I wondered.

Helen's ten-day stay in the hospital, during which she experienced severe pain, had a considerable effect on her. From her letters it was apparent that she was in a sad mood. She sent me a poem, *Madrid*, by Edwin Rolfe, with which she strongly identified. It was a sad poem, pledging never to forget Spain and what had happened during the civil war. I was Helen's Spain. I did not feel that there was anything wrong with Helen's mood; in fact I welcomed it, because some of it rubbed off on me. Oh how I wanted to feel. Joy or sadness, it didn't really matter, but to feel. To feel is to be alive, and the converse is also true.

Probably as a consequence of her mood, Helen for the first time since our agreement implemented her *carte blanche* prerogative. First she wrote me about her intention to have sexual relations with another man, although tentatively, probably not even believing herself that she was about to undertake the move after all the years of loneliness. I wrote back encouraging her to take the step, feeling that the longer she delayed the more explosive the situation might become. Subsequently, in writing me of her experience, she related all the negative aspects of the encounter as though trying to spare me the pain she imagined was mine. I knew that in these circumstances her experience could not be totally satisfactory, but felt that it would be rewarding enough to make it worthwhile. As we had agreed she told her friend that she was doing it with my full knowledge.

While I felt no anxiety, such as might have afflicted me at an earlier period, my own feelings were mixed. I had had time to prepare myself, through our discussions, ever since the question first arose. This allowed me to view it more rationally than would otherwise have been possible, and I had been urging Helen to initiate a liaison, if the opportunity presented itself, and if she felt so disposed, because I felt it was eminently unfair for both of us to be deprived of normal sex activity just because of my imprisonment. But when she wrote me telling me how poorly the whole thing had gone, I felt saddened that she had felt it necessary to reassure me this way. Also, as a part of our understanding Helen went into some detail in describing to me what had taken place, allowing me a certain vicarious pleasure. I was aware that this might be termed "unhealthy" by some, but decided to let my own judgment prevail. I also knew that I might be putting a large load on Helen's shoulders in asking her to tell me about the encounters.

One aspect of Helen's affair troubled me more than any other: that it might be made public by some unfriendly columnist. I knew that people would not have understood, and Helen's image would have been tarnished. We never pondered whether Helen's apartment was bugged or not. We simply assumed it was, since this obviated any dilemma.

Helen would have come to visit me after she had recovered, but with the meeting commemorating the second anniversary of the execution of Julius and Ethel scheduled for June, she couldn't take the time.

Transportation expenses for visits, which might otherwise have proved difficult, were solved by Bernie, a good friend of some means, who told Helen that she should feel free to visit me anytime; he paid the expenses. Thus I didn't have to be concerned that her meager income would be spent to satisfy my personal needs. I always found it difficult to think of the visits as equally satisfying any needs of Helen's despite her constant assurance.

At the end of June Helen and Sydney both came. Sydney was now sixteen, thus falling within the age requirements. As was usually the case after a long hiatus, the first visit did not go too well, but about a week later, at our second visit, we were once more in tune. It was good to talk with a young woman, Sydney, whom I hardly knew anymore. She had just been admitted to the University of Chicago, after only two years of high school, and was on cloud nine. Since Helen did not have the funds, Sydney's father, Casey, agreed to pay her tuition.

Mark was going to begin his schooling in September. We had discussed this and agreed that in view of the nasty political climate it would be safer to send him to a private school rather than risk his getting hurt, psychologically, and possibly even physically, in the public schools, if his identity as my son became known. I was relieved to learn that he had been accepted at the Little Red Schoolhouse, a progressive school, on a partial scholarship. Helen was always telling me how bright our son was, but I discounted that as a mother's prejudices: after all, I said, he couldn't read yet, the way Sydney had when she was his age. She was five and a half when Helen and I were married, so I knew what it was to live with a child of that age, and Mark was a year old when I was imprisoned. It was the ages between that I had missed, and would probably forever be a stranger to. I used to note very carefully those aspects of life which had fled beyond recall, forever lost, as if making up a shopping list.

One of the byproducts of Helen's liaison was that I no longer had the feeling which manifested itself in my telling her that she should leave me and not waste the remainder of her life in pursuit of my freedom. I *knew* that she was still wasting her life, but at least in this one area, which to me was so very important, she was not withering like a raisin in the sun. Of course Helen did not feel her efforts were a waste, but even though we discussed the situation at great length I never seemed able to feel that anything would come of the work of the Committee. This was rough on Helen, because it led to a feeling of inadequacy. I could have tried to feign enthusiasm, but this never occurred to me. Besides, even if I had tried, I couldn't have managed it, and to have lied would have corrupted our relationship.

In 1954, William A. Reuben published a book, *Atom Spy Hoax*, on the case. Under the rules I would never have received permission to get the book, but the lawyers pointed out that they were working on a legal motion which was in part based on the book. Thus I was allowed to receive it as legal material. Ten years later, under much more relaxed conditions, when I tried to get another book on the case, Walter and

Miriam Schneir's *Invitation to an Inquest,* the warden at Lewisburg turned me down, and the lawyers again had to go to Washington.

I could only read the book in A-cell block, where all the other inmate legal material was available, and the only time I was permitted to go to A was on weekends, during yard time. No one was permitted to leave his cell after supper when it would have been more convenient. I was glad to give up the yard period to read the book, though I should have liked to have had it in my cell, where I could read it at my leisure. One unexpected pleasure of reading in A was that I was able to sit on a real wooden chair. In my cell it was the bed or that less than one square foot metal seat/table, and in the mess hall it was a long wooden bench. Somehow the wooden chair appealed to me, I suppose because it represented one of the taken-for-granted artifacts of everyday living.

Reading Bill Reuben's book gave me an overview of the case for the first time, relating it to all the other political cases of the time. Shortly afterwards John Wexley's book was published, and this was also approved as legal material for my perusal. Wexley had done a lot of leg work and uncovered a great deal of material which put into question some of the prosecution evidence. For the first time I read about the last-minute efforts to stop the execution, and of the execution itself. I spent a month of weekends in A-cell block going through the book once and then, later, again. I found it intriguing, reading about *the* case.

Each year, just before August 16, I would recall the last day of freedom, going over all the minute details of the day, from the moment of awakening until the FBI's hired gunmen invaded our apartment. It had been a particularly beautiful day for us, and it was pleasant to recall and re-enjoy. But as with all such recollections, each passing year made the recollection dimmer, and the recollection of the recollection began to take its place. But it wasn't until 1965, when I went to Lewisburg, that August 16 really began to fade and would sometimes pass without my having recalled it even for a moment. On Alcatraz, I had a great need to hang onto that last moment of sweet freedom, and I did so without shame. While I could not live in the day, I would live in yesterday.

In prison things seemed to happen much more abruptly than out there. With no forewarning I was suddenly kicked out of the electric shop. Actually I had some idea this might take place when Mac, a new man, came into the shop. Mac had been an electrician outside, when he wasn't holding up banks. Bill, the other electrician, and I had been having some squabbles. Generally I lost because he weighed about two hundred and fifty pounds, but I must have annoyed him enough for him to have wanted to get rid of me at the first opportunity.

The firing itself was almost humorous. The superintendent of Industries came over to me with a "bill of complaint," a long list of particulars of my failings. I recognized it at once as Bill's handiwork. He had violated one of the prime rules of prison etiquette, going to the *man* to settle matters between himself and another inmate. Maybe he had been shot-gun guard in Arkansas, as rumor had it. The fact that more than a dozen items were detailed would have told anyone that the whole thing was fishy; besides, who ever heard of anyone in the prison system, or even in the civil service, getting fired for not doing his work well? When I tried to point out to the superintendent that his complaints were self-contradictory, he made no attempt to respond.

Almost as a joke I put in a cop-out to see the warden about the firing. Considering the few inmates on Alcatraz, he made himself scarce. It was more than a month later before I was summoned to A-cell block, where in a specially enlarged cell he conducted his infrequent interviews with inmates. He spoke very pleasantly, but said absolutely nothing—and did even less. Ordinarily I would have gone back to the furniture factory, but the new officer in charge had taken a dislike to me, even though I had had no contact with him, and he wouldn't have me. I didn't want to sit down at a sewing machine or desk, so the only thing left was the laundry. Here I tied together bundles of ten pressed sheets, as the men behind the mangle folded them. It involved only ten or fifteen hours of actual work each week. I still earned my full Industrial Good Time, but my pay went down to three or four dollars a month, compared to the more than twenty I had been making. The laundry was operated on a pool basis, and I had to start on fourth class.

I didn't mind my new job. The work was automatic, which meant that I could think while tying the bundles. It was a different kind of thinking, standing on one's feet, physically active. I didn't wonder if I was kidding myself in not feeling regretful that I had lost such a good job, and ended up with a poor one. It wouldn't have done any good. I was stuck with this until an opportunity arose to make a change. If the work became too oppressive I could always find a non-Industries job up on the hill, but I wouldn't earn any Good Time that way.

Joe Belizna was an ex-marine. We would talk politics now and then, and I liked him. He was genuine. He had a good friend, also an ex-marine, now a social worker, with whom he used to correspond. He would show me his letters. When Joe heard how I had been kicked out of my job, he was ready to beat Bill up, even though Bill had at least fifty pounds on him. The only way I could stop Joe was to plead that he would get *me* in trouble if he beat Bill up. I didn't believe this, but I knew that it would be useless to point out that Joe would get himself in trouble. Joe couldn't care less.

After this Joe cooled off toward me, and I suspected why. About a half a year later he blurted out how disappointed he had been that I had only thought of myself. I thought that enough time had elapsed so that I could tell him the truth, and he believed me; we were buddies once more. But about a week later, when he was walking into the mess hall, Bill happened to be sitting at the end of a bench he was passing, and he evidently couldn't resist. The men who saw it told me that Joe lifted Bill off the seat, laying him on the floor with an upper-cut. Joe was immediately taken to the hole and had to spend a couple of months in segregation. Fights in the mess hall were generally considered more serious than anywhere else, but this had been cleanly done; only one blow had been struck, so he didn't lose any Good Time. Usually when there was a fight, even though one of the participants might clearly have been the aggressor, both were sent to the hole, on the theory that both were somehow responsible. Bill was not sent to the hole in this instance. The superintendent of Industries probably intervened on his behalf. He was clearly his boy.

Going to the hole didn't bother Joe. The hole was supposed to be punishment, but some men would deliberately get sent there because they wanted seclusion, and in prison that was the only place they could get it. Running the Rock must have been tough for the administrators. In any other federal prison there was the threat of the Rock to hold the men in line, but here, at the end of the line, no equivalent existed. And for men who had lost all their Good Time, and were not afraid of the hole, there was nothing left. It was surprising how many men stayed "good," when there were no more threats left to make them. I wonder if the "penologists" ever saw it that way?

Thanksgiving, 1955. I had been here three years. Where had they gone? What had I accomplished? Helen visited me, and since we had no immediate problems, we got into a talmudic discussion of love versus duty.

Helen also told me a little about the San Francisco Sobell Committee, of which Warren Billings was an active member. The idea that Billings was helping in the fight for my freedom, after having been imprisoned himself for over twenty years in that other historical political trial of World War I with which I was very familiar, seemed far out. As a child I had learned about the Mooney and Billings case, how they had been convicted of tossing a bomb at a Preparedness Day parade. Governor Olson was elected on a pledge to free Mooney and Billings, which he did.

Some of my confreres had known Billings when they did time with him in San Quentin. They told me he was a good convict, one with whom they could feel at ease. They didn't say the same about Mooney. Billings subsequently became the chairman of the Sobell Committee in San Francisco, and some years after I was released I went to that City and met with him at a friend's house. We talked together for several hours as one ex-con to another, comparing the then with the now. I met him again when we shared a speakers' platform at the protest meeting for the Soledad Brothers. Whenever I met Warren I had the feeling that I was walking in the shadow of history.

It was a bloody December on the Rock. There had been knifings before, but nothing like this. Two inmates died, two others almost died. Besides several less fatal knifings. Christmas season was the likely time; everyone was depressed, and many didn't care if they lived or not. I know how they must have felt, what with their not having a soul on the outside with whom they could commune. I don't know of anything that could be worse than to have to live one's entire existence on the island, with its complete emptiness. All four knifings had homosexual origins. Gambling never led to violence on the Rock. There wasn't much outside of stale cigarettes to gamble with, and in prison gambling and sex are the two major sources of violence. Out in the yard I witnessed one of the killings and one of the near killings.

The killing was weird. One inmate approached the other near some bridge tables, and with a swift upward stroke ripped his belly wide open (it was relatively easy to smuggle an object around the metal detector, going into the yard, by passing it to someone who was taking some of the hassock seats out of the store room). Then for some strange reason, possibly because he was confused, a nearby guard grabbed the arms of the inmate who was stabbed, and held him, while his assailant kept plunging his knife into him. We all stood around dumbfounded, watching the unbelievable scene. Finally the guard must have realized what was happening, and let go, but it was much too late. The wounded inmate took a few steps toward the cell house steps and fell down dead. The inmate who did the killing was never prosecuted, ostensibly because the weapon was never found, but actually because the role of the guard as an accomplice would certainly have come out. The Bureau couldn't afford such bad publicity.

The near killing was almost as weird. I didn't see exactly how it started, but I saw Roland Simcox mounted on the shoulders of "Dog" Mann, plunging a knife into his throat and chest several times before Mann finally fell down, blood spurting from him like water from a faucet. Simcox walked away, and Dog got up and started a weird dance around the yard, yelling *"Help, help, help me."* No one made a move. Mann wasn't one of the best-liked inmates on the Rock. Finally an officer went over and led him up the steps of the cell house, even while the blood was spurting from him.

Surgeons from the Presidio were rushed over, and they worked on Dog all that day, well into the night, to try to save his life. He remained on the critical list for a whole week before word went out that he would live.

Since Mann was knifed in the open, and it was witnessed by several guards, there was no question about who had done it. Simcox was placed in segregation to await trial. The Feds were very careful not to put him in the hole, as they would have had they not intended to try him in federal court. Putting him in the hole would have been a pre-judgment, jeopardizing his prosecution. The court appointed Jack Burnham, a local lawyer, to defend him. Burnham was a fighter and got an acquittal for his client.

The prosecution had stupidly tried to portray Dog as a model of virtue, and it was a simple matter for

Burnham to subpoena his prison record and show he was mixed up with all sorts of deals and had a long homosexual record. The jury acquitted Simcox to show their disgust with the government, rather than because they believed Simcox was innocent. Several inmates testified on Simcox's behalf.

After the trial Simcox was put in the hole (jury verdict notwithstanding) along with the young man who had been the object of his affections, and there was little that Burnham could do about it. The warden was still king here. But six months later Simcox killed his kid and he was tried again, and again he was acquitted in federal court. Again the government had tried to lay it on thick, with a little perjury here and there, and again the jury must have gagged when Burnham exposed it. Of course Simcox once more had the help of inmate witnesses who testified on his behalf.

That holiday I first became really acquainted with Reverend Peter McCormack, the Protestant chaplain. Helen had spoken with him the last time she had visited me, and he had become interested in the case. We talked at length out in the yard, about everything and nothing. He was a warm soul, and all the inmates liked him. He wasn't as naive as some thought. I later learned that his congregation on the mainland found it difficult to understand how he could walk alone in a prison yard filled with desperados, and have no fear. But for every man who might have attacked him, there were a hundred who would have gone to his defense. When Peter McCormack was walking in the yard it was a different place. He was a part of the outside, which he brought in with him.

In November 1957 Reverend Peter McCormack was barred from the Rock by the warden. He had become a thorn in the administration's side, and he was first barred from Industries, on the ground that he was interfering with the men's work. When he sat on the Classification Board the others couldn't be quite as free and easy with their judgments as otherwise. He was finally barred from coming to the island because he had become too interested in the Sobell case, a cardinal sin in the eyes of our Catholic warden. I was sorry to see it happen, because I had gotten to like McCormack. He helped all those he could, whether they came to services or not.

The holiday season was always a time for recalling the past, and I was surprised at how much of the long forgotten I was able to resurrect. I was in the fourth grade, and probably the only Jew in my class. Other Jews moved to a neighborhood for comfort, but we were at St. Ann's Avenue because that was where my father's drug store was located. I had been given a small part in a Christmas pageant at school and joyfully came home expecting to be complimented for such an achievement. Instead I was told to withdraw from the pageant. It was a terrible blow, and I couldn't understand it. Maybe my mother tried to explain it and I couldn't understand; I couldn't recall. But I knew that when I went back to school that afternoon, with a note telling the teacher that I should be taken out of the pageant, I felt a terrible hurt. In one fell swoop my mother had succeeded in setting me apart from my classmates. I had already been having a difficult enough time without that.

Ironically, it was in prison that I first began to learn about Christianity, as I never should have had I remained free. I learned much in prison about which I would otherwise have remained ignorant.

5

Final Years
on the Rock

OVER the years I became aware of a gradual dulling of
my concern for Helen and the children. At first I used
to worry over every little trouble at home, but later,
when Helen wrote me that she or the children had
colds, I hardly gave it a second thought. Further, the
year before my father died, Helen wrote me how his
condition deteriorated with each successive cerebral
stroke, but I could feel absolutely nothing. And when
Helen wrote me how lonely she was, I found myself
unable to respond on any level. Nothing! Absolutely!
This apparent lack of concern grieved me deeply, even
though I recognized that it was far more rational. Oh
how I wanted to experience that tender feeling of concern which I seemed to recall from the past! Anything,
I thought, would have been welcome; a sadness, which
I felt was rightfully mine, evaded me. Reason cried out
that I should be feeling lonely, and yet I had not the
slightest such feeling. Something, to tell me that I was
still a sentient human being. Instead I only could become angry with my lawyers over their legal briefs, or
with Helen when she did not respond to my endless
queries rapidly enough. Except when visiting with
Helen, this seemed to be the limit of my emotions. But
I did achieve some degree of tender feeling on oc-

casion, when I wrote Helen. Any kind of feeling, no matter how painful, would have been welcomed. Perhaps this was why I deliberately created tensions during my visits with Helen, to generate some sort of emotional situation.

In the others around me I could even more clearly see the effects of prolonged confinement on the Rock. They were well institutionalized, although they occasionally rebelled out of desperation, or else went mad and were sent to the Springfield Medical Center. The situation was basically unstable, and the tensions a result of this. I felt that it was due to the high degree of confinement, so much more severe than in other penitentiaries, as to make it qualitatively different. In the first place Alcatraz was much smaller than the usual penitentiary, making for a much greater sameness—in all ways. In addition the ratio of guards to inmates was much higher here, which caused a feeling of great oppression. Everything about the place seemed to bear down on us, although the many guards with the rifles and carbines were the only concrete manifestation of this oppression. Everywhere one could see a guard except when safely locked in a cell for the night. And there, not at all coincidentally, was the only place I could unwind.

The routine was also much more circumscribed than in other prisons, remaining fixed from day to day and year to year. Few essential changes had taken place since the Rock received its first federal prisoners transferred from other prisons in 1934. True there were now movies, and the silent system had been abolished, and correspondence was also a little more relaxed; but beyond these changes the place had remained a citadel of nineteenth-century penological thinking. Through isolation they shall come to recognize the errors of their ways, become penitent and reform. How many of the men or guards were aware of the origin of the term *penitentiary,* I wondered. To most of the men, doing time simply meant paying their debt to society. Once they had done their time they felt the scale was balanced and they didn't owe anyone a thing. Some of the men even preferred doing their time on the Rock and asked to be shipped back from the other prisons to which they were sent. Nobody bothered you here, as long as you followed all the rules. The no-no's were much more clearly defined than at any of the other prisons, primarily because there were so few things one *could* do. In other prisons one had a certain degree of leeway; the rules were not always rigidly enforced. Some men preferred the certainty of punishment—if caught. In addition, some couldn't stand living in the same cell with others.

With all the sameness around me I might reasonably have expected to feel bored. I recalled how (in my youth) a four-hour train ride would bore me "to death." And yet I had no feeling of revulsion against the monotonous situation that existed in Alcatraz. This bothered me. Was I simply anaesthetized against all such feelings? There was absolutely no one in the prison with whom I could discuss the question.

Since a few of the men had real families on the outside, most conversation consisted of the retelling of past exploits. After years of rapping with my confreres I grew slightly weary of their stories. Always the same bank jobs. (For the first year, after leaving prison, I felt uneasy whenever I entered a bank, as if I might somehow find myself holding it up.) Sports—baseball, football, and the rest—were also a favorite topic. I don't think that my confreres differed very much, in this respect, from people on the outside. It was only that I had become sensitized against these continual discussions of the statistics of the ball games and the players, because I couldn't escape them. Otherwise the discussions centered on *facts;* the height of a building or mountain, the population of states or cities, who had won what fight in what round; never any discussions of ideas or theories.

Even though my confreres appeared to be extremely interested in ball games, active sports on the Rock were pursued in a desultory manner. There were no organized teams, as in the other penitentiaries, and only a small percentage of the men played softball. There were usually two or three handball games in progress, with the players going through the motions of the game like zombies. There was little zest in anything any of the men did. Bridge was the most popular "sport." From time to time I would play, especially when I hadn't received a letter from Helen for several days, and knew that I had to kill the weekend, or else it would kill me, while waiting for Monday to arrive. I'd play bridge during the day and bury myself in a book at night, back in the cell. And somehow the weekend would pass, and it would be Sunday night, and I would allow myself to look forward to the following evening, and a letter from Helen. No matter how many times I went through the same scenario, each time it happened I was filled with as much anxiety as if it were the first time. It was as if the gods had doomed me to repeat this self-torture to the end of my days on Alcatraz.

I did not fully realize how Alcatraz had warped my being until after I was transferred away. When I went to the Atlanta penitentiary I found myself fearful of making any move which was not a part of the programed moves of the institution. After the work day was finished, almost all of the men returned to their cells. But since the library was still open, one had the option of going there until count time. For the better part of the first year, whenever I did stop at the library I expected to hear a guard's voice yell out, "Hey you, where do you think you are going?" Each time I reached my cell, and it didn't happen, I felt relieved. Helen told me that during the first visits in Atlanta she found me rigid and lacking in spontaneity. Freedom is never instantaneous. The freedom of the Atlanta visits, where we both sat on a couch, and I could hold Helen's hand and feel her warm body, overwhelmed me. I couldn't relate to it, I couldn't accept it, it meant nothing to me for those first few visits. I was afraid to enjoy this newfound pleasure, I was afraid to emote, as if I might wake up and find it all a dream, with a guard yelling at me, "What do you think you are doing?" But while on the Rock I was totally unaware of what had happened to me.

I had learned to keep my guard up on the Rock, and after I left I was determined not to let it down. Anything could happen to one in prison. I had to be careful, I had to play it cool. This was the dehumanization of Morton Sobell which the authorities had deliberately and calculatedly brought about. There was little overt brutality at Alcatraz, certainly less than at the other penitentiaries. The small population made it dangerous for the guards to be cruel to the men, because brutality was more difficult to conceal and word got around more quickly. But the cruelty of the whole institution exceeded any possible individual cruelties on the part of the guards.

Prisons have always been closed systems, total systems, totalitarian systems. Alcatraz was all this, only more so than the other prisons. At Alcatraz isolation was elevated to an operating principle: isolation of the body and isolation of the soul. It was as closed a system as the authorities dared maintain in the second half of the twentieth century. The toll it took in human lives, as measured by the number who ended up mental wrecks, and those who became warped beyond recall, was greater than anyone would admit. The German people said they didn't know of the existence of concentration camps; similarly the American people didn't know of the existence of Alcatraz. Except as a place, an island in San Francisco Bay, where desperate criminals were kept.

Early during the term of my imprisonment I became aware that life in prison could be analyzed in terms of two distinct components: the real daily existence within the prison, and the life outside. Some of my confreres had been in prison so long and had so little communication with anyone outside, that for them outside life had ceased to exist in any meaningful way. For them it was only a prior existence. Over and over and over again they would recount episodes from this existence, clinging to these as if they were life itself. I tried to carve out an outside existence for myself in the contemporary world, utilizing all available opportunities, and even creating some.

Helen comprised the major source of outside life, but few had Helens who were willing to undergo all the pain I inflicted on her, or who could understandingly cooperate as she did when I sought to break down the rigidity of the system. I had to crowd this existence into about one hundred letters and fifteen hours of visiting time each year. Communication between people is always a problem, even under ideal conditions. For us the difficulty was aggravated by the tremendous difference in our life styles, as well as the problems imposed by the censorship. I was essentially powerless, dependent upon Helen for literally everything relating to the outside. Such an uneven situation was inherently tension producing. Without the basic understanding that called for utter frankness in all areas of our relationship, I doubt that we would have survived the years I spent on Alcatraz.

Helen was loaded with responsibilities almost beyond her capacity. She was the mainspring of the Committee, and had the task of keeping diverse Committee individuals working together. Singlehandedly she was raising a family, and in addition had to try to satisfy my needs and desires. The contrast couldn't have been greater. I had absolutely no responsibilities, having only to care for myself under conditions that allowed me few options. Even while I loaded Helen down with tasks of all kinds I recognized the essential unfairness of our situation. Yet I couldn't stop myself from making all those demands on her; she had chosen to stay in the struggle for my freedom, knowing what it might entail. Whenever I told Helen how our visits satisfied my needs she would be quick to point out that the visits also satisfied her needs. But I felt that while there might be some truth in this, there was still a lopsided situation since my needs in this regard were so much greater than hers. The letter writing was another example of the same situation. I had so much time to write my letters that I could afford to draft them lovingly with great care, while Helen had to dash hers off late at night, when she should have been asleep, or somewhere on the fly. I had too much time on my hands, and Helen didn't have enough. I always asked Helen to tell me in her letters what she could of her daily life, the unimportant as well as the important; what clothes she had worn that day, what she was wearing while writing me, what she had eaten, what meetings she had attended, as well as details of her liaison. We had developed a vocabulary which made it difficult for the censor to understand what we were talking about (I sometimes myself had difficulty interpreting the letters). "Reading a book," with a double dash, referred to the sex act, sometimes alone, sometimes not. The double dash was generally used to denote a hidden meaning. The word *nebulous* referred to something connected with sex. I tried to develop more advanced codes, but it proved too difficult under circumstances where we could not have a single uncensored letter for arranging things.

Whenever we reached an impasse in our correspondence, and were unable to resolve some question, I simply put it aside, waiting for a visit when we could take it up again. With the rapid give and take of conversation, and the nuances possible in personal contact, most of the problems yielded to some sort of solution. And if a solution could not be reached, at least we knew where the difficulty lay. Frequently these questions revolved around the functioning of the Committee, but sometimes they became abstract, as when Helen wrote me, in one of her poems, "And though the leaves of my love shall fall one by one . . . they will come again when you are at my side." This was in response to a letter in which I wrote Helen that we must do all in our power to keep our love alive. I was frightened by the thought that I might have to do any considerable part of this sentence without Helen's love to sustain me. I also doubted that once our love had withered, as Helen's analogy implied, it could be resurrected; I did not feel that love was a perennial. We discussed this point for many months—Helen reluctantly and I with an urgency that is hard to imagine. We never resolved it, as an abstract question, but Helen's love did not wither during the more than eighteen years we were separated.

Frequently I would take Helen's poetic utterances much too literally, and subject them to analytic scrutiny far beyond reason. This was one of the basic differences in our approach which led to frequent tensions. Helen did not feel it was fair to analyze poetry so critically, while I could never get myself to accept the free and easy spirit of poetry.

During our visits it was difficult at first to disregard the guard who was assigned to watch us, and to disremember that each word we spoke was monitored by a guard. But after the first few visits we began to speak to each other as if we were alone. Damn the guard who was listening; if he had no more decency than to listen to a man and his wife make love over the phone, so much the worse for him.

I hardly think our love could have withstood a second five years on the Rock. Love, as I understood it, could not remain alive without communication. The idea that two people could remain in love, without any direct communication, struck me as romantic poppycock. Love, I felt, must develop in accordance with the circumstances; love could not simply remain dormant, to be revived at will. Love like life itself must grow, or else it dies. After I was transferred away from Alcatraz, communication became much easier, and the tensions of misunderstandings were considerably reduced.

With the help of a friend, Helen had a slim volume of her poetry published toward the end of 1957. She left a copy for me with the prison authorities when she visited during the Thanksgiving holidays, but I didn't get it. The warden never explained. As a matter of fact I already had all of the poems, scattered in Helen's letters to me, which I had saved. In the book they were *printed*, and there were also drawings by Rockwell Kent. It took a whole year before Washington relented and told the warden to allow me to receive this dangerous volume of my wife's poetry, entitled *Dearly Beloved*. The book was more meaningful to me than the individual poems, which I already knew quite well. It was a part of Helen, adding a bit of warmth to the otherwise cold cell. Some of the love poems were not directed toward me, but I don't suppose any readers were aware of this. When Helen had initially written them I found that difficult to accept, but with reason I learned to accept them as a part of our agreement, as a part of the Helen I loved. When I loaned the book to some of my confreres they truly appreciated it because so much of it related to experiences they understood only too well.

I was continually probing our relationship, dissecting it with a fine scalpel, analyzing it, and trying to define it with an exactness relationships never have. This "activity" must have served as a substitute for these real aspects of our relationship, which were necessarily missing at the time. This placed a tremendous burden on Helen, psychologically and in terms of the energy expended simply in thinking the matter through.

Sometimes we would get into a silly discussion, like the virtue of an "old" lipstick kiss as compared with a "new" one. A lipstick kiss was an impression

Helen made on a letter by creasing it and pressing her lips against it. One made with newly applied lipstick was a "new" kiss, and one made with lipstick that had been applied earlier in the day was an "old" kiss. I was surprised when the censor allowed the lipstick kisses to pass. But of course the rules didn't say they were verboten. Helen would also send me "nectar" on occasion. Nectar was a very nebulous fluid, with very symbolic connotations. We would alternate between the silly and the serious.

What with my frequent criticisms of Helen, she would sometimes ask me to forgive her failings, and then I would be filled with remorse. I was cognizant of the herculean tasks she was carrying out, and felt that it was not for *me* to forgive *her*. Yet I didn't feel I could remain silent whenever I disagreed with her; this frankness was a part of our understanding, too. I felt that I had to relate to her on this basis to prevent any real blowups. Later in the sentence it became apparent to me that it was this give and take that was a most important component of the formula for my remaining vital through the Alcatraz period. I became a convert to the concept of tension as the *sine qua non* for a vital life. Harmony is important, but it is counterpoint that I prefer, that I cannot live without.

Helen visited me again at the end of March and the beginning of April 1956. We had had a series of particularly good visits, and when she left after the final visit on April 3, I was up on cloud nine. The following day, when I went up to the cell house from Industries at lunchtime, I was told to remain in my cell, I was to have a visit. I immediately knew that something must have happened, since I wouldn't be having an ordinary visit after having used up my allotted visiting time. I guessed correctly that my father had died. He had been hospitalized for some time, having suffered several successive cerebral strokes. Helen hadn't given me any indication that he was critically ill just then; in fact his death was unexpected. Helen remained in San Francisco and visited me that Thursday and Friday, instead of returning for the funeral. She couldn't help my father, but she could help me. During those two visits I talked and she listened, very well. (Those two extra visits were subsequently subtracted from my future allotment.) That night I wrote Helen:

There is no deep pain or hurt. For me he died gradually—ever since they sent me here, where I could no longer see him. It was little enough while I was at West Street—to talk with him for a few minutes every week, and then to watch him, seated on the back row, while I spoke with you, mama, Mark and Syd. He never showed any emotional concern, but I know it was there, deeply buried in his heart. It wasn't his way to exhibit it. They must have hurt him more than they hurt me. A father feels the hurt of a son multiplied manifold. I know, I am a father as well as a son. And then they separated us by distance as well as bars. Can such a hurt kill? I know how easily he could be hurt. I had done it before—as sons sometimes hurt fathers.

I never met another father who was like him. He was warm and gave of himself without thought, but he was so clumsy. Most people misunderstood him, since he didn't express himself along accepted modes. As a business man he was a joke. Profit was never a motive in his life, not even in his drug store. What was he doing there in the first place? He en-

*joyed compounding a difficult prescription a lot
more than making a dollar. Similarly he enjoyed
making his own chocolate syrup for the soda fountain because it was better than any he could
buy. . . .*

*We built our first model airplane in 1926. Then
there were more planes, radios, kites, boats, gadgets
of every description. We used the prescription room
as our workshop. I never learned to carve a propeller
for my airplanes; this was his responsibility. He'd
weigh it on the pharmaceutical balance to make sure
it was correct. . . . I attended my first concerts with
my father, before he bought the store. The radio in
the store was always tuned in to some classical
music. Sunday evenings there was a chess game,
when things in the store were usually quiet. He
helped me with my math, physics and chemistry,
until I went beyond him.*

*He was always a skeptic. When I came home
from school with some "facts" I had learned about
the Haymarket affair, he taught me the meaning of*
cum grano salis.

I was deeply disturbed that I felt absolutely no
grief over my father's death, and wondered what it signi-
fied. I knew rationally that he had ceased to exist
months before he actually died, yet I also knew that
reason is never a good reason in events such as death.
Helen had told me about the last times she had seen
him, when he was already incapable of communication.
I suppose I grieved then, only it was on such a low
level that I couldn't recognize it as grief.

When a father dies, the Bureau of Prisons will
frequently allow the son to attend the funeral, if all ex-

penses for the necessary guards are paid. The Committee offered to pay the expenses for any number of guards the Bureau thought necessary to guarantee my security, but the offer was rejected. While I am generally antipathetic toward funerals, I very much wanted to go to this one. How I longed to grieve, with all my heart and all my soul. Not once did my father write me or tell me—"why did this have to happen to you my son"—much as I knew he wanted to. And I remembered very vividly seeing my father cry when I was ill with diphtheria.

Sometime during the last period on the Rock I began to play a little game with myself (one of many). I would ask myself, "Did I have to be different? Why couldn't I be like everyone else? And save myself a lot of headaches and heartaches." I would allow myself the luxury of yearning to have been born a conformist of conformist parents, and not to be burdened with all these nuisance problems. I would have such an overwhelming desire to be like every other middle-class American that I figuratively bathed myself in the desire.

Then I would begin at the beginning, and explain to myself how it was that I was what I was, how I became what I am, and how meaningless life would be for me if I had chosen any other path but the one I did. I, Morton Sobell, was doomed by whatever gods there were to go on playing the part as long as I lived, or until I saw a different light.

Then I began to feel weary of playing this role, and I wanted so much for the play to end, so I could start all over again. And yet I knew that even if I had the opportunity, I would probably play the same role, even if I knew what the consequences would be. This was me, this was the only role in which I felt comfortable inside myself. Oh yes, here and there I might have acted more cleverly, as hindsight indicated, but my fundamental moves would have remained essentially the same. I was content that I had not soiled myself at any time throughout the ordeal. This would indeed have made life unlivable for me. But I could yearn for that other life, a little. It didn't cost me anything, and I knew that there was no danger that I might go astray.

Helen visited with me the Wednesday before Thanksgiving, in 1956. A Thanksgiving visit had special overtones, since it marked the anniversary of my transfer to Alcatraz. It was a deep visit which left me with a warm diffused afterglow that persisted even into the following day. After such a visit I always realized that the real Helen had seemed to slip away from me, and that probably the most important function of the visit was to bring her back to me.

I spent Thanskgiving morning walking in the yard by myself, looking at the scene, recalling how it had appeared that first day. Now there was plenty of turkey for dinner, but it was all so cold, cold, cold. Why did everything about prison have to be so damn cold? Yes, this was the other important function of a visit, to warm oneself.

I didn't feel like going to the movies that afternoon, I didn't want to lose any of the warmth from the visit. Father Scannel stopped by my cell and we chatted for about an hour. Only in prison would I find myself discussing Christ's divinity with a priest. There were no limits—in prison.

At the end of November Helen came for a second visit, and there was Mark! At last! Alas, I couldn't even recognize my own son, even though Helen had sent me photographs of him all along. I could not correlate the image on the photograph with the person I now saw behind that small window. He had changed too much for me to remember him during that four years when I was not permitted to see him. Communication over the phone was also difficult. Helen could not tune in to our conversation to help ease it along. Finding I could not establish any personal rapport with him I went into some technical matters, explaining how a suspension bridge (Golden Gate) worked. I also wiggled my ears for him, something I hadn't done for years, and I later learned this impressed him. By and large it was an unsuccessful visit, but under the circumstances there was little we could have done to make it better. I was angry at *them* for not having allowed us to have a better visit. It would have been so little, to have allowed us to meet in that room where I met my attorney.

Helen had been pressing Washington to allow Mark to visit me ever since the first fiasco. Some months earlier, when Bennett happened to be visiting Alcatraz, I put in a cop-out to see him. (He usually honored such requests.) Most of the men who saw him realized that whatever he said meant very little. It was all so futile, and yet when one has so little, one grasps at straws. When I asked him about visiting with Mark, he replied that it would be too traumatic for the child to see me. When I pointed out that a bench visit would help minimize the possible trauma, he simply looked at me with a vacant stare.

As always, we never knew what finally made Washington change its mind. After that first visit Mark and I had others, and our communication improved somewhat, but it was only after I was transferred to Atlanta, where we all sat on the couch together, and could talk as a family, that we really began to rap. Yet even that was only comparative. When I got out of prison, I found my son a stranger.

In a sense prison also made me a stranger to myself. While Helen was allowed to send me photographs of herself and the family, she had none of me since my arrest, except, of course, the newspaper ones. However, an informal policy of the Bureau allowed an inmate to have a photograph taken every four or five years, to be sent home; more important, it was placed in his "jacket" for future reference in case he should escape. After trying for over a year I was finally allowed to have a photo taken. I had only the briefest look at it before it was placed in an envelope and sent home. I couldn't recognize myself; the face looked utterly strange. Later, when I went to Atlanta, I had the same shock of nonrecognition when I first looked at myself in a large mirror. On the Rock we only had small five-by-seven-inch shaving mirrors; there were no others. Somehow the size of the mirror seemed to be critical in self-recognition, probably because the larger mirror allowed me to see my face as a part of my head and my whole body. Ordinarily we correlate all these images, because they are all available to us. On the Rock this was not true.

I should have thought that working in the laundry would bother me; yet somehow, despite the apparent monotony of catching sheets all day long behind the mangle, I didn't feel the least bit discomforted, at least I didn't admit it to myself at the time. The job was so damn mechanical that I was able to think about almost anything while I was catching those sheets at the rate of 500 an hour. The thought that it was a time-waster bothered me most—if I allowed it to. I could probably have transferred to the tailor shop or the glove factory, but I actually had to work only fifteen or twenty hours a week here. We usually didn't even go down to work a couple of afternoons a week.

The prison system, under the guise of providing vocational training, was actually providing near-slave-labor for several governmental facilities on the mainland. We were paid by group piece-work, which averaged out to about three dollars a week for all who were on fourth grade, like myself. Actually I didn't care what I was being paid; it was the good time I was making. I was now earning four days a month, which was a lot of time I wouldn't have to do in prison.

In the middle of 1956, the officer in charge of the furniture refinishing factory, who didn't like me, was made a lieutenant. How he made it no one knew, since he was genuinely stupid, much more so than the average hack. By any standards there were many much more qualified men on the force.

As soon as he was out of the factory I applied for a transfer, to get in. I finally made it in January 1957. The officer now in charge wasn't exactly bright, but neither was he actually afraid of a "college man." Once I was out of the laundry I felt a great relief. The idleness had been getting to me, only I couldn't afford to admit it while there was little possibility of a change. Again and again I discovered and rediscovered that one must not admit the real pain of a situation to himself while there is no out, unless he wants to subject himself to needless agony or drive himself crazy. Some do.

Toward the end of 1956 I realized that in order to understand the technical articles I had been trying to read in my electronics magazine I would have to take some kind of course on transistors. Vacuum tubes were on their way out and transistors were replacing them; I would be obsolete, as an engineer, if I didn't do something about it. I was pleasantly surprised at the speed with which my request to take a correspondence course at the University of California, Berkeley (right across the bay) was processed. In one month I received my course notes and text. Since the State of California classified me as a resident, the course cost me $17.50. It would otherwise have cost five dollars more. It felt good to be embarking on a study course.

My initial enthusiasm didn't last too long. I was thirsting for dialogue on the subject matter but my instructor didn't venture a single word of comment, even where I explicitly invited it. Had the FBI spoken to him? Idle speculation. I kept submitting the lessons and getting all of the problems correct, but this was hardly satisfying. In some instances I submitted solutions which were more sophisticated than the ones the book indicated, but still my instructor maintained a deep silence.

In February 1957 I took my midterm in the library with the parole officer as my proctor. That was the only time I was ever in the library during the whole time I was on the Rock. The exam was much too easy to be satisfying, and after the midterm the problems kept getting progressively duller. They were what are called plug-in problems, where one has but to find the right formula and substitute the right values. A lot of plain calculating without any real thinking. I never finished the course—transferring away from the Rock ended it—but I had achieved my objective, getting a better feel for the transistor. I was probably the only one who took a course in transistors without ever seeing one.

By January 1957, after four years on Alcatraz, I was an old-timer, despite the low turn-over rate. I knew my way around, and I had a sense of the place; I could tell when something was up. I also knew that I could do time—though I didn't know what time was doing to me. My situation with respect to the outside world had become somewhat more stabilized; the Committee was now operating on a long-term basis, my lawyers were deeply immersed in a section 2255 appeal motion and, most important, Helen and I had achieved a condition of relative stability. Our private roller-coaster was no longer loop-the-looping, at least not as violently as in the past. I had also finally achieved a transfer down to the furniture refinishing factory. In a way I was sitting pretty.

When I reread Bernard Shaw's *Saint Joan*, I happened to be deeply involved in the *Grunewald* case, as it affected the legality of Saypol's brutal cross examination of Ethel Rosenberg about her having taken the Fifth Amendment before the grand jury. Shaw's epilogue, in which Joan was rehabilitated twenty-five years after having been burned at the stake, brought to mind the idea that any play about this case would also need an epilogue, in which the *Grunewald* decision, which in effect held that Ethel's execution was illegal, could be developed.

As soon as the Supreme Court ruled favorably on the *Grunewald* case my lawyers went directly to the Supreme Court, asking that our original appeal, in which this point had been raised, be reconsidered. We all knew, of course, that the Court would never grant this motion, thus acknowledging that Ethel had been wrongfully killed. We lost the motion, as we did the one concerning the fraud the government had committed in saying that Mexico had deported me. I did think I might win this last one, since it concerned only me, not the Rosenbergs, and was more or less a "techni-cality." While waiting for the opinion I had a dream in which I heard a radio announcer say, "M.S. is granted a new trial." I sobbed so with joy in the dream that I awoke.

After these defeats in the courts I wrote Helen that she ought to stop wasting what remained of her life in trying to gain my freedom—a lost cause, as I saw it. I knew what her response would be even as I wrote her. She would—and did—tell me that she was doing what she felt she had to do. This was the last time we went through that same dialogue. I knew that nothing I could say could possibly change her mind.

Security was the big thing at the Rock. This was the primary way in which the Rock was supposed to differ from the other federal penitentiaries. Quite regu-larly a group of four or five hacks, under the direction of a lieutenant, would descend on the cellhouse and give it a thorough once-over. They would examine the walls of the cells for evidence of tampering; they would tap each of the cellhouse iron bars with a rubber mallet, lis-tening for the tell-tale tone of a cut bar. The whole procedure would take a week. But it didn't prevent the breakout which occurred after I left.

As described to me by the men who were there at the time (half of the men were aware of the prepara-tions for the more than three months it took to carry them out), the bricks in the back of the cells of the men who broke out were removed, put back, and skillfully plastered over to eliminate any evidence. This was all done very quickly with an electric hammer. The bars covering the skylight of the cellhouse, which was only about ten feet above the cell block, were cut and the evidence of this tampering was also disguised. The men had observed that the hacks never went up there in their routine inspections; it was a little out of the way. On the night of the break they removed the loose bricks, climbed up to the roof of the cellhouse, and scaled down the cellhouse wall. Some place on the island they had managed to secrete a rubberized boat which they had constructed from canvas, using gallons of rubber cement. Two of the men got away, though the officials insisted they were swept out to sea. Once some had succeeded in breaking the mystique of the place, others followed in rapid succession, though none made it. In the end the Rock was closed down, having lost its aura of unescapability.

When I first came to the Rock some of the old-timers told me of previous escape attempts, usually by trustees who were assigned to work on the docks. Usually the man was sighted in the water, after a count revealed a shortage, and the guards shot at him, even though there was no possibility that he might get away, once sighted. Several were killed in cold blood, as a warning to others, not to try it. Almost all of the guards' in-service training was devoted to shooting the various firearms.

I didn't listen very much to the radio, but on the night of October 4, I tuned in, after some of my neighbors indicated that an event of unusual importance had taken place. Thus it was that I heard the beeps of the Sputnik, as it winged its way across the skies, and around the earth. I was just as brainwashed as the others; I simply couldn't believe that the Russians could do it—ahead of us.

Our assistant prosecutor, Myles Lane, got into the act, and announced to the media that the Russians' success could only be attributed to our espionage. Naturally he didn't bother to go into any details. This led the *U.S. News and World Report* to republish the Greenglass testimony relating to the "sky platform," which he said Julius had obtained for the Russians. The testimony appeared so ludicrous that I should have thought they would prefer to hide rather than publicize it.

October was a busy month. *Look* magazine published a White Paper on the case, in defense of the government. The article was based on a confidential report prepared by a Justice Department official, Pollack. It was censored out of the magazine, but I was allowed to read it in the law library, in A cell block, as legal material.*

In October I moved into a new cell, after almost five years in the previous one. A "chain" of about twenty men had left the Rock, and we all put in requests for the more desirable empty cells. I was fortunate, or maybe it was just that I hadn't asked for a cell change for so long. My new cell, C-254, was located on the second range, one cell from the end. The new cell was much quieter, since noise came from only one side now, and I had the same beautiful view of the Golden Gate.

I knew George Ellis, who occupied the last cell, quite well, as I had known Pete Dounias, who had occupied my new cell before he was transferred away. George was extremely bright, but had dropped out of the Chicago schools at a precious early age. He had managed to get away from the Atlanta penitentiary

* In 1973, Walter and Miriam Schneir gained access to the Pollack report and found that it contained nothing which had not been known before, despite all of the assertions by the prosecution that they had a great deal of additional evidence against us which they had not produced at the trial.

through a sewer pipe, but was caught about a week later, some hundred miles away, through a fluke. It always seemed to happen that way. George wasn't interested in freedom when he escaped; he just wanted to kill his lawyer, who had double-crossed him. There were too many Georges in prison, men who could have been most productive members of society but for circumstances which directed them toward this life. I had some long discussions with George; even though he didn't have any academic background he could think and reason. Dostoievski said that a society may be judged by how it treats its criminals, but I believe that its treatment of children is a more sensitive barometer. When I saw a magazine photo of a black school girl, all alone in the back of a classroom, ostracized by society, I wept inwardly. How could society be so cruel as to hurt innocent children this way? I recalled that I had once been made to sit on top of a tall stool, wearing a dunce cap, before all the class. I couldn't recall what it was all about, but whatever it was, I had been hurt.

Shortly before I left the Rock I pulled a caper of which I felt proud. When I received my December copy of the *Scientific American,* I was astonished to see that it contained a lengthy article, in the "Amateur Experimenter" section, on Bob Stroud and his ornithological exploits at the Leavenworth penitentiary before his transfer to Alcatraz. I knew there had been a slip-up; with the exception of legal opinions nothing mentioning any inmates was allowed into the prison. It was easy to see how this error had occurred. The censor never thought of looking for an article mentioning an inmate in *Scientific American.* I realized that it would only be a matter of time before the error would be rectified—after someone in Washington had discovered the article and notified the censor.

Usually I kept my copy of the magazine about a month before putting it on the line to be circulated, but now I immediately drew up the route list, crossed off the first three or four names, cut out the Stroud article, and put the magazine on the route the next morning.

Even though Bob Stroud was in isolation up in the hospital, it wasn't too difficult to get the article to him through one of the men who worked up in the hospital. (Later, when I met Stroud in Springfield, he told me how much he appreciated getting it.)

As I had anticipated, several days later the mail censor asked me for my copy of the *Scientific American*. I told him it was already on the route, and gave him a route list. When he located the magazine, with the missing article, he knew it would be useless to question all the men whose names were crossed off. I had to assume that Stroud had got rid of the article after he read it.

Later I got to know Bob well at the Springfield Medical Center; I used to eat with him in a small dining hall. Coincidentally, it was I who found him dead one morning, when he didn't show up for breakfast, the day before President Kennedy was assassinated. He must have been an extraordinarily bright man in his youth, not to have allowed more than fifty years of imprisonment—forty in solitary—to destroy him. Whenever I thought I was doing a long bit, I had only to look at him. Most of the inmates at Springfield didn't like him; he boasted openly that he was a pederast, and they felt that this wasn't good for the public image of the convict. Besides, he ate with his fingers; we were usually alone at the dining table.

That last Christmas on the Rock, Helen, Sydney, and Mark all came to visit me, and we had a wonderful time together. It was a real family visit. Outwardly there seemed to be little reason for the lightheartedness which permeated the visits; I had just lost our appeals in the courts. Yet this removed the weight of decision making, at least for the moment. We were all there together, and that seemed reason enough to be happy.

However, for the last visit Helen came alone, dressed in a beautiful transparent nylon blouse with a black bra, also transparent. It wasn't the kind of visit where I ascended to cloud nine, and then waited for the fall which was sure to follow. We both had our feet firmly planted on the ground, but felt the joy that came from a realization that after all the years of separation, and after all the beatings we had taken, we had not succumbed. Surely this was reason enough for joy and laughter. At one point Helen observed that even under these insufferable conditions we were happier than many couples in the free world. I agreed, but cautioned Helen against voicing such an idea to others, lest it be misunderstood. People would say we were nuts, or even worse. Anyway happiness is never as easy to explain as unhappiness.

Each time a "chain" was about to leave the Rock, word somehow got around and rumors began to fly thick and fast: who was on it, when it was due to leave, and other pertinent data. Only infrequently did the officials succeed in catching us by surprise. Over the years their modus operandi changed. Only a year before, the procedure was to notify the men who were leaving at three in the morning, giving them twenty minutes to pack all their personal possessions. For someone who had been on the Rock five or ten years, and had collected a considerable number of articles, this created a frustrating situation.

A few years earlier Jim had been told he was leaving this way, and he went through the whole procedure, up until the very end, when the men were handcuffed in pairs and checked off the master list. Only then was it discovered that someone had made a mistake. No apologies, nothing. Jim had to go back and do another two years before he was transferred.

The rationale for such procedure was the same as for most other irrational procedures, security. Viz., if the men knew they would be leaving at a given time, it would be possible for them to notify someone on the outside to arrange an escape. Toward the end of my stay, however, the authorities began to relax a little, and the men on the previous shipment had been notified the day before they were scheduled to leave.

On Thursday night, February 20, the first rumors began to circulate around the cell house. No one ever knew who started these rumors, or where the information came from.

By Friday morning I learned from the grapevine that my name was supposed to be on the list. Never before had this happened to me. That afternoon, at work, I asked my superior if he could verify the rumor for me. A short time later he told me that the Associate Warden assured him that I was indeed on the list. I felt absolutely no elation when he told me this; I simply couldn't believe it, or more accurately, I felt I couldn't afford to take the chance of believing it. What if it weren't true? Could I then stand the pain? I had seen how the whole place would go into one big mass depression each time after a chain left. So many had hoped to go, and had seen this hope disappear for at least another half a year. Some men went through this each time a chain left, as if wanting to punish themselves.

Oddly enough, Helen had been to Washington a few weeks earlier, and had been told by well-connected friends there that I was scheduled to leave the Rock, but she didn't write me about it—because she didn't believe it. And as a matter of fact early in January someone who worked in the library had told me he had picked a piece of paper out of the wastebasket of the parole officer which indicated that Washington had given the local officials instructions that I was to be transferred away on the next chain. But I hadn't given this piece of information a second thought. I had heard so much crap over the years that I knew I had to disregard all such reports, or else go crazy.

Saturday morning the rumors became more firm, but then I was told by the men who worked in the kitchen that some of the stewards had seen my name scratched off the list. Now I felt justified in not believing anything. That evening rumors had me back on the list. I fell asleep easily that night, not even thinking about whether I was really going to leave.

Sunday morning after breakfast I started to go to the yard. An officer was standing at the cellhouse door, scanning a list and turning men back. When I reached him he told me to go back and pack my possessions. As I walked back to my cell, for the first time since it all began, I thought that I might leave the Rock after all. But even then I couldn't bring myself to *feel* that I would be leaving. That would have to grow, almost like a religious belief.

That morning I went to A cell block, picked up several cardboard cartons and my legal books, which I packed with the rest of my things. No one scheduled to leave was allowed to go out to the yard that day. The officials were afraid of a last-minute incident. I didn't mind remaining in my cell; it gave me time to think about all the beautiful things out there which would soon become mine. That night I wrote Helen:

February 23, 1958

Tonight I write you in a bare cell, stripped of all my possessions. One doesn't have the opportunity to write a letter under these conditions very frequently. This is my last night on Alcatraz! Do you hear me?

In the early hours of the morning I leave this lonely island, for a very long journey—to Atlanta, I was told. It will be long, not so much in space as in time, with many stopovers and delays . . . and I'm afraid we will become a little separated while I am en route, what with the difficulties of correspondence.

It will be a long journey and tiring, but a welcome one, both in itself and for what it means in terms of progress. Imagine, being able to see the length and breadth of the land, after such a period of close confinement. To see the people, at work, at play: the engines, the rivers, the fields, the houses. In a word, everything—or almost everything (if only you were at my side we could talk about all we saw and felt). . . .

Almost seven years ago—the last time you came to Atlanta—and I remember it as if it were yesterday. The biggest regret is that I won't have Dreyfus working on the 2255 [a new legal motion]. But for the present I'm as happy as one can be in prison. It will be different, going to Atlanta, this time. It has changed, and so have I. Of course I wish it were someplace nearer home, but that may be, in the not too distant future. The thought—the last night I spend in this cell—is almost too much for me.

Part Five

RETURN TO LIFE

1   The Journey Back
to Atlanta

LEAVENWORTH was the first stop on my trip to Atlanta, and from there I wrote the following letter on my first day.

> It was quite a change; five years of the utmost regularity, in every detail, and suddenly freedom—in a way—for three days and nights. Freedom is such a complex concept that a single word cannot be used to embrace the entire realm, meaningfully. Shackled, cuffed, and most closely guarded—and yet I felt free (an illusion?). Free to see life in America from the vantage point of a railroad car hurtling swiftly across the land. This was freedom—when contrasted with the almost absolute isolation of my preceding existence.
>
> Our route was quite circuitous, by way of Los Angeles, where I mentally said hello to some of our friends, and thanked them. Then on to El Paso. It was wonderful, if it only could have been more circuitous.
>
> I was aroused 3 A.M. Monday morning—after hardly closing my eyes. How could I have slept, with the anticipated joy of departure so close at hand? I breakfasted in the still of the night, showered and

got dressed in suitable garb for the occasion. Then I boarded the boat for the return half of the journey begun so many years ago.

As luck would have it, the bay was rough, and by the time the eight mile journey to the railroad depot was over, my stomach had come close to rebelling. The dawn broke just as we made land, and with the rain pouring down I made my way slowly and painfully to the train.

My cloth slippers had become soaked, my ankles (shackled together) were sore, and my spirits confused. But then as I dried out on the train, my spirit did likewise. And with the serving of lunch I began to really enjoy the trip.

Monday night I couldn't sleep. It was quite a feat—trying to sleep on a car with hands and feet restrained, and this was my initial effort. But came Tuesday morning I hardly knew I hadn't slept. This was the life! Looking out of the window and eating all this good food (catered from the dining car). The real coffee was probably best of all.

As evening approached I began to feel miserable. My wrists and ankles were really taking a beating, and what with the lack of activity, the tone of my body began playing all sorts of tricks. I was mighty glad when dawn came on Wednesday. Then I started feeling better, as if I had gone through some sort of crisis and emerged victorious. Strangest of all, I wasn't sleepy or tired. When Wednesday night arrived I felt I could have slept that night, but my destination was at hand, and I never had the opportunity to prove it.

Throughout the trip all my thoughts were on the immediate present. Here was all the wealth of expe-

rience flowing past—and I wanted to absorb it, as much as possible. My mind simply wouldn't function when I tried thinking about serious matters. However, on Wednesday night I started a mystery story and became so engrossed in it that I forgot where I was headed for. It was as if I were simply making an ordinary train journey. It took a positive effort to get back to reality—like when one tries to awaken from a deep dream.

The train reached its destination about midnight and we boarded a bus for the final lap of this phase. Exactly 72 hours after I got out of my old bed I got into a new one and slept the sleep of the deader than dead.

Went to breakfast in the morning, then to the library to get a few books. I don't know how long I'll be here, dearest, but it won't be long enough for you to write me here. What a chopping off of a past! Goodnight, dearest love. Little good things have begun to happen to us. I love thee with all I have within.

Your own Morty

There were many aspects of the trip which I was not permitted to write about in this first letter from Leavenworth. There were twenty-seven of us—eight headed for the Springfield Medical Center, all "certified psychotics"—and the remainder to be distributed mainly between Leavenworth and Atlanta. Each of the mental cases had gone the usual route: D block, the hole, and then the bug ward. An M.T.A. came along on the trip, to keep his wards drugged en route.

The men were paired, handcuffed, and shackled together. Since there was an odd number, one inmate had to be handcuffed and shackled to himself. I was that one.

We traveled in a special prison car, with armed guards in cages at both ends. Our car was always hooked on to the end of regular passenger trains, with baggage cars between us and the other passengers. The guards had a complete assortment of armaments, and were under the supervision of a lieutenant.

I had never before traveled with leg-irons, and before I learned how to cope with them my ankles had become quite sore and swelled up. Adjusting the cuffs and irons was a fine art. Some lieutenants allowed one finger of space, and others two. Our lieutenant was of the more sadistic variety. But I learned how to support the weight of the irons with a string tied to my trousers to relieve the pressure on my ankles. I had one advantage in not having a partner—I didn't have to drag anyone to the toilet with me.

Three times each day twenty-seven meals were brought in, but since those headed for Springfield were all too drugged to eat, we all had plenty of extra food. The lieutenant bought us newspapers, the first we had seen since coming to the Rock.

When the train stopped at the small towns, we all looked out, intently examining the outside world. Alvin Karpis, with the lowest number, hadn't seen it for twenty years. It all looked strange to us. The women appeared ugly; they weren't at all like the actresses we had been seeing on the movie screen (Helen was *sui generis*), but the children were delightful. At one point the men became ecstatic, as they watched a troupe of pre-schoolers following a nun down the street. Such strange behavior for us hardened criminals.

Of the nineteen men who were not drugged, there were only three, including myself, who had more than ten years left to do. Most of the men were due out in a couple of years, and one was due to be released within the week. Yet we were all treated like desperados. The FBI had us covered with rifles when we started the trip at Oakland, and again when we got off the train at Kansas City. To me it seemed like play acting.

At night, when everyone is asleep, a penitentiary is a most depressing place, when viewed from the other side of the bars, both inside and outside the cell house. Leavenworth had a unique institution, well known throughout the prison system, for all newcomers: the digital rectal examination. All the other penitentiaries were satisfied with spread buttocks, but Leavenworth insisted on this added "security" measure.

That first morning, as soon as we returned from breakfast, the captain appeared and asked us if there was anything we wanted, an amazing inquiry for all of us. During the rest of our time there, the authorities leaned over backward to make our stay pleasant. We all agreed we wanted to go to the library. The captain ordered the guard to conduct all of the "holdovers" to the library at once. There were some twenty other holdovers who had been there several weeks, but this was their first opportunity to go to the library. It was evident that we were being treated as privileged characters.

Before long the cell house guard started to bring us boxes of candy which had been given to him by Leavenworth inmates who had previously been on the Rock. They were sending us gifts from their twelve dollar monthly commissary allowance. Ordinarily the rules forbid inmates like ourselves, on holdover status, to receive anything from others. It would be interesting to learn why the captain treated us so kindly. Nor was that all.

That afternoon the cell doors were opened and we were allowed out on the flats, to play checkers, talk, and walk around. Saturday I went to the movie, and saw my first wide-screen filming, *The Helen Morgan Story*. A study in phoniness; the style of singing was 1957, but the songs were of a bygone era.

I was surprised to see, according to the newspaper ads, that the price of foods had not gone up very much during the past five years. This made some connection with my past, but in every other way I was now living in a strange new world. After living for five years in a static situation, I was transplanted into an entirely new ambience. It didn't last long.

Our idyllic existence came to an end on Monday morning when I left for Atlanta—a journey by bus that took place in five stages. First stop was the federal penitentiary at Terre Haute, Indiana. This was a so-called modern penitentiary, without walls. It had a wire mesh, interspersed with guard towers, on the perimeter. Strangely enough we were no longer required to wear leg irons on the bus. It was wintertime and the bus was cold, the landscape was bleak, and the meals were not from a dining car, but it felt good to be traveling on the highways where I could see other cars and people.

After breakfast in a depressing dining hall we started in the midst of a snow storm on the next leg of our trip, to the Federal Correctional Institution for Juveniles, located at Chillicothe, Ohio.

Each night we checked into our new "hotel," and then picked up the bus the following morning. On the third night we arrived at the Lewisburg penitentiary, which was familiar to me. The next two legs of the trip were also familiar to me, since I had been over them twice in 1951.

Except for breakfast, for five days I lived on sandwiches—not very good ones, usually Spam—but I enjoyed myself thoroughly, and wished it could go on five times as long. When I arrived at Atlanta, the usual question arose: for how long would this be my home? I knew it would be a lot easier for me than it had been back in 1951, when I spent a traumatic two months here. I had changed, and so had the place.

2 The Remaining Years and Freedom

I SPENT the next eleven years in three federal prisons before my release in 1969. It was an interesting period during which to do time, if one had to, because it marked the beginning of some long overdue prison reforms. I was a witness to, a beneficiary of, and a participant in these reforms, with the advantage of being able to see how these changes were implemented in each of the three prisons, and how, in certain instances, they were sabotaged.

The first five years I spent in Atlanta. Although still very much a prison, compared to the Rock it was like the free world. There were activities of all kinds going on, and one did have decisions to make, a privilege some men didn't really like. While I was there I saw many rules, which had always been held essential to the running of a prison, abolished in one fell swoop. By the time I left we no longer had to march to the mess hall at a given signal. The authorities apparently forgot their fears about men doubling up on meals. Nor did we all have to go to the yard at a set time. In 1962, eight years after the Supreme Court had ordered the schools to desegregate, I witnessed the beginning of racial desegregation in Atlanta. I had on several earlier occasions tried to eat in the black section with a black friend, but had immediately been ordered to move back to the white section. Disobeying such a direct order would have meant being placed in segregation, losing Good Time, and becoming ineligible for parole. I thought of making a test case of it, but decided that I would probably be killed before it was decided. A guard would have arranged for one of his boys to "hit" me. It was too easy for them to set such things up. I didn't want to be a hero; I just wanted to get out of there alive.

The education department was staffed by total incompetents, but for two years I did attend a Great Books seminar, organized by the librarian and led by an outsider. It was an educational experience in many different ways and I enjoyed it immensely. During the Sunday morning Jewish services I was able to conduct seminars on subjects only indirectly related to Judaism. For example, I spent over five hours discussing Erich Fromm's *The Art of Loving* (which had been denied me on the Rock).

Tennis was a lifesaver for me. Several hours a day, for four months during the year, I played hard at it; during the other months I studied and read. It was this annual cycle, more than anything else, that made me feel alive in Atlanta. Unfortunately, however, my stomach did not take kindly to the greasy southern cooking. Finally, after I had my gall bladder removed, and was reduced to one hundred twenty-eight pounds, I was transferred to the Springfield Medical Center for Federal Prisoners in Missouri.

I remained there almost two years, working in the x-ray department and recovering my health. On the whole my recovery was a question of a proper diet. I enjoyed my work at Springfield. In addition to the x-ray work, I did the electrocardiography and pulmonary function testing. Helen sent me books on each of these subjects and I became an "expert" in each of them. However, the visiting conditions were the best part of the place. The visiting room was tastefully furnished to avoid the usual institutional look, and we were usually able to visit on several days, four hours each day. What a contrast with Atlanta's two two-hour visits in a cold, hard room (although it had looked warm when I first arrived from the Rock).

In Springfield, for the first time, I met several conscientious objectors to the Vietnamese war. It was good to be able to talk with them. Yet with all the mental and physical illness around the place was very depressing and I asked to be transferred away as soon as I felt I'd once again be able to make it on the regular prison diet.

I thought they would send me to Leavenworth that time, although my case worker (formerly called parole officer) had recommended that I be sent to Danbury. They compromised and sent me to Lewisburg which, compared to all the other places in which I had been incarcerated, was only a stone's throw from New York. During the four years I stayed there I witnessed a very determined effort by the Bureau of Prisons to move their system into the twentieth century. I saw a warden transferred when he refused to cooperate; I saw a captain retired when he refused to give up the "coal gang," a punishment detail. If it wasn't the top brass it was the lieutenants and the hacks who sought to impede the move forward.

During the last years I lived in relatively civilized conditions, in a small room with a wooden door which was never locked. While Washington would still not allow me to teach in the education department, I enrolled in the dental prosthetic program and taught several courses there, after finishing my basic training. I took several courses in history and economics, taught by people from nearby Bucknell University. The Protestant chaplain had outsiders of different persuasions come to speak to us, and on two weekends he arranged sensitivity sessions, in which almost half of the participants were from the outside. For me it was a deep and meaningful experience to meet free people on such intimate terms, the closest approach to freedom I achieved in prison.

In the summertime Helen and I were allowed to visit in a green courtyard, without a hack in sight. Washington had finally relaxed its pressure and decided I should be treated like any other prisoner. However, it still refused to give me credit for my jail time, or the time I had spent on West Street while on appeal, despite a change in the law mandating this. Finally, after applications had been made in the courts in Washington, D.C., Lewisburg, and Philadelphia, the Court of Appeals in New York ordered my immediate release on January 14, 1969. Three hours later I was on my way home.

Freedom felt good, but it wasn't realized instantaneously. There was no sudden magic attached to it. I didn't suddenly feel free when the prison guards left me at the Williamsport bus terminal, with a ticket to New York City, alone and on my own for the first time in over eighteen years. I had fifteen minutes to wait before the express bus was scheduled to leave. I looked at all the people moving around me. Somehow the scene did not look unfamiliar, in spite of all the years since I had experienced it. I walked over to the magazine racks and looked at the impressive proliferation of magazines. I bought a package of chewing gum (in prison gum was forbidden, but I used to get a stick now and then). I sat down at the food counter, although I wasn't hungry, and ordered some cherry pie and milk. The pie wasn't very good, even by prison standards.

I was paged; it was Helen on the phone. Friends had already been waiting for me at the front gates of the prison when I was hustled out of the rear. We decided I would go ahead and take the bus which had already pulled in. It left on time, with less than a dozen passengers. I took a seat behind the driver to get a better view. It would have been nice to have had someone to talk with. I thought of what lay ahead. Helen would be waiting for me at the bus terminal, with friends no doubt. I had dreamed of this moment many, many times during those long years—the homecoming. But I had never visualized it quite this way. I felt neither excited nor anxious. It would be a scene with which I was thoroughly familiar.

I recognized the New York City skyline as we approached the Lincoln Tunnel. The four hours had passed rapidly. When the bus pulled into the terminal and I found no one there I knew there must have been a mixup. I wandered around for ten minutes before I located a crowd of people, one of whom recognized me. They opened up and I went up to Helen, but even when I put my arms around her and kissed her she was unaware it was I—for a moment. The police had misdirected her and she had been concentrating on waiting for the bus. It seemed everyone was there that night, friends and family as well as strangers. The police hustled us into a cab, but not before I protested against being shoved around; I had been in too long to come out to this.

That first evening at home was memorable. We talked, we laughed quietly, as if this were not an uncommon event. It was an evening of catching up. I had some Cointreau, my first drink. There would be many more such enjoyable evenings with friends and family. I felt a warmth within such as I hadn't experienced for a very long time.

That first night with Helen was not the most exciting; nor did I feel awed the first time I walked down Fifth Avenue. All that would take time, months and even years. I had to loosen up before I was able to appreciate all the freedom which lay within my grasp— but was not yet mine. A prison mentality cannot be discarded overnight; a slave is not freed by a proclamation.

Barely three weeks after my release I was back at school; it was like going home again (despite what Thomas Wolfe wrote). Sitting in a classroom with all the youngsters and listening to a good lecturer made me feel young and alive again. However, it wasn't easy, trying to span the great gap in time. Electrical engineering had moved ahead at a tremendous rate during the time I was away. I had to struggle to keep my head above water but I enjoyed the challenge. It was proof that I was still alive, and I needed that proof to sustain me.

It was also not easy to learn to live with Helen all over again. A short time before my release I had spoken with Dr. Wolf, the psychiatrist at Lewisburg who was doing two years there in lieu of army time, and was genuinely concerned for the inmates. He cautioned me that it wouldn't be easy; we had each been living alone for too long. Thus I came out forewarned. Helen had been similarly cautioned by a psychiatrist, and we knew that each of us would have to yield. At times our relationship became almost traumatic; such is the irrationality of human beings.

I had also spoken with Dr. Wolf about a question which had begun to bother me now that I faced freedom. Was my lack of bitterness real, or was I simply suppressing my feelings until I could afford to drop the pose? I was afraid that once I was out I might find myself an embittered person—a person with whom I could not live. I felt I had to know the truth about myself.

I frequently stopped at Dr. Wolf's office during lunchtime, on my way to work, to chat with him. To try to resolve this he scheduled several one-hour sessions. Afterwards he assured me that my experience had indeed not embittered me. I could not fully accept his finding at the time; I felt I would have to wait for a definitive judgment.

When I got out, from the first press conference the day after my release, and in every interview until now, I was always asked why I was not bitter. I don't believe that the answer can be found in any single factor, but probably a most important reason is that I did not consider my life wasted by my imprisonment. I always tried to take the long view. I never thought of our conviction as a simple frameup by an unscrupulous United States Attorney, assisted by a judge lacking in principles. Rather I saw our case as an integral part of the Establishment's national policy. Any political trial is used to implement national policy, both domestic and foreign. Being a part of history in this fashion somehow kept me from self-pity and bitterness.

But perhaps even more important, I felt that my life was not wasted because in opposing my continued imprisonment many progressive people were able to reg-ister their opposition to the Establishment's policies. The struggle around this case became the way in which they registered their opposition at a time when most progressive organizations had been decimated during the McCarthy period. Helen made me aware of this during my imprisonment. The basic differences between Helen and myself lay in the relative emphasis we placed on the public fight as compared with the legal fight. This reflected our respective positions, I on the inside and Helen on the outside. By 1965 I felt that the case had outlived its usefulness in public terms, and urged Helen to disband the Committee. However, my view did not prevail.

Certainly not the last reason for my lack of bitterness may be found in the relationship between Helen and myself during all the years of my imprisonment. A person truly loved, as I was, cannot easily become embittered—unless he rejects that love.

If I wasn't bitter, what problems did confront me when I was freed? Most men do not return, as I did, to a warm and loving family. I was fortunate in this regard. It felt good to come back to such a world full of friends and family. But even though my world was not hostile, at first I felt I had to have absolute control over every situation in which I was involved. I was really tight inside. I couldn't allow things just to happen—they might get out of control. I had protected myself that way while in prison, and I couldn't drop this style of living even though I was no longer in a hostile environment.

There was so much I had to learn in order to operate freely in the free world that it was paralyzing. I had to acquire a new taste in clothing before I could purchase any. The styles were all new, and all my former notions were now so much garbage. Yet I couldn't acquire new tastes overnight. What a dilemma! Fortunately the first clothes I bought was with friends whose judgment I trusted, but once that was over I felt I had to be on my own. The simple matter of buying some tools also created a problem for me. Which tools to buy? I no longer had any background in this area. Thus I spent days searching out the few tools I absolutely needed.

Then there were the times I would wake up in the middle of the night in a pool of sweat. At first that happened two or three times a week, but after the first two years it was down to about once a week. I never found out why it happened; I couldn't recall any dreams when I awakened, but I experienced a gnawing anxiety.

Nineteen hundred and sixty-nine was a good year in which to come back to free society. Twenty years earlier the Establishment had the common man on the run, with its cold war, abroad and at home. Ironically the first movement to reassert people's rights arose in the South, among people who had been living under tyranny ever since being brought to these shores. (I had first learned what it was really like to be a black in the South, in prison, from my southern white confreres.) It gave me heart when I read about the Montgomery bus boycott, led by Martin Luther King. (Dr. King later asked Kennedy to free me.) When the civil rights movement began to grow I felt I simply had to get out there to witness it. Then in 1968, when the students blew the lid off the campus, I felt very much a part of them. Nothing would ever be the same again.

Nothing, I felt, should ever be the same for too long. Once the blacks realized that God had not ordained they be second class citizens they were truly free. Oppressed colonial people everywhere in the world were on the march, and I wanted very much to be out where I could join in—in whatever way. Nineteen hundred and sixty-nine also marked the awakening of the American people to the true meaning of the Vietnamese war. What a contrast with the Korean War period twenty years before! Ethel and Julius could never have been executed in 1969. People could no longer be frightened into submission the way they had been in the 1950s.

The first morning after coming out I rode on the subway and saw a startling change. I recalled that the blacks had always held their heads bowed, as if in perpetual submission. Now they all rode heads erect, proudly looking ahead. It made me feel better than anything else could, to be a part of this scene. I knew that I could find a place in it, after so many years of submission to authority in that closed society called prison.